AUTHENTIC
Emilia-Romagna

TOURING CLUB
OF ITALY

Touring Club Italiano
President and Chairman: *Roberto Ruozi*
General Manager: *Guido Venturini*

Touring Editore
Managing Director: *Alfieri Lorenzon*
Editorial Director: *Michele D'Innella*

International Department
Fabio Pittella
fabio.pittella@touringclub.it

Senior Editor: *Paola Pandiani*
Editor: *Monica Maraschi*
Writer and Researcher: *Pietro Ferrario*
with Banca Dati Turistica for Pratical info
Translation and page layout: *Studio Queens, Milan*
Maps: *Touring Club Italiano*
Design: *Studio Gatelli, Milan*
Cover photo: *Bologna, the old town center
(G. A. Rossi)*

Advertising Manager: *Claudio Bettinelli*
Local Advertising: *Progetto*
www.progettosrl.it - info@progettosrl.it

Printing and Binding: *CPM, Casarile*

Distribution
USA/CAN – *Publishers Group West*
UK/Ireland – *Portfolio Books*

Touring Club Italiano, Corso Italia 10, 20122 Milano
www.touringclub.it
© 2006 Touring Editore, Milan

Code K8P
ISBN-13: 978 – 88365 – 3898 – 0
ISBN-10: 88 – 365 – 3898 – 3

Printed in May 2006

SUMMARY

4   What is the Touring Club of Italy?

7   Italy: instructions for use

14   ■ Heritage

110   ■ Itineraries

136   ■ Food

168   ■ Shopping

180   ■ Events

196   ■ Wellness

208   ■ Pratical info

233   Metric convertions

234   Index of names

238   General index

239   Glossary

240   Picture credits

WHAT IS THE TOURING CLUB OF ITALY?

Long Tradition, Great Prestige

For over 110 years, the Touring Club of Italy (TCI) has offered travelers the most detailed and comprehensive source of travel information available on Italy. The Touring Club of Italy was founded in 1894 with the aim of developing the social and cultural values of tourism and promoting the conservation and enjoyment of the country's national heritage, landscape and environment.

Advantages of Membership

Today, TCI offers a wide rage of travel services to assist and support members with the highest level of convenience and quality. Now you can discover the unique charms of Italy with a distinct insider's advantage.

Enjoy exclusive money saving offers with a TCI membership. Use your membership card for discounts in thousands of restaurants, hotels, spas, campgrounds, museums, shops and markets.

These Hotel Chains offer preferred rates and discounts to TCI members!

JOIN THE TOURING CLUB OF ITALY

How to Join

It's quick and easy to join.

Apply for your membership online at
www.touringclub.it

Your membership card will arrive within
three weeks and is valid for discounts
across Italy for the entire year.

Get your card before you go and start
saving as soon as you arrive.

Euro 25 annual membership fee
includes priority mail postage for
membership card and materials.

Just one use of the card will more than
cover the cost of membership.

Benefits

• Exclusive car rental rates with Hertz
• Discounts at select Esso gas stations
• 20% discount on TCI guidebooks
and maps purchased in TCI bookstores
or directly online at
www.touringclub.com
• Preferred rates and discounts available
at thousands of locations in Italy: Hotels -
B&B's - Villa Rentals - Campgrounds -TCI
Resorts - Spas - Restaurants - Wineries -
Museums - Cinemas - Theaters - Music
Festivals - Shops - Craft Markets - Ferries -
Cruises - Theme Parks - Botanical Gardens

ITALY: INSTRUCTIONS FOR USE

Italy is known throughout the world for the quantity and quality of its art treasures and for its natural beauty, but it is also famous for its inimitable lifestyle and fabulous cuisine and wines. Although it is a relatively small country, Italy boasts an extremely varied culture and multifarious traditions and customs. The information and suggestions in this brief section will help foreign tourists not only to understand certain aspects of Italian life, but also to solve the everyday difficulties and the problems of a practical nature that inevitably crop up during any trip. This practical information is included in brief descriptions of various topics: public transport and how to purchase tickets; suggestions on how to drive in this country; the different types of rooms and accommodation in hotels; hints on how to use mobile phones and communication in general. This is followed by useful advice on how to meet your everyday needs and on shopping, as well as information concerning the cultural differences in the various regions. Lastly, there is a section describing the vast range of restaurants, bars, wine bars and pizza parlors.

TRANSPORTATION

From the airport to the city

Public transportation in major cities is easily accessible and simple to use.
Both Malpensa Airport in Milan and Fiumicino Airport in Rome have trains and buses linking them to the city centers. At Malpensa, you can take a bus to the main train station or a train to Cadorna train station and subway stop.

Subways, buses, and trams

Access to the subways, buses, and trams requires a ticket (tickets are not sold on board but can be purchased at most newsstands and tobacco shops). The ticket is good for one ride and sometimes has a time limit (in the case of buses and trams). When you board a bus or tram, you are required to stamp your previously-acquired ticket in the time-stamping machine. Occasionally, a conductor will board the bus or tram and check everyone's ticket. If you haven't got one, or if it has not been time-stamped, you will have to pay a steep fine.

Trains

The Ferrovie dello Stato (Italian Railways) is among the best and most modern railway systems in Europe. Timetables and routes can be consulted and reservations can be made online at www.trenitalia.com. Many travel agents can also dispense tickets and help you plan your journey. Hard-copy schedules can be purchased at all newsstands and most bookstores.

A delightful courtyard of a palazzo in Imola

Automated ticket machines, which include easy-to-use instructions in English, are available in nearly all stations. They can be used to check schedules, makes reservations, and purchase tickets.
There are different types of train, according to the requirements:
Eurostar Italia Trains $ES\star$: Fast connections between Italy's most important cities. The ticket includes seat booking charge;
Intercity IC and **Espresso** E Trains: Local connections among Italy's towns and cities. Sometimes and trains require seat booking. You can book your seat up to 3 hours before the train departure. The seat booking charge is of 3 euro.
Interregionale Trains iR move beyond regional boundaries. Among the combined local-transport services, the Trains are the fastest ones with the fewest number of stops. No seat booking available.
Diretto D and **Regionale** R Trains can circulate both within the regions and their bordering regions. No seat booking available.

DO NOT FORGET: You can only board trains in Italy with a valid ticket, which must be time-stamped before boarding; there are numerous time-stamping machines in every station. You cannot buy or stamp tickets on board.

If you don't have a ticket - or did not stamp before boarding - you will be liable to pay the full ticket price plus a 25 euro fine. If you produce a ticket that is not valid for the train or service you're using (i.e. one issued for a different train category at a different price, etc.) you will be asked to pay the difference with respect to the full ticket price, plus an 8 euro surcharge.

Taxis

Taxis are a convenient but expensive way to travel in Italian cities. There are taxi stands scattered throughout major cities. You cannot hail taxis on the street in Italy, but you can reserve taxis, in advance or immediately, by phone: consult the yellow pages for the number or ask your hotel reception desk or maitre d'hotel to call for you.

Taxi drivers have the right to charge you a supplementary fee for every piece of luggage they transport, as well as evening surcharges.

Driving

Especially when staying in the countryside, driving is a safe and convenient way to travel through Italy and its major cities. And while it is best avoided for obvious reasons, driving in the cities is not as difficult as it may seem or may have been reported to be. It is important to be aware of street signs and speed limits, and many cities have zones where only limited traffic is allowed in order to accommodate pedestrians. Although an international driver's license is not required in Italy, it is advisable. ACI and similar associations provide this service to members.

The fuel distribution network is reasonably distributed all over the territory. All service stations have unleaded gasoline ("benzina verde") and diesel fuel ("gasolio"). Opening time is 7am to12:30 and 15 to 19:30; on motorways the service is 24 hours a day.

Type of roads in Italy: The *Autostrada* (for example A14) is the main highway system in Italy and is similar to the Interstate highway system in the US and the motorway system in the UK. Shown on our Touring Club Italiano 1:200,000 road maps as black. The Autostrada are toll highways; you pay to use them. The *Strada Statale* (for example SS54) is a fast moving road that may have one or more lanes in each direction. Shown on our Touring Club Italiano 1:200,000 road maps as red. *Strada Provinciale* (for example SP358) can be narrow, slow and winding roads. They are usually one lane in each direction. Shown on our Touring Club Italiano 1:200,000 road maps as yellow. *Strada Comunale* (for example SC652) is a local road connecting the main town with its sorrounding. Note: In our guide you will sometime find an address of a place in the countryside listed, for example, as "SS54 Km 25". This means that the you have to drive along the Strada Statale 54 until you reach the 25-km road sign. Speed limits: 130 kmph on the

Autostrada, 110 kmph on main highways, 90 kmph outside of towns, 50 kmph in towns.

The town streets are patrolled by the Polizia Municipale while the roads outside cities and the Autostrada are patrolled by the Carabinieri or the Polizia Stradale. They may set up road blocks where they may ask you to stop by holding out a small red sign.

Do not forget:

- Wear your seat belt at all times;
- Do not use the cellular phone while driving;
- Have your headlights on at all times when driving outside of cities;
- The drunk driving laws are strict - do not drink and drive;
- In case of an accident you are not allowed to get out of your car unless you are wearing a special, high-visibility, reflective jacket.

ACCOMMODATION

Hotels

In Italy it is common practice for the reception desk to register your passport, and only registered guests are allowed to use the rooms. This is mere routine, done for security reasons, and there is no need for concern.

All hotels use the official star classification system, from 5-star luxury hotel to 1 star accommodation.

Room rates are based on whether they are for single ("camera singola") or double ("camera doppia") occupancy. In every room you will find a list of the hotel rates (generally on the back of the door). While 4- and 5-star hotels have double beds, most hotels have only single beds. Should you want a double bed, you have to ask for a "letto matrimoniale". All hotels have rooms with bathrooms; only 1-star establishments usually have only shared bathrooms.

Most hotel rates include breakfast ("prima colazione"), but you can request to do without it, thus reducing the rate. Breakfast is generally served in a communal room and comprises a buffet with pastries, bread with butter and jam, cold cereals, fruit, yoghurt, coffee, and fruit juice. Some hotels regularly frequented by foreign tourists will also serve other items such as eggs for their American and British guests.

The hotels for families and in tourist localities also offer "mezza pensione", or half board, in which breakfast and dinner are included in the price.

It's always a good idea to check when a hotel's annual closing period is, especially if you are planning a holiday by the sea.

Farm stays

Located only in the countryside, and generally on a farm, "agriturismo" – a network of farm holiday establishments – is part of a growing trend in Italy to honor local gastronomic and wine traditions, as well as countryside traditions. These farms offer meals prepared with ingredients cultivated exclusively on site: garden-grown vegetables, homemade cheese and local recipes. Many of these places also provide lodging, one of the best ways to experience the "genuine" Italian lifestyle.

Bed & Breakfast

This form of accommodation provides bed and breakfast in a private house, and in the last few years has become much more widespread in Italy. There are over 5,000 b&bs, classified in 3 categories, and situated both in historic town centers, as well as in the outskirts and the countryside. Rooms for guests are always well-furnished, but not all of them have en suite bathrooms.

It is well-recommended to check the closing of the open-all-year accommodation services and restaurants, because they could have a short break during the year (usually no longer than a fortnight).

COMMUNICATIONS

Nearly everyone in Italy owns a cellular phone. Although public phones are still available, they seem to be ever fewer and farther between. If you wish to use public phones, you will find them in subway stops, bars, along the street, and phone centers generally located in the city center. Phone cards and pre-paid phone cards can be purchased at most newsstands and tobacco shops, and can also be acquired at automated tellers. For European travelers, activating personal cellular coverage is relatively simple, as it is in most cases for American and Australian travelers as well. Contact your mobile service provider for details. Cellular phones can also be rented in Italy from TIM, the Italian national phone company. For information, visit its website at www.tim.it. When traveling by car through the countryside, a cellular phone can really come in handy.

Note that when dialing in Italy, you must always dial the prefix (e.g., o2 for Milan, o6 for Rome) even when making a local call. For cellular phones, however, the initial zero is always dropped.

Freephone numbers always start with "8oo". For calls abroad from Italy, it's a good idea to buy a special pre-paid international phone card, which is used with a PIN code.

Internet access

Cyber cafés have sprung up all over Italy and today you can find one on nearly every city block. The Italian national phone company, TIM, has also begun providing internet access at many of its public phone centers.

EATING AND DRINKING

The bar

The Italian "bar" is a multi-faceted, all-purpose establishment for drinking, eating and socializing, where you can order an espresso, have breakfast, and enjoy a quick sandwich for lunch or even a hot meal. You can often buy various items here (sometimes even stamps, cigarettes, phone cards, etc.). Bear in mind that table service ("servizio a tavola") includes a surcharge. At most bars, if you choose to sit, a waiter will take your order. Every bar should have a list of prices posted behind or near the counter; if the bar offers table service, the price list should also include the extra fee for this.

Lunch at bars will include, but is not limited to, "panini," sandwiches with crusty bread, usually with cured meats such as "prosciutto" (salt-cured ham), "prosciutto cotto" (cooked ham), and cheeses such as mozzarella topped with tomato and basil. Then there are "tramezzini" (finger sandwiches) with tuna, cheese, or vegetables, etc. Often the "panini" and other savory sandwiches (like stuffed flatbread or "focaccia") are heated before being served. Naturally, the menu at bars varies according to the region: in Bologna you will find "piadine" (flatbread similar to pita) with Swiss chard; in Palermo there are "arancini" (fried rice balls stuffed

with ground meat); in Genoa you will find that even the most unassuming bar serves some of the best "focaccia" in all Italy. Some bars also include a "tavola calda". If you see this sign in a bar window, it means that hot dishes like pasta and even entrées are served.

A brief comment on coffee and cappuccino: Italians never serve coffee with savory dishes or sandwiches, and they seldom drink cappuccino outside of breakfast (although they are happy to serve it at any time).

While English- and Irish-type pubs are frequented by beer lovers and young people in Italy, there are also American bars where long drinks and American cocktails are served.

Breakfast at the bar

Breakfast in Italy generally consists of some type of pastry, most commonly a "brioche" – a croissant either filled with cream or jam, or plain – and a cappuccino or espresso. Although most bars do not offer American coffee, you can ask for a "caffè lungo" or "caffè americano", both of which resemble the American coffee preferred by the British and Americans. Most bars have a juicer to make a "spremuta", freshly squeezed orange or grapefruit juice.

Lunch and Dinner

As with all daily rituals in Italy, food is prepared and meals are served according to local customs (e.g., in the North they prefer rice and butter, in South and Central Italy they favor pasta and olive oil).

Wine is generally served at mealtime, and while finer restaurants have excellent wine lists (some including vintage wines), ordering the house table wine generally brings good results (a house Chianti to accompany your Florentine steak in Tuscany, a sparkling

Prosecco paired with your creamed stockfish and polenta in Venice, a dry white wine with pasta dressed with sardines and wild fennel fronds in Sicily). Mineral water is also commonly served at meals and can be "gassata" (sparkling) or "naturale" (still).

The most sublime culinary experience in Italy is achieved by matching the local foods with the appropriate local wines: wisdom dictates that a friendly waiter will be flattered by your request for his recommendation on what to eat and drink. Whether at an "osteria" (a tavern), a "trattoria" (a home-style restaurant), or a "ristorante" (a proper restaurant), the service of lunch and dinner generally consists of – but is not limited to – the following: "antipasti" or appetizers; "primo piatto" or first course, i.e., pasta, rice, or soup; "secondo piatto" or main course, i.e., meat or seafood; "contorno" or side-dish, served with the main course, i.e., vegetables or salad; "formaggi", "frutta", and "dolci", i.e., cheeses, fruit, and dessert; caffè or espresso coffee, perhaps spiked with a shot of grappa.

The pizzeria

The pizzeria is in general one of the most economical, democratic, and satisfying culinary experiences in Italy. Everyone eats at the pizzeria: young people, families, couples, locals and tourists alike. Generally, each person orders her/his own pizza, and while the styles of crust and toppings will vary from region to region (some of the best pizzas are served in Naples and Rome), the acid test of any pizzeria is the Margherita, topped simply with cheese and tomato sauce. Beer, sparkling or still water, and Coca Cola are the beverages commonly served with pizza. Some restaurants include a pizza menu, but most establishments do not serve pizza at lunchtime.

The wine bar (enoteca)

More than one English-speaking tourist in Italy has wondered why the wine bar is called an enoteca in other countries and the English term is used in Italy: the answer lies somewhere in the mutual fondness that Italians and English speakers have for one another. Wine bars have become popular in recent years in the major cities (especially in Rome, where you can find some of the best). The wine bar is a great place to sample different local wines and eat a light, tapas-style dinner.

CULTURAL DIVERSITY

Whenever you travel, not only are you a guest of your host country, but you are also a representative of your home country. As a general rule, courtesy, consideration, and respect are always appreciated by guests and their hosts alike. Italians are famous for their hospitality and experience will verify this felicitous stereotype: perhaps nowhere else in Europe are tourists and visitors received more warmly. Italy is a relatively "new" country. Its borders, as we know them today, were established only in 1861 when it became a monarchy under the House of Savoy. After WWII, Italy became a Republic and now it is one of the member states of the European Union. One of the most fascinating aspects of Italian culture is that, even as a unified country, local tradition still prevails over a universally Italian national identity. Some jokingly say that the only time that Venetians, Milanese, Florentines, Neapolitans, and Sicilians feel like Italians is when the national football team plays in international competitions. From their highly localized dialects to the foods they eat, from their religious celebration to their politics, Italians proudly maintain their local heritage. This is one of the reasons why the Piedmontese continue to prefer their beloved Barolo wine and their white truffles, the Umbrians their rich Sagrantino wine and black truffles, the Milanese their risotto and panettone, the Venetians their stockfish and polenta, the Bolognese their lasagne and pumpkin ravioli, the Florentines their bread soups and steaks cooked rare, the Abruzzese their excellent fish broth and seafood, the Neapolitans their mozzarella, basil, pizza, and pasta. As a result of its rich cultural diversity, the country's population also varies greatly in its customs from region to region, city to city, town to town. As you visit different cities and regions throughout Italy, you will see how the local personality and character of the Italians change as rapidly as the landscape does. Having lived for millennia with their great diversity and rich, highly heterogeneous culture, the Italians have taught us many things, foremost among them the age-old expression, "When in Rome, do as the Romans do."

NATIONAL HOLIDAYS

New Year's Day (1st January), Epiphany (6th January), Easter Monday (day after Easter Sunday), Liberation Day (25th April), Labour Day (1st May), Italian Republic Day (2nd June), Assumption (15th August), All Saints' Day (1st November), Immaculate Conception (8th December), Christmas Day and Boxing Day (25th-26th December).

In addition to these holidays, each city also has a holiday to celebrate its patron saint's feast day, usually with lively, local celebrations. Shops and services in large cities close on national holidays and for the week of the 15th of August.

EVERYDAY NEEDS

State tobacco shops and pharmacies

Tobacco is available in Italy only at state licensed tobacco shops. These vendors ("tabaccheria"), often incorporated in a bar, also sell stamps.

Since 11 January 2005 smoking is forbidden in all so-called public places - unless a separately ventilated space is constructed - meaning over 90% of the country's restaurants and bars. Medicines can be purchased only in pharmacies ("farmacia") in Italy. Pharmacists are very knowledgeable about common ailments and can generally prescribe a treatment for you on the spot. Opening time is 8:30-12:30 and 15:30-19:30 but in any case there is always a pharmacy open 24 hours and during holidays.

Shopping

Every locality in Italy offers tourists characteristic shops, markets with good bargains, and even boutiques featuring leading Italian fashion designers. Opening hours vary from region to region and from season to season. In general, shops are open from 9 to 13 and from 15/16 to 19/20, but in large cities they usually have no lunchtime break.

Tax Free

Non-EU citizens can obtain a reimbursement for IVA (goods and services tax) paid on purchases over €155, for goods which are exported within 90 days, in shops which display the relevant sign. IVA is always automatically included in the price of any purchase, and ranges from 20% to 4% depending on the item. The shop issues a reimbursement voucher to present when you leave the country (at a frontier or airport). For purchases in shops affiliated to 'Tax Free Shopping', IVA may be reimbursed directly at international airports.

Banks and post offices

Italian banks are open Monday to Friday from 8:30 to 13:30 and then from 15 to 16. However, the afternoon business hours may vary.

Post offices are open from Monday to Saturday, from 8:30 to 13:30 (12:30 on Saturday). In the larger towns there are also some offices open in the afternoon.

Currency

Effective 1 January 2002, the currency used in many European Union countries is the euro. Coins are in denominations of 1, 2, 5, 10, 20 and 50 cents and 1 and 2 euros; banknotes are in denominations of 5, 10, 20, 50, 100, 200 and 500 euros, each with a different color.

Credit cards

All the main credit cards are generally accepted, but some smaller enterprises (arts and crafts shops, small hotels, bed & breakfasts, or farm stays) do not provide this service. Foreign tourists can obtain cash using credit cards at automatic teller machines.

Time

All Italy is in the same time zone, which is six hours ahead of Eastern Standard Time in the USA. Daylight saving time is used from March to October, when watches and clocks are set an hour ahead of standard time.

Passports and vaccinations

Citizens of EU countries can enter Italy without frontier checks. Citizens of Australia, Canada, New Zealand, and the United States can enter Italy with a valid passport and need not have a visa for a stay of less than 90 days.

No vaccinations are necessary.

Payment and tipping

When you sit down at a restaurant you are generally charged a "coperto" or cover charge ranging from 1.5 to 3 euros, for service and the bread. Tipping is not customary in Italy. Beware of unscrupulous restaurateurs who add a space on their clients' credit card receipt for a tip, while it has already been included in the cover charge.

USEFUL ADDRESSES

Foreign Embassies in Italy

Australia
Via A. Bosio, 5 - 00161 Rome
Tel. +39 06 852721
Fax +39 06 85272300
www.italy.embassy.gov.au.
info-rome@dfat.gov.au

Canada
Via G.B. de Rossi, 27 - 00161 Rome
Tel. +39 06 445981
Fax +39 06 445983760
www.canada.it
rome@dfait-maeci.gc.ca

Great Britain
Via XX Settembre, 80/a - 00187
Rome
Tel. +39 06 42200001
Fax +39 06 42202334
www.britian.it
consularenquiries@rome.
mail.fco.gov.uk

Ireland
Piazza di Campitelli, 3 - 00186
Rome
Tel. +39 06 6979121
Fax +39 06 6792354
irish.embassy@esteri.it

New Zealand
Via Zara, 28 - 00198 Rome
Tel. +39 06 4417171
Fax +39 06 4402984
nzemb.rom@flashnet.it

South Africa
Via Tanaro, 14 - 00198 Rome
Tel. +39 06 852541
Fax +39 06 85254300
www.sudafrica.it
sae@flashnet.it

United States of America
Via Vittorio Veneto, 121 - 00187
Rome
Tel. +39 06 46741
Fax +39 06 4882672
www.usis.it

Foreign Consulates in Italy

Australia
2 Via Borgogna
20122 Milan
Tel. +39 02 77704217
Fax +39 02 77704242

Canada
Via Vittor Pisani, 19
20124 Milan
Tel. +39 02 67581
Fax +39 02 67583900
milan@international.gc.ca

Great Britain
via S. Paolo 7
20121 Milan
Tel. +39 02 723001
Fax +39 02 86465081
ConsularMilan@fco.gov.uk

Lungarno Corsini 2
50123 Florence
Tel. +39 055 284133
Consular.Florence@fco.gov.uk

Via dei Mille 40
80121 Naples
Tel. +39 081 4238911

Fax +39 081 422434
Info.Naples@fco.gov.uk

Ireland
Piazza San Pietro in Gessate 2 -
20122 Milan
Tel. +39 02 55187569/02 55187641
Fax +39 02 55187570

New Zealand
Via Guido d'Arezzo 6,
20145 Milan
Tel. +39 02 48012544
Fax +39 02 48012577

South Africa
Vicolo San Giovanni Sul Muro 4
20121 Milan
Tel. +39 02 8858581
Fax +39 02 72011063
saconsulate@iol.it

United States of America
Via Principe Amedeo, 2/10
20121 Milan
Tel. +39 02 290351
Fax +39 02 29001165

Lungarno Vespucci, 38
50123 Florence
Tel. +39 055 266951
Fax +39 055 284088

Piazza della Repubblica
80122 Naples
Tel. +39 081 5838111
Fax +39 081 7611869

Italian Embassies and Consulates Around the World

Australia
12, Grey Street - Deakin, A.C.T.
2600 - Canberra
Tel. 02 62733333, 62733398,
62733198
Fax 02 62734223
www.ambitalia.org.au
embassy@ambitalia.org.au
Consulates at: Brisbane, Glynde,
Melbourne, Perth , Sydney

Canada
275, Slater Street, 21st floor -
Ottawa (Ontario) K1P 5H9
Tel. (613) 232 2401/2/3
Fax (613) 233 1484 234 8424
www.italyincanada.com
ambital@italyincanada.com
Consulates at: Edmonton,
Montreal, Toronto, Vancouver,

Great Britain
14, Three Kings Yard, London
W1K 4EH
Tel. 020 73122200
Fax 020 73122230
www.embitaly.org.uk
ambasciata.londra@esteri.it
Consulates at: London, Bedford,
Edinburgh, Manchester

Ireland
63/65, Northumberland Road -
Dublin 4
Tel. 01 6601744
Fax 01 6682759
www.italianembassy.ie
info@italianembassy.ie

New Zealand
34-38 Grant Road, Thorndon,

(PO Box 463, Wellington)
Tel. 04 473 5339
Fax 04 472 7255
www.italy-embassy.org.nz
ambwell@xtra.co.nz

South Africa
796 George Avenue, 0083 Arcadia
Tel. 012 4305541/2/3
Fax 012 4305547
www.ambital.org.za
ambital@iafrica.com
Consulates at: Johannesburg,
Capetown, Durban

United States of America
3000 Whitehaven Street, NW
Washington DC 20008
Tel. (202) 612-4400
Fax (202) 518-2154
www.italyemb.org
stampa@italyemb.org
Consulates at: Boston, MA -
Chicago, IL - Detroit, MI - Houston,
TX - Los Angeles, CA - Miami, FL -
Newark, NJ - New York, NY -
Philadelphia, PA - San Francisco, CA

ENIT (Italian State Tourist Board)

Australia
Level 4, 46 Market Street
NSW 2000 Sidney
PO Box Q802 - QVB NSW 1230
Tel. 00612 92 621666
Fax 00612 92 621677
italia@italiantourism.com.au

Canada
175 Bloor Street E. Suite 907 –
South Tower
M4W3R8 Toronto (Ontario)
Tel. (416) 925 4882
Fax (416) 925 4799
www.italiantourism.com
enit.canada@on.aibn.com

Great Britain
1, Princes Street
W1B 2AY London
Tel. 020 7408 1254
Tel. 800 00482542 FREE from
United Kingdom and Ireland
italy@italiantouristboard.co.uk

United States of America
500, North Michigan Avenue
Suite 2240
60611 Chicago 1, Illinois
Tel. (312) 644 0996 / 644 0990
Fax (312) 644 3019
www.italiantourism.com
enitch@italiantourism.com

12400, Wilshire Blvd. – Suite 550
CA 90025 Los Angeles
Tel. (310) 820 1898 - 820 9807
Fax (310) 820 6357
www.italiantourism.com
enitla@italiantourism.com

630, Fifth Avenue – Suite 1565
NY – 10111 New York
Tel. (212) 245 4822 – 245 5618
Fax (212) 586 9249
www.italiantourism.com
enitny@italiantourism.com

Emilia-Romagna is a region where cultural events and art live side by side with its people's passion for good food and enjoying life to the full. In an atmosphere imbued with an old-fashioned charm, its historic monuments are decorated with bright colors. Under the Torre degli Asinelli in Bologna, the trattorias are alive with the gentle buzz of good humor which typifies the locals. People who know how to enjoy themselves and give others a good time, but, at the same time, hard-working creative people who have succeeded in exploiting their a fertile land. Here, historical events and the genius of the people of Emilia and Romagna have resulted in a

Abbey	→ Abbazia	Museum	→ Museo
Cathedral	→ Duomo	Oratory	→ Oratorio
Chapel	→ Cappella	Park	→ Parco
Castle	→ Castello	Parish church	→ Pieve
Church	→ Chiesa	Hall	→ Sala
Doorway	→ Porta	Theater	→ Teatro
Fountain	→ Fontana	Sanctuary	→ Santuario

large number of splendid cities of art, fascinating towns and isolated monuments of great architectural merit.

A region which is worth exploring in detail, because there are wonderful surprises in store in terms of art treasures and beautiful landscape, from the Apennines and the plain down to the coastal strip.

Highlights

- The refined, elegant castle of the Este family in Ferrara
- The elaborate decoration of Modena cathedral
- The splendid gold and brightly-colored mosaics in Ravenna

> Bold, stars and italics are used in the text to emphasize the importance of places and works of art:
>
> **bold type **** → **not to be missed**
> **bold type *** → **very important**
> **bold type** → **important**
> *italic type* → **interesting**

Inside

16 Bologna
31 Ferrara
45 Forlì-Cesena
54 Modena
67 Parma
77 Piacenza
83 Ravenna
95 Reggio Emilia
103 Rimini

15

In the urban landscape of Bologna, the monumental buildings blend into the fabric of minor buildings, hidden behind their red and ochre-colored walls and rows of porticoes. The porticoes, which, end-to-end, amount to almost 38km in length, lend harmony to the city landscape, attenuating the breaks between buildings with different architectural styles. Its nicknames, Bologna "the Learned" and Bologna "the Fat", refer to the city's famous university and its gastronomic tradition. Traces of the Roman and medieval origins of this city of art and culture, built at the foot of the Apennine foothills, can still be perceived today, but the predominant impression is of architecture of the 17th and 18th centuries, interspersed with buildings erected in the following two centuries. The history of Bologna begins with Roman colonization and the building of the Via Aemilia, which still forms the backbone of the modern city. In the 11th century, Bologna's reputation as a center for law led to the founding of the oldest part of the university (1088). In medieval times, many towers and tower-houses were built by feudal lords who came to live here and the newly-emerging merchant classes, as were the porticoes, which provided a setting for craft and commercial activities. The city's appearance changed radically in the 15th century under the rule of the Bentivoglio family. When Bologna was incorporated into the Papal States, an oligarchy of nobles, the Senate, held economic power and ruled the city. Bologna now began to take on the appearance which still predominates today, with its senators' palaces, its convents and monasteries being made ever more beautiful. After Italian Unification (1861), there was an attempt to recover Bologna's image as a Gothic commune, in contrast to the Baroque city, and restoration work was carried out in an endeavor to emphasize its medieval character. Bologna is a city with a human dimension, a place where past and present live side by side. The streets of the city center are pervaded by an atmosphere of days gone by. The noises of the city are muffled and fade into the background. What predominates is the feeling of being in a medieval town, but, walking under the porticoes, you encounter the university city. Jolly groups of students, street musicians and the colorful signs above the trattorie are indications of a relaxed and hard-working city.

Fontana del Nettuno ❶

The famous bronze statue in the center of the Fountain of Neptune depicting the god in the process of placating the waves, popularly known as *"il Gigante"* (the Giant), is the work of Giambologna (1563-66). It stands on a base designed by Tommaso Laureti. Giambologna also executed the four *putti* (cherubs) with dolphins and the four mermaids. The square named after the fountain was laid out in 1564 to provide access to the city's largest square, Piazza Maggiore, which the people of Bologna refer to as *"la piazza"*.

Piazza Maggiore ❷

The noble monumental center of the city was laid out between 1200 and 1203, and assumed its current appearance in the first half of the 15th century. It has always been the setting for the city's most important civic and religious ceremonies and festivals. Until 1877, it was also the market square. Splendid public buildings overlook the square: **Palazzo del Podestà***, **Palazzo Comunale*** and the **basilica of S. Petronio****. On the south-west side of the square, Palazzo dei Notai is a late 14th-century palace which was radically restored in 1908; on the east side, Palazzo dei Banchi is actually a facade erected (1565-68) to harmonize the east side of the square like a sort of stage-set, with the two great arches which lead into the animated streets where the market is held.

Palazzo del Podestà ❸

This palazzo adjoins the Palazzo di Re Enzo behind, forming a single block, situated above the crossroads of two passageways. The tall Torre dell'Arengo (1212) was built daringly above the crossroads of the passageways below; the large bell at the top of the tower, called the *Campanazzo* by the locals (brought here in 1453), is rung to mark important civic occasions.

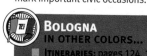

BOLOGNA
IN OTHER COLORS...
- ITINERARIES: pages 124, 125
- FOOD: pages 142, 147, 151
- SHOPPING: pages 176, 178
- EVENTS: page 182
- WELLNESS: pages 199, 203
- PRACTICAL INFO: page 211

View of Piazza Maggiore from north-east, with Palazzo Comunale at the far end

The porticoed facade of the building overlooking the square was re-designed with Renaissance forms in 1485. **Palazzo di Re Enzo**, whose facades overlook Piazza del Nettuno and Via Rizzoli, owes its name to the son of Emperor Frederick II who, when he was captured at the battle of Fossalta (1249), was imprisoned here until he died (1272). It was built in 1244 as a palace for the city magistrature, but its present appearance is the result of radical restoration work (1913). In the vault of the crossroads of the covered passageways are terracotta statues of the four patron saints of the city by Alfonso Lombardi (1525). This complex is now used for permanent exhibitions, conferences, and other events.

Palazzo Comunale ❹

Also known as Palazzo d'Accursio, this palace was built and added to subsequently. The original part of the palazzo (13-14C) is the porticoed building with the tower. The rest is the result of defenses added in 1365 which, on three sides of the building, give it the appearance of a fortress. The facade is graced by large 15th-century windows and a terracotta **Madonna and Child** by Niccolò dell'Arca (1478). The former municipal offices are now a cultural center for the city. The central part of these facilities is the impressive former Stock Exchange: below the glass floor you can see Roman and early medieval remains. The building is entered through a 16th-century doorway; beyond the courtyard, a large sloping ramp with long, shallow steps leads up to the first floor and the Sala d'Ercole, with a

statue of Hercules by Alfonso Lombardi (1519) and a fresco of the **Madonna of the Earthquake** by Francesco Francia (1505). On the second floor, the Sala Farnese leads into the Farnese chapel. Off the Sala Farnese is the entrance to the **Museo Giorgio Morandi***, which contains 281 works (paintings, watercolors, drawings, etchings and two sculptures) by the great Italian 20th-century artist. It also contains the entrance to the **Municipal Art Collections***, which include paintings from the 13th-19th centuries of the Bologna and Emilia Schools, furniture from the 17th and 18th centuries, 17th- and 18th-century miniatures, tapestries, ceramics, clocks, decorations and frescoes from the 16th-19th centuries and 19th-century paintings.

Palazzo Comunale, a large building with a square plan and palace-cum-fortified town

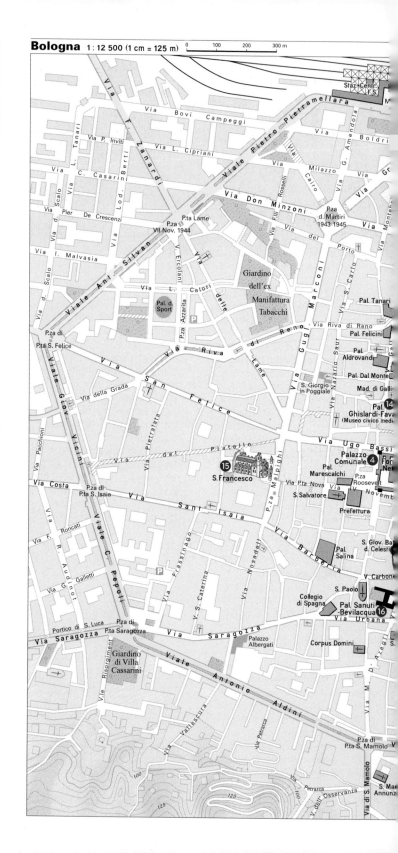

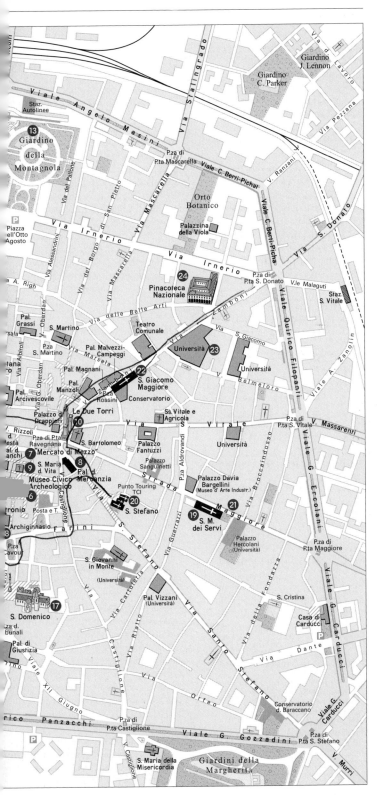

S. Petronio ⑤

The imposing basilica of S. Petronio, a fine example of the Italian Gothic style, dominates the square from a platform which accentuates its size and symbolic image. Dedicated to Petronius, bishop and patron saint of Bologna, but never a cathedral, the church is proof of the city's ideals of independence. In fact, it was the civic authorities who decided to erect the church at the end of the 14th century. The construction of the basilica, designed by Antonio di Vincenzo, began in 1390 and was not completed until the mid-17th century. Note the decoration in Istrian stone and pink Verona marble. The three doorways are decorated with marvelous **sculptures**** by Jacopo della Quercia (1425-38), a masterpiece of the transition between the Gothic and Renaissance styles. On the right of the church is the bell tower, erected in 1492. The side-chapels *inside the church* have carved marble or wrought-iron screens (15-17C). In the right aisle, the second chapel has 15th-century frescoes and a polyptych attributed to Tommaso Garelli; in the third chapel, a frescoed polyptych of the Lombard School (15C); in the fourth chapel, *stained-glass windows* by James of Ulm (1466); in the fifth chapel, a **Pietà** by Amico Aspertini (1519) and a *wooden Crucifix* (1462); in the sixth chapel, **St Jerome**, a panel by Lorenzo Costa (1484); in the eighth chapel, carved and inlaid **stalls** (1521); opposite the eleventh chapel, a painted terracotta group of figures depicting the **Lamentation of the Dead Christ** by Vincenzo Onofri (late 15C). In the presbytery, the tribune by Vignola (1548) was altered in the 17th century. With regard to the two organs, the one on the right is one of the oldest in Italy (1475). In the left aisle, the first chapel has a **St Roch** by Parmigianino. A little further on is the beginning of the meridian line which stretches as far as the west wall, traced by Gian Domenico Cassini (1655). This feature was regarded by travelers on the Grand Tour as one of the most curious sites of the city. In the seventh chapel, a **Madonna and Saints** by Lorenzo Costa (1492); in the fifth chapel, a **Martyrdom of St Sebastian** of the Emilia School (second half 15C); in the fourth chapel, *frescoes* by Giovanni da Modena and assistants (1410-15).

The pilasters are decorated with early 15th-century frescoes; the beautiful second chapel, where the relic of the head of St Petronius is kept, has rich decoration by Alfonso Torreggiani (1750); in the first chapel, frescoes by Giovanni da Modena. The **Museo di S. Petronio**, accessed from the far end of the left aisle, has two rooms containing drawings and designs for the facade of the basilica, the instruments used by Gian Domenico Cassini to mark out the meridian in the church, some 16th-century low reliefs, a model of the basilica dating from about 1515; vestments and furnishings dating from the 16th to 18th centuries, reliquaries, chalices and gold- and silver-work from the 13th century, and illuminated corals (15-16C).

Basilica di S. Petronio

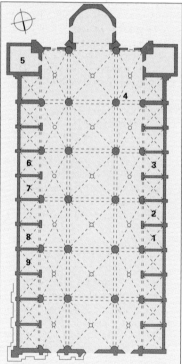

1 Pietà by A. Aspertini
2 St Jerome by L. Costa
3 Choirstalls dated 1521
4 Terracotta sculpture by V. Onofrio
5 Museo di S. Petronio
6 St Roch by Parmigianino
7 Madonna by L. Costa
8 15th-century St Sebastian
9 Frescoes by Giovanni da Modena

Museo Civico Archeologico ⑥

Via dell'Archiginnasio runs along the left side of S. Petronio. On the opposite side of the street, the *portico del Pavaglione* is

The nave of S. Petronio

always crowded. At No. 2 is the entrance to the Museo Civico Archeologico, one of Bologna's most prestigious institutions, housed in the former hospital of S. Maria della Morte, a 15th-century building converted by Antonio Morandi (1565). It has a vast and very prestigious collection. The prehistoric section contains objects dating from the Paleolithic to the Bronze Age, mostly from the Bologna area. The finds from the Villanova culture (a modern name applied to a prehistoric culture, dating from the 9C to the mid-6C BC, it refers to the town of Villanova, where the remains of a necropolis were found in the 19th century) consist of groups of grave goods. The museum's **Etruscan finds** include the *Certosa situla*, a bronze-plated bucket with reliefs depicting scenes from daily life and religious processions, and some *votive bronze statuettes* (early 5C, BC). The museum has some good Greek and Roman displays and the **Egyptian collection** is one of the finest in Europe.

Mercato di Mezzo ⑦

"Mercato di Mezzo", the old name for the area between Piazza Maggiore and Piazza della Mercanzia, is lined with all kinds of shops interspersed with high-quality craft workshops. With its own particular atmosphere, for centuries this was the market-place, (the "stomach of Bologna", as it was sometimes described). Today the late-Roman street plan is still there and the names of the streets hark back to the

trades that used to flourish here: Via Clavature (referring to the locks made by blacksmiths) and Via Drapperie (referring to upholsterers).

Palazzo della Mercanzia ⑧

Palazzo della Mercanzia, erected in the late-Gothic style under the supervision of Antonio di Vincenzo and Lorenzo da Bagnomarino (1384-91), was originally a customs house. Built of brick and Istrian stone, it has a splendid loggia with two pointed arches and three pilasters decorated in various architectural styles with flowers on the capitals.

S. Maria della Vita ⑨

This Baroque church overlooks Via Clavature (no. 10). Built on a central oval plan, the space inside the church is dominated by its height. To the right of the high altar is a wonderful sculpture of the **Lamentation of the Dead Christ***, composed of seven life-size polychrome terracotta figures, an work by Niccolò dell'Arca (1463). In the adjoining oratory (1617) is another fine composition of 14 statues depicting the **Transito della Madonna**, by Alfonso Lombardi (1522).

Due Torri ⑩

The Two Towers (Due Torri), also called the *Torri Pendenti* (Leaning Towers), are the most famous of the many towers built during the medieval period and are the best-known site in the city. These huge towers, which, during the Medieval period, were built not only in towns, but also in villages and tiny country hamlets, were not only for defensive purposes. The families and institutions which promoted and sponsored the building of the towers celebrated and reinforced their power and wealth. The **Torre degli Asinelli*** (97.20m high) was named after the family who built it in the early 12th century; the small fort at the bottom of the tower was added in 1488. Those who wish to brave the 498 steps of the tower, which leans west 2.23m off the perpendicular, will be rewarded with magnificent views over the city. **Torre Garisenda*** (48.16m), built in the same period and owned by the Garisendi family, was originally 60m high. The height was reduced amid fears that it might collapse (1351-60); a plaque recalls the verses written by Dante Alighieri inspired by the tower.

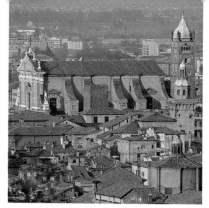

The bell tower of the Metropolitana of S. Pietro

Via dell'Indipendenza ⑪

This long, porticoed street was laid out in 1888 to connect the city center to the station. On the right of Via dell'Indipendenza (nos. 3-5) stands *Palazzo Scappi*, which incorporates a tower built in 1220 by the Scappi family. Further along on the right, beyond the Metropolitana di S. Pietro, at no.11, is the portico known as the *Monte di Pietà*, re-built in 1758. In the adjoining Via del Monte is a courtyard with a double loggia (second half of the 15C). At no. 8 Via del Monte is **Palazzo Boncompagni**, built in the early 16th century. It was owned by the Pope Gregory XIII Boncompagni, who was born in Bologna and is also famous for promoting (1582) the Gregorian calendar.

Chiesa Metropolitana di S. Pietro ⑫

The original church of the Metropolitana di S. Pietro was altered several times, but the present structure dates from the re-building work executed in 1605 by Floriano Ambrosini. Its imposing brick facade with marble decoration was designed by Alfonso Torreggiani (1747). Inside, the nave is flanked by communicating side-chapels, and the presbytery was designed by Domenico Tibaldi in 1575. The terracotta figures of the **Pietà** by Alfonso Lombardi (1522) and the Romanesque (12C) holy water stoups on each side of the main doorway and the side entrance in the right wall of the church are worthy of note; in the large lunette above the apse is an *Annunciation* by Ludovico Carracci, his last work (1619). The *Museo del Tesoro della Cattedrale* has a fine collection of superb early examples of sacred art.
Outside the church, the **bell tower*** is important both from an architectural and historical point of view; it was begun in 1184 and the pinnacles on the top were

added in 1426. Next to it, the Portico dell'Episcopio (12C) surrounds the *Palazz Arcivescovile* (Archbishop' Palace), designed by Domenico Tibaldi (1575) and restored in the mid-19th century. The district around the church of the Metropolitana contains many medieval houses and towers, and is the part of Bologna which best evokes the medieval flavor of the city.

Montagnola ⑬

An impressive late 19th-century staircase leads up to the top of the hill, which was laid out as a garden in 1662 and is now a public park. Reliefs and groups of statues depict events in the history of the city. At the bottom of the Montagnola is Porta Galliera, dating from 1661.

Museo Civico Medievale ⑭

No. 4 Via Manzoni, the majestic **Palazzo Ghisilardi-Fava**, is a typical example of local late 15th-century architecture. Today, it houses the city's medieval collection, with material dating from the Middle Ages and the Renaissance. Highlights of the museum include sculptures from the 14th-17th centuries, bronze figurines and plaquettes dating from the Renaissance, sacred vestments, Byzantine ivories (10-12C), fibulas, military bracelets and early medieval gold-and-silver-work; various works of figurative art from the period of rule of the Bentivoglio (15C) and a fine weapon collection dating from the 16th and 17th centuries. The museum also has many interesting exhibits relating to natural history and the exotic from private collections made in previous centuries.

S. Francesco ⑮

This Franciscan chrurch was built between 1236 and 1263, restored in the 19th century and re-built after the Second World War. The larger bell tower, by Antonio di Vincenzo, was erected in about 1402 while the other dates from the 13th century. The most interesting feature of this building is the apse, with a choir and deambulatory with chapels arranged around the edge and rampant supporting arches, in the late-Gothic style. The facade, the lines of which are Romanesque (completed in about 1250), rises to a point, and has a doorway with a porch. Inside, Renaissance tombs decorate the base of the walls, including the *monument to Pietro Fieschi* (second on right, 15C), the tomb of *Pope Alexander* V (fourth on left), and the tombs of Nicolò Lamberti and Sperandio di Bartolomeo (1424-82). At the high altar is a precious **altar-piece*** with marble low reliefs, statues and fretwork sculpted by Pier Paolo dalle Masegne (1392). The *sacristy*, dating from the late 13th century, is by Antonio di Vincenzo. The adjoining monastery, where, in the 13th century, the "Universitas Artistarum" (University of Artists) used to meet, contains the *Chiostro dei Morti* (late 14C), and the tombs of the rectors of the university. Behind the church, in Piazza Malpighi, are the **tombs of the Glossatori***, the authors, in the medieval university of Bologna, of the comments (or *glosse*) on legal texts. The tombs are located in raised platforms protected by sloping roofs and decorated with majolicas.

alazzo Sanuti-Bevilacqua ⑯

This palazzo is one of the finest expressions of early Renaissance architecture in Bologna. Built between 1477 and 1482, it is completely decorated with rusticated ashlars, with two tiers of elaborate one- and two-light windows. The porticoed **courtyard**, with its loggia and double tiers of arches, has worked columns and capitals and a frieze around the edge.

5. Domenico ⑰

The church of S. Domenico overlooks **Piazza S. Domenico**, an irregularly-shaped cobbled square in the urban fabric, the site of two votive 17th-century columns and the **tombs*** of two doctors of law. The church, with a monastery attached, was built in the late-Romanesque style between 1228 and 1238 and altered in 1727-33. The facade

culminates in a single point. Inside, the nave and two side-aisles reflect the tenets of classic 18th-century elegance. Half-way up the right aisle is the *chapel of St Dominic*, built in 1597-1605 on a Greek-cross plan, with a dome and a *Glory of St Dominic* by Guido Reni (1613-15) in the vault; below is the **tomb of St Dominic****, a startling sculptural composition executed by artists from different periods. The sarcophagus is by Nicola Pisano, assisted by Arnolfo di Cambio, Pagno di Lapo and Fra' Guglielmo (1265-67). Behind the tomb is the *reliquary of the head of St Dominic* (Jacopo Roseto, 1383). In the chapel in the right transept, a *St Thomas Aquinas* by Guercino (1662); in the chapel on the right of the presbytery, a **Mystic Marriage of St Catherine** by Filippino Lippi (1501). In the presbytery are beautifully inlaid wooden **choirstalls***. In the left transept, a painting of the **Crucifix** by Giunta Pisano (1250) and a *funerary monument to Taddeo Pepoli*, the work of a Tuscan sculptor dating from the 14th century. In the left aisle, in the chapel of the Rosary, at the altar, is a *series of small paintings* by Ludovico Carracci, Bartolomeo Cesi, Guido Reni, Francesco Albani and others; in the vestibule beyond it, the **monument to Alessandro Tartagni**, an elegant work by Francesco di Simone Ferrucci; in the second chapel, **Raymond of Peñafort** by Ludovico Carracci. At the end of the right aisle is the entrance to the **Museo di S. Domenico**, which contains gold- and silver-work, holy vestments, reliquaries, codices and illuminated choir-books (from the 13C) belonging to the church, and some important paintings and sculptures, including a terracotta **bust of St Dominic** by Niccolò dell'Arca (1474). The right transept leads into the *Chiostro dei Morti*

THE OSTERIE OF BOLOGNA

The old osterie of the city are places where Bologna's glorious traditions of fine wines and cuisine are jealously preserved. They started as locande, inns with rooms, which offered food and drink to their guests. These locande became particularly popular in Bologna in the second half of the 13th century, both as a result of the city's increasing importance as a stopping-place on the main route between north and south, and because of the growing numbers of students attracted by the prestige of the university founded in 1088. There were once more than 150 of them. There were probably a similar number in the 16th century, when the city witnessed the building of the basilica of S. Petronio. Of course, today's osterie are different, and the differences between these and wine bars, pubs and trendy bars are becoming gradually more attenuated. What has remained is the jolly atmosphere, which is still to be found – albeit in a more modern version – in the approximately 200 venues of this kind to which Bologna owes much of its lively reputation.

Basilica di S. Domenico

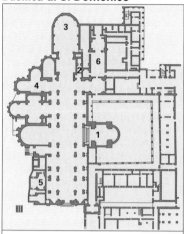

1 Cappella di S. Domenico
2 St Catherine by Filippino Lippi
3 16th-century wooden choirstalls
4 Crucifix by Giunta Pisano
5 Painting by L. Carracci
6 Museo di S. Domenico

(14-15C), dominated by the Romanesque Gothic bell tower of S. Domenico. From Piazza S. Domenico, we can walk along the 19th-century street of Via Garibaldi, to Piazza dei Tribunali. Here, the majestic **Palazzo Ranuzzi** was converted into a "seat of law" in 1870 and is therefore also called Palazzo di Giustizia. This work of Palladian inspiration (1584) contains a magnificent double staircase (1695) worthy of a stage-set.

Archiginnasio ⑱

Palazzo Archiginnasio is a long, porticoed building with a square internal courtyard and a double loggia. Like almost all the rooms, the walls of the courtyard are decorated with painted or sculpted coats-of-arms of rectors, priors and students who attended the Studio (as Bologna University is called) between 1500 and 1700. Off the courtyard on the ground floor is the *chapel of S. Maria dei Bulgari* and, on the first floor, the **anatomy theater**: the design is by Antonio Levanti (1649), and the 18th-century wooden sculptures are by Ercole Lelli and Silvestro Giannotti. Since 1835, the palazzo, which was the main part of the university until 1803, has housed the prestigious **Municipal Library**, which contains more than 650,000 volumes, 12,000 manuscripts, letters, maps and prints.

S. Maria dei Servi ⑲

The Gothic church of S. Maria dei Servi, begun in 1346 and finished in 1545, has a elegant four-sided portico dating from different periods (late 14C to mid-19C). Th interior, consisting of a nave and two side aisles, is late-Gothic in style. The most interesting part of the church is the ambulatory, decorated with fragments of frescoes by Vitale da Bologna (1355). On the walls: a *Madonna Enthroned with Saints*, attributed to Lippo di Dalmasio, and a *Madonna and Child with Saints*, a polychrome terracotta altar-piece by Vincenzo Onofri (1503); in the third chape a **Maestà**** by Cimabue and a fresco by Lippo di Dalmasio; near the side-door, a holy water stoup with a marble griffon (14C). In the presbytery are some fine wooden inlaid choirstalls (15-17C) and, on the left wall, a *Virgin with the Seven Founder Saints* by Giuseppe Maria Crespi (1734). In the left aisle, at the sixth altar, an *Annunciation* by Innocenzo da Imola and frescoes by Bagnacavallo.

Complesso di S. Stefano ⑳

Via S. Stefano is one of the most characteristic streets of the old city of Bologna. The part of the street which lead from Piazza della Mercanzia towards the monumental complex, in front of which lie a picturesque series of buildings, is also called Piazzola di S. Stefano. The square is overlooked by **Palazzo Bolognini** (16C),

The old anatomy theater in the Archiginnasio

which has unusual anthropomorphic decoration on the facade, the picturesque group of houses of **Case Tacconi**, where Renaissance features blend with Gothic, and *Palazzo Isolani*, with its 18th-century facade, and Palazzo Bolognini (15C), also decorated with faces of animals and monsters. The complex of S. Stefano is one of Bologna's most important religious centers and dates back more than a thousand years. It incorporates a series of religious buildings, also known as the Sette Chiese (Seven Churches), which were built and altered in different periods, with features which date back to late Antiquity. Much of what you see today is the result of restoration work conducted between 1870 and 1930. From left to right, the following buildings overlook the square: the church of the Crocifisso, the octagonal church of S. Sepolcro and the church of Ss. Vitale e Agricola. The church of the Crocifisso has a Romanesque facade culminating in a single point and a pulpit dating from 1488. Inside there is a single nave and a raised presbytery dating from the 14th century, altered in 1637. Suspended from the arch above the choir is a wooden painted *Crucifix* by Simone dei Crocifissi; below the presbytery is the crypt. A door on the left of the church leads into the **church of S. Sepolcro** (12C). Built on a dodecagonal plan, the church has an ambulatory, matroneums and incorporates a number of re-used Roman capitals. The **church of Santi Vitale e Agricola**, which dates from the 11th century, has a nave and two side-aisles divided by cruciform pilasters alternating with Roman columns. The side-apses contain the tombs (11C) which once held the remains of the proto-martyrs Vitale and Agricola. From the church of Santo Sepolcro you can access the rectangular **Cortile di Pilato (Pilate's Courtyard)**: in the center is an 8th-century marble bowl with a Lombard inscription; the two side-chapels contain 16th-century frescoes. From the courtyard you enter the *church of the Trinità*, with a nave and transepts, restored in 1924. The chapel on the left contains a wooden sculpture of the **Adoration of the Magi** (14C) by Simone dei Crocifissi. The courtyard also leads into the **Chiostro dei Benedettini (Cloister of the Benedictines)** (12-13C), with two tiers of loggias: the lower tier has arches resting on large pillars and groups of four small columns, while the upper tier is supported

Complesso di S. Stefano

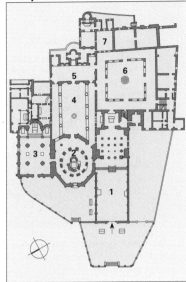

1 Chiesa del Crocifisso
2 S. Sepolcro
3 Ss. Vitale e Agricola
4 Cortile di Pilato
5 Chiesa della Trinità
6 Chiostro dei Benedettini
7 Museum

by pairs of small columns and capitals with plant, animal and human motifs. Off the cloister lies the **Museo di S. Stefano**, with a remarkable collection of paintings of the Bologna School from the 14th and 15th centuries, statues, low reliefs, reliquaries and church furnishings (14-18C).

Strada Maggiore ㉑

For centuries, as its name suggests, Strada Maggiore, the part of the Via Aemilia which crosses the city center, lay on the main route to Rome. Cutting straight through the city, it has porticoes on each side in the section below the Torre degli Asinelli. Almost every building on the street has some feature of interest, whether medieval houses, palaces or churches. The senatorial **Palazzo Hercolani** dates from the 18th century. On the ground floor is an atrium, a loggia, a grand courtyard and an English-style garden; a neo-classical monumental staircase leads up to the piano nobile (upper floor). Facing Piazza di Porta Ravegnana, on the right, beyond *Palazzo Poggi Tartagni*, with its 15th-century capitals, the neo-classical facade of the 16th-century *Palazzo*

The Renaissance doorway of S. Giacomo Maggiore

Sanguinetti incorporates the medieval Torre Oseletti. Beyond **Casa Isolani** (13C) with its tall wooden piers are the classic 16th-century facades of *Palazzo Fantuzzi* and *Palazzo Gessi*, and *Casa Valori* and *Casa Bonfanti*, which date from the 15th and 14th centuries respectively.

S. Giacomo Maggiore ㉒

This church dedicated to St James the Greater, one of the city's most important monuments, was built by Agostinian monks between 1267 and 1343. In the second half of the 15th century, the interior was re-designed in the Renaissance style. An elegant **portico** decorated with terracotta friezes and grooved sandstone columns was added to the side of the church. The Gothic facade of the church culminates in a small shrine containing a statue of the saint. It has a rose-window (replaced in 1954), two tall two-light windows, a doorway with two lions supporting columns, and niches with tombs on either side. The interior has a single nave, and side-chapels in groups of three, under large arches joined at the top by a gallery adorned with statues. In the seventh chapel on the right, a *Mystic Marriage of St Catherine* (1536) and other frescoes by Innocenzo da Imola; in the ninth chapel, a **St Roch Consoled by an Angel** by Ludovico Carracci; further on is the **Poggi chapel**, designed, decorated and frescoed by Pellegrino Tibaldi (mid-16C). The ambulatory contains several works (14-15C): in the second chapel, a **polyptych** by Paolo Veneziano and a Crucifix by Jacopo di Paolo; in the third chapel,

a *Coronation of the Virgin and Saints* by Jacopo di Paolo and, on the left, a *Crucifix* by Simone dei Crocifissi (1370); the sixth chapel is the **Bentivoglio chapel****, built on a square plan with a dome (1486): above the altar, a **Madonna Enthroned with Child and Saints**, a painting by Francesco Francia (c.1494), in the upper lunette, the *Vision of the Apocalypse* is a fresco by Lorenzo Costa; on the walls, also by Costa, are (on the left), a **Triumph of Death and Triumph of Fame** (1490) and (on the right) a *Madonna and Child with the Bentivoglio family* (1488). Opposite, next to the edge of the presbytery, is the **tomb of Anton Galeazzo Bentivoglio** executed by Jacopo della Quercia and his assistants (1435). The portico outside leads into Via Zamboni, and the *oratory of S. Cecilia* which contains a remarkable **fresco cycle*** depicting scenes from the life of Sts Valerian and Cecilia, by Francesco Francia, Lorenzo Costa and others.

The church overlooks **Via Zamboni***, an old street which begins in Piazza di Porta Ravegnana. The street was altered in the second half of the 15th century by the Bentivoglio, where the street widens out is the neo-classical facade of the 16th-century Palazzo Manzoli. Opposite, *Palazzo Malvezzi de' Medici* has a large staircase which leads up to the first floor. Beyond it, Palazzo Magnani was designed by Domenico Tibaldi (1577-87) and belonged to a family of blacksmiths (*magnano* in the dialect of Padua means blacksmith); in the grand hall is a fine frieze with frescoes depicting **stories of Romulus** (1590-92) by three of the Carracci and an interesting art collection. Next-door is the splendid **Palazzo Malvezzi** (16C) **Campeggi**, with an elaborate portico.

Università ㉓

The heart of the cultural city is **Palazzo Poggi** (1549); originally the seat of the Institute of Sciences (1711) it became the seat of the university in 1803. Founded in 1088, **Bologna University**, called the "Studio", is regarded as the oldest in Europe. A century later it had already acquired great prestige. Palazzo Poggi is dominated by the two parts of the *Torre della Specola* (1721). Once an astronomical observatory of primary importance, today it houses the interesting **Museo di Astronomia**, with a fine collection of instruments including medieval astrolabes.

The headquarters of the Academy of Sciences has frescoes depicting **stories of Ulysses** by Pellegrino Tibaldi (1549). In the main seat of the university, the **Musei di Palazzo Poggi** incorporate the old laboratories of the 18th-century Istituto delle Scienze. The rooms of the museum, which was conceived in a way that links teaching, research and conservation, focus on the following themes: *Boats and seafaring; Military architecture; Human anatomy; Obstetrics.* The *Museo Storico dello Studio*, housed in the same building, has a multimedia section which, with documents and memorabilia, tells the story of the university. Next to Palazzo Poggi is the entrance to the **University Library**, with a large reading-room and 18th-century walnut bookshelves. Other rooms contain 16th-century friezes. The library contains rare manuscripts, a collection of incunabula and ancient papyruses. Further along Via Zamboni is the interesting **Museo di Geologia e Paleontologia Giovanni Capellini***, with the largest paleontological collection in Italy. It includes early collections, fossilized plants and vertebrates, and geological specimens. There is a remarkable life-size (24m) model of a Diplodocus (species of dinosaur).

Pinacoteca Nazionale ㉔

The gallery is housed in a palazzo in Via delle Belle Arti which dates from the second half of the 17th century. The collection began as the private collection of the Accademia di Belle Arti, established here in 1804. It was subsequently enhanced in the second half of the 19th century and mainly contains paintings by artists from Bologna and Emilia from the 14th-18th centuries. The collection reflects the artistic development of the city. Highlights of the collection include: **St James at the Battle of Clavijo*** by Pseudo Jacopino di Francesco (first half of the 14C); a polyptych of the **Madonna and Child with Saints*** by Giotto and his workshop (1333-34); a number of works by Vitale da Bologna: a **Last Supper** (a fresco fragment), a **St George and the Dragon*** and four panels depicting the **stories of St Anthony Abbot**. There are also works dating from the late-Gothic and Renaissance periods, works of the Ferrara School, including the **Merchants' altar-piece*** by Francesco del Cossa (1474), and by painters from Bologna, such as the **Ecstacy of St Cecilia*** by Raphael. Works from the Emilian Mannerist School include a **Madonna and Child with Saints*** by Parmigianino. Other works document the Golden Age of the Bologna School between the late 16th century and the second half of the 17th century, including a **Madonna degli Scalzi*** by Ludovico Carracci; a **Madonna of St Louis*** by Annibale Carracci; a **Slaughter of the Innocents**, Samson Victorious** and Portrait of a Mother** by Guido Reni. The 18th century is mainly represented by the works of Giuseppe Maria Crespi (**Courtyard Scene***), Donato Creti and the three Gandolfi: Ubaldo, Gaetano and Mauro.

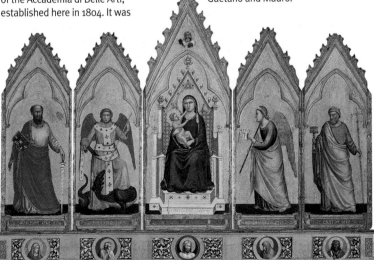

The beautiful polyptych of the Madonna and Saints by Giotto in the Pinacoteca Nazionale

BUDRIO [18 km]

The ancient town of Budrio is surrounded by fruit plantations. A castle was added to the medieval fabric between 1363 and 1379. Today, a few round towers are all that survive of the town's 15th-century walls. Economic growth between the 16th and 18th centuries resulted in the building of many palaces and porticoed houses. On the main street, Via Bissolati, stands the austere *Palazzo Gandolfi* and *Casa Tubertini*, with a *relief of the Trinity* on the facade. In *Piazza Quirico Filopanti* (1864) is the **Church of S. Lorenzo**, altered in the 18th century. The church is preceded by a portico and has a facade with a 15th-century clock-tower. Opposite the church, across the square, is *Palazzo Comunale*, built in the neo-Gothic style, crowned with Ghibelline merlons. Next to it is the 15th-century *clock-tower*, restored in 1871, formerly the watch-tower at the entrance to the old castle, with a belfry on the top. Below the tower is the entrance to the *Church of S. Maria del Borgo*, which contains a *Flight into Egypt* by Mastelletta. In Via Giuseppe Garibaldi, next to *Palazzo*

Boriani Dalla Noce, is the *theater*, built in the 17th century (altered in 1924-28), and *Palazzo della Partecipanza* (entrance in Via Mentana), which houses the **Pinacoteca Civica Domenico Inzaghi** and the *Museo Civico Archeologico e Paleoambientale*. The art gallery contains valuable works by artists from Emilia from the 14th to 18th centuries. From Piazza Matteotti, at the end of Via Bissolati, it is only a short walk (1km), to the *little church of Ss. Gervasio e Protasio*. Founded in 401, it has a Baroque facade preceded by a large portico, a curved tympanum, and a contrasting 14th-century bell tower. The interior is a jewel of early medieval art. There is a white marble cross with Lombard and Carolingian decoration.

IMOLA [33 km]

Imola is a typical Romagna town, situated on the Via Aemilia which bisects it. The old part of the town is compact and uniform and easy to identify because of the orthogonal street plan. In the town center, **Piazza Matteotti** ❶ is a pleasant, well-proportioned square (1474-84) overlooked by the broad, austere facade of **Palazzo Sersanti** (1480-84), once occupied by the lords of the town; its harmonious

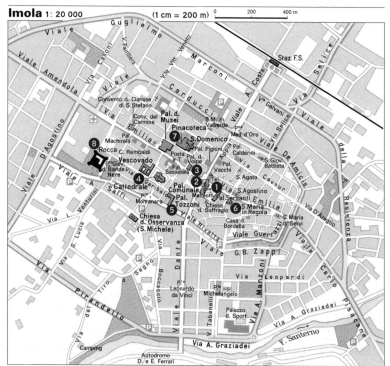

Imola 1: 20 000 (1 cm = 200 m)

Renaissance lines are reminiscent of the style of Brunelleschi, especially in the use of dosserets which support the capitals, making the arches more slender. Opposite, **Palazzo Comunale** ❷ dates from the 13th and 14th centuries and was re-structured in the second half of the 18th century. You can see traces of the old building on the right-hand side, in the pointed arches with Romanesque capitals. From the piazza we can turn into **Via Emilia**, where we find **Palazzo Della Volpe** ❸ (c.1480), with terracotta decoration in the facades. Across the street is Palazzo dei Musei, built in the 18th century above the foundations of the former *Franciscan monastery* (14C). The remains of the lower church are still clearly visible (part of the nave and the apse, with traces of frescoes), whereas the upper church has been converted into a *theater*. The complex now houses the **Museo Civico G. Scarabelli** (temporarily closed). The rooms with geological and archeological exhibits are particularly interesting (with finds dating from the Villanova period to the early Middle Ages). The palazzo also houses the municipal library, which has a rare Latin *psalter* dating from the 13th century and incorporates the rooms of the 18th-century Franciscan library.
The **Cathedral** ❹ of Imola towers majestically above the surrounding buildings. Dedicated to St Cassian, it dates from the 12th century, but was completely re-built in 1781. However, the proportions and the inner essence of the old Romanesque church were left intact. The facade is of a later date (1850), but the bell tower dates from the 15th century. In the classical spacious interior there is a splendid wooden **Crucifix**, possibly of Spanish origin (15-16C). The somber palazzo opposite the cathedral houses the **Museo Diocesano d'Arte Sacra**, with a collection of paintings (some remarkable paintings of the 15th and 16th centuries by artists from Bologna and Romagna), sculptures, church furnishings, architectural fragments and a priceless collection of illuminated codices from the 13th and 15th centuries. There are also two splendid 18th-century carriages. Nearby is the **church of the Osservanza**, dating from the late 15th century, which has been radically restored. Not far away, in Via Garibaldi, is **Palazzo Tozzoni*** ❺ (1726-38), with a late Baroque facade with curved

motifs, one of the finest creations of Domenico Trifogli. Inside is a majestic *staircase* with statues and stucco decoration. The most interesting aspect of the palazzo is its period furnishings, which give an insight into the domestic side of life and the tastes of a noble family in the 18th and 19th centuries. It also contains some eclectic collections including paintings, terracottas, coins, archeological finds, drawings, prints and collections of books. The paintings include works by Bartolomeo Passerotti, Lavinia Fontana, Bartolomeo Cesi, Ferraù Fenzoni and Antonio Beccadelli. Walking back towards Piazza Matteotti, we come to the **Church of S. Maria in Regola*** ❻, an example of purist architecture with Palladian influences (1780-86). Its picturesque old **bell tower**, which is egg-shaped, dates from 1181. Inside, the church, built on a square plan, has 6th-century Byzantine **screens** at the altar. Other important monuments include **Palazzo Calderini**, a fine Renaissance building in the Tuscan style, which has an unusual facade with three different tiers of wall decoration, and, more particularly, the **Pinacoteca Comunale** ❼, housed in the former *Dominican monastery*. Its collection concentrates on works by painters from Romagna and Emilia (15-18C).
The Rocca* ❽ is the most representative of the fortresses in Romagna. It was built in 1472-74 above a medieval fort of the 11th century, re-built in 1259 and reinforced in 1322. Set in a lovely park, it has a square plan with round towers the same height as the curtain walls. It incorporates a massive rectangular keep dating from the previous fort. To enter the fort, cross the drawbridge spanning the moat. Inside there is a fine weapon collection (14-19C) and an impressive collection of medieval ceramics and majolicas. There are good views from the top of the keep over the town.

SAN GIOVANNI IN PERSICETO
[21 km]
The name of the village of Persiceto, famed for its traditional carnival, probably derives from the local name for a peach-tree (*persico*). There is evidence of Roman occupation in the way the land is divided into centuries. You can still see the layout of the primitive, early medieval town, with the streets arranged in concentric circles, and districts laid out on a grid plan.

One of the town's most interesting buildings is a defense tower built in 1306. It was damaged and re-built several times. Corso Italia crosses the town from north to south, connecting *Porta Vittoria* to *Porta Garibaldi*. The 18th-century *Palazzo della Partecipanza* is situated on this street, and if we turn off along Via Gramsci we come to the *Palazzaccio* (14C), which has a fine portico with a wooden colonnade. The focal point of the town is *Piazza del Popolo*, site of the *collegiate church of S. Giovanni Battista*, begun in 1671 and re-built in the late 18th century. The interior of the church, based on a Latin-cross plan, is decorated in the Baroque style with some fine 18th-century stuccoes and there is a *baptismal font* in pink Verona marble (1450). The rooms of the 17th-century sacristy house the *Museo d'Arte Sacra* which has paintings of the Bologna School (16-19C), objects used during mass, and splendid vellum illuminated choir-books. Opposite the church is the *Palazzo Comunale*. It was restored in the 18th century and contains a fine *staircase* and the *municipal theater*.

SANTUARIO DELLA MADONNA DI S. LUCA [5 km]

The famous Sanctuary of the Madonna di S. Luca, where the municipal cemetery is now located, can easily be reached by car or by public transport. It is also very pleasant to walk there (takes almost an hour) by climbing the hill under the portico which leads up to the sanctuary from the town. To reach the church, start at Porta Saragozza, follow the street of the same name and then continue along Via di S. Luca. Opposite the 19th-century fortified Porta Saragozza stands a monumental tribune (1675) marking the beginning of the **Portico di S. Luca***. The portico has 666 arches, is 3,796m long, and was built between 1674 and 1715 to connect Bologna to the *sanctuary*, a clear reference to its link with the world's most porticoed city. If we turn left off Via Saragozza after about 1km, into Via di Casaglia, we come to the neo-classical *Villa Spada* (early 19C), which houses the **Museo Storico Didattico della Tappezzeria***. Its collection includes more that 6,000 pieces of fabric from Italy and Europe.

The **Sanctuary of the Madonna di S. Luca*** is the most important in the city's religious and civic history. It stands on the Colle della Guardia hill (289m), on the site of an old hermitage (12C). The place later became a pilgrimage site where the faithful came to venerate an image of the Virgin Mary thought to have been painted by St Luke. The present building (18C) is oval in shape and preceded by a curved narthex, with tribunes at each side and a dome. Inside, where an optical illusion gives the impression that it is built on a Greek-cross plan, the church is decorated with frescoes, statues and stuccoes. At the third altar on the right, a *Madonna and Child*, and a *St Dominic and the Mysteries of the Rosary* by Guido Reni (1597-98). Above the high altar, a Byzantine icon of the *Madonna and Child* (12C). In the sacristy, *Christ Appearing to the Madonna*, a fine painting by Guercino.

The church of the Madonna di S. Luca and the long portico leading up to it from Porta Saragozza

FERRARA

Ferrara's geographical position in the territorial context of Emilia Romagna h destiny in historical terms with regard to both its social and economic devel s out of the way in relation to the important route of the Via Aemilia on uninterrupted urban development took place all the way from Milan to Rimini, ... an unusual and constant pressure to develop. The position of Ferrara, removed from the area from which much of the rest of the region has benefited, and almost subordinate to it, has had positive repercussions, particularly from a physical and environmental point of view. In fact, the area of Ferrara and its province has avoided the scourge of industrialization and has thus been spared the often negative consequences of such things. As a result, the area has been able to preserve its natural environment, the high quality of which led to Ferrara to being designated a UNESCO World Heritage Site in 1995. In 1999, this prestigious award was extended to the Po Delta and the Delizie Estensi (as the summer palaces built by the Estes are called). Thanks to extensive restoration work and considerable human effort, the city's urban and architectural resources have made it possible to launch an impressive cultural initiative based on a program of urban quality. Gradually, the city has built up an image which now attracts a discerning and assiduous type of tourism. Ferrara, the "bicycle city", is pervaded by the peaceful atmosphere typical of its province, but is enlivened by its cultural and historical heritage.

Palazzo dei Diamanti ❶

The 'diamonds' in the name refer to the pointed, faceted ashlars which decorate the façade. As the light changes, they alter the appearance of the building. This is certainly one of the most famous palaces of the Italian Renaissance. It houses the **Pinacoteca Nazionale****, which plays an important role in conserving and reconstructing that 'lost paradise' which once constituted Ferrara's artistic heritage. The left wing contains works of the 14th and 15th centuries, including two *tondi* with **Stories of St Maurelius*** by Cosmè Tura. The grand hall, which forms part of the monumental apartments, houses the gallery's larger works, such as the magnificent frescoes depicting the **Slaughter of the Innocents***, a beautiful **polyptych of St Andrew **** (c.1530) and a **Death of the Virgin***, dated 1508. Works from the 16th and 17th centuries include a **Madonna and Child*** by Gentile da Fabriano, **Christ with the Soul of the Madonna*** by Andrea Mantegna and a **Madonna and Child in the Rose Garden*** (c.1480).

Castello Estense ❷

From Palazzo dei Diamanti, **Corso Ercole I d'Este***, which marks the transition from the Renaissance to the medieval part of the city, leads to the castle. The Corso has the aura of a princely street, with its palaces and gardens, and reflects the Renaissance concept of what a city should be. There are many gardens between the noble palazzi, including the majestic **Palazzo di Giulio d'Este** (late 15C), with its fine terracotta **cornice**. The castle's evolution from being a powerful military structure to a sumptuous ducal residence has resulted in the Castello Estense being the city's most emblematic monument. It was built with four towers and is surrounded by a wide moat which not only reminds us of its original function but has the effect of isolating it from its urban context. The visit begins under the portico at the entrance to the *Museo Provinciale del*

Palazzo dei Diamanti is interesting both in terls of the architecture and history

31

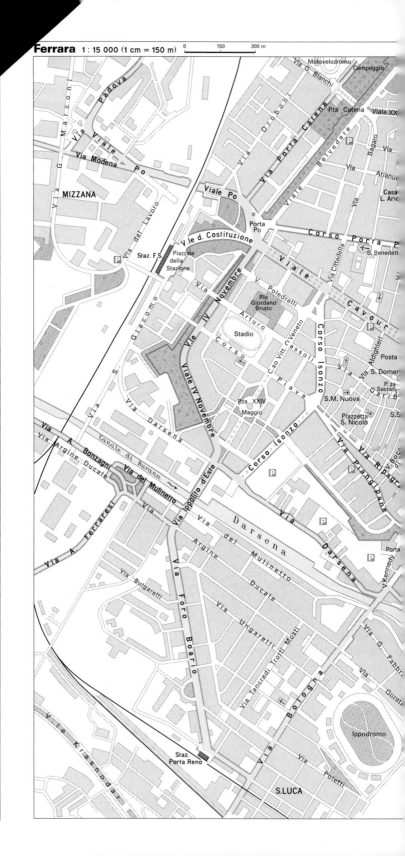

Ferrara 1 : 15 000 (1 cm = 150 m)

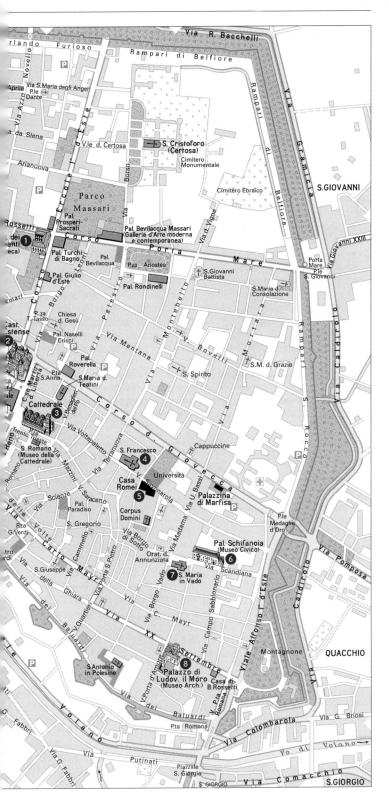

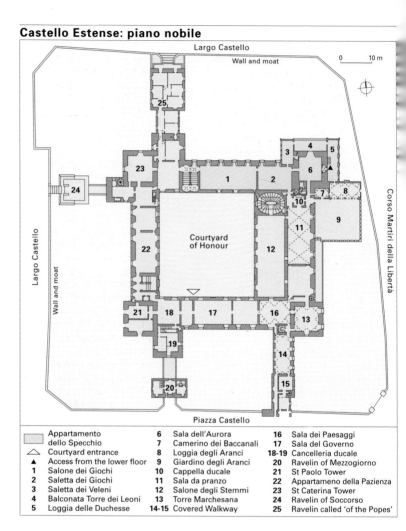

Castello Estense: piano nobile

Map labels:
Largo Castello
Wall and moat
0 — 10 m
Courtyard of Honour
Largo Castello
Wall and moat
Corso Martiri della Libertà
Piazza Castello

Legend:

	Appartamento dello Specchio	**6**	Sala dell'Aurora	**16** Sala dei Paesaggi
	Courtyard entrance	**7**	Camerino dei Baccanali	**17** Sala del Governo
▲	Access from the lower floor	**8**	Loggia degli Aranci	**18-19** Cancelleria ducale
1	Salone dei Giochi	**9**	Giardino degli Aranci	**20** Ravelin of Mezzogiorno
2	Saletta dei Giochi	**10**	Cappella ducale	**21** St Paolo Tower
3	Saletta dei Veleni	**11**	Sala da pranzo	**22** Appartameno della Pazienza
4	Balconata Torre dei Leoni	**12**	Salone degli Stemmi	**23** St Caterina Tower
5	Loggia delle Duchesse	**13**	Torre Marchesana	**24** Ravelin of Soccorso
		14-15	Covered Walkway	**25** Ravelin called 'of the Popes'

Castello. The Gothic rooms, in the oldest part of the complex, and the other rooms, have exhibits associated with the history of this castle-palace. The itinerary includes the dungeons. An *artillery ramp* leads up to the first floor to the *Loggia delle Duchesse* (with a vaulted ceiling), the Loggia degli Aranci and the **Giardino pensile degli Aranci***, a small terrace-garden with citrus trees in pots; from the loggia, cross the frescoed *Stanzino dei Baccanali*, to the **Cappella Ducale*** (Ducal chapel, 1590-91), traditionally called the **chapel of Renée de France**: small and compact, it is decorated with polychrome marble and devoid of images, except for the Evangelists on the ceiling. Next to it is the **Appartamento Ducale,** (c.1570), with

richly decorated rooms (Sala dell'Aurora, Saletta dei Veleni, Saletta and Salone dei Giochi). The visit includes climbing the 13th-century **Torre dei Leoni**, from the top of which there are marvelous views over the city.

Cattedrale ❸

The facade of the cathedral, the bottom of which is Romanesque and the top Gothic, has a handsome central **doorway*** and a **porch**, crowned by a loggia. On the right-hand side of the cathedral, which faces *Piazza Trento e Trieste* is the **Loggia dei Merciai** (built in 1473 to house the shops which, in the 13th and 14th centuries, had been set up under the cathedral wall). The **bell tower** (1441-42), designed partly by Leon Battista Alberti,

is unfinished. It has a beautiful **apse***
(1498) and, at the foot of the cathedral,
is a long inscription of the city statutes
carved in stone (80m long).
The interior, preceded by a narthex,
with objects in stone and marble,
is a fascinating mixture of different
periods and styles. In the right
transept, an altar with a **Martyrdom of
St Lawrence***, by Guercino, and another
with a bronze statue of **Christ on the
Cross, the Virgin Mary, St John,
St George and St Maurelius*** (1450-56)
by Nicolò Baroncelli and Domenico
di Paris. Around the curved apse are
wonderful **wooden choirstalls**
(1500-25), while the fine late 16th-
century stuccoes draw attention to the
vault of the apse, where there is a
visionary **Last Judgement*** painted by
Bastianino in 1577-80. In the sixth
chapel of the left aisle, a splendid
Coronation of the Virgin by Francesco
Francia. Close to the cathedral is the
deconsecrated **church of S. Romano**,
dating from the 15th century. It now
houses the important **Museo della
Cattedrale***. The collection includes
interesting **tapestries**, four **panels****
by Cosmè Tura (1469) and other
interesting works. On the walls are fine
marbles, including the twelve **reliefs
of the months*** (13C). On the first floor
are 22 splendid **illuminated choir-
books*** (executed between 1477 and
1535), together with an illuminated
hymn-book and *psalter* (1472), and
precious marbles. By walking west we
come to the *ghetto*, created around the
mid-15th century. Under the rule of
Ercole I d'Este (1471-1505), Ferrara
became a veritable center of Jewish
culture in Italy. The old synagogue is in
Via Mazzini. The streets of the
ghetto and the places
associated with
the Jewish

community and references to the
cultural peculiarities of some of its
inhabitants are described throughout
the works of Giorgio Bassani, author of
the famous book "The Garden of the
Finzi Contini", on which the film by
De Sica was based.

Basilica di S. Francesco ④

The formal quality of this church, with
its vast brick facade, finds expression
inside, where the Brunelleschian
dimensions seem to "breathe" the
light and the atmosphere of the Ferrara
Renaissance. However, this
equilibrium was affected in 1956
by the replacement of the terracotta
floor with a floor in *botticino* marble.
Amongst others, Girolamo da Carpi
worked on the *triple fresco cycle* with
a Franciscan theme painted on the
ceilings between the 16th and 19th
centuries. On the pilaster between the
sixth and seventh chapel of the right
aisle, a terracotta *Flagellation*,
attributed to Nicolò Baroncelli; in the
eighth chapel, a 14-15th-century fresco
of *St Anthony of Padua*. In the right
transept is the *tomb of Ghiron
Francesco Villa*, a military man; in the
chapel to the right of the presbytery,
a *Madonna Glykophilousa* (Madonna
of the sweet embrace), a 16th century
Venetian icon by a Cretan painter,
and a beautiful ciborium in the form
of a temple dating from c.1636.
In the left transept, a 5th-century
Roman *sarcophagus* in the Ravenna
style, re-used as the tomb of Francesco
Ariosto, uncle of the famous poet.
In the first chapel on the left, a
good fresco by Garofalo depicting
the **Arrest of Jesus in the Garden
of Gethsemane** (c.1524).

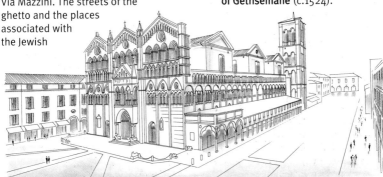

The cathedral, **a splendid blend of different styles and consecrated in 1135**

Casa Romei ⑤

Dominated by the high transept of S. Francesco, Casa Romei, begun in 1442, was built for Giovanni Romei, a rich noble at the Este court. It is one of the best examples in Ferrara of a 15th-century aristocratic residence, although the facade is very simple. Conversely, the interior is richly decorated. The *grand central courtyard* is dominated by a large *monogram of Christ* surrounded by terracotta angels. On three sides of the courtyard is a portico and a loggia with remains of wall painting. On the ground floor, the Sala delle Sibille (named after the sybils depicted in the paintings in the mid-15C), has a monumental fireplace decorated with terracotta; next-door, and similar, the *Saletta dei Profeti*. Some rooms on the first floor have wall paintings dating from the second half of the 16th century, figurative works and grotesques by Camillo Filippi and his sons Cesare and Sebastiano: in particular the *Chapel of the Principesse*, the *Salone d'Onore* and the *Studiolo* of Giovanni Romei. The rooms of Casa Romei also contain precious objects such as marbles, sculptures and detached frescoes from abandoned churches and palaces around Ferrara.

THE METAPHYSICAL SILENCE OF FERRARA

In the difficult years leading up to the beginning of the First World War, the "lonely peacefulness" of Ferrara, as the poet Carducci describes it in his ode dedicated to the city, was witness to an interesting phenomenon of the international avant-garde movement: metaphysical painting. Giorgio De Chirico, captivated by the mystery of its famous squares, used his vivid imagination to transform Ferrara's geometric shapes into a setting for his disturbing mannequins. His nude, complicated, motionless figures are set in a place to which only they give a meaning. Art becomes "severe and cerebral, ascetic and lyrical", with no connection to reality, dictated only in relation to the significance of the painting. But why Ferrara? In 1915, De Chirico came here to do military service and, in 1916, met Carlo Carrà, who was a patient at the military hospital. The fact that they were far from action at the front, the city's historical charm, the opportunities to meet important writers and artists, and, more particularly, Ferrara's secretive, secluded atmosphere resulted in Carrà helping De Chirico to launch metaphysical painting. One of De Chirico's most important works of metaphysical painting, The Disturbing Muses, was inspired directly by Ferrara: the old Castello Estense,

 the modern silo and chimney-stacks in the background; everything in the picture is static and seemingly suspended in time. This undefinable moment is inhabited by the only beings possible: mannequins. Dominating the silent scene is the great discovery of the psycho-analysts, the absolute "Ego".

Palazzo Schifanoia ⑥

Close to Palazzo della Schifanoia, which overlooks **Corso della Giovecca***, the street connecting the medieval and Renaissance parts of the city, is **Palazzina di Marfisa d'Este**, daughter of Francesco d'Este, a good example of Mannerist architecture (1559). Palazzo della Schifanoia, the most famous of the palaces built by the Este family, houses part of the collection of the **Musei Civici di Arte Antica**; these museums, dotted about the city, include the *Lapidario Civico* in the former church of S. Libera (opposite the palazzo), the Palazzina di Marfisa, *Palazzo Bonacossi*, the *Cella di Torquato Tasso* (the cell where the poet was confined) in the Arcispedale S. Anna, the house of the poet Ludovico Ariosto and the Museo della Cattedrale. The palace was built in the late 14th century but altered in the next century by Leonello d'Este to "*schivar la noia*" (prevent the duke from getting bored, hence its name). The marble **doorway*** has low reliefs, some of which depict the achievements of Duke Borso d'Este, who had the palace enlarged to make room for his grand new apartments. The great hall contains the delightful **frescoes of the months**** (c.1470), the most eloquent expression of the Renaissance in the Ferrara area. By 1467, the magnificent **ceiling of the Sala degli Stucchi** had been completed. The *Sala delle Imprese* contains numerous heraldic crests of the Este family. Palazzo Schifanoia houses some important collections: archeological finds, medals and coins, Renaissance ceramics with graffito decoration, prints, paintings and bronzes. The collection of **illuminated codices***, with choir-books and an incunabulum is particularly interesting. There are also some fine terracotta **statues**, an English alabaster **polyptych** depicting the *Passion* (early 15C) and a collection of Gothic and Renaissance ivories.

Chiesa di S. Maria in Vado ❼

Of medieval origin, the church once stood next to a ford (*guado* in Italian, hence *vado*) on the Po. Built on a Latin-cross plan with a nave and two side-aisles, the focal point of worship is the **chapel of Preziosissimo Sangue** in the right transept: this is the site of the altar cloth over which, on March 28, 1171, blood spurted out of a wafer broken by a priest who had doubts about the Sacrament of the Eucharist. The richly decorated little church with a pronaos dates from the late 16th century. Between 1617 and 1630, the painter Carlo Bononi came here to work on one of the most important decorative projects in the history of the art of Ferrara. His painting of extremely high quality can be found on the arches and ceiling above the nave, in the

presbytery and in the vault of the choir. There are other important paintings by Domenico Mona (sixth chapel of the left aisle and the presbytery) and Camillo Filippi, who painted the *Annunciation with St Paul* above the fine wooden choirstalls.

Palazzo Ludovico il Moro ❽

This palazzo, also known as **Palazzo Costabili**, is a majestic and very harmonious architectural complex. It now houses the **Museo Archeologico Nazionale***. Its beautiful square **courtyard** is decorated with porticoes and loggias with recurring pairs of windows. From it, a *grand staircase* leads into the museum. This contains a huge number of finds, including grave goods from 21 burials, datable to 500-400BC, most of which are of Attic origin and some of Italic origin. The painted vases depict scenes from the Greek myths, with which the Etruscans were also familiar. Nearby is the *Museo dell'Architettura* (Musarc), located in the *Casa di Biagio Rossetti*, the house which the architect designed for himself (note the double-window motif and the terracotta decoration). Not far away you can see the old **walls*** of Ferrara, which still run almost all the way round the city. Not only are they of historical and environmental importance, but they add to the city's charm.

DAY TRIPS

ABBAZIA DI POMPOSA [50 km]

The abbey of Pomposa is very important from a historical, artistic, cultural and spiritual point of view. The **basilica of S. Maria**** is the focal point of the complex, which includes the monastery, with its museum, and Palazzo della Ragione. The church was supposedly built in the mid-8th century, although work probably continued until the 9th century, but it may date back even earlier, possibly to the 7th century. Its present appearance is the result of four different periods of restructuring work. This included the building of the crypt (rebuilt in the 20C) and the narthex, with its two-light windows (9-10C). The narthex was later

FERRARA
IN OTHER COLORS...
  ▪ **ITINERARIES:** pages 127, 132
  ▪ **FOOD:** pages 142, 147, 152
  ▪ **SHOPPING:** page 176
  ▪ **EVENTS:** pages 183, 189
  ▪ **PRACTICAL INFO:** page 219

incorporated into the church in the (10-11C), increasing the original seven bays to nine. At about the same time, a rectangular **narthex** was added with three arches, decorated with bands of brick, ceramic bowls, recessed panels, low reliefs and two round windows with calcarenite screens decorated with animal motifs and stylized trees. **Inside**, the church has a nave and two side-aisles. The first two bays, added later, let in more light. The great apse, following the style of Ravenna, is semi-circular inside and polygonal outside. The smaller apses were added in about 1150. The nave and aisles are separated by re-used Roman and Byzantine columns, with dosserets and capitals. The beautiful *inlaid* marble floor was made in several stages between the 6th (the earliest part is near the apse) and the 12th centuries (the last part, with very fine geometric patterns). Next to the first column on the left is a 12th-century Romanesque *holy water font*, supported by four telamones. The walls of the nave are adorned with a single **cycle of frescoes*** of the Bologna School, executed just after the middle of the 14th century, however the most precious **fresco cycle**** is in the apse (1351). The **bell tower**** (1063), 48m high, rises above the complex and is a familiar reference point for miles around. It is square, with nine tiers of small arches. The facade of red and yellow bricks incorporates the occasional **ceramic bowl** with tree, fish, bird and flower motifs. These can be dated to the 11th century and come from Egypt, Tunisia and Sicily, and are of Arabic origin. The *refectory* of the **monastery**, in addition to the 14th-century decoration on the west wall, is decorated with interesting **frescoes*** painted in 1316-20. In the chapterhouse are more lively 14th-century **frescoes**, attributed to the so-called Maestro del Capitolo, a

painter who trained with Giotto in Padua. In the dormitory where the monks used to sleep, on the first floor of the monastery, is the **Museo Pomposiano**. It contains about 200 exhibits associated with the history of the monastery, including capitals, columns, column bases, pilasters, and panels, some of which come from other churches in the Ravenna style. There are many frescoes detached from the walls of the basilica and Palazzo della Ragione. The collection also has liturgical objects, Etruscan cippi dating from the 5th century BC and Attic vases.

Opposite the basilica stands **Palazzo della Ragione**. Its name is associated with the fact that the abbot used to administer justice in the territory under his jurisdiction. Built in the 11th century, it was altered in 1396. The apparently "Romanesque" loggia on the side facing the church was replaced in the 20th century.

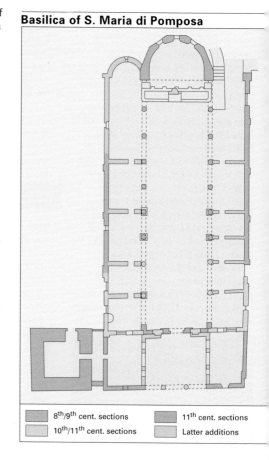

Basilica of S. Maria di Pomposa

8th/9th cent. sections

10th/11th cent. sections

11th cent. sections

Latter additions

negative impact both on the small population of red deer, because of the fierce competition to find food, and on the vegetation, since the undergrowth has virtually disappeared except for swallow-wort (*Vincetoxicum hirundinaria*). This is the only plant which fallow deer will not eat, since it is toxic. Nocturnal animals on the reserve include the badger (*Meles meles*) and a large population of tawny owls (*Strix aluco*).

CENTO [35 km]

The main public square of Cento, dedicated to its most famous son, Giovan Francesco Barbieri (the painter's nickname "Guercino" refers to the fact that he had a pronounced squint), is **Piazza Guercino**, meeting-point of the four roads leading into the town. There were once four gates: the only one left is *Porta Pieve*, on the Pieve di Cento side of town. Monuments in the square include Palazzo del Governatore with a 17th-century *clock-tower*, and *Palazzo Comunale* (1612) with an elegant 18th-century facade. The **Palazzo del Governatore** (1502), is now the *Galleria d'Arte Moderna A. Bonzagni* and houses important works by Carrà, Manzù, Guttuso, Fontana and Guidi. In **Via Provenzali** it is worth stopping at *Casa Provenzali* (no. 6) to admire Guercino's lovely frescoes. Further along the portico stands the 14th-century *church* (since altered) *of S. Pietro*, which has fragments of 14th-century frescoes and 17th-century paintings. Another interesting building, at the end of the street, is the *church of Ss. Sebastiano e Rocco*, founded in the 16th century but restructured in 1764-70. The **ghetto**, located between Via Provenzali and Via Malagodi, is accessed through the atrium of Casa Provenzali. This district, where the Jewish community was obliged to live from 1636, has houses with little wrought-iron balconies typical of the Spanish tradition (some date from the 18C), and the neo-classical *Palazzo Modena*, later Palazzo Carpi (1820). Nothing remains of the synagogue. The British statesman Benjamin Disraeli (1804-81) was descended from a family from Cento which emigrated in the 18th century. The two parts of **Corso del Guercino** meet in the main square. In one part of the street (left of the Palazzo Comunale), set back in a small square, is the former *church of S. Lorenzo* (now an

The Rocca of Cento and the monument to Guercino

BOSCO DELLA MÉSOLA [56 km]

Not far from the abbey of Pomposa, the Bosco della Mésola (which locals refer to as the 'Boscone'= big wood) is worth a visit. If you are lucky you may be able to spot fallow deer, terrapins sunning themselves by the water, or iridescent green lizards. The whole wood is now a nature reserve. The wildlife routes in the park can be followed by bike or on foot. The dominant type of vegetation here (known as *Quercion ilicis*) is typical of thermophylous Mediterranean areas, with a large number of holm oak (*Quercus ilex*), which commonly grows above the dunes. Because of the diverse morphology of the area, there are different types of vegetation according to the altitude. The low-lying areas close to the water table where cool, humid conditions prevail are populated by the Caucasian ash (*Fraxinus oxycarpae*) and sedge (*Cladium mariscus*); slightly higher up, there are groups of common oak (*Quercus robur*) and hornbeam (*Carpinus betulus*). The fauna here is particularly interesting. Many different species of birds inhabit the woods, but there are also fallow deer and a population of deer that occurs only in the Bosco della Mésola and is a protected species. Because they have been isolated for centuries, their morphological and genetic characteristics have changed, so that the colony has become almost a sub-species of the European red deer. The excessive density of the fallow deer population, on the other hand, is having a

auditorium), a fine example of local Baroque, and, on the opposite side, the imposing **Casa Pannini** with its wooden structural features, dating from 1360; some of the frescoes from here (by Guercino and his School) are now at the Pinacoteca Civica.

On the other part of the Corso stands *Palazzo Rangoni* (1766) and the *Teatro Comunale* (1856-61). The **Rocca**

The crenellated Palazzo del Governatore, after the changes and restoration works

and Porta Pieve are all that remains of Cento's fortifications. The castle dates from the second half of the 14th century, was rebuilt a century later, and then altered and extended. It is a compact, rectangular building with massive towers at each corner and a tall keep. The **Pinacoteca Civica*** is housed in *Palazzo del Monte di Pietà e dell'Archivio notarile* (1782). It is a monument to Cento's most famous son, Guercino, and his School. On the first floor, one work rivals the masterpieces by Guercino and his assistants: the **Madonna Enthroned with St Joseph, St Francis and Donors***, by Ludovico Carracci (1591). Three other churches in the town are worth a visit: *S. Maria Addolorata dei Servi*, the *basilica of S. Biagio*, an old church rebuilt in the Baroque style (1730-45) with a richly decorated interior, but, best of all, the **church of the Rosario**, where Guercino was a member of the confraternity, and which contains five of his works. Less than 3km from Cento is **Castello della Giovannina**, built in about 1490. Part castle and part villa, it is a massive, square building with a tower at each corner. The interior was frescoed by Guercino and other artists.

The origins of **Pieve di Cento** are similar to those of Cento, from which it is separated by the Reno River, marking the boundary between the provinces of Ferrara and Bologna. The town still has obvious traces of the medieval settlement, three 14th-century gate and a fourth gate which was rebuilt in the 18th century. The old *pieve* (parish church) after which it is named overlooks the main square. The *collegiate church of S. Maria Maggiore*, which has a richly decorated Baroque interior, contains two important works: a monumental *Assumption of the Virgin Mary*, by Guido Reni (1599), and an equally enormous *Annunciation* by Guercino (1646). To the left of the church is *Palazzo Comunale*, which incorporates the 19th-century *municipal theater*. Another building worthy of note is the *oratory of the SS. Trinità*, with a richly decorated interior. Pieve di Cento also has some interesting buildings with original wooden features, such as *Casa degli Anziani* (Home for the Elderly) (13C) and *Casa Vedrani* (14C).

COMACCHIO [52 km]

Set in a unique environment from a wildlife point of view, Comacchio was founded and grew up on thirteen little islands joined by bridges. The **cathedral** stands by the *Canale Maggiore* (main canal), in the oldest part of the town. Founded in 708, it was rebuilt in 1694-1720. The bell tower was built in 1766 on an enormous base of Istrian stone, which is still there, but it was never finished. Inside the cathedral are some fine *paintings* and the richly decorated *chapel of the Sacro Cuore*, the dome of which is decorated with frescoes and stuccoes. Other buildings on the main street include the *Loggia dei Mercanti* or *Loggia del Grano*, built in 1621, and the *clock-tower* (1824). Following the characteristic *Via Fogli* beside Canale Maggiore, we come to *Ponte degli Sbirri* or *Ponte delle Carceri* (1631-35), opposite the **Trepponti***, an unusual architectural feature (1634) spanning the crossing-point of two canals, which has become the symbol of the town. Together with the two bridges, the *Pescheria* (18-19C), the neo-classical *former Ospedale S. Camillo* (1778), and the aristocratic *Palazzo Bellini* (19C) form an attractive scenario. A nearby building houses the *Museo della Nave Romana*, which contains a 1st-century BC ship 20m long found in the riverbed of Valle Ponti. Continuing along *Corso Garibaldi* from the clock-tower, we come to the *church of the Rosario*, founded in 1618 and altered subsequently. It contains a 17th-century *Annunciation*, a striking **Beheading of John the Baptist** (c.1630), and two fine wooden sculptures: a Baroque *Crucifix* (1641) and a *Madonna and Child* dated between the 15th and 16th century. Nearby is the picturesque *Via del Rosario* which leads to the *Ponte del Carmine* (18C).

Corso Mazzini is the north-west section of the longitudinal axis of old Comacchio, with smaller buildings which were once the dwellings and warehouses of fish merchants.

Finally, the Sanctuary of **S. Maria in Aula Regia** or dei Cappuccini is connected to the town by a portico with 142 arches built in the 17th century. The origins of the church date from the 16th century but the facade dates from 1888. The jewel of the decoration inside is a much revered 15th-century painting of the **Madonna Enthroned with Child**. For centuries, this image of Maria "Madonna del Popolo" appeared on leaflets, permits, panegyrics, images of saints and prayer-books. It

appeared on the figure-heads of boats, too and, even today, in the streets of Comacchio, many small shrines and altars contain a small statue of the Madonna Enthroned from this church. There is also a beautiful altar-piece of the *Crucifixion with the Virgin Mary, St Mary Magdalene and St John the Evangelist* (c.1600) and a *St Felix the Capuchin Friar* (1706).

Not far away lies the **Parco Naturale del Delta del Po****, which is well worth a visit.

OASI DI CAMPOTTO [40 km]

One place not to be missed on any tour of the Ferrara area is the Oasi di Campotto, an extraordinary landscape of wetlands and woodland, a peaceful haven where the only noise is natural, especially birdsong. The golden reed-beds which provide refuge for ducks and reed warblers are reflected in the shallow, muddy water, the ideal habitat for water lilies and water gentians. In the distance, on the horizon, woods of elm, poplar, willow and ash provide nesting grounds for egrets and cormorants. In 1988, when the Parco Regionale del Delta del Po was created, the oasis became a headquarters for the park. The starting-point for any visit to the Oasi di Campotto is the **Casino**, the center of operations for all the park has to offer in terms of wildlife and culture. The Casino itself is interesting from a historical point of view. Built between the late 18th and early 19th centuries as a farmhouse for working the local farmland and exploiting the resources of the reclaimed land, the building originally had three floors: the

The picturesque Trepponti, built in 1634, is the symbol of Comacchio

Parco Naturale del Delta del Po

As the water in the Po nears the Adriatic Sea, it slows down, depositing sand and fine silt. The posits create new lands and cause the river to divide into minor branches that, prior to flow to the sea, create the type of river mouth known as a delta. The delta area is continually growi changing since its is dependent on the water level and t tides; this also creates numerous different land and sea e tems. Starting from the sea, you find wide beaches and c dunes, covered in 'pioneer vegetation', marking the edge of the so 'inlets'. Next, you come to vast expanses of water located behi dunes or lagoons cut off from the sea with variable levels of sa Further inland, the belts of dunes, which marked the coast line sands of years ago, are often bordered by tamarisk and caneb and function as the edge of the lagoons that have become sa panses of water. In other places, these dunes are completely cc

Spoonbill

Great reed warbler

Avocet

Black-winged stilt

Avocet ch
Sheldrake with chick

Salicornia

Valli di Comacchio is probably the most important brackish wetland in the delta, with a diversity of nature and an ecology influenced by the water's salinity and depth. The small islands covered with vegetation that requires salty climes, such as statice and glasswort, are home to avocets, black-winged stilts and, in recent years, the rare spoonbill. The salt pans that border the northern water valleys, although no longer producing salt, are conserved because of their habitat: the semi-dry tanks are the nesting sites for many slender-billed and Mediterranean gulls, white terns and sandwich terns. Around 1600 flamingos come to the delta and, from 2000, a colony of 200 couples have been reproducing in the salt pans. During the spri and autumn migrations, the water valleys are stopover points for many wading birds, like the go and sandpiper. Thousands of ducks, swans and geese spend the winter months here.

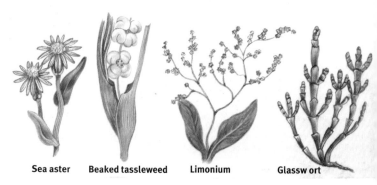

Sea aster   Beaked tassleweed   Limonium   Glassw ort

warm-weather plants
ch as pines, holm oak and
glish oak, sometimes
eating places like the
esola wood. Today,
e delta has largely
en reclaimed and
ained, and the influ-
ice of humans is ever-
owing, nonetheless, it
ill represents one of the
ost important wetlands
Europe.

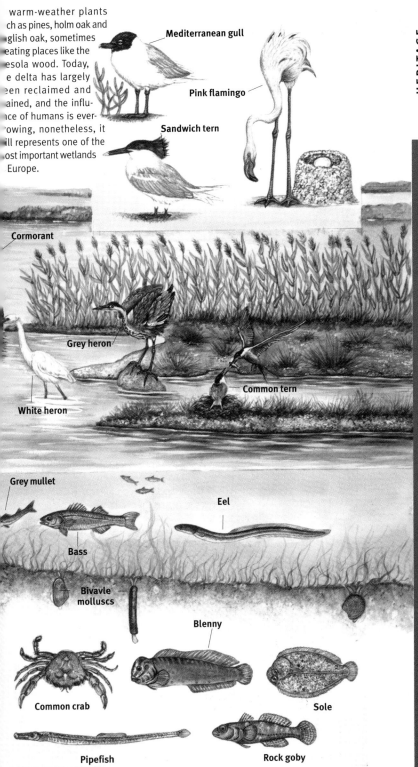

Mediterranean gull

Pink flamingo

Sandwich tern

Cormorant

Grey heron

White heron

Common tern

Grey mullet

Eel

Bass

Bivavle
molluscs

Blenny

Common crab

Sole

Pipefish

Rock goby

threshing ground, the farmhouse and the cowshed – on the first floor, safe from flooding – and the rice store above. The mud deposited here by numerous floods eventually buried the area occupied by the threshing ground, leaving only the two floors we see today above ground. The farm now houses the **Museo delle Valli di Argenta***, a museum documenting the history and wildlife of the area, showing how the land, the fauna and the flora of these wetlands have evolved. There is a *mechanical model* showing how the water is controlled using water-pumps and sluice-gates. *Guided tours* to the valli and the Bosco del Traversante start at the Casino where it is also possible to hire binoculars and bikes. Through the Casino it is also possible to visit the **Museo della Bonifica***, opposite the parish church of S. Giorgio. The museum display has an exhibition about the local area and methods of land reclamation, an open-air exhibition of machines and tools, and you can visit the *Saiarino water-pump*, built in 1925 and still in use. Immediately to the south of the Reno, almost completely hidden among the trees of the park, is the **parish church of S. Giorgio***, which, despite its small size, is one of the most important monuments in the Ferrara area. It was built in 569 close to a settlement that was probably Roman. The little church had a single nave at that time, but in 1122 it was restructured and given a nave, two side-aisles, and a beautiful **Romanesque doorway***, consisting partly of re-used pieces of Roman marble. Notice the sculptures of the months on the door

jambs, and the *Martyrdom of St George* in the lunette. The current building dates from 1571, when the side-aisles were removed, the church was again given a single nave, the outer walls were raised and the altar was built. From the early phase you can still see the apse, which is polygonal outside and semi-circular inside, a typical feature of churches near Ravenna. On the lower parts of the outer side walls you can see the arches of the previous church with a nave and two aisles and, inside, fragments of early frescoes. On the north side of the church there are two small hanging arches, above which the masonry is different. This shows how the height of the church was raised in the post-medieval period, necessary because of the deposits of mud left by flooding.

The low-lying areas of **Valle Santa, Cassa Campotto** and **Bassarone** are used as emergency overspill tanks where water can be stored temporarily whenever the rivers are in spate. The hydraulic purpose of the tanks prevail over any other type of use, but this has not stopped the typical vegetation and fauna of fresh-water wetlands from becoming established. As a result, it has become an area of international importance because of the wildlife it supports. Walking or cycling along the embankments of the *valli*, you may see carpets of white water lilies and water gentians, whereas the edges of the *valli* are populated by fields of reed mace and ditch reeds. On the higher embankments you sometimes see thick patches of Ravenna grass. From the hides, you are likely to see great crested grebe, coot, mallard, grey heron and little egret. The area is very important for wildlife with both species of heron, cormorant and the smaller birds. In spring, many waders stop here on passage. In winter thousands of ducks, coot and lapwing winter here. Between Cassa Campotto and Valle Santa lies the **Bosco del Traversante**, one of the last remaining woods in the Po Delta. Woods were very common here before the land was reclaimed and, over centuries, the trees were cleared. Now, elm, white poplar and ash are the most common tree species. In some areas of the reserve, efforts are being made to improve the environment, with projects such as tree-planting and the re-flooding of unproductive farmland, in the hope of recreating the wetland environment.

The parish church of S. Giorgio

FORLÌ

ocated in the hart of Romagna, Forlì lies on a plain on the line of the ancient Via Aemilia.
In addition to having cosiderable industrial, crafts and trading sectors, the town also enjoys
high standard of living because of the facilities available and an active cultural life. The old
wn, built largely of brick, has some interesting architectural monuments and strikes a fine
lance between the 15th- and 16th-century buildings and those in Baroque and neo-classical
yle. Interesting architectural work and building has also been carried out from the second
lf of the 18th century on, including the reconstruction work following the bombing during
e Second World War.

Mercuriale

Part of the abbey-church of S. Mercuriale
is built on the site of an early medieval
church. The basilica is the most
important monument in Forlì, both in
architectural and religious terms. Rebuilt
with a nave and two side-aisles in 1173-
81, additions were made in the 15th and
16th centuries and it was modified again
in the 17th, 18th and 20th centuries. Early
parts of the brick facade include the
cornice of small arches and the lovely
marble doorway. The lunette is
decorated with a high relief from the
early 13th century (**Dream and
Worship of the Magi***). The elegant
bell tower** in the Lombard style
stands 72 m high and dates from
1180. It is normally regarded as the
town's most important symbol. The
inside is spacious and austere.
The nave has a ceiling with cross-
beams and a 14th-century floor. In
the right aisle, the **tomb of
Barbara Manfredi***, created
in the 15th century, and, in the
left aisle, the **Arcata Ferri,**
an elegant arch of Istrian stone
(1536).

Piazza Aurelio Saffi ②

The piazza is named after the
politician from Forlì, Aurelio
Saffi (1819-1890), to whom the
monument in the middle of
the square is also dedicated.
The focus of town life, the mix
of architectural periods and
styles in the buildings
surrounding the piazza can
be regarded as a synthesis of
Forlì's cultural history. They
include the basilica of S.
Mercuriale, Palazzo
Comunale, and **Palazzo del
Podestà**, built in 1459-60

and restored in 1912 and 1926. The
facade is predominantly Gothic and has
a portico with pointed arches; it is
adorned with terracotta and decorated
capitals. To the left stands the lovely
Palazzo Albertini. It was built in the late
15th and early 16th centuries, but was
restored and substantially restructured
in 1929. This building with a portico and
Venetian windows has an elegant loggia
at the top. In the south-east corner of
the square, next to the mock-classical
Palazzo Talenti Mangelli (1800), at
the beginning of Corso della
Repubblica, stands the 18th-century
church of the Suffragio. The facade
was executed by Cesare Bazzani in
1935. The oval interior has a dome
with frescoes by Jacopo Guarana
and Serafino Barozzi. Cesare
Bazzani also designed the massive
post office (1932) and *the
government offices* (1935-36)
next door.

Corso Garibaldi ③

This follows the line of the
north-western section of the
ancient Via Aemilia. The series
of mansions resulting from the
reconstruction work carried
out in the 17th and 18th
centuries bring a degree of
prestige to this road. In the
17th-century Palazzo Albicini is
a giant canvas depicting
Aurora (c.1673). *Palazzo
Guarini Torelli* has retained its
16th-century architectural
features in the corner balcony
and the elegant courtyard; in
the upper floors are paintings
by Felice Giani and Gaetano
Bertolani (c.1814). On the
other side of the road stands
Casa Palmeggiani; it has a

The monument to Aurelio Saffi

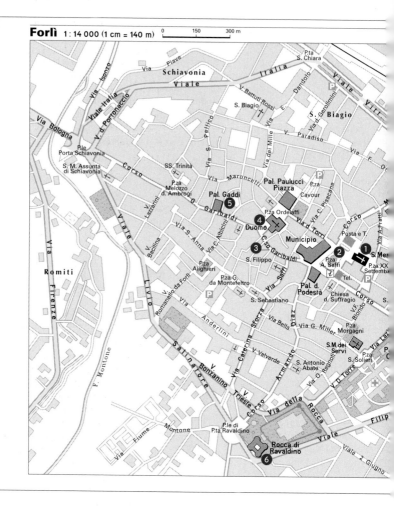

Forlì 1:14 000 (1 cm = 140 m)

15th-century facade characterized by a portico with an unusual double pair of hanging arches, ending in a drop-shaped wall capital, decorated at the bottom with a rose.

Duomo ❹

The cathedral was originally a Parish church in the 10th century, then a Gothic

Piazza Aurelio Saffi, the heart of town life

building that was enlarged and modified at the end of the 15th and during the 16th centuries. The current appearance is practically due to work carried out in 1841. This gave it a mock-classical appearance, as can be clearly seen on the facade with the pronaos supported by brick columns, crowned by a tympanum. Two elements of the original building remain: the *chapel of the SS. Sacramento* (1490-1539), and the *chapel of the Madonna del Fuoco* (1619-1636), with frescoes in the dome by Carlo Cignani depicting the **Assumption**. It is also worth seeing the huge Romanesque painted wooden **Crucifix** (late 12C); the hexagonal *font* (in the baptistery), with relief sculptures executed in 1504 and, in the chapel of SS. Anna e Gioacchino, a *St Sebastian* (1497) by Nicolò Rondinelli and a *St Roch* by Palmezzano.

Cesare Martuzzi and his 'Canterini Romagnoli' (little singers from Romagna), the show-girl Ines Lidelba and the actor Ermete Novelli. The remaining two rooms focus on the destroyed Teatro Comunale of Forlì and various different types of musical instruments that were either made by craftsmen from Romagna or belonged to Italian musicians, dating from the 19th and 20th centuries. A wonderful collection of puppets has recently been added to the museum collection.
The **Museo Etnografico** has quite a substantial collection of pieces related to farming, as well as reproductions of numerous shops and workshops: barber, grocer, saddler, rope maker, farrier, bookbinder, carpenter and frame-maker. There are also some rooms dedicated to seafaring.

Rocca di Ravaldino 6

The name of the fortress comes from the ancient ravelin around which, in the second half of the 14th century, the first set of fortifications were built. Work on the present building began in 1471 on the orders of Pino III Ordelaffi (who belonged to the family who ruled between the end of the 13th and the beginning of the 16th century), who, the following year, ordered work on the construction of the fortress to begin, completed in 1483. The stronghold ceased to be used as a military structure in the 16th century and it became a prison in the 19th century. In Piazzale di Porta Ravaldino, you can access the Canale di Ravaldino. In the Middle Ages this canal ran uncovered across the city, but, for some time, it has been completely covered over. Today, it is navigable for about 1,900m: organized boat trips give an unusual and interesting insight into the underground town.

Palazzo Gaddi 5

The palazzo, which faces Corso Garibaldi, dates from the 16th century, but its appearance is that of an 18th-century noble residence. On the *piano nobile* is a neo-classical apartment dating from the early 19th century, which has a series of paintings completed by Felice Giani and Gaetano Bertolani in January 1820. Palazzo Gaddi now houses the Museo del Risorgimento, the Museo del Teatro, and part of the Museo Etnografico.
The **Museo del Risorgimento 'Aurelio Saffi'** has pieces ranging from the Napoleonic period (1796) to the Second World War. The **Museo Romagnolo del Teatro** has eight rooms; six of these are dedicated, in the following order, to tenor Angelo Masini, the soprano Maria Farneti, the conductor and composer

FORLÌ-CESENA
IN OTHER COLORS...
- **ITINERARIES:** pages 124, 133
- **FOOD:** pages 147, 159, 165
- **SHOPPING:** page 175
- **EVENTS:** page 184
- **WELLNESS:** pages 198, 200, 202
- **PRACTICAL INFO:** pages 216, 221

CESENA

Cesena is immersed in a countryside of gentle rolling hills covered, in spring, with peach a
cherry tree blossom. As a town, it is both welcoming and discreet, reserved but with an acti
cultural life. It has produced considerable talent in both the artistic and entrepreneur
spheres. The old town center, shaped rather unusually like a scorpion, is surrounded by we
preserved late-medieval walls. It has managed to combine its traditional vocation of agric
ture with the modern world. The Cesuola Stream flows through the town and the Savio Riv
down one side. Cesena is situated at the foot of the Garampo hill. The ancient Via Aemilia w
built in a wide curve around the foot of the hill (hence the local name of *Curva Caesena*).

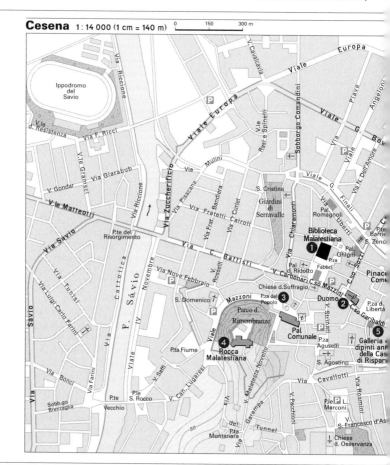

Biblioteca Malatestiana ❶

The Biblioteca Malatestiana (Malatesta Library) is the most important monument in the city, and the only completely preserved Humanist monastic library with its original structure, furnishings and book collection. It was built as a public library by Malatesta Novello (the last lord of the city, 1418-65), between 1447 and 1452, in the monastery of the Friars Minor of St Francis. In addition to the Biblioteca

Malatestiana, the complex houses the **Biblioteca Piana**, the **Museo Archeologico**, the *Museo Lapidario*, the *Biblioteca Comunale* and the *Biblioteca Comandini*. In the tympanum above the lovely **doorway*** leading into the reading-room o
the library, is an elephant, the symbol of the Malatesta family, always accompanied by the maxim "*Elephas indus culices non timet*" (the Indian elephant does not fear mosquitoes). As soon as you step into the

library—a blend of a long reading-room and a basilica with a nave and two side-aisles—you enter a different dimension: an impression created by the rhythm of the columns and the light flooding in from the row of low pointed windows at the sides, and from the rose-window in the center, below which the ashes of the patron Malatesta Novello are buried (the location of the tomb is marked on the wall by a relief of the family crest with three

heads). In the side-aisles are 58 reading-desks made of umbrella-pinewood, to which precious **illuminated manuscripts**** are tied with the original chains in the form of wrought-iron pine-cones or acorns. The ante-chamber of the Biblioteca Malatestiana is the **Biblioteca Piana**, the private collection of the Pope from Cesena, Pius VII Chiaramonti. It contains more than 5,000 volumes, including manuscripts from the 12th to 15th centuries, incunabula

and rare editions, including 15 splendidly decorated 15th-century **choir-books**. One of its more curious possessions is the smallest book in the world that can still be read without the aid of a magnifying glass. Near the library is the **cloister of S. Francesco** (15C); the rounded arches on each side of the square cloister are supported by columns decorated with capitals carved with plant motifs, and bearing the Malatesta crests. Off the cloister is the **Museo Archeologico**. It has a collection of finds from archeological excavations around Cesena dating from prehistory to the 15th century, with many finds from the Roman period.

Duomo ❷

The cathedral, dedicated to St John the Baptist and built at the wishes of Galeotto Malatesta (Lord of Cesena) between 1378 and 1416, has the original Romanesque-Gothic design. The lower part of the facade is divided by slender pillars while the upper part has Venetian Renaissance features. Inside, the nave and two side-aisles are divided by slender pillars supporting pointed arches, with delightful use of color. The nave is illuminated by a row of Romanesque windows below a ceiling with visible trusses. Many of the numerous works of art are worth seeing: G.B. Bregno's the **Corpus Domini altar*** (1494-1505), the marble triptych of **Sts Christopher, Leonard and Eustachius** (1514) and the Baroque **chapel of the Madonna del Popolo** with the fresco of the same name (early 16C): a gloriously rich combination of shapes and colors, enhanced by the marble decoration, stuccoes, the angels on the doors, its curved windows and, above all, the *Genealogy of the Virgin Mary*. From outside the cathedral, you can see the *chapel of St Tobias*, with Renaissance features. It now houses the **Museo della Cattedrale**, which contains church vestments and paintings, such as the well-known and elegant icon of the **Madonna of the Pear*** (1347) by Paolo Veneziano.

Piazza del Popolo ❸

The Malatesta family ordered this square to be built as the new heart of the town in the 15th century. It is paved with river cobblestones and is also the setting of the elegant and well-known **Fontana Masini****. This familiar symbol of the town was made in 1590 of Istrian stone and is richly carved with motifs and figures. On the south side of the square is the 18th-century **Palazzo Comunale**. Features worth noting include the *great hall* with 19th-century frescoes, the *Sala degli Specchi* and *frescoed friezes*. On top of the high wall linking the **polygonal tower** to the palazzo is the **Loggetta Veneziana**, originally an uncovered walkway.

This building (1466), sometimes called the Rocchetta di Piazza, houses the *Museo di Scienze Naturali*. This has some old instruments once used for teaching science. On the other side of the square, much of which is porticoed, there are other delightful palazzi and the Baroque church of *Ss. Anna e Gioacchino*.

Rocca Malatestiana ④

This stronghold is situated at the top of the Garampo hill and surrounded by the **Parco della Rimembranza**, a green park criss-crossed by footpaths. Not much remains of the *Rocca Vecchia* (16C): just two arches called '*occhi di civetta*' (eyes of the owl). The irregularly-shaped pentagonal building we see today was finished in 1480. A curtain-wall with a chemin-de-ronde connected the fort to the Rocchetta di Piazza and continued to the Palazzo Comunale. In the vast area surrounded by the walls are two towers, one (called *maschio* or 'keep') has a square plan and the other (called *femmina*) has a rectangular plan, with a polygonal bastion at one of the corners. The keep has been converted into an **exhibition area for archaeology displays** of finds from the Malatesta period (the Renaissance and post-Renaissance). The *femmina* now houses the **Museo di Storia dell'Agricoltura** where various farming environments have been reproduced as well as displays of the production cycles associated with farming. Charming **chemins-de-ronde**, walkways connecting the seven towers, run along the inside the mighty defence walls, with superb views as far as the sea. A wonderful example of defensive structures, these inner walkways allowed the soldiers to move around the fortress under cover. In addition, the internal courtyards could be defended because of the arrow slits all around the walls. The courtyard of the fortress is overlooked by a graceful loggia with six arches.

Galleria dei Dipinti Antichi della Cassa di Risparmio ⑤

This art gallery is located on the corner of Via Tiberti and Corso Garibaldi and contains about 70 paintings from the 15th-18th centuries, the majority from the Emilia and Romagna Schools.

Pinacoteca Comunale ⑥

The public art gallery was instituted in 1883. Its collection represents the various Schools of painting in Romagna (15-18C), but it also has a contemporary section, with works of the Cesena School by Guttuso, Morandi and Schifano.

S. Maria del Monte ⑦

This basilica stands at the summit of the Spaziano hill, overlooking Cesena from the south-east. It's only a short walk from the town. On entering, your gaze is drawn to the central staircase leading to the raised presbytery, called the **Grand Chapel**. Above the chapel is a wonderful frescoed dome. Behind the main altar are the Giuseppe Scalvini's walnut-wood **choirstalls*** (1560-62) with figures depicted in clever depictions of perspective, each one different, with grotesque figures on the armrests. The ambulatory is where the famous **votive collection**** is displayed: these little tablets, which normally represent the malady which is the object of the votive offering, are not only an indication of popular devotion, but also give us an insight into the local customs from the 15th century to the present day.

DAY TRIPS

BAGNO DI ROMAGNA [56 km]

Famous since Antiquity for its thermal springs, Bagno di Romagna is set in the lovely **Parco Nazionale delle Foreste Casentinesi, Monte Falterona e Campigna****. The park has forest ecosystems which are host to numerous tree species and a rich undergrowth which forms the habitat for a large number of plants and animals. In the center of the town, the **basilica of S. Maria Assunta** (9C) overlooks *Piazza Ricasoli*. The church has some remarkable art treasures, especially of the Tuscan School of the 15th and 16th centuries. The town has been awarded the TCI's Orange Flag.

BERTINORO [15 km]

The truly wonderful panoramic position of this town has lead it to be called the 'balcony of Romagna'. At the heart of the medieval town, surrounded by defensive walls, with its delightful little cobbled streets and an atmosphere of days gone by, is **Piazza della Libertà****, with a view which, on good days, stretches as far as the Dalmatian coast. Overlooking the square is *Palazzo Comunale* (1306) with its characteristic crenellations, the *cathedral* and the *Torre Civica* (or clock tower). At the bottom of the square stands a column that symbolizes the hospitality of the town. Known as the **Colonna delle Anella***, it was erected during the 13th century to end a dispute among local noble families about who should host visitors to the town. It was decided that the families would be able to 'own', on a rotating base, one of the twelve rings attached to the bottom of the column. Then, it would be the guests themselves who would 'choose' their hosts, depending on which ring they tied their horse to on arrival. Above the town towers the imposing thousand-year-old **Rocca***, superbly restored. Inside, a wonderful frescoed *dining room* (1613).

CASTROCARO TERME [11 km]

Piazza Garibaldi, situated at the heart of the grand-ducal part of town, is the site of the 18th-century *Palazzo Piancastelli* and the **church of Ss. Nicolò e Francesco**, built in 1520. Beyond *Porta di S. Nicolò* lies the **medieval part of town***; notable buildings here include the late-Gothic *church of S. Nicolò*, **Palazzo dei Commissari**, a typical building of the grand-ducal period, the **Torre Campanaria**, a harmonious cylindrical building with a 1.3-ton bell, and the **Baptistery of S. Giovanni**, a small church dating from 1292. Beyond the *Porta della Postierla* is the imposing **Fortezza Medievale***; the *keep*, *dungeon tower* and the *Cortile delle Armi courtyard* are worth seeing. *Palazzo della Guarnigione* houses an exhibition of old weapons, majolicas and antique furniture. The town has been awarded the TCI's Orange Flag.

CESENATICO [35 km]

Cesenatico is quite a compact town filled with terraced houses lining each side of the famous **canal-harbor**** designed by Leonardo da Vinci. Once a seaport (it used to be the port for Cesena), the town is now an important holiday resort – it has been awarded the Ministry of the Environment's Blue Flag for the quality of its beaches on various occasions – and a fishing town. The **Museo Galleggiante della Marineria*** (an unique floating museum) is located in the oldest and most inland section of the canal-harbor. It has an interesting display of boats used between the disappearance of the lateen sail and the arrival of motor-driven vessels.

Next to the museum is *Palazzo degli Anziani*, now the **Antiquarium Comunale**, a museum with finds from the Roman period. On the eastern side of the canal-harbor is the **church of S. Giacomo**, not far away from the **Piazzetta delle Conserve**. The name of the square comes from the ice-stores that can still be seen today. These truncated, cone-shaped receptacles were filled with snow and ice and used to store fish and other commodities.

FORLIMPÒPOLI [8 km]

The **Rocca****, the majestic castle built in the 14th century. This imposing granite building on a rectangular plan has four cylindrical towers, one at each corner, and a splendid chemin-de-ronde. Located in the interesting subterranean rooms of the fortress, the **Museo Archeologico Civico**** has wonderful mosaics, sculptures and bronze and glass artifacts, all relating to the town's Roman period. There is also medieval and prehistoric material. One of

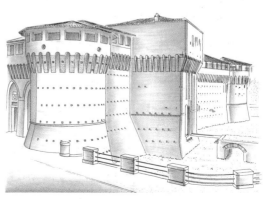

The Rocca, a majestic castle built in the 14th century, dominates Piazza Garibaldi, the heart of the old town center

the major religious buildings in the town is the **church of the Servi**, built in the early 16th century, and above all the early-Christian (6C) **collegiate church of S. Rufillo**. It was rebuilt in the 14th century and then restored in 1821.

GALEATA [33 km]

The town, dominated by the massive vertical cliff, lies on a flat ledge, ensuring a breezy climate. An unusual feature of the town center is its fine and rather unusual low porticoes. The **Museo Archeologico Civico 'D. Mambrini'*** has some important Roman, pre-Roman and Barbarian finds. On a panoramic promontory, 3 km from the center of Galeata, stands the splendid Romanesque Parish church of the **abbey of S. Ellero****. The abbey is set in a beautiful park and dates from the 5th century. The church has largely retained its original structure, although later styles are also evident (Byzantine and Romanesque features outside, and Baroque inside). The facade has a fine Romanesque doorway.

LONGIANO [32 km]

This town, which has been awarded the TCI's "Bandiera Arancione" (Orange Flag), has a fascinating medieval center, built on the slopes of a hill and culminating in the imposing **Castello Malatestiano***, which has retained its original 13th-14th-century layout. In the courtyard stands a tower, (the *Torre Civica*) and an elegant *Venetian-style fountain basin* (1506). The rooms of the castle house the prestigious **Fondazione Tito Balestra**** which has a display of *paintings and drawings* by artists from Italy and elsewhere. Interesting buildings in the town include: the **Sanctuary of the SS. Crocifisso** (1755-64), named after the **Crucifix** of the Pisano-Giuntesca workshop, painted on canvas and fixed onto wood (13C), in a niche above the choir; and the **collegiate church of S. Cristoforo** (18C). The *Baroque Oratory of S. Giuseppe* (1703-1728), built on a Greek-cross plan, is now the **Museo di Arte Sacra** which takes full advantage of the setting created by the elegant *stuccoes* and late 18th-century *statues*. Another interesting museum is the **Museo Italiano della Ghisa** (Cast-iron Museum) with a display of furnishings from various Italian cities used in the 19th and 20th centuries.

MODIGLIANA [34 km]

The ruins of a fortress of the Guidi counts, called the 'Roccaccia' (great fortress), dating from the 12th-13th century, overlook the town. The old town center still has fields among its old frescoed houses and is crossed by a little stream. To reach the center, you must pass through the so-called *Tribuna* (16C), a rather unusual building comprising a cylindrical tower, two bell towers and an edicule. The center of the old town was Piazza Pretorio. On the square stands **Palazzo Pretorio**, which now houses the **Pinacoteca Comunale Silvestro Lega****, with works by Silvestro Lega and some other artists. Silvestro Lega, born in Modigliana in 1826, was a founder of the Macchiaioli art movement. The Macchiaioli painters believed in an artistic reawakening that translated into the rejection of linear drawings and the use of patches of color and chromatic contrasts, as well as a preference for subjects relating to everyday life. On the outskirts of the town, heading towards Faenza, is the *Ponte della Signora* (18C). This spectacular hump-backed bridge has three arches, the central one stands high above the river.

MONTELEONE [43 km]

The *Castello di Monteleone* is quite well preserved and most of it is original (first documented in 1233). It is associated with the love story between Lord Byron and Countess Teresa Gamba Guiccioli, who used to meet here. Inside is a garden with a *bell tower* and two smaller towers. In front of this is a balustrade overlooking the sea. The little medieval town, which has been awarded the TCI's "Bandiera Arancione" (Orange Flag), lies in a semi-circle around the foot of the castle.

PORTICO AND SAN BENEDETTO [35 km]

Portico di Romagna and the little town of San Benedetto, which form a single municipality, have been awarded the TCI's "Bandiera Arancione" (Orange Flag). The town, which has retained its original layout, is built in three levels sloping gradually down towards the river: the highest part of the town contains the castle and the Parish church; the middle part contains palazzi which once belonged to the nobility; and the lowest level has the old houses once inhabited by peasants and artisans.

The **passeggiata***, or walk around the old town, is definitely worthwhile for the wonderful views. San Benedetto in Alpe used to be a favorite haunt of hermits and spiritual retreats because of its wild landscape. In fact, that is why the thousand-year old Benedictine abbey founded by the Cluny monks came to be founded here. Today, it still overlooks the old part of the town known as *'il Poggio'*. You should not miss an outing to the **Cascata Acquacheta****, a lovely waterfall described by Dante in his 'Divine Comedy', an enchanting place where the woods, water and old footpaths paths blend to create a most harmonious whole. Here and there, the stream flows over rapids and into small pools; the actual waterfall is rather unusual because the rocks are arranged in a terrace-like pattern of small steps, so that the water has to jump down a step at a time. The plateau above the waterfall is also delightful. 4 km south of Portico, near the village of Bocconi, is a pretty area near the river that is well worth visiting: there is an old mill, a small waterfall and a hump-backed bridge, **Ponte della Brusia*** (18C), with three arches.

PREMILCUORE [50 km]

This village overlooked by the spurs of the mountains has long been a summer holiday resort. The old town center clings to a ridge above the river and it is one of the best remaining examples, especially in terms of layout, of a fortified medieval village with its walls, towers and steep little streets, which have earned it the TCI's Orange Flag. **Porta Fiorentina**, one of two

Ponte della Brusia at Bocconi

ancient gates, has an old, mechanical *clock* (1593), which is still in good working order: two big stones pull a long hemp rope the entire height of the tower, driving the original mechanism. Piazza Ricci is dominated by *Palazzo Giannelli* and *Palazzo Briccolani*, both examples of grand-ducal architecture. Nearby is the **oratory of S. Lorenzo** which has an interesting altar-piece above the high altar (17C-Tuscan School). Slightly out of the center is the *parish church of S. Martino*.

TERRA DEL SOLE [9 km]

Terra del Sole, founded with the name of Eliopoli (city of the sun) by the Grand Duke of Tuscany, Cosimo I de' Medici, in 1564, was completed in 1579. It is a fortress town that was carefully planned and built in line with the Renaissance principles of the 'ideal city'. The old town center is surrounded by an imposing set of rectangular walls with bastions, almost 13m high, with two gates, *Porta Fiorentina* and *Porta Romana*. The gates were each guarded by a castle, named, respectively, *del Capitano delle Artiglierie* and *del Governatore*. There are two types of terraced houses, which were built differently according to their final use, either as ordinary houses or as part of the military garrison. At the end of the 18th century, some of the walls were removed to make space for the main road. As such, the current road passes along a slightly different route to the original road that connected the two entrances. Even today, when you enter Piazza Garibaldi, once the parade ground, you have the impression of entering a 'city-museum' still pervaded by the spirit of the Renaissance. **Palazzo Pretorio** is almost completely intact and is a wonderful example of Renaissance architecture. The town has been awarded the TCI's Orange Flag.

Modena is situated in the plain on the line of the Via Aemilia. Founded by the Etruscans in about 600BC, it was destroyed by serious flooding after the Fall of the Roman Empire. The city was later reconstructed and the first medieval walls were built. During the 11ᵗʰ century, the Canale Naviglio was dug, the surrounding land was reclaimed and the first Palazzo Comunale and tower were erected. The city has a typically dense medieval urban fabric, with narrow, winding streets and irregularly-shaped blocks following the course of canals, built above the ruins of the Roman town.

Piazza Grande ❶

Piazza Grande was begun in the age of the communes. It has always been the seat of civic and religious power and was the focal point of the medieval street system. Set around the square is the cathedral (1099), Palazzo del Comune and the Torre della Ghirlandina (1169). This broad piazza with its round cobbles is still the heart of the city today. It has always been the place where people meet and conduct business, and, since 1931, has also been the setting for the weekly fruit and vegetable market. Palazzo Comunale occupies the north and east sides of the square. In front of the palazzo is large red granite stone called the **pietra ringadora** (haranguing stone) which, according to some, came from the walls of the Roman town, Mutina: it was used for making speeches and for publicly humiliating debtors, as well as for civic and judicial purposes.

Cattedrale ❷

The cathedral is the city's most important monument. A prototype of the Romanesque in Emilia, together with Piazza Grande and the Torre della Ghirlandina, it has been designated a UNESCO World Heritage Site. Its very walls seem alive, so thickly is it adorned with carvings. Begun in 1099 by the architect Lanfranco, it is

usually called the Duomo, or '*domus clari Geminiani*' (house of the illustrious St Geminianus) as it is described in the inscription on the foundation stone on the facade of the church. The building work was executed by master stonemasons from Campione in the 12-14ᵗʰ centuries. The **facade** is divided into three parts by pillars surmounted by octagonal edicules which augment the vertical quality of the central section; the large, Gothic rose-window is by Anselmo da Campione, who also executed the side-doors (late 12C); a loggia with small arches spans the facade horizontally and the motif is repeated on the sides and the apse of the edifice, creating a visual effect of harmony and rhythmical movement. The porch in front of the **main doorway*** has a loggia on the top and its columns are supported by lions of Roman date; the door-jambs are decorated with tendrils, symbolic motifs and twelve figures of *Prophets and Patriarchs* executed by Wiligelmo; at the sides and above the side-doors are panels depicting the **Story of the Creation**, a masterpiece by Wiligelmo, in which Romanesque sculpture achieves convincing volume and great expressive energy. On the south side of the church is the *Porta dei Principi* or *del Battesimo*, with stone lions supporting the columns of the

The Romanesque cathedral

porch. The door-jambs and the archivolt are decorated with plant motifs and sculptures of the *Life of St Geminianus*, by a follower of Wiligelmo called the Master of St Geminianus. Further along is another porch with a loggia, also with columns supported by lions, the *Porta Regia*, almost a second facade facing Piazza Grande, the work of Anselmo da Campione (c.1175). On the north side of the building is the **Porta della Pescheria***: the door-jambs have carvings depicting the *months*; in the archivolt, a *Story of the Breton cycle of King Arthur* (1120-30), executed in the French Burgundian style; in the architrave, sculptures with *animal motifs*. The austere brick **interior of the cathedral*** is flooded with light filtering through the stained glass of the rose-window (c.1450). The basilica has a nave and two side-aisles separated by cruciform pillars alternating with columns; high up, fake matroneums recall the loggia motif on the facade; the rib vaults date from the 15th century. Inside the entrance, two Roman capitals function as holy water fonts; halfway up the nave is a 14th-century pulpit. In the right aisle, a brick arch frames frescoes of the Modena School of the 15th century. At the far end of the nave is an ambo and a splendid **rood screen*** executed by Masters of Campione in the 12th and 13th centuries; supported by telamones and lions bearing columns, there are remarkable low reliefs in the marble plutei of the parapet, and there are traces of paint in the *scenes of the Passion*. Above the rood screen, under the triumphal arch, a wooden 14th-century *Crucifix*. The crypt is divided into a nave and two side-aisles by 60 columns with fine capitals (late 11C); in the central apse, the *tomb of St Geminianus* (4C); in the right apse, a ploychrome terracotta sculpture of the **Virgin Suckling the Infant Christ** (c.1480). The presbytery has a fine balustrade with two tiers of small columns and beautiful inlaid wooden *choirstalls* (1465). The bell tower (86m high), known as the **Ghirlandina*** is joined to the cathedral by two pointed arches. Two balconies surrounded the top of the tower which dominates the houses below. Begun by Lanfranco, the height of the bell tower was raised by

the Masters of Campione (1319): in fact, you can see the Romanesque motifs in the lower part of the structure, and the Gothic motifs higher up in the octagonal part and the spire. The apses are underground at the original level of the church; you can see the inscription on the foundation stone in the central apse and, below it, original models of the old units of measurement used in Modena (the *mattone*, *tegola*, *pertica* and *braccio*) reminding us that the piazza has always been a center of commerce. From the loggias of the tower there is a splendid view over the town, with its bell towers, domes and numerous

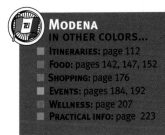

MODENA
IN OTHER COLORS...
- **ITINERARIES:** page 112
- **FOOD:** pages 142, 147, 152
- **SHOPPING:** page 176
- **EVENTS:** pages 184, 192
- **WELLNESS:** page 207
- **PRACTICAL INFO:** page 223

wooden roof-top terraces. From here you can see as far as the gardens of the ducal palace and the green circle of trees marking the beltway, with the hills behind.
Next to the cathedral, the **Museo lapidario del Duomo*** contains architectural fragments and sculptures, some of which come from the church; they include eight *metopes* carved with imaginary and grotesque figures dating from 1125-30.

Palazzo Comunale ❸

Palazzo comunale is a complex combination of medieval buildings dating from the 10th to 15th centuries. They were later altered and unified behind a single austere porticoed facade dating from the 18th and 19th centuries. The front of the building is divided into the *clock-tower* and the 13th-century popular assembly hall which was altered in the 16th century; a broad niche contains a *statue of the Immacolata* placed there in 1805. On the edge of the building stands the *Bonissima*, a marble statue of a woman holding what was once the top of some scales (12C). According to tradition, it

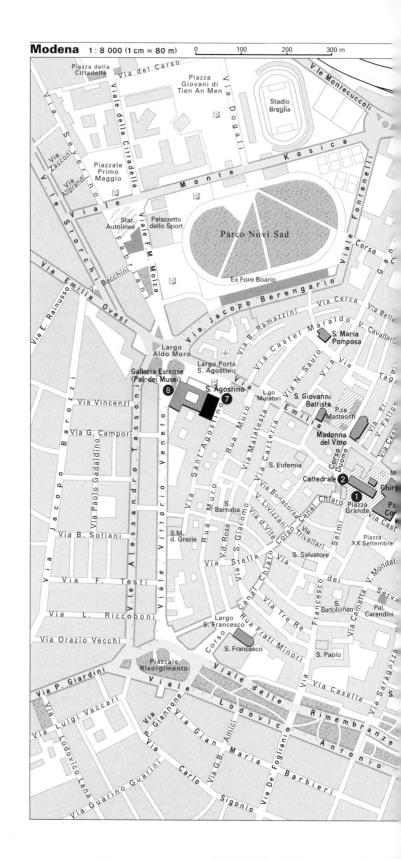

Modena 1 : 8 000 (1 cm = 80 m)

0   100   200   300 m

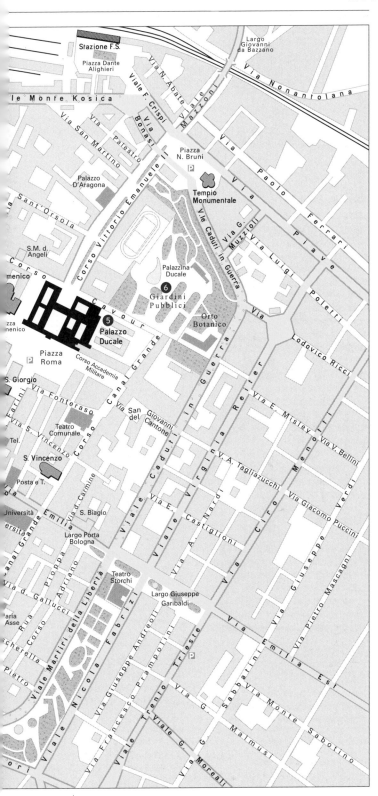

represents a very rich, charitable woman called Bona, or Matilda of Canossa in person; in fact it was the emblem of the municipal office ("*Buona stima*", literally, good estimate, hence Bonissima) which controlled weights and measures. Off the portico is a *monumental staircase* (1563) which leads up to the frescoed rooms on the first floor: **Sala del Fuoco**, with frescoes depicting scenes from the Roman era of the city, *Sala del Vecchio Consiglio* (17C), *Sala degli Arazzi*, and *Sala dei Matrimoni*.

Chiesa di S. Pietro ④

According to the legend, the church of St Peter was built above the ruins of a Temple of Jupiter dating from the 1st century. It was annexed to a Benedictine abbey in the 10th century. In the square in front of the church is the *cross of St Peter* (14C), perched on top of a column with a capital carved with lion's heads (12C). This church is an important testimonial of Renaissance art in Modena, and, at that time, the city's second most important church after the cathedral. Its large harmonious brick facade is divided by pilaster strips and cornices, with beautiful terracotta decoration. This is particularly obvious in the horizontal frieze depicting *satyrs on sea-horses*. It is also enhanced by three marble doorways and three rose-windows. The interior is divided into a nave with two aisles on the right and two on the left, separated by cruciform pillars, and has semi-polygonal apses. In the nave are *terracotta statues* and a remarkable painted organ. The 16th-century sacristy has carved wooden benches.

Palazzo Ducale ⑤

This majestic building, the most characteristic features of which are its size and harmonious lines, was begun in about 1634 and finished in the mid-19th century. Built partly over the ruins of the old castle founded by the Este family in 1288, it was rebuilt between 1336 and 1340, providing the city with an alternative focus to the cathedral. The role of the building changed when the court of Ferrara moved here in 1598, and it became one of the most interesting Baroque princely residences in Italy. Its long, imposing facade has a tower at each end and is higher in the center. It has three tiers of windows grouped in pairs (1651) and is topped by a balustrade decorated with statues. The main part of the palace is its most striking feature, being imposing but not too serious. Guided tours of the interior, now the Military Academy, can be booked at the Tourist Office. The grand courtyard is decorated in the Baroque style, with two rows of loggias with columns interspersed with pillars; note also the splendid monumental staircase. The loggia leads into the ducal apartments overlooking the square: the *grand hall* with its frescoed ceiling (1696); the *Sala di Psiche*, with a ceiling fresco depicting the *Marriage of Cupid and Psyche* (c.1695); the *Salottino d'Oro*, a small

Modena: chiesa di S. Pietro

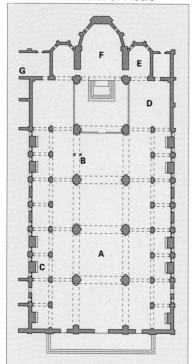

A Nave with 6 terracotta statues by A. Begarelli

B 16th-century organ by G.B. Facchetti

C Chapel with altar-piece by F. Bianchi Ferrari

D Right transept with the "great niche with statues" decorated by A. Beganelli

E Right apse, Pietà by A. Beganelli

F Presbytery with 16th-century inlaid wooden choirstalls by G. F. Testi

G Door leading into the sacristy

room with beautiful stucco Rococo decoration covered in gold leaf (1742). Near the palace stand the churches of S. Giorgio and S. Domenico. The **church of S. Giorgio***, also known as the Sanctuary of the Beata Vergine Ausiliatrice (1647-80), was built in the flamboyant Baroque style. It has a curved pediment, pinnacles and a split tympanum above the door; the elegant interior, built on a Greek-cross plan and visually melodramatic, has composite pillars and columns interrupted horizontally by rows of matroneums. **S. Domenico**, the 13th-century Dominican church, was rebuilt between 1708 and 1735. This very striking building has a facade in the late-Mannerist style, with pilaster strips in the Ionic style, and a tympanum below its curved pediment. Inside the oval church, to the left of the entrance is a delightful terracotta sculpture depicting *Jesus in the House of Martha and Mary with the Apostles Peter and Andrew and Two Women* (c.1546).

Giardini Pubblici ⑥

The park situated to the north of the castle is a typical Renaissance Italian-style garden divided into geometric shapes, completed 1602 with the addition of a pool. The *Palazzina Ducale* (1632-34), extended by adding two exedra-shaped wings (c.1750), is a very elegant building. It has a long facade, with two statues of Roman emperors and a tower in the middle with an octagonal top. The present layout dates from the 19th century and comprises a mixed garden, part formal and part woodland, with mazes, a small asymmetrical

lake, and paths meandering around a fake 'wild' area. Not far away is the *Botanical Garden* of the University of Modena, created in the mid-18th century. The collection contains more than a thousand species of plant. The most interesting sections are the ducal glasshouses, built in 1765, which contain a huge variety of exotic species, and the area devoted to trees. Other parks in the city include the **Parco**, which occupies the area between Viale delle Rimembranze and Viale Martiri della Libertà in the older part of the city and the area between Viale L.A. Muratori and Viale N. Fabrizi further out of the center, **Parco della Resistenza**, which occupies a huge area behind the provincial train station, **Parco della Repubblica, Parco Amendola Sud, Parco Enzo Ferrari**, south of which is the extension to *Parco Corassori*, and **Parco Novi Sad**, situated right next to the historic center.

Chiesa di S. Agostino ⑦

The church (c.1665), designed as a setting for the funerals of the dukes, a sort of pantheon of the d'Este family, is richly decorated with statues and busts of saints and men of the Church related to the Estes; notice the beautiful coffered ceiling with scenes depicting the *Glorification of the Estes*; in the first arch on the right, a large terracotta sculpture of the *Deposition* (c.1530); at the fourth altar on the right, below the gallery, a detached fresco of the

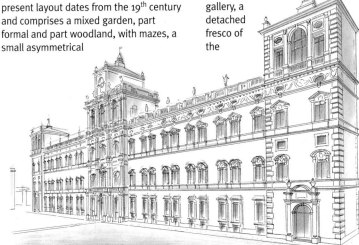

Palazzo Ducale became one of the most interesting Baroque princely residences in Italy when the court of Ferrara moved here in 1598.

Madonna and Child, by Tommaso da Modena (c.1350). In front of the church is **Largo di Porta S. Agostino****, a vast rectangular area laid out in 1750-60, which once featured one of the town gates, demolished in 1912. The square is the setting for some of the most important architectural projects commissioned by Francesco III d'Este. On the south side of the square is the majestic, somber facade of the *Grande Ospedale Civico degli Infermi*, known as the Ospedale Vecchio(1753-56); it has beautiful wrought-iron work, with small Baroque-style volutes on the pediments and a large wrought-iron gate in the entrance hall.

Palazzo dei Musei ⑧

Palazzo dei Musei, an imposing building in the neo-Mannerist style, has been the city museum since 1884. It incorporates several of the important collections left to the city by the Este dynasty, and expresses their artistic and cultural taste. In the middle of the atrium is a *bust of Duke Borso d'Este* (1830). As well as housing permanent collections, the museum is often used for exhibitions of a high cultural standard. The collection of the **Museo Lapidario Estense** is displayed in the loggia surrounding the the the four sides of the courtyard of the Palazzo dei Musei. It includes Roman, medieval and Renaissance material from the Modena area. There are fragments of sculptures, milestones, cippi, sarcophagi, funerary steles, inscriptions, crosses, tombstones, funerary monuments, coats-of-arms and architectural fragments. On the first floor of the palazzo is the **Biblioteca Estense***, one of Italy's most important libraries. It has an extremely fine collection of books, manuscripts, and valuable incunabola, the core of which formed the library of the Duke of Ferrara in the 14th century. There are three sections: the Este library, with 4,102 manuscripts, the Archivio Muratoriano and the musical section, also the Fondo Campori collection of original

A wonderful illuminated volume

manuscripts. On request, it is possible to visit an exhibition of beautiful illuminated manuscripts from Italy and abroad, dating from the 14th to 16th centuries. The numerous books on display include the famous **Bible of Borso d'Este****, one of the most beautiful books ever created, a masterpiece of the Renaissance courts of the Northern Italy. It comprises two volumes (1,200 pages) in vellum, which was specially treated in Bologna, and was made in Ferrara (1455-61). It is a magnificent work of figurative art, built up around the text and almost engulfing it; the richness of the images, the decoration of the pages with different edges and cornices, the illuminated first letters of each paragraph and a series of pictorial illustrations dominate the text throughout. Illuminated texts like these were typical of the period. The wood-engraving collection includes an edition of *The Garden of Polifilo*, with beautiful illustrations by the Venetian printer, Aldo Manuzio 1499. The **Musei Civici***, which occupy the upper floors of the palazzo, comprise the *Museo Civico di Storia e Arte Medievale e Moderna* and the *Museo Civico Archeologico Etnologico*. The former contains all kinds of material, much of it the result of collections made by aristocrats in the Modena area and almost all of it made by local artists and craftsmen. The archeological museum, which has retained its rather charming 19th-century look, has finds dating from the Paleolithic and an important collection of Neolithic and Eneolithic finds made in the province of Modena, including artifacts made of pottery, flint and bone. The Terramara culture (settlements of houses on stilts dating from the Bronze Age) is represented by pottery and bronze artifacts. Iron-Age finds include pieces from the Villanova and Etruscan cultures. There are many finds from the Roman city of Modena. The ethnological section of the museum contains objects from tribes in South America and New Guinea, but also from Japan, Africa and Egypt. The **Galleria**

Estense**, located on the top floor, is one of Italy's most important art collections, and contains paintings, sculptures and drawings, medals and other objects which belonged to the d'Este family. The gallery has a large number of works by artists from Emilia and other parts of North-Eastern Italy dating from the 15th to 18th centuries, but also important works from other parts of Italy from the 15th and 16th centuries, and by European masters (Flemish and German painters of the 15th and 16th centuries). In the atrium is a marble bust of Duke **Francesco I d'Este*** by Gian Lorenzo Bernini (1650-51). One work not to be missed is the **triptych*** by El Greco with *Moses Receiving the Tables of the Law* and the *Last Judgement* in the central panels, and *Adam and Eve in front of the Eternal God*, an *Annunciation*, a *Baptism of Christ* and an *Adoration of the Shepherds* in the side panels. Some of the rooms are specially equipped for blind visitors. The **Civica Biblioteca di Storia dell'Arte "Luigi Poletti"**, which specializes in architecture and art history, contains more than 50,000 books dating from the 16th to 19th centuries, as well as collections of antique and modern drawings and prints.

DAY TRIPS

CARPI [18 km]

This small country town has one of Italy's largest squares: **Piazza dei Martiri*** ❶. It has always been the setting for the town's religious, lordly and commercial functions. A lovely *portico* with 52 arches 212m long runs along the west side of the square. The palazzo overlooking the piazza is the headquarters of the Cassa di Risparmio di Carpi which has a fine art collection; another interesting building is the *Farmacia dell'Assunta* (1853), an old pharmacy with its original 19th-century decoration and furnishings. On the south side, the high portico of the *Loggia del Grano* (c.1510) faces the main street (Corso Alberto Pio). Overlooking the north side is the Baroque facade of the Cathedral of S. Maria Assunta while **Palazzo dei Pio*** ❷ overlooks the east side of the square. A small round tower known as the *Uccelliera* (1480), a massive tower

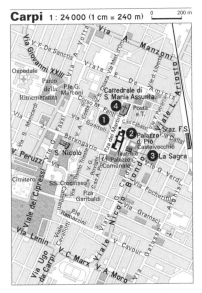

Carpi 1 : 24 000 (1 cm = 240 m)

(1320) on the north side and the *Torrione di Galasso Pio* (15C) on the south side contrast with the 17th-century *clock-tower* in the center of the building. On the first floor, near the entrance to the Museo Civico "Giulio Ferrari", are the *monumental apartments* and various richly decorated rooms, including the *Salone dei Mori*, a delightful Renaissance frescoed *chapel* (early 16C), the *Stanza del Forno*, the *Stanza della Torre di Passerino*, the *Stanza Ornata*, the *Stanza dei Trionfi*, the *Studiolo di Alberto Pio* and the *Stanza dell'Amore*. The **Museo Civico "Giulio Ferrari"*** (temporarily closed) contains important collections of paintings, furnishings, ceramics, engravings, archeological finds and material from the Risorgimento, all associated with local art and history. Behind the Palazzo is the **parish church of S. Maria in Castello**, or **La Sagra** ❸ (8C), which has the typical appearance of a military church. In 1515 it was altered and given a new Renaissance facade. The tall 13th-century **bell tower** with its pinnacles and spire is located at the center of the old town. The Renaissance **Cathedral of S. Maria Assunta*** ❹ has a Baroque facade, however the interior has retained its original lines. Built on a basilica plan, the cathedral has a Latin-cross plan, with a nave and two side-aisles separated by composite pillars. It

Carpi, the doorway of parish church of S. Maria

contains several works of art. Another building overlooking the same square is the neo-classical *Teatro Comunale* designed by Claudio Rossi (1857-61).

CASTELVETRO DI MODENA
[21 km]

The "Castel" in its name probably refers to the fort of Roman date. The early-medieval castle and town were built above the ruins of the Roman structure. An earthquake in 1501 destroyed much of the town and radical changes were made in the 1930s, however Castelvetro di Modena is a picturesque place, with its outline of towers and bell-towers, and has been awarded the TCI's "Bandiera Arancione" (Orange Flag). All that remains of the 10th-century *castle* are some of its defensive walls, its *clock-tower* and *Palazzo Rangoni*. On the esplanade in front of the castle stands the majestic neo-Gothic *parish church of Ss. Senesio e Teopompo* (1897-1907).

FANANO [65 km]

This small, well-preserved Renaissance town in the Apennines, which has been awarded the TCI's "Bandiera Arancione" (Orange Flag), has a rich artistic heritage, especially its churches. Its streets, decorated by artists of international standing, constitute a veritable open-air museum. The **parish**

church of S. Silvestro, regarded as one of the most beautiful late-Romanesque churches in the Apennines, is worth visiting. Restructured in the 16th century, it has a splendid east door (1502); the nave and two side-aisles are separated by twelve stone columns with capitals, probably carved by master stonemason from Campione.

FIUMALBO [84 km]

Dominated by the shape of Monte Cimone, in the heart of the Parco Regionale dell'Alto Appennino Modenese, Fiumalbo's historic center is well-preserved and has been awarded the TCI's "Bandiera Arancione" (Orange Flag). At the entrance to the town, with its medieval cobbled streets, stone houses and slate roofs, is the rustic *oratory di S. Rocco*, built in the 15th century, with frescoes dating from 1535-36. The *parish church of S. Bartolomeo Apostolo* has some 13th-century features and a beautiful Renaissance facade with an elegant porch; inside, there is a Baroque ceiling above the nave and two side-aisles, and some *Romanesque sculptures* (13C). Set around the little square in front of the church are the *oratory of the Immacolata* and the *oratory of S. Caterina*.

NONÀNTOLA [10 km]

Nonàntola's history is closely linked to that of its famous **Benedictine abbey***. Founded in the mid-8th century, it was one of the most powerful in Northern Italy, with its own scriptorium. It was handed over to the Cistercians (1514), and suppressed in 1769. The medieval structure of the square castle, with the *Torre dei Modenesi* (1261) and the *Torre dei Bolognesi* (1307), 36m high, can be seen in the layout of the porticoed streets of the old town. The abbey complex includes the **church of S. Silvestro**, with Lombard Romanesque forms dating from the 12th century, a feature particularly obvious in the apse. On the facade, there is an original doorway with a porch and **low reliefs** by the workshop of Wiligelmo. Mighty composite brick pillars separate the nave and side-aisles; it has a raised presbytery above the large and very beautiful **crypt**, where there are 64 columns with capitals dating from the

8th and 12th centuries and some fine works of art. South of the church stands the Benedictine *monastery* with a 15th-century double loggia overlooking the courtyard. The nearby Palazzo Comunale still contains the **refectory,** which has some fine frescoes dating from the 11th and 12th centuries. The abbey has a **treasury,** containing what remains of the abbey's considerable assets, and an **archive,** with documents dating from between the 8th and 14th centuries. This is one of the most important archives in Europe and contains numerous parchments and documents associated with eminent figures such as Charlemagne, Matilda of Canossa and Frederick Barbarossa. Left of the abbey stands the Renaissance *church of S. Filomena.* Other buildings of interest include the *parish church of S. Michele Arcangelo,* with a lovely Romanesque apse, and *Villa Emma* (1898), which has a double portico on the facade and various outbuildings. The villa is associated with a touching episode during the Second World War: it provided shelter for about 900 Jewish children who were helped by local people to escape to Switzerland.

SASSUOLO [17 km]

The **Palazzo Ducale**** stands on Piazzale della Rosa, a beautiful square also overlooked by the Paggerie and the *church of S. Francesco.* Its rooms are decorated with frescoes and stuccoes,

especially the **Galleria di Bacco** (17-C frescoes) and the *Salone delle Guardie,* which occupies two floors of the palace, a masterpiece of architectural perspective by artists of the Bologna School. In the courtyard, the Fountain of Neptune was executed by Antonio Raggi according to a design by Bernini. Features in the garden include the splendid Baroque **Peschiera** (fish-pond) or **Teatro delle Fontane** and the *Casino del Belvedere* (the tempera paintings inside depict the *Delizie Estensi* or residences of the d'Este family). The palazzo contains the paintings and furnishings of Galleria Estense in their original location. Religious buildings here include the 17th-century *parish church of S. Giorgio,* the *church of S. Giuseppe* and the small, elegant *church of the Madonna del Macero.* Fine examples of civic architecture include the *clock-tower, Villa Vistarino dei Pioppi* or *Giacobazzi,* a large mansion (18C) set in a vast park, *Villa Amalia* and *Villa Bontempelli,* a building dating from the 17th-18th centuries with a fine doorway and tower. The *Palazzina della Casiglia,* which has features typical of the Ferrara tradition, dates from 1560. Next to it are the ducal stables (1783). This small palazzo houses the *Centro di Documentazione dell'Industria Italiana. delle Piastrelle di Ceramica,* where an interesting exhibition traces the development of the local ceramic-tile tradition.

Abbazia di Nonantola: plan of the crypt and the presbytery

Altar with the relics of St Anselmo

Tomb of St Sylvester

Polyptych by Michele Di Matteo

High altar

Plan of the crypt

Plan of the presbytery

Modena Cathedral

Begun in 1099 on the foundations of a five-aisled basilica dating from the previous century which housed the tomb of St Geminianus, Modena Cathedral is the masterpiece of the architect Lanfranco, "*mirabilis artifex, mirificus aedificator*" (wonderful building, outstanding creator). According to the tenets of Romanesque architecture, it is built on a basilica plan with a nave and two side-aisles, its facade being divided into three parts by prominent pillars. In the center, the tympanum has a spire on either side and the main doorway has a porch supported by lions of Roman date. A continuous series of blind loggia with three-light windows under broad arches spans all the facades, a motif repeated in the nave in the form of a fake matroneum. The white marble side-facades are decorated with complex sculptural decoration by Wiligelmo. The same artist was responsible for the four friezes on the main facade depicting the Stories of Genesis. Wiligelmo also decorated the door-jambs of the doorway with plant motifs representing the jungle of life – Man's struggle to live. The Masters of Campione (late 12-14C) were responsible for the Gothic-style rose-window, the Porta Regia in pink marble facing Piazza Grande and the rood screen with the pulpit inside, where the entrance to the crypt is decorated with scenes from the Passion. On the north side of the cathedral is the bell tower, 87 m high, known as the "Ghirlandina": the first five storeys are Romanesque, whereas the sixth storey and the octagonal spire are late additions by Anselmo da Campione.

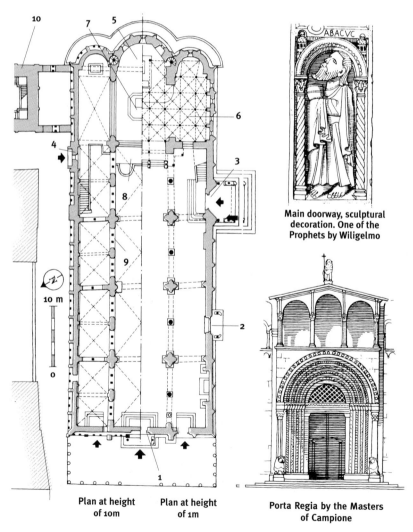

Main doorway, sculptural decoration. One of the Prophets by Wiligelmo

Plan at height of 10m

Plan at height of 1m

Porta Regia by the Masters of Campione

gende:
   Main doorway
   Porta dei Principi
   Porta Regia
   Porta della Pescheria
   Choir
   Crypt
   Presbytery
   Rood screen with
lpit
   Three-light window
   of the fake
atroneum
. The "Ghirlandina"
   bell tower

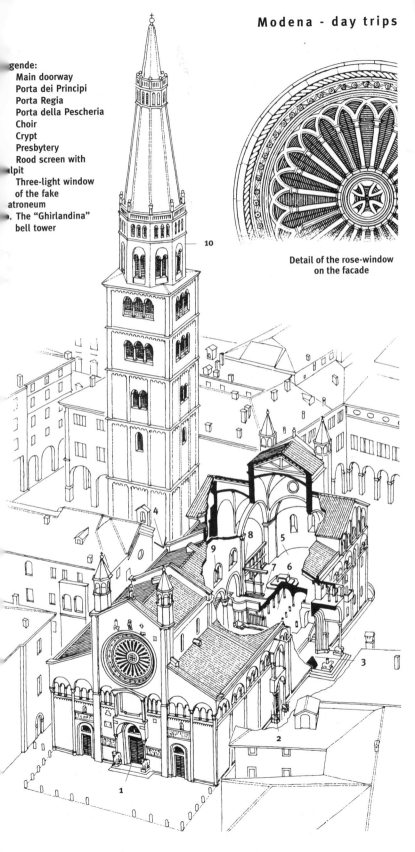

Detail of the rose-window
on the facade

SÈSTOLA [71 km]

This medieval town and mountain resort below **Monte Cimone** has been awarded the TCI's Orange Flag. Buildings of note include the *Casa di Via del Forno* with a lovely carved doorway (18C), and *Casa Le Volte*, with a double arched passageway. The *parish church of S. Nicolò* is built on a basilica plan with a nave and two side-aisles separated by solid stone columns and contains several good artworks. Opposite the church, is a *fountain* with an elegant portico (1812). The **fort**, surrounded by 16th-century walls, looks down on the town from a rocky spur. It is divided into several different parts: the 'borgo', the military area and the 'rocca', or seat of local administration and government.

Rocca di Vignola, a late-Gothic fresco in the chape

VIGNOLA [23 km]

In spring, the flowering cherries provide an unforgettable spectacle. The capital of cherry production, Vignola, set in a strategic position controlling the old *Via Claudia*, is situated between the bed of the Panaro River and the hillside. Its famous **Rocca***, is crowned with corbels and crenellations, the merlons still have a few traces of frescoes. Defending the entrance is a fortified gateway. A drawbridge leads into the castle courtyard. On the ground floor are the receptions rooms with heraldic decoration (16C). The living quarters are upstairs and the chapel has a late-Gothic cycle of **frescoes***. Adjoining the Rocca at the bottom of a small lookout tower is the *oratory of S. Maria*. The **oldest part of town*** is a huddle of houses near the fort. Situated on Piazza Cavour is *Palazzo Boncompagni* (16-17C), built in the Mannerist style; inside is an unusual oval staircase with hanging steps. Nearby is the *Torre dei Galvani* with an interesting weather-vane in the shape of a cock. In Via Garibaldi, the delightful heart of the town, the facade of the *parish church of Ss. Nazario e Celso* dates from the 19th century; built in 1416, it was extended and completed in the Corinthian style in 1685; the interior, with a nave and two side-aisles, contains some fine paintings. Opposite the church, under the old walls, is *Villa Galvani*, with the hanging garden of the original neo-classical design along with a coffee-house, a panoramic footpath, a box-hedge theater and botanical collections.

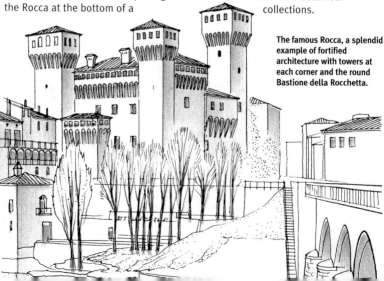

The famous Rocca, a splendid example of fortified architecture with towers at each corner and the round Bastione della Rocchetta.

PARMA

Parma, whose heritage of cultural traditions derives from its inspired aristocracy, has many art treasures and a historic center with some remarkable buildings, the legacy of its former e as the capital of the Duchy of Parma, Piacenza and Guastalla. It is also famous because of e artists who worked here, including Antelami, Correggio, Parmigianino and Verdi.

iazza del Duomo ➊

Piazza del Duomo is a quiet, charming place which has retained much of its medieval atmosphere. The facade of the Duomo, austere and solemn, the octagonal Baptistery in pink Verona marble and the **Palazzo Vescovile**, originally dating from the 11th century, transformed in the 13th and the beginning of the 16th, form an exceptionally beautiful architectural whole. Housed in the basement of the Palazzo Vescovile is the **Museo Diocesano***. The display of the museum starts with the Roman city and pagan cults, and includes structures uncovered during restoration work, highlighting the development of the episcopal complex between the early-Christian era and the Middle Ages.

Parma: Duomo

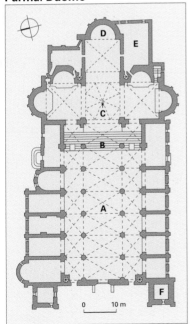

```
0        10 m
```

A Nave	**D** Apse
B Stairs	**E** Sagrestia dei
C Dome	Consorziali (sacristy)
	F Bell tower

Duomo ➋

Dedicated to the Assumption, the cathedral is regarded as one of the finest expressions of Romanesque architecture in the Po Valley. The **facade**, built of sandstone blocks, has a gable roof, emphasized by a loggia motif which follows the sloping lines of the roof and is repeated in two horizontal tiers. In front of the central doorway is a tall porch with colums supported by stone lions, dated 1281. To the right is the tall 13th-century brick **bell tower** (63m), with stone outlines. Above the narrow top perches a gilt embossed copper angel, the original of which is conserved inside the church. Along the sides of the edifice you can see the chapels which were added to the original structure, relieved by a long series of small loggias which continues the motif of the facade and continues around the apsed ends of the transepts, the presbytery and the apse. A rather unusual feature for a medieval building is the octagonal dome resting on a drum. The majestic **interior**, based on a Latin-cross plan, is full of atmosphere. The ceilings and walls are decorated with frescoes by painters of the local Mannerist School, which, however, do not detract from the austere medieval charm of the building. A 16th-century staircase of red Verona marble leads up to the transept; on the right is the famous relief depicting the **Deposition***, the first dated work by B. Antelami (1178) and one of the finest examples of Romanesque sculpture, showing clear Provençal influences. In the center of the presbytery, above the high altar of Verona marble (late-12C) with reliefs and pilaster strips, is the huge dome. In the vault, Correggio's frescoes with chiaroscuro of the **Assumption of the Virgin*** (1526-1530) dominate the space. Below the transept and the presbytery is the **crypt**, supported by columns which differ in material and size, and in the shape of the capitals, which are decorated with plant motifs and date from the earliest construction phase of the building (late 11-early 12C).

Battistero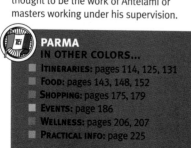

The great octagonal baptistery built of pink Verona marble is decorated with four superimposed tiers of open loggias with architraves and crowned with a series of blind arches. It is one of the most extraordinary testimonials in Italy of the transition between the Romanesque and Gothic styles. Work on the building, begun in 1196 by the same Lombard craftsmen who worked on the Duomo, was later continued between 1260 and 1270, probably by the Masters of Campione. It was completed in 1302-07 with the addition of the gallery of blind arches, the balustrade and the pinnacles crowning the top. Above the **Portale della Vergine*** (doorway) is a lunette depicting scenes of the *Adoration of the Magi* and *Joseph's Dream*; in the lintel surrounding the arch, the *Twelve Prophets*; in the architrave, exquisite reliefs depicting biblical scenes including the *Baptism of Christ*, the *Banquet of Herod* and the *Beheading of John the Baptist*. To the right of the **Portale del Giudizio*** there is a lunette depicting the *Savior* with *angels* and the symbols of the Passion. The **Portale della Vita*** is so called because of the parable depicted in the lunette, where a young man up a tree is eating honey while two rodents and a dragon wait below. The **interior*** is vast, with slender, elegant lines, and twice as many sides as the octagonal exterior. The lower register has 16 small apses set into the walls. Higher up, the two tiers of small trabeated loggias resting on slender columns are separated by the long stone ribs which support the pointed ceiling like the spokes of an umbrella. This is probably the work of master stonemasons from Campione. The high relief sculptures of the **months***, the **seasons*** and the **signs of the Zodiac*** in the recesses of the first loggia are the most famous of all: they date to the early 13th century, and are thought to be the work of Antelami or masters working under his supervision.

PARMA
IN OTHER COLORS...
- **ITINERARIES:** pages 114, 125, 131
- **FOOD:** pages 143, 148, 152
- **SHOPPING:** pages 175, 179
- **EVENTS:** page 186
- **WELLNESS:** pages 206, 207
- **PRACTICAL INFO:** page 225

Parma 1 : 13 500 (1 cm = 135 m)

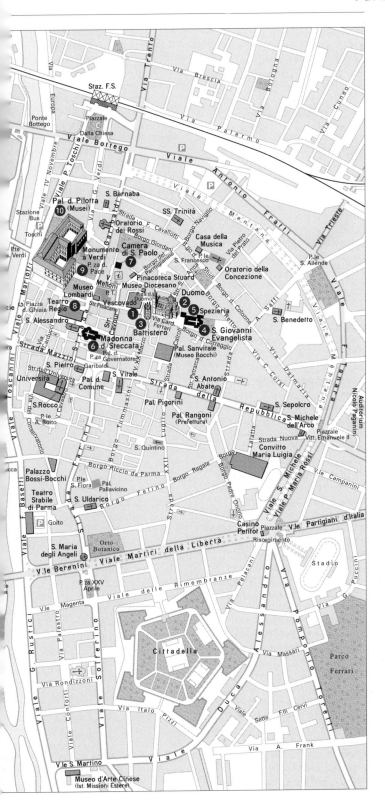

Parma: Battistero (plan and vertical section)

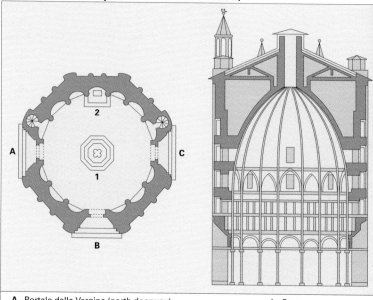

A Portale della Vergine (north doorway)
B Portale del Giudizio finale (west doorway)
C Portale della Vita (south doorway)

1 Font
2 Altar

S. Giovanni Evangelista ④

The origins of the church of S. Giovanni Evangelista are very old. Founded in the 10th century, it was rebuilt between 1498 and 1510 for the Benedictine order. Contrasting with the Renaissance architecture of the complex and the lovely cloisters of the adjoining monastery, the church has a fine Baroque white marble facade dating from 1604-1607. The tall, slender bell tower dates from the same period (1613). The spacious **interior**, with a Latin-cross plan, is famous for the fresco cycle by Correggio. The nave and side-aisles are separated by classical-style grooved gray stone pilasters. The **fresco cycle**** executed by Correggio in about 1520, represents the *Death of St John*: the Evangelist is depicted as an old man turning his gaze heavenwards, while, in the center, the figure of Christ is approaching his dying disciple to accompany him on his journey to Heaven. The light, color and shapes of the clouds on which the apostles are seated in pairs transform the vault of the dome into a convincing optical illusion: the real architectural features fade into the background, leaving the field clear for the unregimented, dynamic composition of the figures in the painting. Correggio also worked in the presbytery, where he executed the grotesques above the transept and the vault of the apse (*Coronation of the Virgin*). This work was destroyed in 1587 when the original apse was replaced with the present larger one: the fresco you see today is a faithful copy of Correggio's original, painted by Cesare Aretusi in 1587. The only remaining fragment of the original is now in the Galleria Nazionale. Around the edge of the apse are beautiful *wooden choirstalls* by Marcantonio Zucchi (1513-31). Do not miss the fresco in the lunette above the door leading into the sacristy. Painted by Correggio in about 1523, it depicts the *Young St John the Evangelist* writing the Book of Revelations. Close to the church is the **Benedictine monastery**, famous for its Renaissance cloisters.

Storica Spezieria di S. Giovanni Evangelista ⑤

The interior of this old pharmacy, documented as early as 1201, but probably even older, dates from the 16th-17th century. It has frescoes, wooden furnishings and period pharmaceutical paraphernalia. On the shelves is a fine set of vases of different origin and different periods, which vary also in terms of shape and size: majolica jars, flasks, beakers and mortars used in the preparation of medicinal compounds. The rooms in this historic pharmacy belonging to the monks include the *Sala del Fuoco*, where there is a counter with very precise antique scales where the medicines were weighed, the *Sala dei Mortai*, where there is a frescoed lunette depicting masters of early medicine and the *Sala delle Sirene*.

ladonna della Steccata 6

This splendid Renaissance church, one of the city's finest, was begun in 1521. This elegant building has obvious references to the style of Bramante. Built on a Greek-cross plan, it has semi-circular apses and square chapels at the corners. Pilaster strips, plain windows alternating with two-light windows and a cornice with pairs of oculi add interest to the extraordinary exterior, which is capped by a marble dome with a loggia and lantern. The decoration at the top of volutes, festoons, statues, vases and a large balustrade was added in 1696. The **interior** of the church is based on a central plan, with four wings with apses and four square chapels in the corners. The higher architectural features are decorated with lovely 16th-century *frescoes* of the Parma School. The finest work is the refined **painting cycle*** on the arch above the presbytery, executed by Parmigianino in 1530-39.

amera di S. Paolo 7

The Camera di S. Paolo was originally part of the private apartments of the abbess of the convent of the Benedictine Sisters

Frescoes by Correggio in the dome of S. G. Evangelista

of St Paul. It was restructured and decorated from 1514. The extraordinary **painted decoration**, regarded as one of the masterpieces of the Italian Renaissance, was executed by Correggio in 1519.

Teatro Regio 8

The Teatro Regio was commissioned by Marie Louise of Austria and built in 1821-29. The front of the theater, in the neo-classical style, rests on ten Ionic columns, with a double string-course above; next to the large window are two reliefs depicting allegories of fame. The internal decoration is by G. Magnani, whereas the ceiling and the huge stage curtain depicting Marie Louise dressed as Minerva is by the Parma painter G.B. Borghesi.

Piazza della Pace 9

Piazza della Pace, recently redesigned to recall the landscape of the Po Valley (with poplars and water features), is sealed off on the north side by the 18th-century *Palazzo dell'Intendenza* whereas, on the west side stands Palazzo della Pillotta. The garden to the left of the palazzo contains the *Monument to the Partisan* by Marino Mazzacurati (1955); to the right, on its own, is the *Monument to Verdi*. On the east side of the square is *Palazzetto di Riserva*, an elegant neo-classical building housing the **Museo "Glauco Lombardi"**. The rooms of the museum, which have stuccoes on the ceilings and walls, are an interesting example of late 18th-century architectural and decorative taste. The museum contains a collection of documents and objects which once furnished the ducal residences of Parma under the Bourbons and Marie Louise of Austria (1748-1859). The display begins in the *Sala delle Feste* and continues through various rooms where some of the most moving testimonials of the Imperial period (1810-1814) are kept. *Sala Dorata* and *Sala Toschi* contain works by the great engraver Paolo Toschi (1788-1854). *Sala dei Francesi* contains mementos of the first period of Bourbon domination (1732-1802). In *Sala Petitot* there is a display of a works by the court architect Ennemond Alexandre Petitot who, for twenty years, supervised building and town-planning work in the Duchy, and was instrumental in the transition from Rococo to neo-classicism. *Sala degli Affetti* and *Sala Maria Luigia* are the last two rooms.

Palazzo della Pilotta ⑩

Palazzo della Pilotta, named after the Basque game of *pelota*, was erected in the second half of the 16th century to accommodate the services of the court and the State. Under the Farnese, some of the vast palace was used to house the ducal library and picture collection, to which the collection of the Accademia di Belle Arti (1752), finds from the excavations at Veleia (1760) and vast collection of books (1761) were later added. These art collections, still housed in the same building, formed the nucleus of the great institutions created in the first half of the 19th century, namely, the Galleria Nazionale (1822), the Museo Archeologico Nazionale and the Biblioteca Palatina (1834). The **Biblioteca Palatina** contains almost 700,000 volumes, 6,000 manuscripts, 70,000 original manuscripts, more than 3,000 incunabula and a body of more than 5,000 wood and copper engravings, many of them extremely rare. In the second part of the library is a cartoon by Correggio depicting the *Incoronata* (the detached fresco kept in the Galleria Nazionale), whereas the third part of the library is called the *Sala di Dante* because it is decorated with paintings of scenes from the "Divine Comedy". The monumental *Sala di Lettura* is decorated in the neo-classical style and has a bust of *Marie Louise* by Antonio Canova. The rooms of the **Museo Archeologico Nazionale*** occupy two floors of the palace: the first floor contains examples of Greek, Roman, Italiot and Etruscan art which were not found locally; the ground floor houses the collections of prehistoric and proto-historic finds and Roman material. There is an *Egyptian collection* in one of the rooms on the first floor. The finds discovered at Veleia are very interesting and include a *cycle of statues* depicting famous members of the Imperial Julius-Claudian family and some fine bronzes. The most famous is the **tabula alimentaria***, the largest bronze inscription of Roman date to have survived. The large prehistoric and proto-

historic collection, arranged in the rooms on the ground floor, includes some interesting examples of Celtic culture. The Roman finds displayed in the following rooms were discovered in and around Parma. The **Galleria Nazionale**** is one of the most important collections in Italy in terms of the number and sheer quality of the works on display, many of which bear the signatures of great masters. The collection includes paintings from the 13-19th century attributed to the main Italian Schools of painting and art movements, but there is no shortage of masterpieces by Flemish, Dutch, Spanish and French painters. However, the main part of the collection comprises paintings of the Parma and Emilia Schools dating from the 15th to 18th centuries. The entrance to the gallery is through an imposing wooden door crowned by the ducal crest. Sudden we find ourselves in the **Teatro Farnese**** one of the most imposing and captivating historic theaters in the world, which now forms the magnificent atrium of the art gallery. Built in 1618-19, this marvelous building is a perfect example of the great theatrical tradition of the courts of the Po Valley (16-17C). A wooden walkway suspended behind the stage leads to the west wing and, subsequently, the north wing of the palace. These contain the precious collections of the Galleria Nazionale and are arranged in various sections according to the period and the different schools of painting. The first section is devoted to Romanesque art,

with architectural fragments from the 11th to 13th centuries and panels of the Tuscan School from the 14th and 15th centuries. These are followed by detached frescoes and paintings, including a delightful monochrome **Head of a Girl*** attributed to Leonardo da Vinci, known as "La Scapigliata" (The Dishevelled). Another important section of the gallery contains works (16C), including a famous **Portrait of Erasmus of Rotterdam*** by Hans Holbein the Younger. From here we move on to the north wing, devoted mainly to the Parma School (16-17C). The huge room below is devoted to 17th-century Venetian painting and another section is devoted to 18th-century Venetian painting. The 19th-century rooms contain some of the best works by Correggio and Parmigianino. Note Correggio's detached frescoes of the *Annunciation*, the **Madonna della Scala**** and the **Madonna dell'Incoronata***, also the paintings of the **Deposition** and the **Martyrdom of Four Saints**. Great masterpieces by this painter include the famous **Madonna della Scodella**** and the **Madonna of St Jerome****, also called "Il giorno" because the picture is flooded with golden late-afternoon light. Works by Parmigianino include a series of drawings, a fine **self-portrait** and the portrait known as the **Turkish slave****.

Palazzo Ducale ⑪

A straight avenue cuts across the park to the large complex of the ducal palace. In front of it are four 18th-century statues of divinities. The palace was enlarged and altered in the 18th century by Ennemond Petitot, who added pavilions to the four corners. However, the central part has retained Vignola's original 16th-century design. Inside, the rooms are decorated with frescoes by painters of the Mannerist School and 18th-century stuccoes. On the south side of the garden of the ducal palace is the **Palazzetto Eucherio Sanvitale**, an example of Renaissance architecture (1520). Few European cities can boast a rare example of a historic princely garden such as the **Parco Ducale**. In 1561, Ottavio Farnese entrusted Vignola with the task of creating it. He designed an Italian-style garden, based on the gardens of Roman villas. In 1690, the creation of the large *oval fish-pond* sparked off the transformation of the garden into a French-style garden, completed in the 18th century under the Bourbons. The present garden is the work of Petitot, who chose a classic style and completed it by adding marble statues, sculptures and vases.

DAY TRIPS

BUSSETO [38 km]

The historic center of Busseto, which has been awarded the TCI's Orange Flag, is partly surrounded by walls with towers at the corners. The whole length of Via Roma, Busseto's main and oldest street, is porticoed. On each side are old shops and

Palazzo Ducale is surrounded by a princely garden

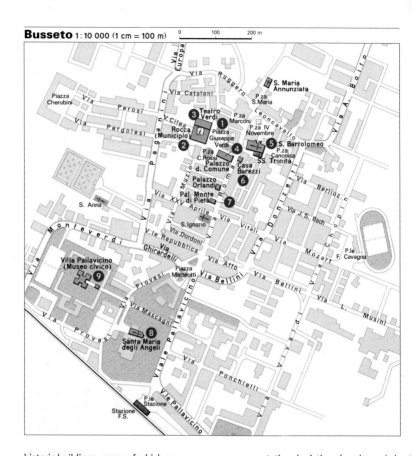

Busseto 1 : 10 000 (1 cm = 100 m)

historic buildings, many of which are associated with the memory of Giuseppe Verdi. At the end of it is the square named after the town's most famous citizen. Set around **Piazza Giuseppe Verdi** ❶ are the Rocca, the collegiate church of S. Bartolomeo and Palazzo Comunale Vecchio. In the center is the bronze *monument* to Giuseppe Verdi. The **Rocca** ❷, founded in the 13th century, is a combination of late-Gothic and Renaissance motifs. It has Ghibelline merlons in the shape of a swallow's tail, two-light windows with pointed trilobate arches, and one-light windows framed by terracotta panels. It now houses the **Teatro Verdi** ❸, built between 1856 and 1868. The interior decoration is by the Parma painters Giuseppe Baisi and Alessandro Malpeli, whereas the *medallions* on the ceiling date from 1865. The rooms of the foyer are also interesting, with a gilt tribune and a large mirror. South of the square is the **Palazzo Comunale Vecchio** ❹, a 15th-century edifice which has one-light windows with terracotta

ornamentation depicting cherubs and vine tendrils. In the frieze on the string-course there are panels depicting harpies linked by their tails, and classical vases. East of the piazza is **Palazzo del Bargello or del Capitano**. The ground floor of the facade has a portico with polygonal pilasters and, higher up, windows with beautiful 15th-century terracotta frames by craftsmen from Cremona. Nearby is the **collegiate church of S. Bartolomeo** ❺, erected in 1437-50. The facade is adorned with beautiful terracotta decoration in the Lombard style. The interior, decorated in the mid-18th century with rocaille stucco-work, has some important *paintings* and **frescoes** dating from the 16th, 17th and 18th centuries. The **Tesoro della Collegiata,** kept partly in the 17th-century sacristy and partly in the church, comprises sumptuous vestments, hangings, 15th-century illuminated choir-books, ivories (early 15C) and splendid embossed sculpted silver-ware. The most important exhibit is the gilt silver *processional cross* (1524). Off the right aisle is the **oratory of the SS. Trinità,** founded in about 1110. It contains 18th-century stuccoes and a splendid high altar in polychrome marble (1749); in the apse, a *Holy Trinity with St Apollonia and St Lucy* (1579) by Vincenzo Campi. Nearby, on Via Roma, stands **Casa Barezzi** ❻, where Verdi lived for many years, and taught the daughter of the house, Margherita, whom he later married. The late 18th-century *salone* of the house is possibly the place most closely associated with Verdi in Busseto. Everything in it speaks of the composer: his Tomaschek piano, the portrait of Antonio Barezzi, Margherita's father, and the charcoal portrait of the young Verdi, his letters and appeals for patriotism (1859). The house also has the *discoteca Schipper-Suppa*, a collection of more than 500 recordings. The rooms before the *salone* contain the *Collezione Stefanini*, an exhibition of Verdi memorabilia. On the same street, the neo-classical **Palazzo Orlandi** and **Palazzo del Monte di Pietà*** ❼ were built between 1679 and 1682. Inside are frescoes detached from the portico (1682), antique furniture and some fine silver-ware. Behind the palazzo is the **Biblioteca del Monte**, dated 1768, which has 40,000 books, including 20 incunabula and 495 books printed in the16th century. Outside the old walls of the town stands the austere Gothic church of **S. Maria degli Angeli** or **dei Frati** ❽ with its Franciscan monastery, built between 1470 and 1474. The facade has a beautiful doorway with a terracotta frieze, a large rose-window and polygonal apses. The interior is plain and bare. The nave and two side-aisles are separated by massive pilasters, decorated in different styles, which support the cross-vaults. Nearby is **Villa Pallavicino** ❾, which stands alone at the end of an avenue of poplars, surrounded by a square fish-pond. This is one of the most splendid villas in the Parma area, built on a five-module checkered plan. The entrance is a rather splendid pavilion with doorways on three sides, and niches containing statues. The semi-circular vault of the main part of the villa is frescoed with grotesque mythological figures dating from the second half of the 16th century. The ceilings of the rooms are painted with allegorical frescoes and stuccoes. The villa now houses the **Museo Civico** (temporarily closed). The exhibits include mementos of Giuseppe Verdi, antique furniture from

various periods, exhibits associated with local history, and paintings and ceramics from the 17th and 18th centuries. There is a good section devoted to the paintings and drawings of the Busseto painter Isacco Gioachino Levi.

FIDENZA [23 km]

Piazza del Duomo is situated in the center of the medieval town, and has retained an atmosphere of days gone by. The quiet, secluded square, paved with cobbles, is dominated by the majestic facade of the Duomo. East of the square is a line of old houses and, to the north, the Porta di S. Donnino. The **Duomo***, one of the finest examples of Romanesque architecture in the Po Valley, was built in three stages: the basilica with the nave and two side-aisles dates from between the late 11th and early 12th centuries; towards the end of the 12th century, the School of Benedetto Anselmi created the facade, with two towers, and the vaulted roof; finally at the very end of the 13th century, the apse was rebuilt in the Gothic style and rib vaulting was added to the highest part of the church. The side-chapels were not added until the 16th century. The **facade**** below the gable roof has twin towers on each side and three doorways richly decorated with sculptures and framed by elaborate porches. Next to the bell tower (1569) is a beautiful apse dating from 1287, decorated with Romanesque reliefs depicting the four seasons, with a lovely loggia above. The **interior*** is composed of a nave and two side-aisles, with composite piers, and a tall, narrow structure crowned with matroneums, showing the influence of Lanfranco, the architect of the Modena Cathedral. Above the nave, the ribbed vaults date from the late 13th century. Many of the sculptures inside the Duomo date from the early 13th century, and demonstrate the skill of Antelami and his workshop. The **crypt***, a broad structure with a short nave and side-aisles, houses the furnishings used during the festival of St Domninus. The **Museo del Duomo** is divided into two separate parts: one occupies a wing of the Palazzo Vescovile and the other is located inside the cathedral. It has a display of architectural fragments and objects from the treasury of the saint. Nearby, **Casa Cremonini** and the **medieval tower** form a single unit: it has a section focusing on the sculptures by

Antelami and his workshop in the cathedral and an archeological section with the remains of the old *Roman bridge*. In Piazza Verdi, the **Teatro "Girolamo Magnani"** was built between 1812 and 1861. Notice the rich internal decoration with stuccoes and gilt-work, created by stage-set designer Girolamo Magnani, after whom the theater is named. **Palazzo Comunale** (1191) is a porticoed building on the south side of Piazza Garibaldi, the town's main square. The current appearance of the building is the result of restoration work and additions begun in the 14th century and completed in the second half of the 19th century. The **church of the Vergine Madre** was constructed in the late 17th century. It has a Baroque facade and a single nave, crowned with a broad dome supported by a drum. The chapel adjoining **Palazzo delle Orsoline** is now the **Museo del Risorgimento "Luigi Musini"** which contains documents and mementoes relating to the period of the Risorgimento in the area around Parma. Palazzo delle Orsoline also houses the **Museo dei Fossili dello Stirone**. The gradual erosion of the Stirone Stream made it possible to build up a fine collection of fossils, especially the shells and skeletons of mollusks, starfish and even whales, which illustrate the geological history of the area. Not far away is the church of **S. Michele**, erected in the 14th century and restructured between 1528 and 1548. It has a Greek-cross plan and contains 16th-century frescoes.

FONTANELLATO [19 km]

The little town of Fontanellato, which has been awarded the TCI's "Bandiera Arancione" (Orange Flag), is dominated by the majestic edifice of its merloned 15th-century **Rocca***, one of the most interesting castles in the region. It is a splendid example of military and residential architecture, with precious antique furniture, furnishings and frescoes, including a very important cycle by Parmigianino (**Saletta di Diana e Atteone****, painted in 1524). The interior is extremely well preserved. In the square surrounding the castle is the **church of S. Croce**, built in 1447. Note the lovely Baroque wooden furnishings in the sacristy, dating from 1673-82. Just outside the town is the **Sanctuary of the Beata Vergine del Rosario**, an edifice dating from

between 1641 and 1660. The forms of the facade echo the Baroque style, however it dates from 1913. Inside, the ceiling of the church is covered with frescoes dating from the first half of the 18th century.

TORRECHIARA [18 km]

This small medieval town is inextricably linked to the fame of its splendid medieval **Castle**** which towers above it. Its famous castle, one of the largest and best-preserved in the area, was erected between 1448 and 1460. It has a triple outer wall and towers at the four corners, connected by curtain walls. The two loggias on the east side are later additions. Inside is a fine *courtyard* with porticoes and windows with terracotta decoration in the Lombard style. The *oratory of S. Nicomede* and the rooms beyond have splendid 16th-century frescoes. In particular, the *Salone degli Stemmi* was partly frescoed by Baglione, who also painted the **fresco cycle** in the *Salone degli Acrobati*. The **Camera d'oro** deserves special attention. It contains a rare **fresco cycle** with a secular theme, painted before 1464. Set in an isolated position, the **Badia di Torrechiara** is an old monastery complex built in 1471. Inside the *church*, on the pilaster separating the two chapels, is a 15th-century fresco depicting the *Madonna and Child*, by a master of the Lombard School.

Fontanellato: Rocca

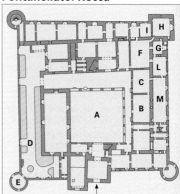

A Courtyard	G Sala degli Amorini
B Ticket office	H Sala delle Grottesche
C Book shop	I Saletta di Diana e
D Hanging garden	Atteone
E Optical Chamber	L Saletta con teatrino
F Sale delle Donne Equilibriste	M Sala delle Mappe

PIACENZA

Situated on the western edge of Emilia, Piacenza has always been a land of transit, a land of beginnings and ends, set in a key strategic position between the Po, the great northern-Italian plain and the Apennines. It attracts mainly business tourism and weekend visitors who often ignore the opportunities offered by a city where there is much to explore. Its old town center has buildings dating from Roman times to the present day, including many fine churches and palazzi.

S. Savino ❶

One of Piacenza's earliest churches (founded early 5C), S. Savino was rebuilt in 1107, altered in 1630 and later restored to its Romanesque lines (early 20C); a Baroque portico (1720) with pairs of columns obscures the facade. The interior is representative of the Romanesque Lombard style; the nave is separated from the side-aisles by granite pillars decorated in various styles. Fine capitals carved with animal and plant motifs support the round arches. In the presbytery, an interesting *floor mosaic* (12C); the black-marble altar with bronze decoration (1764) contains a sarcophagus with the relics of St Savinus. Above it, a beautiful Romanesque wooden **Crucifix** (12C). The **crypt** is supported by small graceful columns dating from the 11th century, with delicate capitals carved with plant motifs and human figures; the fine mosaic floor depicts the months and *signs of the Zodiac* and the farming activities which correspond to them (12C).

Duomo ❷

The complex structure of the Duomo was built in two stages: the first between 1122 and 1160, the second between the beginning of the 13th century and 1233. It has a gable roof, and the facade is built of red Verona marble and sandstone, divided into three sections by pillars; in the center is a large 14th-century rose-window, whereas, on each side, small blind loggias echo the loggias at the top which, in turn, emphasize the lines of the sloping roof. Above each doorway is a porch with a loggia (the central one is decorated with the signs of the Zodiac), supported by lions and telamones, decorated with carvings by masters of the Piacenza School. On the left, the solid **bell tower*** (1333), 71m high, has a tapering spire with a gilt copper weather-vane on the top in the form of an angel. The **interior** is built on a Latin-cross plan, with a nave and two side-aisles and a raised presbytery above the crypt. The Romanesque style can be seen in the 26 mighty cylindrical pillars joined by semi-circular arches while the Gothic style can be seen in the upper part of the church and in the vaults. At the top of the arches are reliefs of *Saints and Prophets*. The octagonal dome cladding above the crossing of the transept has frescoes (1625-27) by Guercino in the segments. Guercino also painted the **Sybils** in the lunettes below. In the

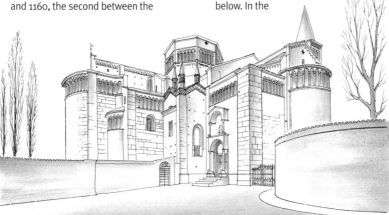

Influenced by Anglo-Norman models, the Romanesque Duomo has some Gothic features

presbytery, at the high altar, there is a remarkable wooden polychrome **altar-piece** (1447). Two flights of steps below the altar lead down to the large *crypt* dedicated to St Justina; a forest of 108 columns with beautiful carved capitals divides the space into five longitudinal aisles and three transverse ones.

S. Antonino ❸

Founded *extra moenia* (outside the city walls) between 350 and 370, rebuilt in the first half of the 11th century, the church was later altered several times (15-16C) and subsequently restored (19-20C). As a result, it is a combination of many different styles. However, two architectural features dominate the building: the imposing *octagonal tower* (1004) with three tiers of two-light windows, built above the crossing of the transept, and the tall, graceful Gothic pronaos known as '*il Paradiso*' (Paradise, 1350), which stands in front of the left wing of the transept; it shelters a marble doorway (1172) with *high reliefs* on the jambs by masters of the Piacenza School (12C). The **interior**, in the neo-Gothic style, is built on an interesting upside-down Latin-cross plan, with a nave and two side-aisles, each with an apse; it has a remarkable gilt wooden *organ gallery* on the right of the nave and frescoes in the vaults of the apses; at the third altar on the right, a fine 15th-century polychrome terracotta **Crucifixion**. The small museum adjoining the church has three 15th-century *polyptychs*. South of the church, a late 15th-century cloister.

Piazza dei Cavalli ❹

Laid out in the 13th century, the square is the civic heart of the city. In the middle are two **bronze equestrian statues**** (1620-25) depicting *Duke Ranuccio I* and his father *Alessandro Farnese*, set on pedestals adorned with low reliefs. The way the horses have been expressed is particularly striking. The monument to Ranuccio is more static and composed, while that of his father throbs with the expressive vitality created by the flow of his cloak and the horse's mane. The square is dominated by Palazzo Pubblico, known as **il Gotico**** (the Gothic), one of the most significant examples of 13th-century civic architecture in Italy. It has the typical structure of a Lombard

Piacenza 1 : 17 000 (1 cm = 170 m)

broletto (town hall) with an open ground-floor area supported by broad pointed arches; the pillars are faced with white marble but, higher up, the white marble alternates with stripes of red Verona marble and eventually meets the warm colors of the of the brick upper floor. Broad three- and four-light windows decorated with terracotta illuminate the vast hall (inside, tie-beams support the roof). The small towers at the corners are joined by walls with 'Guelph' crenellations (1870); the slender square tower above the palazzo, called the '*Lanterna*', is 40m high. Set back slightly is the former *Palazzo dei Mercanti* (1676-97); opposite is the elegant neo-classical facade of *Palazzo del Governatore* (1787), with a large sun-dial and a perpetual calendar (1793), the top of which is

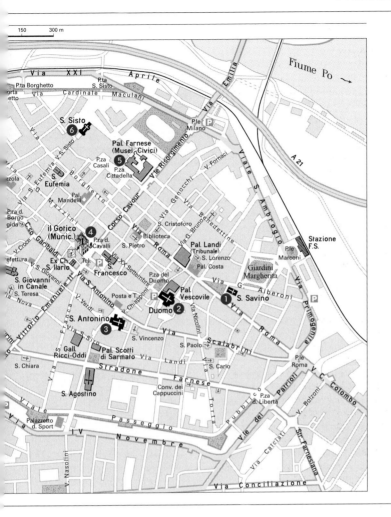

decorated with statues of pagan gods. Just off the east side of the square, beyond the *monument to Gian Domenico Romagnosi* (1867), the **church of S. Francesco**, erected in 1278, again embodies the transition from the Romanesque to the Gothic style. The high brick facade below the gable roof is spanned by pilaster strips which reach almost up to the blind arcading at the top, crowned by three tall pinnacles. The remarkable marble **doorway,** with an embrasure, is richly decorated. The interior comprises a nave and side-aisles separated by columns which support pointed arches, and an ambulatory with chapels radiating out from it. The nave is higher than the aisles and ends in a pentahedral apse.

Palazzo Farnese ⑤

This is one of Piacenza's most important buildings. It comprises two adjoining but separate parts: the remains of the **Cittadella Viscontea** (1373) and the actual palazzo. With regard to the old fortress, the remaining parts include the west part, with a loggia, two corner-towers and the curtain-wall running between them. The palazzo is built around a vast courtyard. Two monumental tiers of loggias with arches rest on niches where

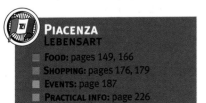

PIACENZA
LEBENSART

■ **FOOD:** pages 149, 166
■ **SHOPPING:** pages 176, 179
■ **EVENTS:** page 187
■ **PRACTICAL INFO:** page 226

you can see the attachment points of the semi-oval theater planned by Vignola. The palazzo is a powerful, solid brick building relieved by stone corners and string-courses which alternate with three tiers of windows and squared arches. On the upper floors, on either side of the *grand staircase* (note the lovely 17th-century wrought-iron *gateway*), are the rooms of the ducal apartments, including the Alcova della Duchessa and the ducal chapel. The palazzo houses two important cultural institutions, including the **Museo Civico**, which has an interesting display with works of great artistic importance, and the **Pinacoteca**, which contains works mainly from churches in and around Piacenza, the *Fasti Farnesiani* (frescoes depicting the Life of the Farnesi) and a beautiful collection of paintings by Genoese and Flemish masters. The paintings of the 16th and 17th centuries are particularly fine. In the basement is the marvelous **Museo delle Carrozze***, a collection of 40 carriages (18C and 19C).

S. Sisto ⑥

This very old complex dates from the 9th century, but was completely restructured during the Renaissance. The church (1499-1511) dedicated to St Sistus was radically changed by the innovations wrought by Bramante and Biagio Rossetti. A massive 17th-century doorway in the 'rustic' style leads into a courtyard with a portico on three sides (1591-96), masking the late-Renaissance facade. The **interior**, adorned with frescoes, wrought-ironwork and 18th-century decorative features, is built on a Latin-cross plan. The first transept near the entrance makes it possible to see the nave and two side-aisles almost in cross-section: the side-aisles with their smaller domes and the nave with a barrel vault decorated with painted recessed panels; at each end of this first transept are two unusual models of churches built on a Greek-cross plan, decorated with niches and five small domes; above the crossing between the nave and the second transept is the tiburium, surrounded by a loggia of small columns. In the presbytery, note the lovely wooden **choirstalls** (1514-25) with wonderful carvings and marquetry work; at the far end, the original *Sistine Madonna*

The interior of S. Sisto with 18C decoration and wrought-ironwork

painted by Raphael in 1512 has been replaced by a copy. Notice the large gilt carved wooden gallery, and the *organ* (16C) by the Facchetti. To the right of the church is the former **monastery**, built in the second half of the 16th century. This vast complex includes a beautiful cloister with a portico on the ground floor supported by small, slender columns, from which you can see the majestic *bell tower* (1506-7). It is decorated with pilaster strips, with a belfry surrounded by three-light windows and has a small dome on the top.

Madonna di Campagna ⑦

This church, documented as early as 1030, is a very important example of Renaissance art. Rebuilt in 1522-28, the solid main part of the church is built on a Greek-cross plan, (the shape was altered when the presbytery was extended in 1791), with exactly the same features inside and outside; the height of the brick building is emphasized by the large octagonal tiburium, made taller and more slender by the lantern and the four smaller tiburia above the chapels at each corner. The harmonious space inside the church is divided up by four central pillars, which support the dome and the barrel vaults of the four arms of the building. The whole interior is covered with elegant painted decoration, dominated by figurative scenes and a bold use of color.

DAY TRIPS

BOBBIO [45 km]

Bobbio is a holiday resort for people who come to visit the nearby river and spa. The town's history is closely linked to the **abbey of S. Colombano,** founded by the Irish missionary monk in 614. It was one of the most important medieval centers of religious culture in Italy, with a famous scriptorium and library. The network of narrow streets and paved alleys, with its old houses and noble palazzi, lends a medieval atmosphere to this town, which grew up around the monastery, and has been awarded the TCI's "Bandiera Arancione" (Orange Flag). Piazza Fara, the heart of the town, is overlooked by the apse of the basilica and the long loggia (1570) of the monastery which now houses the **Museo dell'Abbazia** (a collection of archeological material and works associated with the figure of St Colombanus (from 4 to 18C). To the left of the basilica stands the *bell tower* which dates from the 9th century as does the small right-hand apse. The facade of the basilica, divided into three parts, with a porch, overlooks Piazzetta di S. Colombano. The whole building, which dates from the reconstruction of 1456-1522, incorporates the remains of the original church dedicated to St Colombanus. The interior, built on a Latin-cross plan, with a nave and side-aisles separated by pillars decorated in different styles, has splendid *wooden choirstalls* (1488). There are some important works of art in the crypt; note the **floor mosaic,** really a Bible for the illiterate, who, despite not being able to read, could learn by looking at mosaics like these, with their symbolic Romanesque motifs (first half of the 12C). Contrada Porta Nuova, the town's main shopping street, leads to the porticoed *Piazza del Duomo.* The *Duomo,* documented in 1075, has a 15th-century facade and two towers dating from the first church; inside, it is decorated in the neo-Gothic-Byzantine style (1896), and has some 14th-century frescoes. The highest part of Bobbio is dominated by the *castle,* built in 1440. The enormous keep and the remains of the entrance stand on the ruins of an early monastic settlement; it houses a small museum with antique furnishings. Outside the town, the unusual twisted outline of the **Ponte Gobbo,** one of the symbols of Bobbio, attracts the eye; its eleven arches of varying dimensions have been restored to provide a pedestrian route across the Trebbia River. Possibly of Roman date, it is documented from 1196 onwards and was restructured in the 16th and 17th centuries.

CASTELL'ARQUATO [32 km]

The extremely picturesque hill-town of Castell'Arquato, which has retained its medieval atmosphere, has been awarded the TCI's "Bandiera Arancione" (Orange Flag). The layout of the town is divided into two main parts: the town at the foot of the hill and the monumental part at the top. The end of the tarmac marks the beginning of the old town. Via Dante, the charming street which winds up to the monumental part of town, leads to the *Torrione Farnesiano,* a 16th-century keep with huge concave arches. Next to it is *Palazzo del Duca* (13-14C), which overlooks a fountain with several spouts, dating from 1292. Beyond the *church of S. Pietro* (15C), a long ramp leads under the huge vault which supports the neo-Gothic *Stradivari castle.* The 16th-century former *Ospitale S. Spirito* now houses the **Museo Geologico,** which has collections of scientific importance. At the top of the hill is the fascinating **Piazza Alta** or **Piazza del Municipio.** Set around it are Palazzo Pretorio, the apse of the collegiate church and, protruding slightly, the fortress. **Palazzo Pretorio** is a massive building (1293) with crenellations, a pentagonal tower (14C), a small loggia and an external staircase (15C); the great council chamber has a

The Gobbo Medieval bridge, symbol of Bobbio

coffered ceiling and very fine painted decoration. The **collegiate church of S. Maria** is a Romanesque structure dating from the early 12th century, with a 14th-century bell tower and an imposing apse. Under the left-hand side of the portico, known as the 'Portico del Paradiso' (15C), there is a Romanesque **doorway** with an embrasure. The golden sandstone facade of the church overlooks a charming little square. Off it is the entrance to the gardens of the fortress. Inside the church, you can still see many features of the original building, including carved capitals (early 12C), Romanesque sculptures (12C; ambo and altar) and frescoes (15C). Note the lovely monolithic *font* dating from the 8th century. The 14th-century cloister provides access to the **Museo della Collegiata** which has a collection of church gold- and silver-ware and religious paintings. The huge **Rocca**, built in 1343, has two walled areas, built on different levels; the higher enclosed area includes the keep (47m above the moat) which is also the entrance (over a drawbridge); the lower part of the fortress has towers at the corners.

FIORENZUOLA D'ARDA [22 km]

The Via Aemilia, or "*contrada dritta*" (straight street), now **Corso Garibaldi**, is the town's main street; the oldest part of town still has features that date back to the Roman town. One of the buildings on the main street is the 18th-century *Palazzo Bertamini Lucca* with its vast public park: in the small chapel, a fresco cycle (1723-25); nearby, the 15th-century *Palazzo Grossi* has large windows with pointed arches, and is adorned with Renaissance friezes and decorative motifs. In Via Liberazione, *Teatro Verdi*, built in 1847 and enlarged in 1914, has retained the appearance of a 19th-century theater, with three tiers of boxes in the auditorium. Not far away is the former monastery of *S. Francesco* (mid-16C). The **collegiate church of S. Fiorenzo** has features that are typical of the Romanesque and Gothic styles in the Piacenza area; the facade was partly altered in the 19th century; the detached bell tower stands over the remains of a pre-Roman structure. A brick Renaissance doorway leads into the church, with a tall nave and side-aisles; in the apse, a vast cycle of *frescoes* (late 15C-early 16C). The right aisle contains an interesting *chapel of the Sacramento* (1656) and the high altar has beautiful marble decoration. At the top of the same street is the elegant Baroque facade of the church known as the *Beata Vergine del Caravaggio* (1731-49). The former convent and church of *S. Giovanni* has a lovely portico and 18th-century loggia.

VIGOLENO [43 km]

This medieval town surrounded by fertile farmland is one of the most charming in the area of Piacenza, and has been awarded the TCI's "Bandiera Arancione" (Orange Flag). Surrounded by defensive walls with crenellations, it is dominated by the tower of the *castle* (12C). A strong *fortified gateway* leads into an elegant piazza with a fountain with cobbled streets radiating out from it; set around the square are the *oratory of the Madonna del Latte* (featuring a panel with a relief of a pilgrim). In the Romanesque Parish church of *S. Giorgio*, there is a lunette depicting *St George and the Dragon* (early 13C); the interior has a nave and two side-aisles with the remains of some 15th-century frescoes, including one of *St George, the Dragon and the Princess* (in the apse).

Vigoleno, view of the castle and fortifications

RAVENNA

Ravenna, the mosaic city, has a host of architectural masterpieces and mosaic art dating from the times of Galla Placidia, Theodoric and Justinian (c.400-550). The 'Byzantium of the West' has retained its unique appeal in its treasure of early-Christian basilicas, its baptisteries, its cylindrical 10th- and 11th-century bell towers, its Romanesque churches with examples of Renaissance architecture left by the Venetians and its 17th- and 18th-century palazzi. The city has a surprising vitality which would make it interesting even if it did not have a great, albeit distant, past; even if it had not preserved the monuments that have made it famous the world over, eight of which have been designated UNESCO World Heritage Sites; even if it were not situated in the great basin of the Romagna Riviera. However, the discerning tourist will soon discover that the city has many surprises in store and that, behind its mask of art and history, there is much more to see beyond the great early-Christian and Byzantine remains. Here, the impetuous wind of modernization, which has destroyed much and which has brought much that is new, has spared the 'soul' of the historic city. Not only the soul jealously preserved inside the basilicas and baptisteries, protected and exalted, strangely, by their ancient, rough brick walls; not only its 'nocturnal' soul, which is to be found in the most secluded corners of the city (Galla Placidia, the area associated with Dante). But also the more familiar soul, which is to be found all over the historic center. The old and the new live side by side, forming an unusual symbiosis, creating an atmosphere which is not only fascinating but difficult to put into words.

Mausoleo di Galla Placidia ❶

The most famous Placidian monument deserves special attention. This small squat building on a Latin-cross plan demonstrates its function as a tomb particularly through the symbolism of its **mosaics****. Despite being almost certainly some of the oldest in the city, possibly dating from before 450, they are in an excellent condition. The quiet, dark setting of the tomb and feeble light filtering through the alabaster windows enhance its beauty and charm. In the lunette above the doorway is a depiction of the *Good Shepherd*; in the opposite lunette, *St Laurence with his gridiron in front of a cupboard with the four Evangelists*. In the four arms of the building are three large *sarcophagi*: the one on the left is late 5th century, the one on the right, early 6th century, and the undecorated middle one is of Roman times.

Basilica di S. Vitale ❷

The new entrance leads to steps down which you can enter the basilica through its oldest ceremonial entrance: the monumental narthex, which formerly widened into the original, and now lost, four-sided portico. The basilica was built on the site of an earlier oratory (5C), visible in the submerged enclosure. In the famous **mosaics*** in the *vault of the apse*, the most prominent figure is Bishop Ecclesius who stands to the left of Christ, while, to the right of the Savior is the soldier martyr, St Vitalis, patron saint of Ravenna, after Apollinaris, its first bishop. The four main parts of the mosaic cycle in the apse and the dividing arch are: 1. The holy scene of the *Theophany of the Heavenly Christ*, assisted by archangels Michael and Gabriel, giving the crown of glorious martyrdom to St Vitalis *while Bishop Ecclesius presents a model of the church*, as if to Christ; 2. *The Imperial procession of Justinian and Maximian*, with magistrates, soldiers and clergy, bearing bread for the Holy Communion (Justinian is holding the paten) in the church towards the altar; 3. The *Imperial procession of Empress Theodora* bearing the chalice of wine for the Holy Communion, in the ceremonial act of entry led by officials with a following of court ladies; 4. The Imperial significance of the apse arch where *two Imperial eagles*, to the right and left of the central Christological clipeus, with unfolded

RAVENNA
IN OTHER COLORS…

- **FOOD:** pages 153, 160, 166
- **SHOPPING:** pages 175, 177
- **EVENTS:** pages 187, 194
- **WELLNESS:** pages 199, 201, 203, 205
- **PRACTICAL INFO:** page 227

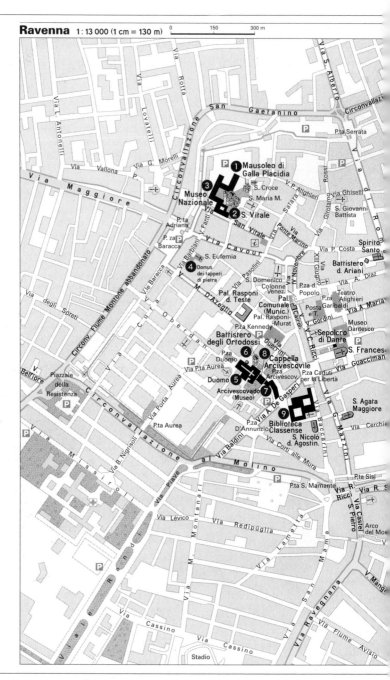

Ravenna 1:13 000 (1 cm = 130 m)

wings, *support the clipeus* containing a stylized monogram (Imperial Constantinian) of Christ. In the *presbytery*, the **mosaic cycle*** is divided into two pictures of Biblical sacrifices: on the right, the *sacrifices of Abele and Melchizedech*; and, on the left, the *sacrifice of Abraham*.

Museo Nazionale ❸

Ravenna's leading cultural institutions include the national museum, known as S. Vitale after the monastic complex in which it is housed, although it originated and developed in the monastery of Classe. A complement integration and extension of Ravenna's

the *large refectory* of the monastery, is the entire 14th-century *cycle of frescoes* from the *choir* of the medieval convent church of S. Chiara – masterpieces by Pietro da Rimini.

Domus dei Tappeti di Pietra ④

This is one of the most important archaeological sites uncovered in Italy in recent decades. It is the only private dwelling found so far in the city, a large noble mansion, the full layout of which has been reconstructed. A succession of different construction phases (at least ten) ranging from the 4th-3rd century BC to the 16th century AD are revealed down to a depth of about 7 m. Of these, it was decided to highlight the one illustrating city life in the 6th century AD. The Domus has 14 rooms and two courtyards paved with geometric marble mosaics (*opus sectile*). Access to the site, situated three metres below the present road level, is via the **church of S. Eufemia** (1742-47). The circular-plan church hall leads, to the left of the main altar, into the sacristy, or *Sala dei Cento Preti*, which conserves the well-head used as a baptismal font by the bishop of the city, Apollinaris; the painting above the niche and the frescoes in the lunettes are attributed to Andrea Barberini (1757) and his School. The remains of St Euphemia are in a Greek marble sarcophagus in the center. A short staircase descends to the rooms of the Domus. The visitor route winds along a raised walkway that roughly follows the perimeter of the ancient walls and crosses all the rooms in the house, allowing you to admire the floor mosaics. Note the mosaic of the Good Shepherd, which does not really belong to the mansion but to a domus that stood on the same spot in a previous period (4-5C).

Duomo ⑤

Visitors are invited to search for evidence of Ravenna's older Ursiana basilica beneath today's large cathedral, commenced in 1732. The materials (24 columns, floor marble, four columns in the atrium and the entrance) came from the Ursiana cathedral and the monumental **ambo of Archbishop Agnello*** (556-569) is the most notable work to have survived from that time.

whole monumental heritage, the Museo Nazionale occupies the former monastery's first and second cloisters. The first, Renaissance one contains the most important materials of Roman Ravenna (and Classe). The museum display continues on the first floor with important monuments from Classe. In

Also old (5C) are the *sarcophagi of Esuperanzio (and Maximian)* and the **sarcophagi of Barbaziano and Rinaldo***. The *high altar*, a fine work dated 1760, has a dual mensa, just like the earliest altars. The **bell tower*** of the Duomo (9-10C) is perhaps, from a historical point of view, the most important of all the round bell towers; certainly, it seems to be the oldest and it was probably the prototype for the other bell towers of Ravenna.

Battistero degli Ortodossi ⑥

The baptistery is well preserved and famous for the splendor of its **mosaics**** and the cultural symbolism of their cycles. There are five iconographic registers: three are found in the dome, one in the tambour and the fifth in the base wall structures. 1. **Christ being baptized by John the Baptist** 2. The **Group of Apostles**, depicting the main Christian preparatory rite for baptism, the so-called *traditio symboli*, i.e. giving the catechumen candidates the Creed. 3. The **Heavenly Paradise**, an iconographic description of the garden of the Heavens, the place where those who pass through the shadow of death, via baptism, to enter the realm of light and life will be eternally blessed. 4. The **Sixteen Prophets**. 5. The **bottom register** of the building, in keeping with its square foundation structure, was decorated with marble *tessellae* (*opus sectile*), *vine* tendrils, *human figures* in mosaic, four apses containing the Biblical scenes (lost) described by the four Latin *inscriptions*. As well as the baptismal font which is a mixed blend of the 16th-17th centuries, be sure to see three other important features: the original marble *ambo* of the baptistery; the bronze *cross* ordered by Archbishop Theodore (c.688); and the *altar*, dating from the 5th century, which was not associated with the original use of the building.

Baptism of Christ with the Twelve Apostles, Ortodossi

Museo arcivescovile ⑦

This museum is famous both for its precious collection and because it is housed in the historic **Episcopate** of Ravenna, an extremely old building foundation (pre-396) comprising the fine 5th-century Cappella Arcivescovile (see below).
It houses numerous important relics, including one of the most precious monuments of all Christian antiquity: the **chair of Maximian****, an Episcopal throne commissioned by the famous theological archbishop of Ravenna (546-556).

Cappella Arcivescovile ⑧

Also known as the Cappella di S. Andrea (St Andrew's Chapel), this is the old oratory of the bishops of Ravenna, built at the beginning of Ostrogoth rule in the city as a response by the Orthodox Catholic Episcopate to the massive presence of the Arian Church. Arianism, condemned as heresy by the Councils of Nicaea (325) and Constantinople (381), was named after Ario, a priest of Alexandria (280-336). This heresy denied the divine nature of Christ, that he was of the same 'substance' as God and the fact that he was eternal. Christ was regarded as a man of high moral standing, but only a man. Despite being condemned by the Church of Rome, Arianism spread throughout the Christian world and the Barbarian tribes who occupied the territories of the fallen Roman Empire (Visigoths, Ostrogoths, Vandals, etc.) became Arians. In fact, the controversial message is obvious in the symbolism of the atrium with *Christ the Warrior driving out the beasts of heresy*. The cross vault is decorated with splendid **mosaics*** which have been gleaming since the early 6th century.

Biblioteca Classense ⑨

The city's main library, and one of Italy's most important and monumental libraries, is based in the historic Via Baccarini: the Classense. It was named after the **monastery** that houses it; this was the monastery of S. Apollinare in Classe but, transferred to Ravenna after the battle of 1512, was then called 'Classe Dentro'. The building complex was constructed over a couple of centuries and is one of Ravenna's most significant urban acquisitions. The monastery building presents a harmonious broadness, and the *large cloister* inside is very grand. Rich and important, the *Aula Magna* is a jewel of Baroque art. Its collection consists of early medieval and medieval codices (approximately one thousand), incunabula (approximately 800), 16th-century editions and later printed collections, forming in all more than 600,000 volumes. The most important manuscripts include the 10th-century Greek **parchment codex***, containing eleven plays by Aristophanes (main archetype for the printed editions).

Museo d'Arte della Città di Ravenna (MAR) ⑩

Housed in the former *Lateran Canons Monastery* (1496-1508), this is of special worth for its beautiful **Renaissance cloister***, and, overlooking the public gardens, the **Loggetta Lombardesca***, thus called for its general attribution to the circles of the Lombardo family; an elegant construction with two rows of arches constructed after 1503. The gallery is particularly interesting because of the insight it gives to painters from Romagna: Nicolò Rondinelli da Lugo, Francesco Zaganelli da Cotignola and Bartolomeo Ramenghi, known as 'il Bagnacavallo'; but there are also paintings by Marco Palmezzano and Baldassarre Carrari from Forlì; and others, of the Ferrara, Bologna, Venetian and Tuscan schools. The Basilica of S. Francesco provided the most famous work in the collection: the **funerary monument of Guidarello Guidarelli*** (a military man from Valentino, mortally wounded in Imola in 1501), by Tullio Lombardo (1525). Of no lesser importance are the modern and contemporary sections of the museum, which offer a rich collection of artists from Ravenna and Romagna datable to around the second half of the 19th century and the first half of the 20th century. Also linked to the city's great mosaic tradition is the *collection of contemporary mosaics* (produced in the second half of the 20C) on permanent display on the ground floor, in the setting of the cloister of the Loggetta Lombardesca.

Basilica di S. Apollinare Nuovo ⑪

Historically and culturally, this is perhaps the most important monument of the Imperial and early-Christian Roman period in Ravenna. Here, in fact, two impressive walls covered with **mosaics*** (unique in the art history of Antiquity) represent both the Catholic faith of the great ancient Church and the Arian faith. The commissioning Arian bishops of court had the two series of pictures of the life of Christ placed in the register above the windows. The series should be observed starting from the apse, i.e. the altar. In this way, the first scene on the right and the first scene on the left correspond perfectly; they show the two suppers that prompt respective sequels: the supper in Cana that marks the beginning of the Saviour's public life, and the Jewish Easter supper that starts the '*historia*' of the Passion, Death and Resurrection, i.e. the mysteries of the Christian Easter celebrated in Holy Week. The cycle of mosaics is completed by two large facing panels of *Christ the King* and the *Virgin Mother seated on the throne and assisted by the four archangels, Michael, Gabriel, Raphael and Uriel.*

S. Giovanni Evangelista ⑫

In assessing the historical and cultural value of the monumental complex of the Palatine basilica of St John the Evangelist, the visitor should not only bear in mind that he/she is in Ravenna's oldest church, but that he/she is entering the Roman basilica which, in the ancient mosaics (destroyed in the 16C), celebrated the pomp of the Roman-Christian Empire. Important monuments apart from the *protesi* and the *diaconicon* (chapels on the right and left of the apse) include the original marble altar with a Latin inscription from the same period, the medieval bishop's chair, the 10th-century bell tower, the mosaic floor dating from 1213 in the large fragmented squares next to the perimeter walls, the main **doorway** with sculptures in the Romanesque-Gothic style (13-14C), and the beautiful 16th-century Benedictine **cloister**.

Mausoleo di Teodorico ⑬

The Tomb of Theodoric is the only monument in Ravenna without wall mosaics. This recognition is well deserved, not only for its uniqueness (it is the only religious building in Ravenna built entirely in stone) but also because it is of remarkable historical importance within the context of Ostrogoth monuments. This can be seen by interpreting the perfect Greek-cross plan of the lower cell and a perfect circle in the upper cell, a true funerary chamber. This round cell is, moreover, crowned with a perfectly round 'capstone', an whole monolith that acts as a roof; a unique architectural feature. Admire in particular the Barbarian *frieze*, i.e. a tongs-shaped frieze: the most striking of the two rings of decoration on the upper part of the building. At the top, in the center of the monolithic capstone, is a *cross* in clipeus with colored traces of what appears to be mosaic decoration. On the outside, high up, are the names of some of the Apostles and Evangelists.

The Mausoleum of Theodoric has been declared a world heritage site by UNESCO

DAY TRIPS

BAGNACAVALLO [19 km]

The town has a well-preserved historic center, which has a radial plan of medieval origin with picturesque porticoed streets. **Piazza della Libertà** is the largest square, featuring medieval and 18th-19th-century buildings: the **Torre Civica** or *Torre dell'Orologio*, perhaps of the 13th century, and *Palazzo Vecchio* (12-13C but repeatedly restructured), which probably formed part of the defense system of which the so-called *Castellaccio*; the neo-classical porticoed **Palazzo Comunale** (1791-1803), and the *Teatro Comunale Goldoni*, inaugurated in 1845. **Via Mazzini**, the old main street winds forward and features, on the left, the Baroque *collegiate church of S. Michele Arcangelo*, which has retained the 15th-century polygonal apse of the previous church. On the right is the 18th-century *Palazzo Longanesi-Cattani*. A must, in the south part of the old town, reached along Via Battisti, is the picturesque **Piazza Nuova**, with its beautiful elliptical shape, created in 1758-59 as a covered food market. The **complex of S. Francesco** is the oldest convent in Bagnacavallo. Constructed in

the 13th century, it was repeatedly modified and partially rebuilt in the 18th century. The charming new refectory, completed in 1766, is situated on the north-west side. This vast hall is lined with fine 18th-century wooden seating and is embellished with two large paintings: the *Wedding at Cana* and the *Coronation of Pope Clement XIV*. The **church** contains a much revered image of the *Blessed Virgin of Jerusalem*, brought from the Holy Land by a Franciscan tertiary in 1490 and placed in a *chapel*. The church contains other works of certain major historic and artistic merit: a 14th-century *Crucifix* painted with tempera on a gold background, by a master of the Rimini School, an interesting 19th-century low relief portraying Tiberto V. Brandolini, and a *Madonna Enthroned and Child, St Joseph and Sts Roch and Sebastian* by Ferraù Fenzoni and fragments of the old 14th-century fresco decoration. The **Centro Culturale le Cappuccine** is housed in the former 18th-century convent of the *Capuchin nuns*. It houses the *municipal art collections* comprising works of the 16th-19th centuries, and the **Pinacoteca moderna**, a collection of small sculptures with a special section devoted to the painter Enzo Morelli. On the ground floor is the **Gabinetto delle Stampe Antiche e Moderne**, the *Biblioteca Taroni*, a major history and archive collection with more than 400 parchments and rare 18th-century editions. A rich **wildlife section** organizes educational initiatives to encourage children to get to know and help protect the wildlife of the Romagna area. This section is linked to the *Podere Pantaleone*, situated in the immediate vicinity of the old center; it is an area set aside for ecological and environmental reasons and survives as an example of the old Romagna countryside.

The **parish church of S. Pietro in Sylvis***, the most famous monument in Bagnacavallo, is one of the best-preserved Parish churches in Romagna. It very probably dates from the early decades of the 7th century; the interior, with a nave and two side-aisles, has fine marbles, and important frescoes executed in the first half of the 14th century by an unknown painter of the Rimini School. Do not miss the vast, charming crypt.

BRISIGHELLA [43 km]

This pleasant holiday resort, which has been awarded the TCI's "Bandiera Arancione" (Orange Flag), is much appreciated for its picturesque appearance and its curative waters. It has an unmistakable silhouette, dominated by three hills, on the top of which stand the most representative buildings. The first hill is dominated by the Torre dell'Orologio (clock-tower), of 19th-century appearance but medieval foundation. It houses an exhibition of clocks and various measuring instruments called 'La signora del tempo' (temporarily closed). A small gorge, cultivated with vines, separates the first hill from the second, surmounted by the majestic **Rocca** (fortress), one of the best-preserved in the whole region. It was erected in 1310 and given a tower, the *Torre Maggiore* (1503), five storeys high. The third hill, known as Monticino, is the site of the *Sanctuary of the Madonna*, a small 18th-century church. At the foot of the clock tower lies the most picturesque part of the town. The picturesque **Via degli Asini***, raised and covered, is lit by half arches all different one from one another The hub of the town is *Piazza Carducci*, lower down, on which stands the 17th-century **collegiate church of Ss. Michele e Giovanni Battista**. The interior contains some fine art-works. Via Roma descends from the square to the *church of S. Maria degli Angeli* or *dell'Osservanza* and the adjoining *convent* (16C). Inside it contains, on the left, the *chapel of St Elizabeth* and an altar-piece by Marco Palmezzano depicting the *Madonna Enthroned and*

Child with Angels and Saints and, in the lunette, the *Everlasting Father* (1520), a work dating from the mature period of the great painter from Forlì. Near the convent is the lovely *Parco Giuseppe Ugonia*, with a remarkable anti-heroic monument to the *Sleeping Infantryman*.

The **parish church of S. Giovanni in Ottavo** or **del Thò*** is situated just outside Brisighella. The first mention of the church dates from 909, but it is certainly earlier. Its present lines are the fruit of work done in 1572 on the previous Romanesque structure. The interior, which can only be visited by appointment, incorporates much re-used material. The *crypt* is typically Romanesque. The room next to the crypt houses a collection of fragments of ancient vases, Faenza ceramics, and a fragment of Roman floor mosaic. In the inner courtyard there is an old olive-press.

CERVIA [23 km]

Passing time has produced close cultural and everyday links between the old town and the busy strip of land facing the sea, the beautiful saltpans and the ancient pinewood. Strolling at random past the sights and monuments mentioned here is a good way of appreciating the urban design and environmental worth of old Cervia. The bustling core of town life, **Piazza Garibaldi** is the fulcrum of Cervia's original urban layout, an example of 18th-century town planning with a rectangular structure. The **Cathedral of the Assunta**, near which stands a pine-cone-shaped *fountain* (1882), was built in the 18th century and has a well-made high altar, with an altar-piece of the *Assumption and Saints* (17C). **Palazzo Comunale**, begun in 1702 to a design by Francesco Fontana, is a porticoed construction with a distinctive clock-tower; a fine 18th-century terracotta *statue of Our Lady of the Assumption* appears prominently above the Baroque balcony. Behind this building is **Piazza Pisacane**, formerly the market-place, a delightful place featuring notably the former *fish market*. The old town is clustered around Piazza Garibaldi, with the distinctive terraced **houses of the saltworkers**.

Nearby, on the left of the **Canale delle Saline***, is the little *church of the Suffragio* (1722; worth a stop for a Gothic wooden *Crucifix* of the early 14th century and a fine organ attributed to Gaetano Callido). This watercourse can today more correctly be described as a canal-harbor, flanked by picturesque surroundings which have an aura of Cervia's past. These include – a remarkable example of industrial archaeology partially converted to the **Museo del Sale (MUSA)** – the 18th-century **magazzini del sale** (salt warehouses). On the right bank is the *fountain of the Tappeto Sospeso* and the mighty *Torre di S. Michele*, dating from 1691. Continuing towards the sea, you come to the *Borgo Marina* and the elegant promenade of *Lungomare Gabriele D'Annunzio* and *Lungomare Grazia Deledda*. South-west lie the small towns of **Pinarella** and **Tagliata**, enhanced by a small and well-tended pinewood.

Milano Marittima was created as an addition to Cervia (with which it forms a single administrative unit, with the Canale delle Saline as the demarcation line). From the outset, it had the aspirations and characteristics of a 'garden town'. Today it is a first-class tourist resort and it remains one of the most significant planning projects on the Romagna Riviera pinewood. Situated behind Milano Marittima is the **Pineta di Cervia*** (Cervia Pinewood), where the unusual environment, comprising the pools of the nearby saltpans and a composite ensemble of vegetation, is very important for wildlife. Numerous paths wind through the **nature reserve**. The **saltpans** are the southernmost point of the Parco del Delta del Po and, resembling a vast chess-board formed by different-sized pools, include the little deconsecrated church of the *Madonna della Neve*, a relic of the old town of Cervia, which stood here from the 8th until the 17th century. The millenary system of artisan saltpan management has been replaced by an industrial system. Production has recommenced in the saltpans, thanks to the creation of the **Società Parco della Salina**, which currently markets an excellent 'sweet organic. The saltpans are also important as a wetland which supports wildlife, especially waders and seabirds, and other species. Certain species of gulls, ducks, avocets and black-winged stilts breed here, while cranes, storks, egrets flamingoes and spoonbills stop to feed on passage. There is no shortage of halophytes, the typical plant species of saline marsh habitats. Visitors must be accompanied by a park guide.

Faenza: Cathedral

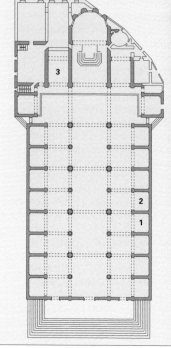

1 Innocenzo da Imola altarpiece
2 Sarcophagus of San Terenzio
3 Sarcophagus of San Savino

FAENZA [31 km]

The **cathedral*** is the city's main monument and stands with its imposing and unfinished facade overlooking the very central *Piazza della Libertà*. Built in two stages between 1474 and 1511, at the height of the Renaissance, the cathedral is the most significant indication of the influence exercised over Faenza by the Tuscan culture for centuries. However, there are many features peculiar to the Romanesque architecture found in the Po Valley (alternating pillars and columns, ribbed vaults). Works of particular interest include: a **Madonna and Child with Saints** by Innocenzo da Imola (1526), an altar-piece still surrounded by its original frame; the **sarcophagus of St Terence*** (1461), with low reliefs of the Tuscan School; and, finally, the most celebrated piece in the cathedral, behind the altar: the classic **sarcophagus of St Savino***, deemed by recent studies to be the joint work of Benedetto Da Maiano and Antonio Rossellino. **Piazza della Libertà** is overlooked by the cathedral facade, before which rises the *Portico dei Signori* or *degli*

Orefici (early 17C) and partially remodelled in the Art-Nouveau style (c.1907). The **Piazza Fountain** is decidedly Baroque in design (1619-21). At the point where the two main urban thoroughfares meet stands the *clock-tower*, a faithful reconstruction of the old one, erected in 1604 and destroyed in 1944.

A mirror-reflection of Piazza della Libertà, **Piazza del Popolo*** is the busy fulcrum of the city's public life; it is surrounded by two porticoes that present an elegant, harmonious appearance although they were constructed, rebuilt and altered over a long period of time (from 1470 to 1932). Beside the tower is **Palazzo del Podestà** (the oldest nucleus dates from 1177) although its present appearance is largely the product of period restoration (late 19–early-20C). Opposite is **Palazzo del Municipio**, erected in the 13th century. Its extremely heterogeneous appearance perpetrates the memory of the various figures in power who succeeded each other and ranges from the oldest medieval structures to the late-Baroque façade on Corso Mazzini, which dates from 1770-80. If you visit Faenza, don't miss the **Museo Internazionale delle Ceramiche***, a worthy showcase for Faenza's great ceramic tradition, the local pride and the reason for the city's fame around the world. The collections are divided into three large sections (Italian ceramics, civilization and continents, contemporary ceramics) and these form a highly enjoyable encyclopaedia of the ceramic art, from its beginnings to the flourishing of several schools, in Italy and abroad, and the most modern present-day expressions of the art with works by great artists of the 20th century (including Matisse, Picasso, Chagall, Léger, Martini, Fontana). Another first-rate collection is the **Pinacoteca Comunale***, including some masterpieces, and its oldest sections date from the late 18th century. It is housed in the 19th-century *Palazzo dei Gesuiti*. Highlights of the collection include: a wooden sculpture of **St Jerome*** by Donatello and a marble bust of the **Infant St. John***, attributable to Antonio Rossellino. There is a large section of important 15th-16th-century paintings, whereas the 17th century is represented by the works of Ferraù Fenzoni, Alessandro Tiarini and a **Portrait of a Magistrate**, by an unknown artist, who was possibly Dutch. There are also pictures from the neo-classical, Romantic and Realist periods. Close to the municipal art gallery is the **church of S. Maria Vecchia**, with its splendid **bell tower**.

The **Museo del Neoclassicismo*** is the name given to the collections now housed in the old rooms of **Palazzo Milzetti**, a building by the architect Pistocchi. The building has added value as the finest neo-classical artists at work in Faenza were involved in its decoration: from Felice Giani to the Ballanti Graziani brothers. The decoration of the interiors, often devoted to a theme associated with classical mythology, provides insight into the tastes of the times, captured in Homer's poems (*Sala delle Feste*), the history of Rome (*Sala di Compagnia*), Graeco-Roman paganism (*Gabinetto d'Amore*), and archeological finds at Herculaneum and Pompeii (*Sala da Bagno*). Not far away is the **church of S. Maria Nuova dell'Angelo**, which has a beautiful **high altar***.

LUGO [25 km]

The fabric of the old town center is manifestly of good urban quality, with well-preserved buildings based upon a complex system of squares, with the Rocca and the Pavaglione acting as counter-fulcrums. The system created by the **central piazzas** started to take shape in the early 18th century as an expression of the town's consolidated economic and cultural vitality. It is closed to the north-east by Piazza Martiri della Libertà, where the entrance to the **Rocca** is located; the crenellated round keep, with its present 15th-century appearance, is all that survives of the medieval fortress, erected in or around 1297; the rest of the complex, arranged around a central courtyard with ramparts, a hanging garden, towers and walls, reflects the restructuring work executed in 1568-70. Facing the Rocca is the **Pavaglione***, a rectangular square (measuring 132m x 84m), the conceptual hub of the urban layout. The first design of 1570, completed in 1783, was conceived to house the silkworm cocoon market. Devised as a four-sided portico, enclosed and lined with shops, it surrounds *Piazza Mazzini*. *Piazza Baracca* lies between the Rocca and the Pavaglione: on it is a *monument to Francesco Baracca* (1936), hero of the Great War and born in Lugo. **Corso Matteotti** leads into the area once designated as the Jewish ghetto.

Basilica of S. Vitale

The audacity of construction and its splendid mosaics make the Basilica of S. Vitale, founded around 540, one
the loveliest central-plan Byzantine churches. The external lines of the building – simple and clear-cut in expos
brick with an animated combination of volumes, particularly so in the apse – only hint at the beauty of the in
rior. Those entering the basilica are immediately plunged into a centric and enveloping space, where a skilful p
of solids and voids, flat and curved surfaces, mosaics, marbles and frescoes produce effects of light and sha
ow that bring an impression of remarkable lightness to the whole construction. The 16m diameter dome is a m
terpiece of engineering and was constructed using numerous slender terraco
pipes inserted one inside the other. The central space is divided by eight
lars and elegant niches or semi-circular spaces, with a double row

Bell tower

Dome

Dosseret

Women's gallery

Ambulatory
or lower loggia

Pillar

Votive chapel of San Vitale

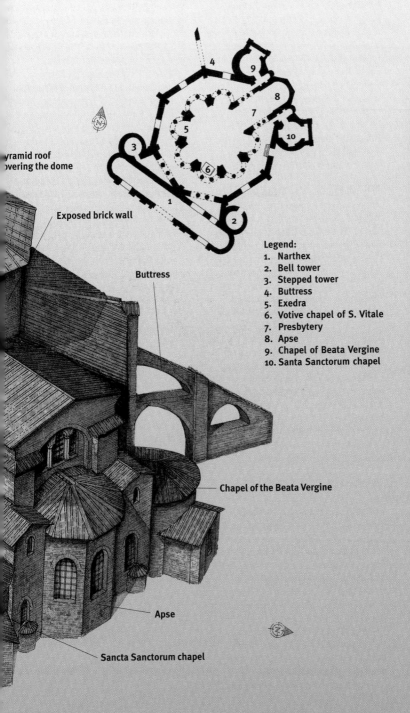

...umns. The lower loggia is at the same height as the women's gallery, the place of prayer and worship reserved ...women, which was reached via the stepped towers, situated at the sides of the narthex. The right-hand tow-...preceded by a vaulted ceiling bearing precious Byzantine stuccowork, raised and repeatedly reconstruct-...has been turned into a bell tower.

...yramid roof
...overing the dome

Exposed brick wall

Buttress

Legend:
1. Narthex
2. Bell tower
3. Stepped tower
4. Buttress
5. Exedra
6. Votive chapel of S. Vitale
7. Presbytery
8. Apse
9. Chapel of Beata Vergine
10. Santa Sanctorum chapel

Chapel of the Beata Vergine

Apse

Sancta Sanctorum chapel

Completing the system of squares, at the back and right side of the Pavaglione respectively, are *Piazza Trisi* and Piazza del Teatro. The former is distinguished by *Palazzo Trisi*, erected in 1764-75, *Palazzo della Congregazione di Carità* (1768) and the side of the *church of the Carmine*, rebuilt in the 18th century. In *Piazza del Teatro* stands the splendid **Teatro Rossini**, designed by Petrocchi and completed in 1760-61 by Antonio Galli 'il Bibiena'. From Piazza Trisi, Via Baracca leads to the *oratory of S. Onofrio* (1679), where there are some paintings by Ignazio Stern, also known as "lo Stella". Continue along Via Codazzi to the **collegiate church of S. Francesco**, preceded by a portico with three arches; it has Romanesque and Gothic features construction (13C).

PINETA DI S. VITALE [8 km]

Having long been owned by Ravenna's abbey of the same name, this old pinewood stretches out on the left of the Strada Romea and is the most illustrious survivor of the dense mass of pinewoods, which, until the 18th century, used to cover the entire coastal strip from the mouth of the Reno to Cervia. Of environmental importance, it is crossed by paths leading to the Ca' Vecchia Visitors' Centre. On the other side of the Strada Romea is the **Valle Mandriole-Punte Alberete** complex, crossed by the embanked course of the Lamone River. This is a freshwater wetland which was declared a fauna oasis in 1968 and, today, is one of the most important in Europe, because it preserves the typical marsh habitat of the coastal-plain areas. Its vegetation is home to a rich avifauna, particularly aquatic species.

S. APOLLINARE IN CLASSE
[5 km]

Set in the vast plain south of Ravenna, the view of the buildings of S. Apollinare in Classe is very striking: the main basilica, the high atrium and the soaring bell tower. Bishop Apollinaris, founder of the Church of Ravenna was buried here. Having died as a martyr, he was buried 'in Classe' around the year 180 and, since then, has been central to the community. As a result, the great commissioning client and theologian Maximian had the figure of the saint exalted in the center of the **apse vault** (the whole presbytery, with its triumphal arch, is covered with **mosaics***

executed at various times). The iconolog of S. Apollinare in Classe therefore, plac the bishop – in the mystery and greatest sacrament of the communion of worshippers, the Holy Communion – in t center of all. Outside the church is the round **bell tower***, probably erected in th 10th century. Inside the basilica, notice t two large uncovered sections of the original *floor mosaics*. The church contai some treasures of early-Christian sculpture: *sarcophagi*, **capitals**, *inscriptions*, the **ciborium of Eleucadio**, the early-medieval *crypt* and the *chair of Bishop Damiano* (693-709). When descending from the presbytery towards the doors, it is worth stopping in the righ hand aisle to look at the first two sarcophagi: the one called the **sarcophagus of Archbishop Theodore** because, (clearly, reused for his burial) it a beautiful 5th-century piece, as, too, is th second, called the **sarcophagus of the Twelve Apostles** because it represents th group of Twelve receiving the appointmer to teach the Gospel. The *portraits of the archbishops of Ravenna* in the tondos on the nave walls, a work ordered by the Camaldolensian custodians of the basilic and by the Biblioteca Classense also bear witness to the great ecclesiological importance of S. Apollinare.

S. Apollinare in Classe

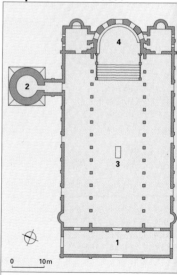

1 Atrium
2 Bell-tower (10th cent.)
3 9th-century altar
4 Presbytery (6th-9th cent. mosaics)

REGGIO EMILIA

city with a down-to-earth, generous nature, rooted in the farming tradition, its people are hard-working, combining quality of life with great civic commitment: the culture of ·ggio is based on study, solidarity, sociability and services. Situated on the Via Aemilia, e old town is enclosed within the hexagon formed by its circular roads, which follow the mond-shape of its old walls. City of art, it has a strong cultural tradition and an portant historical and artistic heritage. Its many layers of building reflect various styles, that Roman remains mingle with medieval, masterpieces of the Renaissance with roque and neo-classical monuments, endowing the city with a formal, very balanced pearance, full of color and atmosphere.

iazza Camillo Prampolini ❶

This large rectangular square is the city's main public space and is closed and surrounded on all sides by buildings; access points are not noticeable, as they are hidden or concealed under large vaults. The overall impression is somber, the only decoration being the statue of Cròstolo from Palazzo Ducale of Rivalta. The east side is occupied by a complex of religious buildings: **Palazzo Vescovile**, the facade of which incorporates the profile of the **Baptistery of S. Giovanni Battista**, dating from the 11th century, the Duomo and Palazzo dei Canonici. Opening between these is the **Broletto**, a bustling, partially covered street. The piazza is also overlooked by **Palazzo del Comune**, built in 1414-94 and rebuilt 1583, with a composite architecture resulting from gradual additions. It has a graceful 18th-century facade, decorated

The interior of the Duomo

with large arches, and a three-arched portico. Inside, the **Sala del Tricolore** is a magnificent oval hall with three tiers of balconies (1774-75). Towering above **Palazzo del Monte**, the hub of the city, is the Torre dell'Orologio (clock-tower). 47m high, it reflects the *crenellated tower* erected in 1216.

Duomo ❷

Dating from the Romanesque period (9C), the cathedral has been modified several times over the centuries. The facade with its gable roof, decorated by small hanging arches, is crowned by an original octagonal tower with a niche containing an image of the *Madonna Enthroned and Child and Donors*, in gilt, embossed copper, by Bartolomeo Spani (15C). The structure resembling a *westwerk* (a northern architectural model used in the Romanesque period), on an

axis with the nave, gives a vertical dimension to the facade. The partial marble decoration dates from the Renaissance; the doorway is enhanced by two *statues of Adam and Eve* in the style of Michelangelo, by Prospero Sogari, known as 'il Clemente' (1557), who also executed the statues (*Sts Chrysanthus and Daria*) in the niches. The interior is built on a basilica plan with a nave and two side-aisles; the

REGGIO EMILIA
IN OTHER COLORS...

- **ITINERARIES:** pages 114, 135
- **FOOD:** pages 143, 149, 153, 160
- **SHOPPING:** page 175
- **EVENTS:** page 188
- **WELLNESS:** page 201
- **PRACTICAL INFO:** page 228

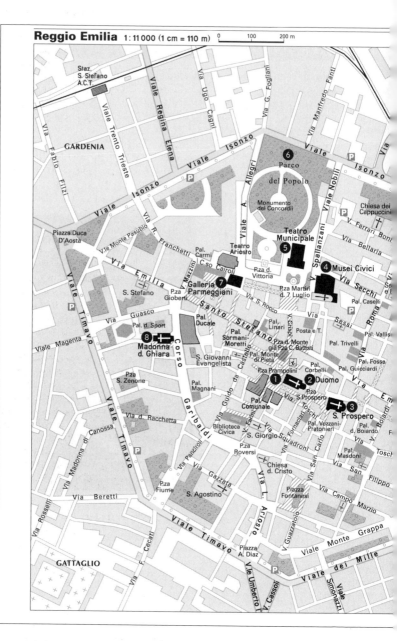

Reggio Emilia 1:11 000 (1 cm = 110 m)

crypt below the transept has cross-vaulting supported by 42 columns (an underground room has a Roman polychrome marble floor dating from the 3-4C AD).

Basilica di S. Prospero ❸

The church, founded in the 10th century, is one of the oldest in the city. Reconstructed in 1514-23, it is adorned with a striking carved facade (1748-53) with mixtilinear cornices, a play of niches and eleven *statues* (18C) portraying the patron saints of the city and the Doctors of the Church. On the edge of the parvis are six large lions of red Verona marble (1504). There is a strong contrast between the 18th-century forms of the church (in brick) and the adjacent **bell tower** (in gray stone), a remarkable octagonal construction, one of the most significant local Renaissance buildings. The interior of the church is built on a Latin-cross plan, illuminated by an

by neo-classical facades on the north and south sides, with porticoes and numerous shops around the edge – a busy market and trading place. Scenographically, the apses of the cathedral are balanced by the Baroque facade of the Basilica of S. Prospero.

Musei Civici ❹

The atrium has mosaics of Roman date and figurative floors (12-13C) from the Duomo and other local churches. The **Museo Spallanzani di Storia Naturale*** has zoological, mineralogical and paleo-ethnology collections, as well as anatomical and botanical collections. The **Museo di Paletnologia "Gaetano Chierici"*** is a priceless example of late 19th century museological culture, preserved with its original furnishings and as arranged immediately after Chierici's death; it has good *ethnographical collections* of native American material from the great plains of North America. The **Galleria dei Marmi** (Marble Gallery) has a large collection of cippi, epigraphs, marbles, miscellaneous pieces, sculptures and decorations of local origin, dating from Roman times to the 18th century. In the adjacent cloister is a recomposition of Roman architectural marbles including some funerary monuments of centurions. The **Museo di Reggio in Età Romana** has finds dating from the town's foundation to Barbarian times; the archaeology of late Antiquity is illustrated by the Roman-Barbarian treasure (late 5C) with gold-work and coins of the Imperial and Barbarian periods, and from Constantinople. Upstairs is the **Pinacoteca "Antonio Fontanesi"**, with a vast collection of local interest, with 16th-19th- century works. The **Museo "Renato Marino Mazzacurati"** (1907-69), offers an extensive review of the works by the artist. The **Raccolte di Preistoria e Protostoria fino all'Età del Ferro** include material from prehistoric times up to the Iron Age, such as the famous neolithic *Venus* and *cippi* from Rubiera, and Etruscan funerary tablets (5-7C BC) with friezes and inscriptions. The **Museo dell'Arte Industriale** displays artistic craftsmanship, some of it local, and an exhibition of fabrics and records relating to the silk industry.

oculus and divided by Doric columns covered with imitation marble stucco-work. It displays several works by local artists of the 16th and 17th centuries. A riot of form and color draws visitors to the splendid cycle of **frescoes** in the choir and presbytery. Above the high altar 'del Santissimo' is the **altar-piece of the Assumption**, a masterpiece by Tommaso Laureti and Ludovico Carracci (1602). Next to the basilica is **Piazza S. Prospero**, an attractive space, entirely surrounded

Teatro Municipale "Romolo Valli" ⑤

Standing imposingly in the tree-lined public gardens is the impressive neo-classical theater, erected in 1852-57. One of the most beautiful and functional in Europe, this is the hub of the city's cultural life. Inaugurated in 1857, it is dedicated to a famous local actor (1925-80). The facade, composed and elegant, lends distinction to the long architraved portico; its upper order is divided by pilaster strips, and crowned with allegorical statues. Inside is the magnificent horse-shoe-shaped hall, with four tiers of boxes and a balcony; white and gold decorations and a splendid chandelier contrast with the dark red wall covering. Note the famous **curtain** by Alfonso Chierici.
A visit backstage shows the rigging, balconies and winches for the scenery and special effects. The foyer areas include the notable *Hall of Mirrors*, adorned with mirrors featuring carved gilt frames.

Giardini Pubblici or Parco del Popolo ⑥

The gardens occupy six hectares of green space in the area of the former Citadel (14C) demolished in 1848. A walk round the park, created from 1864 on, provides an opportunity to admire a large number of botanical species (evergreens in particular, including grandiose cedars of Lebanon). Various works adorn the gardens: the **funerary monument of the Concordi** (1C AD), the *statues* of Boiardo and Ariosto by Riccardo Secchi, and the *four seasons*, taken from Palazzo Ducale of Rivalta.

Civica Galleria "Anna e Luigi Parmeggiani" ⑦

This is in an eccentric building by Ascanio Ferrari (early decades of the 20C), which stands in the south-west corner of Piazza della Vittoria. An unusual example of eclectic architecture, it was designed as a museum, in a combination of French and Spanish forms, a mixture of Gothic and Renaissance styles. The gallery presents a collection formed in France, between the late 19th and early 20th centuries, by the Asturian painter and benefactor Ignacio Leòn y Escosura, the painter

Cesare Detti (1848-1919) and Parmeggiani himself. The arms, gold-work, fabrics, paintings and furnishings are mostly 19th-century fakes in medieval and Renaissance style. In the atrium are marbles, terracottas and stone capitals; next is the *Sala dei Gioielli*, with Limoges enamels (12-13C); the *Sala delle Armi*, containing bayonets, firearms and armor (15-17C); of note among the paintings in the central hall is a **Christ of the Benediction** by Domenico Theotocopulos, known as El Greco and, in the center, *works* formerly attributed to Velázquez and Van Eyck; the *Sala Detti* has family paintings and self-portraits in historic costumes, and the *Sala Escosura* has paintings based on historic subjects; the *Flemish, English and French rooms*; the Spanish room exhibits the most comprehensive collection of Spanish art in Italy; the *Sala dei Costumi* and the *Sala dei Velluti*, with 18th-19th-century garments and clothing accessories.

Santuario Beata Vergine della Ghiara ⑧

Built to a design by Alessandro Balbi (1597-1619) and completed by Francesco Pacchioni, the church is preceded by a large parvis. The facade, in brick with marble adornments, is in two rows, animated by pilaster strips and serlianas, and crowned at the top by acroterions. The whole culminates in a soaring dome and the unfinished bell tower. Three doorways lead into an interior built on a Greek-cross plan with a deep apse. The decorative unity of the interior highlights the chromatic contrast between the decorations and the architectural space. Sumptuous 17th-century decoration in gilt stucco-work frames a fine *cycle of frescoes* that covers the vaults. Beside the convent cloister is the *Museo della Ghiara* (temporarily closed), with the rich legacy of the lay vestry consisting in silver-ware, fabrics, votive offerings, sacred furnishings of the 17th-19th centuries and a drawing of the **Madonna of the Ghiara** by Lelio Orsi (1569). In the Sala del Tesoro is a remarkable painting, the *Salvation of Laura da Correggio* by Luca Ferrari and a precious 17th-century crown of the Virgin.

Sanctuary of the Madonna della Ghiara

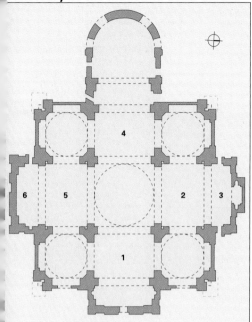

1 Panels of *Adamo ed Eva*
2 Paintings by *Lionello Spada*, including *Esther and Ahasuerus*
3 Altar of the Madonna by G.B. Magnani
4 Frescoes by Alessandro Tiarini, including *David and Solomon*
5 Frescoes by Luca Ferrari, including *Rachel and Job*
6 Town Altar by G.B. Magnani, with a work by Guercino, *Christ on the Cross consoled by the Angel*

DAY TRIPS

CASTELLO DI CANOSSA [23 km]

Founded in 940, the castle of Canossa was the setting for the famous encounter, in 1077, between the German Emperor, Henry IV and Pope Gregory VII (see page 112). The strategic importance of the stronghold was, together with the geological instability of the rock, one of the contributory causes that decreed the castle's ruin over the centuries. Today it appears as a secluded but beautiful place, with a only few ruins testifying to its past greatness. Inside the historic area is the crypt of the *church of S. Apollonio* and the small *Museo Nazionale "Naborre Campanini"*, which has some precious exhibits, including a monolithic font of the 12[th]century. In the nearby town of **Rossena** stands the **castle*** built by Matilda of Canossa, one of the most beautiful and best-preserved in the area. It is situated on a promontory of red volcanic rock which gives the town its name, in a panoramic setting. Besides the castle with its medieval keep, the fortifications and curtain-walls with protruding bulwarks, the town inside the castle walls is also interesting; it has retained its original layout, built around the only street. Opposite Rossena stands the isolated square *Torre di Rossenella*, on a rocky peak dominating the area.

CASTELLARANO [28 km]

The town already appears in documents of the years 898 and 900, while the *parish church of S. Maria Assunta* is mentioned in a 945 document of the bishop of Reggio (it is interesting to visit the crypt, which has Romanesque features, including a lunette carved in the old doorway). The settlement of Castellarano is, however, much older. An example of a fortified river town, it has a large **old center*** in an excellent state of conservation, with the original medieval layout. At the base of the hill, against the backdrop of Piazza XX Luglio, is the **Rocchetta*** (15C), a fortress with three gates, one of which is pointed, a central tower and two side towers, and a parade ground. Via Torre, still paved with river pebbles, skirts the ring of walls and climbs to the Aia del Mandorlo, the antechamber to the *castle*. At the side is the *Torre dell'Orologio* (clock-tower). Inside the tower is a 17th-century clock mechanism, worked by weights. Other features of monumental interest include the 17th-century *Casa Barbanti* in Via Toschi, a *flight of steps* in Via del Monte, the 18th-century *aqueduct* in Via Migliorini, and the deconsecrated *church of Santa Croce* (17C). Sites in the vicinity include **Roteglia**, a castle associated with the parish church of Castellarano and, in a pleasant side-valley, the town of **San Valentino** (11C). It has a fine *castle*, with a 14th-century tower, a loggia and four stone columns, and a Romanesque *parish church*, dating from 1517.

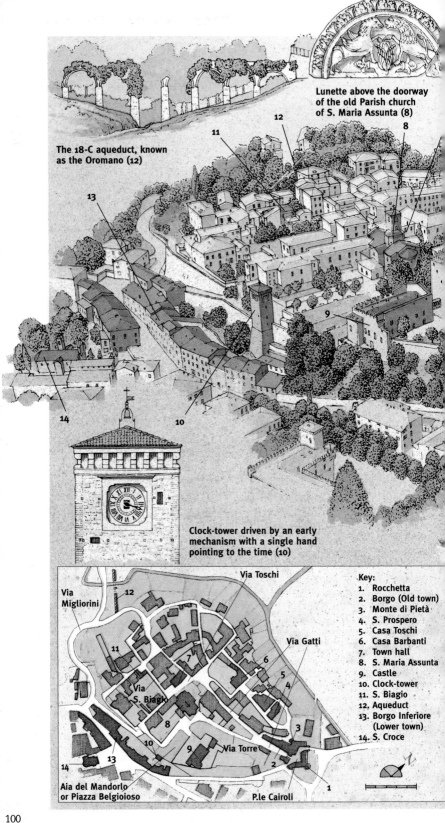

The 18-C aqueduct, known as the Oromano (12)

Lunette above the doorway of the old Parish church of S. Maria Assunta (8)

Clock-tower driven by an early mechanism with a single hand pointing to the time (10)

Key:
1. Rocchetta
2. Borgo (Old town)
3. Monte di Pietà
4. S. Prospero
5. Casa Toschi
6. Casa Barbanti
7. Town hall
8. S. Maria Assunta
9. Castle
10. Clock-tower
11. S. Biagio
12. Aqueduct
13. Borgo Inferiore (Lower town)
14. S. Croce

Via Toschi

Via Migliorini

Via Gatti

Via S. Biagio

Via Torre

Aia del Mandorlo or Piazza Belgioioso

P.le Cairoli

The old town of Castellarano

The old town is situated on a sandstone spur overlooking the Secchia River. Various tributaries flow into the river and further downstream some of the water is conveyed via the Canale di Reggio to Reggio Emilia. The entrance to the town, which was once surrounded by fortifications, used to be a fortified gate called the Rocchetta (or Porta Maggiore). The gate is defended by a moat and once had a draw-bridge. The seven-sided tower next to it was built during the Renaissance period when, as fire-arms became more widespread, towers were built with many edges in order to deflect cannon-balls from several angles. As the town's military role diminished, the areas and buildings inside the walls were converted for civic purposes. The urban fabric is still composed of narrow streets, small squares and courtyard houses which once belonged to the town's more important families. Many of the monumental and private buildings were built using stones from the riverbed, a cheap, plentiful source of building material. In recent years, the historic character of the town has been enhanced by paving the streets with cobbles, repairing the defensive walls and other buildings, leaving the original masonry visible in some cases, and restoring the Rocchetta.

Torre "Cappellana"

Torre della Rosa

South-west Gate

East Bastion

en-sided er

North Bastion

Porta Maggiore

Bridge

Drawbridge

ROCCHETTA (1)

CORREGGIO [17 km]

A beautiful little town, with many porticoed streets and delightful views. The old city is still well preserved within the old fortifications (1452). The backbone of the town is **Corso Mazzini**, the old main street, lined by grand buildings; it is a broad cobbled street accompanied throughout its length by pastel-colored porticoed houses and adorned with 18th-century and neo-classical embellishments. Set on the Corso Cavour-Piazza S. Quirino-Via Antonioli axis is the theater, Palazzo dei Principi and the Basilica of S. Quirino with the civic tower. At the beginning of the street is the Rocchetta (1372), with the remains of medieval walls, crenellations, corbels and decorations in brick. **Palazzo dei Principi**, a refined Renaissance building erected in 1507, is the city's main monument. Of clear Ferrara style, it incorporates a fine compositional balance. The pink brick facade has a lovely, finely carved **doorway** (School of Pietro Lombardo), with a little balcony above. The courtyard, with a portico resting on columns featuring composite capitals, is adorned with two *well-heads*. A large staircase leads to the counts' apartment, now the *Civic Library*, with precious incunabulae and editions dating from the 16th-18th centuries, and the **Museo Civico**. Note the **Sala del Camino** with a rich coffered wooden ceiling (1508), a frieze depicting *Tritons with Mythological Figures* and a large, carved fire-place. The **Basilica of Ss. Quirino e Michele** was built between 1513 and 1587 and stands in the square of the same name, with the **Monument to Correggio** by Vincenzo Vela (1880). Beside it, acting as a bell tower, stands the civic *tower*. Inside it has a nave and two aisles, with six chapels on each side and a raised presbytery over the crypt.

CORREGGIO: AN ARTIST AND HIS CITY

Antonio Allegri (1489-1534), a famous painter of the Italian Renaissance, owes his nickname 'Correggio' to his native town. In his day, the town was the seat of an Imperial *contea* with a court which was famous for its Humanist culture. As a young man, Allegri was sent to Mantua to train in the workshop of Mantegna. Later he met Leonardo da Vinci in Milan, the great Venetian painters (16C) and saw the works of Michelangelo and Raphael. Correggio worked for a long time in Parma, where he was offered the job of painting three domes: in the convent of S. Paolo, the church of S. Giovanni and the Duomo, where he painted marvelous mythological and heavenly scenes and opened the way for the glories of the Baroque all over Europe. As his biographers describe, Allegri's association with Correggio was extremely close. He was born here, he decorated its churches, he was married here; in the studio in his house, he created the last marvelous mythological paintings; he died here at an early age, and was laid to rest here in the church he loved, S. Francesco. Today, it is possible to follow an itinerary of places in and around Correggio associated with the painter: his house in Borgovecchio, his tomb in the church of S. Francesco, where some of his masterpieces were formerly located; the monument erected to him in Piazza di S. Quirino and, lastly, the room devoted to his work in the town museum and art gallery, in Palazzo dei Principi. It includes one of works depicting the *Face of Christ* and a sheet worked on both sides, bearing his signature, with preparatory sketches for the frescoes in the Parma Cathedral.

SCANDIANO [12 km]

The old center of Scandiano used to be called the "*scatola dipinta*" (painted box), on account of the profusion of painted decoration on the facades of the houses. The element that originally led to the building of the town is the **Rocca dei Boiardo***, an architectural construction of great importance. The incomplete Renaissance castle was converted to a noble residence in the Baroque period, with the addition of the fine south facade and the west tower called the 'Torrazzo'. The main entrance has an elegant *tower* with Ghibelline crenellations, and there was once a drawbridge. The apartments have late 17th-century stucco-work by Antonio Traeri.

RIMINI

Situated in the south-east corner of the plain of the Po, Rimini, capital of seaside tourism, has grown up as a result of the presence of its bathing institutions which offer first-class facilities, (see page 122). The tourists who come here want not only the beach with all its comforts, but also summer leisure activities, venues, and a continuous offering of shows and exhibitions. Parallel to this phenomenon is Rimini's strong attraction as a city of art, with a remarkable artistic heritage, fruit of its interesting history.

Piazza Cavour ❶

The piazza is the city rendez-vous point and the hub of local political, social and religious life for the people of Rimini. The most important public buildings are situated here. In its center stands the 17th-century **statue of Paul V** with, beside it, the **Pigna Fountain**, the round lines of which enliven the square. It was built in 1543, but the drum supporting the pine-cone, with its lovely low reliefs, is of Roman date; the marble bases date from the 15th century. The beauty and harmony of this water feature even enchanted Leonardo da Vinci, whose comment is inscribed on the monument. Various splendid buildings overlook the square. **Palazzo Comunale** is composed of a loggia with seven round arches, raised above a flight of steps, and an upper floor with two corner balconies and broad windows. **Palazzo dell'Arengo*** was built between 1204 and 1207. The building, with its majestic Romanesque-Gothic lines and crenellations, has an open ground floor with pointed arches which are echoed in the row of elegant windows on the first floor. Under the portico, the pointed windows are modern. Under the second arcade, look for the original old wooden municipal measures. On the right of the building, an external staircase leads up to the **Salone dell'Arengo** on the first floor, which has exposed roof trusses and is one of the finest halls in Italy. **Palazzo del Podestà** was erected in 1330 and an external flight of steps links it to Palazzo dell'Arengo. On the other long side of the square stands the **Vecchia Pescheria** (Old Fish-market). It has a two-tiered loggia with three round arches; the area under the arches is flanked by two rows of counters in Istrian stone, and there are four lion

fountains at the corners. The Vecchia Pescheria and the adjacent Piazzetta di S. Gregorio, still known by the locals as 'Piazzetta delle Poveracce' (the 'poveracce' being the old women who used to sell fish here), has become the hub of life for the city's youth, and is full of restaurants, bars and meeting-places. The neo-classical facade of **Teatro "Amintore Galli"** (1842-56) also overlooks the piazza. Behind the theater stands the mighty **Castel Sismondo**, the lines of which give a hint of its former splendor. Built between 1437 and 1446, the main part of its original structure has survived. Castel Sismondo is now an important location for cultural events.

S. Agostino ❷

Also known as *S. Giovanni Evangelista*, the art treasures kept here make it one of the most important churches in the city. It was built in 1247 in the Romanesque-Gothic style. These features are still visible in the sides, apse and **bell tower** (55m) – the tallest in Rimini. The interior has one nave and contains some of the most important examples of the Rimini School of the 14th century, namely the **frescoes*** in the apse, attributed to the Maestro dell'Arengo. The same master is also attributed with the large **Crucifix** kept in the baptistery to the left of the presbytery.

Piazza Cavour: on the right-hand side, Palazzo del Podestà and Palazzo dell'Arengo

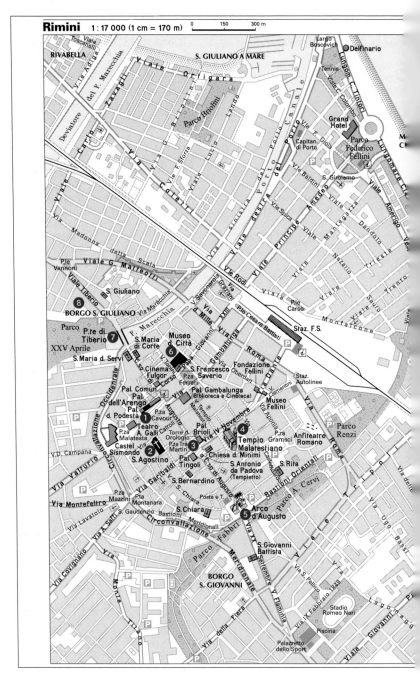

Piazza Tre Martiri ③

This square is a symmetrically harmonious space and stands on the site of settlement of the old Roman forum, paved with large rectangular stones, some of which are visible in closed-off areas around the square. Gothic and Renaissance capitals adorn the portico on the west side of the square. On the east side is the **Torre dell'Orologio** (clock-tower), dating from 1547. The clock mechanism dates from 1562, and the clock face with a perpetual solar-lunar calendar dates from 1750. Beside the tower are *Palazzo Brioli* and *Palazzo Tingoli*. At the south-

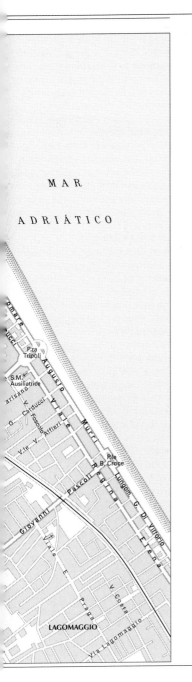

MAR

ADRIÁTICO

Rubicon. The great condottiere is also portrayed in a bronze *statue*, a copy of an original Roman one, that towers over the square.

Tempio Malatestiano ❹

This is the greatest monument in Rimini and one of the most important churches of the Renaissance. For the execution of the project, Leon Battista Alberti, the great architect who instilled the highest canons of Classicism in the structures, and leading artists such as Piero della Francesca and Agostino di Duccio were summoned. The **exterior** is particularly impressive, especially on account of the innovative architectural concept underpinning the whole project. Alberti's talent was expressed in the creation of a marble casing that would cover the existing medieval church, enveloping it without distorting its form – a contrast of styles contained in sublime harmony and culminating in a dome in the place of the old transept. As well as being an illustrious product of the Renaissance, the church harks back to the greatest examples of Roman Classicism. The **facade*** is marked, at the bottom, by three arches and fluted columns supporting the trabeation. The central arch contains the entrance doorway, with a tympanum and frieze in porphyry; marble fruit festoons decorate the sides. The top of the facade, clearly incomplete, reveals the springer of the central arch, flanked by raised triangular sides. A plinth decorated with Malatesta symbols runs around the whole building, also adorning the sides. The **sides** are marked by the seven great arches, divided by pillars, which frame the pointed windows of the old construction. The bell tower (15-16C) stands at the end of the bare left side of the building. The **interior** contains treasures rightly numbered among the most important of the Italian art

east tip stands the **Tempietto di S. Antonio da Padova** (1518), an elegant, octagonal building. Beside the 'tempietto', a 16th-century *cippus* (column of Julius Caesar) commemorates the tradition by which Julius Caesar climbed onto a stone and spoke to his soldiers after crossing the

RIMINI
IN OTHER COLORS...
- **ITINERARIES:** pages 122, 129
- **FOOD:** pages 143, 153, 166
- **SHOPPING:** pages 175, 179
- **EVENTS:** page 188
- **WELLNESS:** pages 204, 205
- **PRACTICAL INFO:** page 220

heritage. The cathedral has a single nave, with a wooden trussed roof, beneath which open the pointed arches of the numerous side chapels, raised by a step and closed by ornate marble balustrades. The contrast between the richly decorated Malatesta part and the bare presbytery is very striking. Note, in particular, the sinopia of the fresco depicting **Sigismondo Malatesta kneeling before St Sigismund****, by Piero della Francesca (1451), and the **Crucifix**** on a panel by Giotto, painted specially by the great artist in 1312 for the previous 13th-century church.

Rimini: Tempio Malatestiano

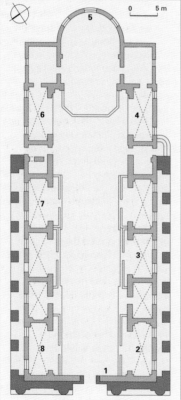

1 Tomb of Sigismondo Malatesta
2 Angels by Agostino di Duccio
3 Tomb of Isotta degli Atti
4 *Sigismondo Malatesta kneeling before St Sigmund* by Piero della Francesca
5 Crucifix by Giotto
6 *St Francis receiving the stigmata* by Giorgio Vasari
7 Bas-reliefs by Agostino di Duccio
8 *Sarcophagus of the Forefathers and Descendants* by Agostino di Duccio
■ Work by Leon Battista Alberti

Arco d'Augusto ⑤

Created in 27BC in honor of Octavian Augustus, the arch is one of the oldest monuments to survive from Roman times In Istrian stone, it has an arch framed by Corinthian semi-columns supporting a tympanum with richly and elegantly decorated cornices. Not far away is the **Roman Amphitheater**, built under Hadrian in the 2nd century AD, with a brick, oval structure. Surviving parts of this grand edifice, which once had a seating capacity of 12,000, include the two arcades of the outside portico and part of the arena and the cavea (rows of seating).

Museo della Città ⑥

This museum is housed in the former Jesuit convent and school erected between 1746 and 1755. It serves as a point of reference for the history and art of the entire Rimini area and beyond. At present, more than 40 rooms display approximately 1,500 works. In the **archeological section**, the most interesting find from Imperial Roman Rimini (2-3C AD) is a mosaic depicting a **mooring scene in the port**. The inner courtyard-garden contains a **Lapidario** (Roman stone museum) displaying a collection of *inscriptions* dating from the 1st century BC to the 4th century AD. The **Pinacoteca** has a display featuring works from the 11th-20th centuries. This comprises masterpieces by the 14th-century Rimini School, an unusual elaboration on Giotto's teachings, including a fresco showing the **Last Judgement** and a **Crucifix** by Giovanni da Rimini (first half of the 14C). Next come works linked to the Malatesta family, and local 17th-century paintings by Benedetto Coda and his school; 17th-century Emilia-Romagna is represented by works by Guido Cagnacci, Guido Reni, Guercino and Simone Cantarini. See also the series of Flemish tapestries (17C), a collection of pottery and bronzes (14-17C) and numerous architectural fragments and aristocratic coats-of-arms. The last rooms contain still-life works, neo-classical painting and, finally, a collection of 20th-century portraits.

Ponte di Tiberio ⑦

The bridge connects the city to Borgo S. Giuliano and is one of the greatest monuments in Rimini dating from Roman

The Arch of Augustus, one of the earliest surviving monuments of Roman date

times. Work on the bridge was begun under Augustus in 14AD and completed under Tiberius in 21AD. The bridge is built of Istrian stone, is 62m long, and has five arches, the last (northern) arch was removed in 522, but redone to a smaller scale in the 17th century. The piers are built at an angle to the axis of the bridge so as to guide the flow of the water underneath. The whole structure rests on a bed of wooden piles. The decorations on the seaward side of the bridge lend weight to the theory that it was designed as part of the original entrance to the harbor: between the piers are four rectangular blind windows, with vases, pateras and civic crowns carved in relief on the keystones.

Borgo S. Giuliano 8

This is one of the oldest popular districts in the city and one of Fellini's favourite places. Its name derives from the church of the same name, which was part of a Benedictine abbey complex first documented in 816. It is a district of sailors and fishermen, full of atmosphere, with tiny houses and narrow streets, where brightly-colored murals commemorate Fellini and the characters in his films. Viale Matteotti features parts of the ring of defense walls dating from the 15th-16th century.

DAY TRIPS

BELLARIA IGEA MARINA [14 km]

Located at the southern tip of the province of Rimini, Bellaria and Igea Marina are two typical seaside resorts that come administratively under a single municipality. **Bellaria** is one of the liveliest resorts on the Rimini Riviera, with plenty of beaches and excellent facilities, especially for families with children. It hosts the Bellaria Film Festival (first week of June), a major event for independent Italian filmmakers. **Igea Marina** has many avenues bordered with flowers, where it is pleasant to stroll. However, the most popular promenade is through the *Parco del Gelso* (Mulberry Park), in the town center, an enchanting place where pubescent oaks and pines alternate with flowering meadows.

CATTOLICA [20 km]

In the center of **Piazzale I Maggio** is the **Fontana delle Sirene** (Mermaid Fountain), a symbol of the city. This is the heart of the tourist resort of Cattolica. On summer evenings, the piazza with its park and water features become the setting for a show in which the water of various fountains, set on a raised platform, dances to the notes of symphonies and waltzes. The tree-lined *Viale Bovio*, a famous shopping street, leads to Piazza Nettuno, surrounded by lines of trees. From here, Via Mancini is another popular street with holiday-makers and tourists, which leads to *Piazza Mercato*. This is the commercial hub of the town, dominated by the **covered market**. Nearby, the church of **S. Pio V** and the 13th-century church of **S. Apollinare** are worth a visit. The **Museo della Regina***, housed in the *Ospedale dei Pellegrini* (1584), has an interesting collection. The display is divided into two sections: the *archeological section* contains everyday objects from the 1st century BC, and the *marine section*, with models of boats of different periods and an extensive collection of boat-building tools, fishing equipment, ex-votos and nautical charts. The **Parco "Le Navi"*** (see page 118) is worth a visit.

MONTEFIORE CONCA [23 km]

The **Castello Malatestiano** at Montefiore Conca, with its severe geometric lines, rendered even more massive by the lack of crenellations, stands on a high hill and contains some rare examples of **frescoes***. The **town** set on the slopes below it must be one of the most beautiful in Italy, and has been awarded the TCI's "Bandiera Arancione" (Orange Flag). Of medieval origin, it consists in a walled, almost circular center, the streets of which all converge on the castle, and the part of the town outside the walls, which grew up near the main town gate (**Porta Curina**).

REPUBBLICA DI SAN MARINO [26 km]

The Republic of San Marino is regarded as the oldest republic in the world; tradition dates its foundation to the year 301. The urban layout is pleasant and of good quality, and the town has retained its medieval flavor. One of the highlights here is its marvelous views, but there are also charming corners of the town with simple stone houses and hanging gardens, small allotments, steep alleyways and flights of steps, some of which are cut out of the rock, and oddly-shaped squares. The old town is still surrounded by its 16th-century **walls**. The gate of *Porta di S. Francesco* or *Porta del Loco* leads into the town. Immediately beyond it is the church of **S. Francesco**, built from 1361 onwards by master builders from the local area and from Como. In front of the facade is a *porch* dating from

1631. Opposite the church, Via Basilicius leads to the highly animated, busy **Piazzetta del Titano***. Overlooking the square is *Palazzo Pergami Belluzzi*, now the *Museo di Stato*. The museum has archeological and art treasures associated with the history and legends of the Republic of San Marino; it has a section with finds dating from the Neolithic to the Middle Ages, and a *Pinacoteca* with paintings from the 14th-19th centuries, including works by Guercino. Walking down **Contrada Omerelli** from Piazzetta del Titano, you come to the 18th-century Walloon church and the rebuilt *Palazzo Valloni*, which now houses the *state library*, the *government archives* and, since 1989, the University of San Marino. By walking up the same street, you come to **Piazza della Libertà**, which looks out onto the wide expanse of the Montefeltro hills. It is surrounded by the 17th-century *Palazzo Mercuri*, *Palazzo delle Poste* and *Palazzo del Governo* or *Palazzo Pubblico Piazzale Belvedere* commands wonderful views over the valley. Next, as you continue up along **Contrada Omagnano**, after passing the loggia of Casa Gozi, you come to Piazzale Domus Plebis. There, you can see the *Basilica of S. Marino*, begun in 1826 and designed by Antonio Serra. Built on the site of the old parish church, it has a neo-classical facade preceded by a Corinthian hexastyle pronaos.

The Republic of San Marino, traditionally held to be the oldest republic in the world, lies behind the majestic Porta di S. Francesco and is dominated by the daringly located Torre Rocca

The street in front of the basilica is **Contrada della Pieve**, which winds through the oldest part of the town. Daringly sited on a sheer cliff, the **Torre Rocca** or **Torre Guaita** dates from the 11th century and has two sets of walls: the outer wall, crowned with merlons, and strengthened by corner towers, leads into a picturesque *courtyard* of irregular shape; stairs climb up to the top *gate* which leads into the castle proper. From here there are *wonderful views*. Protruding from the walls are the *bell tower* and the old *lookout tower*. From the fortress, a narrow path cut out of the bedrock follows the edge of the precipice for a while (known as '*Passo delle Streghe*' or Witches' Path) and goes beyond the *Mura della Fratta*, to the **second tower**, called **Cesta** or **Fratta**; this houses the *Museo delle Armi Antiche*. By continuing along a paved path through a delightful wood, you come to the **Torre del Montale** which stands alone on the far peak of the hill, surrounded by a thick wood of young oaks. It was probably built at the turn of the 13th century, and rebuilt in 1935.

RICCIONE [11 km]

The 'Green Pearl of the Adriatic' is one of the most famous and popular holiday spots along the Romagna coast. The image of this small town is inextricably linked to the idea of summer holidays, sea and fun, and this notion is reinforced by its numerous restaurants, shops, hotels, bars and night clubs. **Viale Ceccarini*** is the throbbing heart of Riccione, one of the most famous places in the whole Rimini Riviera, with elegant boutiques and other shops, attractive cafés and trendy venues: a veritable cross-section of the 'sweet life' for which the Romagna Riviera is renowned. The **Museo del Territorio*** is housed in the Centro Civico della Pesa and shows how human colonization has evolved in and around Rimini, focusing on the physical transformation of the area from a natural environment to an environment dominated by human intervention. The **Castello degli Agolanti** stands isolated on a hill and is now used for important exhibitions and other events. There are also a number of **theme parks** (see page 118-119).

SANTARCANGELO DI ROMAGNA [10 km]

The layout of the **medieval town**, which is very harmonious architecturally speaking, is well preserved. It has silent little squares, winding streets and picturesque flights of steps with charming views. Here it's worth visiting the **Castello Malatestiano**, a square castle with polygonal towers, and the **MUSAS – Museo Storico Archeologico*** (Archeological Museum).

Castello degli Agolanti (once owned by lords of the *contado* of Riccione), now an exhibition venue

VERUCCHIO [17 km]

The medieval town of Verucchio has many fine historical buildings, such as the **Rocca Malatestiana** and the monastery of **S. Agostino**. This town stands on a very ancient site: between the 9th and 6th century BC, it was one of the most important settlements of the Villanova culture (in fact it has a fine museum, the **Museo Civico Archeologico Villanoviano****). The town has been awarded the TCI's "Bandiera Arancione" (Orange Flag).

VISERBA [4 km]

This old fishing-port is now a popular holiday resort, although it is also known for its spring water which gushes from the *Fonte Sacramora*. The water is supposed to be good for general health and has diuretic properties. The main attraction in this town is its theme park called **Italia in Miniatura**, consisting of 270 scaled-down reproductions of the most famous monuments in Italy and Europe.

HISTORICAL ITINERARIES

PARKS

CHILDREN

BEACHES

DISABLED

BIKING ROUTES

INDUSTRY MUSEUMS

CINEMA

Emilia-Romagna, with its exceptionally rich and diverse natural and cultural wealth, can satisfy practically every possible need in terms of tourism. From the sea to the plain, and from the hills to the mountains, everything comes together to form a delightful mosaic of landscapes where the abundance of parks, reserves and protected areas provide immense scope for walking, hiking or cycling in a beautiful, natural and pristine environment. The coastal stretch, with its wonderful sea and beaches, is for literally everyone to enjoy, with an array of options. There are play areas, entertainment for kids, beach-sports and water sports, with facilities that will meet everyone's needs, no matter what their level of ability is. Emilia-Romagna is a region well worth exploring, where the warm welcome extended by the local people makes visitors feel utterly at home.

Itineraries & special interest

Highlights

- An amazing tour amid Romanesque architecture around Modena
- Four interesting suggestions of parks to visit: a wonderful blend of fun and learning about wildlife
- A vast range of beaches catering for all needs: "technological" beaches, eco-compatible beaches, beaches with libraries, cinemas and discos, not to mention beaches with sports facilities and other entertainment
- The pristine Parco Nazionale dell'Appennino Tosco-Emiliano

Inside

112 **Historical itineraries**
114 **Parks**
118 **Children**
120 **Beaches**
124 **Disabled**
125 **Cinema**
130 **Industry museums**
132 **Biking routes**

ROMANESQUE ARCHITECTURE AROUND MODENA

In the province of Modena, Romanesque architecture is found in three different settings: the city, the plain and the Apennine hills. It is an extraordinary collection of works, built in the 11th and 13th century, which has features in common, sometimes linked to the figure of Matilda of Canossa (1046-1115), promoter of many works. Matilda was the countess of Canossa and played a leading role in the Investiture Conflict between the Emperor and the Pope. When, in 1076, she succeeded her father as state governor, she became an important ally of Pope Gregory VII, determined to confirm the superiority of the spiritual power of the Church over the temporal power of the Emperor. Matilda played a prominent role in relations between the Pope and Emperor Henry IV, his cousin. During the Investiture Conflict, Henry IV had the Pope kidnapped during mass at the basilica of Santa Maria Maggiore in Rome at midnight on Christmas Day in 1075. The Pope was taken to Germany and at this point the intervention of the countess of Canossa became fundamental. Excommunicated by the Pope, Emperor Henry IV passed into history due to his famous humiliation at Canossa. Thanks to the intercession of Matilda, Henry IV was received by the Pope at Canossa castle, but only after he had begged to be allowed to enter after standing barefoot in the snow for three days as penitence. The emperor finally obtained a pardon. In the following years the struggle between Henry IV and the papacy continued and Matilda sealed her devotion to the Church by donating all her possessions to the Papal States. Church architecture in the province of Modena uses a simple form of sculpture influenced by artists from Como, in Lombardy, and the area of Campione, on Lake Lugano. They are mainly basilicas with three naves divided by pillars and terminating with semicircular apses. Small arches, saw-tooth or diamond shaped brick friezes, shelves with figurative anthropomorphic elements, sculpted capitals with weaving and foliage are the main decorative elements.

Modena is one of the principal capitals of Romanesque in the Po Valley. Its cathedral (1099), a masterpiece designed by great artists such as the architect Lanfranco and sculptor Wiligelmo, followed by the Masters of Campione, has been added to the list of UNESCO world heritage sites. Of particular interest are: the main doorway with the Stories of Genesis, a masterpiece by Wiligelmo; Porta dei Principi or Battesimo, decorated with episodes from the life of St Geminianus; Porta Regia; Porta della Comunità, almost a second facade onto Piazza Grande, built by Anselmo da Campione (c.1175); a true gem of medieval sculpture, Porta della Pescheria, with an episode from the Breton cycle of King Arthur with a clear French-Burgundy influence in the archivolt. The ambo and pier by the Masters of Campione are also of great significance. In nearby Nonàntola there is the majestic abbey dedicated to St Sylvester, founded in 752 by the Lombard Anselmo. In the doorway, whose lintel bears the famous inscription documenting the restoration work carried out after 1117, there are some precious low reliefs depicting evangelical tales and events in the history of the abbey. On the south side there is a rare cycle of frescoes dating back to the Romanesque period. Still in Nonàntola there is the parish church of S. Michele. The parish church in Carpi (1184), the remains of which are part of the church of the Sagra, and the church of San Giorgio di Ganaceto, with its lovely, richly sculpted apses, both have features in common. The former has a lunette on its doorway portraying the Crucifixion in different colors and an ambo with the symbols of the evangelists, attributed to the School of Nicolò, who worked on the cathedrals of Ferrara and Verona, while in the church of Ganaceto there is a precious holy-water font designed by the celebrated sculptor of the metope of the Modena Cathedral. The pulpit of the parish church of Quaràntoli, consecrated in 1114, with its symbols of the four evangelists was clearly influenced by Wiligelmo's Modena School. The Romanesque architecture of San Cesario and Sorbara are instead emphatically perpendicular in the Lombard and Nordic fashion. The large abbey of Frassinoro (1071) and the parish

Romanesque architecture

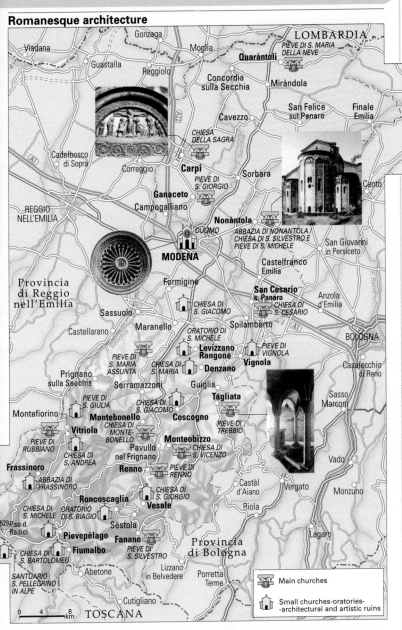

Main churches

Small churches-oratories--architectural and artistic ruins

church of Santa Maria di Rubbiano are the most important examples of architecture close to the province of Reggio. There are lesser works in the churches of Santa Giulia a Monchio, San Andrea a Vitriola, San Michele di Pievepèlago and San Bartolomeo di Fiumalbo. Along the via Giardini, in the central part of Frignano, two other parish churches mark the route: the parish churches of Rocca Santa Maria and

Renno. The eastern part of the province in the foothills is not so prolific, with the relics of the apses of the parish church of Vignola and the church of Denzano, the small chapel of San Michele a Levizzano, the church of San Giacomo a Colombaro and, above all, the parish church of Pieve di Trebbio, an exquisite example of Romanesque architecture which is also said to have been founded by Matilda of Canossa.

NATIONAL PARK TUSCAN-EMILIAN APENNINES

PROVINCES OF LUCCA, MASSA CARRARA, PARMA, REGGIO EMILIA

AREA: 22,300 HECTARES. MOUNTAIN RIDGE BETWEEN EMILIA-ROMAGNA AND TUSCANY WITH STRATIFIED SANDSTONE RELIEFS.

HEADQUARTERS: VIA EMILIA ALL'OSPIZIO 2, REGGIO EMILIA, TEL. 0522434366

WEBSITE:
WWW.PARKS.IT/PARCO.NAZIONALE.APP.TOSCO.EMIL; WWW.APPENNINOPARK.IT

VISITORS' CENTER: PARCO DI BUSANA (REGGIO EMILIA) TEL. 0522891209. OPEN ALL YEAR ROUND FROM MONDAY TO FRIDAY, 9.00 TO 16.00. FROM MARCH TO OCTOBER ALSO SATURDAYS AND SUNDAYS, 9.30 TO 12.30.

ENTRANCE: PASSO DEL CERRETO (COLLAGNA, REGGIO EMILIA). FROM SS 63 ROAD, AULLA-PASSO DEL CERRETO; AULLA HIGHWAY EXIT (A15-A12).

Man's abandonment of the Apennine mountains and the creation of parks and protected areas have favored the return of the wolf, generating small local packs.

Situated on the border between Tuscany and Emilia, Parco dell'Appenino Tosco-Emiliano is one of the most admired Italian parks. The panoramas the visitor can enjoy from the ridge are some of the loveliest in the Apennine hills. From the summit of some of the peaks (Mt Prado 2,054m, Mt Cusna and Alpe di Succiso, both over 2,000m) the eye can see as far as the Po Valley or the Apuan Alps, the Tyrrhenian Sea or the Ligurian Sea, or linger on the woods and meadows, valleys and ridges spread out below which are gentler on the Emilian side and more rugged in Tuscany, towards the Apuan hills. The park combines

different territories such as Alto Appennino Reggiano (Parco del Gigante), Alta Val Parma e Cedra (Parco dei Cento Laghi), Pietra di Bismantova, mentioned by Dante in the Divine Comedy, and the Triassic chalks of Secchia Valley. These jewels on the Emilian side are joined by those on the Tuscan side. Near Mt Vecchio (1,981m) there is a jutting spur which joins the majestic limy massif of Pania di Corfino (1,603m) and the Natural Park of Orecchiella, the southernmost outpost of the Park.

Glacial relicts and splendid beech woods

The geological history of this part of the Apennines has profoundly influenced its flora. High altitude habitats, isolated by the sea of ice which surrounded them, became a shelter for glacial relicts for which the peaks of the park represent the southernmost limit of distribution in Italy.
Mountain crowberry (*Empetrum hermaphroditum*) grows among the blueberries while in these damp habitats it is not rare to find the white cottongrass and the alpine bulrush.
It is often environmental factors which influence the type of vegetation present. In windier areas the moss campion grows next to the dwarf rush while in the more sheltered valleys, where snow stays on the ground for a large part of the year, there are true rarities such as the tiny herb willow, the dwarf cudweed or the alpine catchfly (*Lychnis alpina*).
Descending to lower altitudes, once below the blueberry moors interspersed on the Tuscan side with vast areas of grassland where pinks, gentians and primulas bloom, you see the first signs of the enormous beech woods which reach altitudes of 900 to 1,000m. Favored by the fresh, damp climate, the beech is the dominant tree species, but there is no lack of relict groups of spruce, silver fir and yew.
The so-called royal fir wood of Valle di

The unmistakable square bulk of the Pietra di Bismantova (Rock of Bismantova), which is also mentioned by Dante in the 4th canto of Purgatory, is visible from most of the Apennines in the Reggio area. It is a limestone block which rises an impressive 1,047m

above the plain. It was formed by a process known as "selective erosion" and once lay at the bottom of a sea. Due to the wealth and variety of its environments the rock has an extremely high degree of bio-diversity, which makes it an ideal place for carrying out research and taking pleasant walks to the summit, along a path with lovely views. Its natural fort-like shape has meant it has often been used as a refuge over the years.

Dolo, in upper Apennines in the Reggio-Emilia area, which was once part of the Royal woods of Montagna Reggiana, and which provided the Duchy of Este with precious wood for their building projects and shipyards, is especially important. Crossing the dense beech woods it is not uncommon to see traces of the presence of man, who exploited these woods for centuries before proceeding to reforest them, transforming the copses into forests of tall trees. At higher altitudes these beech woods are joined by sycamores, alpine laburnums and mountain ashes while lower down, where the hills begin, there are chestnut trees and broad-leaved oak woods. Downy oaks and turkey oaks are mixed with hop-hornbeams and a enormous number of other tree and shrub species such as flowering ash, field maple, hazel tree and hawthorn, which encourage a dense undergrowth where the delicate flowers of primulas, violets and dog's-tooth are conspicuous.

Rare species and welcome returns

The medium high altitude and glaciations have also had interesting consequences for the local fauna. One result is the presence of so-called "glacial relicts" such as the snow-vole (*Microtus nivalis*), typical of the primary meadows of the ridges and always quick to vanish down one of the many holes of its intricate subterranean burrows, the common frog and the alpine newt. The reappearance of the wolf is a significant result of the protection a large part of this territory has enjoyed for some time and the scarcity of human settlements. The return of this typical Apennine predator was also encouraged by reintroducing some of it chosen prey such as the roe-deer, the deer, the increasingly numerous wild boar and the mouflon. The latter was successfully introduced in the nineteen-sixties and seventies to the rocks and stony ground of Pania di Corfino, in the Tuscan part of the park, where in more recent times another emblematic species, the golden eagle, whose hunting territory now reaches as far as Pietra di Bismantova (Rock of Bismantova), has begun to nest again.

As long as it's water

All newts need water (water-holes, lakes or springs, with a predilection for stagnant or very still water) in order to breed, lay their eggs and spend the early phase of their lives or the larva stage. In the absence of anything better, the alpine newt (*Tritirus alpestris*) quite often has to be content with the drinking holes of Alpine pastures. These waters, in which the faeces of cattle accumulate, are so murky that it is often almost impossible to make out the colors of the newts, despite the contrast between the bluish-brown of their upper bodies and the bright orange-yellow of their lower bodies.

Mt Cusna (2,121m) has been known since time immemorial as "dead man" or "the giant" due to its peculiar shape when seen from below.

The woods are also home to more common small and medium-sized predators, although these are often hard to see as they are nocturnal creatures such as foxes, polecats, stone martens and weasels. One of the key functions performed by these predators is to keep the resident population of micro-mammals (bank voles, field mice, dormice) under control. The vastness of the wooded areas and variety of habitats are responsible for the abundance of species of sedentary and migrant nesting birds. The passes of the ridge are in fact transitory passages for birds of prey, Ciconiiformes, woodpigeons and thrushes. The blackbird, the long-tailed tit, the blackcap, the treecreeper and the spotted and green woodpecker nest in the beech woods and forests of broad leaved trees while in clearings with hedges and fruit trees you will find the wryneck. Woods with numerous glades make an ideal habitat for the shrike, the woodlark and common birds of prey such as the buzzard and the kestrel or rarer birds like the peregrine falcon, which however tends to nest on rock-faces. The bird population living at other altitudes is also interesting. On stony ground and in meadows in the summer you can see the water pipit, the Alpine accentor, the redstart and the linnet. This mix of habitats and species makes up the park's rich legacy. It is up to the men who will take it over to learn from the experience of their colleagues and make it a center where civilisation, considerable traces of which remain (villages, precious mountain architecture, ancient roads) and nature can harmoniously coexist with benefits for both.

Cepe mushrooms (**Boletus edulis**) grow in the undergrowth of the beech woods.

117

LE NAVI – CATTOLICA AQUARIUM

PIAZZALE DELLE NAZIONI 1/A, CATTOLICA (RIMINI) TEL. 05418371/0541837910

WEB: WWW.LENAVI.IT

OPEN: APRIL TO DECEMBER

OPENING TIMES: FROM APRIL TO MID-JUNE EVERY DAY 9.30 TO 17.30. FROM MID-JUNE TO MID-SEPTEMBER EVERY DAY 10.00 TO 22.30. FROM MID-SEPTEMBER TO 1 OCTOBER EVERY DAY 9.30 TO 17.30. FROM OCTOBER TO DECEMBER SUNDAY AND HOLIDAYS 9.30 TO 17.30.

ADMISSION: FULL-PRICE € 15, REDUCED (UNDER 12, OVER 65, PARTIALLY DISABLED PEOPLE AND PEOPLE ACCOMPANYING DISABLED PEOPLE) € 11. FREE ENTRACE: CHILDREN LESS THAN 1 M TALL AND DISABLED PEOPLE.

GETTING THERE

BY CAR: A14 HIGHWAY, EXIT CATTOLICA, ABOUT 4 KM FROM THE HIGHWAY ON THE SEAFRONT.

BY TRAIN: CATTOLICA STATION AND BUS NO. 125 STOP 71

Le Navi is a park-aquarium dedicated to environmental education, measuring over 110,000m² and containing vast green spaces. Its attractions include: the deep sea elevator which descends virtually to 3,200 m beneath the sea, the undersea laboratories of Geopolis, dedicated to the formation of the earth, the dynamic Planet Hall, which houses tanks with living fossils. A 3D film reveals the secrets of ocean creatures, introducing you to the show tanks of Acquapolis, the kingdom of marine flora and fauna. The park houses over 3,000 examples of 400 different species of Mediterranean and tropical fish and invertebrates. The park's main attractions are: the large shark tank and the jelly-fish tanks. Finally there is the Touch tank where you can stroke stingrays, skate and eagle-rays.

AQUAFAN

VIA ASCOLI PICENO 6, RICCIONE (RIMINI) TEL. 05414271/0541603050

WEB: WWW.AQUAFAN.IT

OPEN: JUNE TO MID-SEPTEMBER

OPENING TIMES: 10-18.30; SOMETIMES OPEN IN THE EVENINGS

ADMISSION: FULL-PRICE € 21, REDUCED (AGE 6-11 AND OVER 65) € 14; FREE ENTRANCE: CHILDREN UP TO 5 YEARS OLD

GETTING THERE

BY CAR: A14 HIGHWAY, EXIT RICCIONE

BY TRAIN: RICCIONE OR RIMINI STATION

Aquafan is one of the legendary temples of amusement on the coast of Romagna and has become well-known not just as an aquatic park but also as a venue for nightly musical entertainment. It covers 150,00 m² and the indoor area alone measures approximately 11,500m².
The park can be reached by public transport from Rimini, Riccione, Cattolica and Cesenatico. Aquafan has thrilling water chutes and other more sedate forms of entertainment,

such as the lazy river which winds through a reproduction of a tropical atoll, the large wave pool and the Jacuzzis. The setting of Baby Antarctic beach is also picturesque. It is a 800m² swimming pool set at the South Pole. Moreover, children can enjoy the Fairytale Hill where many fairy-tales are told, the Dance with the Puppets disco and the Bigbaboland toy theatre, where amusing shows are staged.

MIRABILANDIA

Adriatica road km 162, Savio
(Ravenna), Tel. 0544561156

WEB: WWW.MIRABILANDIA.IT

OPEN: mid-April to mid-September, Until
mid-October, only Saturday and Sunday

OPENING TIMES: 10.00-18.00; July-August
also 10.00-23.00.

ADMISSION: Full-price € 23.50,
reduced (children up to 1.50 m tall and
up to 12 years old) € 18; Free entrance:
children up to 1 m tall, second
consecutive day, day of birthday.
Disabled access.

GETTING THERE

BY CAR: A14 highway, exit Cesena Nord,
E45 towards Ravenna, exit Mirabilandia

BY TRAIN: Lido di Savio-Lido di Classe
station, free bus to the park

Mirabilandia stands out from other
Italian and European amusement
parks. It covers approximately 85
hectares (30 hectares of actual park)
and is subdivided into 7 themed
areas spread around a lake: Pirate
Cove, the pre-Columbian city of Sian
Ka'An, Adventureland, Bimbopoli (an
area of 10,000m² built using non-toxic
materials and according to stringent
safety criteria), the Dolce Vita studios,
the Caribbean beach of Mirabilandia
and finally Motorworld, the
area dedicated to engines.
Each area offers stunning and thrilling
rides, with something for everyone.
You will find performances, parades
and entertainment with stuntmen
and clowns everywhere.

PARCO OLTREMARE

Via Ascoli Piceno 6, Riccione (Rimini)
Tel. 05414271/0541603050

WEB: WWW.OLTREMARE.ORG

OPEN: April-November

OPENING TIMES: April 10.00-18.00; May-
June 10.00-18.30; July-August 10.00-12.00;
September 10.00-18.30; October-
November (only Sunday) 10.00-18.00

ADMISSION: Full-price € 21, reduced (aged
6-11 and over 65) € 17; Free entrance:
children up to 5 years old

Disabled access.

GETTING THERE

BY CAR: A14 highway, exit Riccione

BY TRAIN: Riccione station

This park covers 110,000m² and was
created with the intention of promoting
the conservation of the environmental
heritage of the Adriatic coasts. The park
is divided into themed itineraries. You
begin with the formation of the cosmos
and the earth and then proceed to
Darwin's garden of evolution, a
fascinating walk between iguanas and
crocodiles with sound and visual effects,
to reach the Po Delta, through marshy
waters populated with eels, reptiles,
amphibians and numerous birds. Don't
miss the nature trails through habitats
which are typical of the area. Other park
attractions are the seahorse aquariums,
the dolphin lagoon (9,000m²) and the
animal farm, where you may encounter
birds of prey, predators and farmyard
animals. In the space dedicated to
technology, life-sized reproductions of
whales, sharks and other Mediterranean
creatures complete the experience. The
park is well served by public transport
from Riccione, Rimini, Cattolica, Cervia
and Cesenatico.

With its 120km of coastline Emilia-Romagna is an ideal destination for beach-lovers. The resorts on the shores of Romagna were among the first to have water purificatic plants and all those infrastructures required for making a stay at the beach more comfortable and fun. Despite the pressure exerted on them by the number of tourist the coasts still offer precious natural areas such as the lagoons and reclaimed land Comacchio or the pinewood of Ravenna, representative of the typical coastal vegetation. The low-lying, flat and sandy Romagna coast lends itself to tourism providing amenities and facilities which satisfy the demands of all age groups.

Lido di Volano

(Province of Ferrara). This is in one of the most picturesque spots on the Adriatic coast, at the south-east end of Mesola wood, between Emilia-Romagna and Veneto. Lido di Volano is a precious natural oasis with its characteristic gentle, sandy beach, its system of dykes, its many saltwater inlets, islands and Mediterranean vegetation. It can be reached from Ferrara, by heading east and taking the Via Romea and then continuing for about 18km until you find the sign for the beach. Once you have arrived, it is worth continuing to the lake called Taglio della Falce, a true gem. Don't forget the pinewood of Volano and the Bertuzzi Valley which stretches for about 2,000 hectares, with its rich fauna of nesting birds, such as the dwarf heron, the stilt-plover and the purple heron.

Ancona di Bellocchio Beach

(Province of Ferrara) Over 3km of public beach north of the mouth of the Reno River, in the park of the Po Delta, lying between the territories of Ferrara and Ravenna. The beach, a favorite of nudists, is surrounded by a solid dune belt and entrance is from the foreshore of Lido di Spina. Behind it you will find Ancona di Bellocchio and Lake Spina, different biotopes in a precious wetland. Both zones, which have large bird populations can only be observed from the outside.

Marina Romea Beach

(Province of Ravenna) The beach stretche for 2km between the southern mouth of the Lamone and the start of the Porto Corsini coast. In the pinewood undergrowth to the rear, a state nature reserve crossed by 9 narrow roads suitable for vehicles and 2 footpaths, you may find orchids. Behind the built-up area there are some pinewood relicts and the start of the Prato Barenicolo which penetrates into the Piallassa della Baiona an important wetland and a European Union protected site, with important vegetation found in harsh environments such as saltwater plants, and various species of heron, the rare ferruginous duck, pink flamingos, spoonbills and avocets. There is an observation tower on the edge of the Piallassa.

A beautiful sandy beach on the Riviera

orto Corsini Beach

(Province of Ravenna) A southern extension of Marina Romea beach, this public beach (400m long and 70-80m wide) has a lovely pinewood to the rear with interesting tree species and undergrowth. The dune between the shore and the pinewood is part of the perimeter of the Parco Regionale del Delta del Po and is 100-120m wide in parts. The protected dune belt is accessible on foot from the north and south and by a footpath through the wood.

x Colonia CRI Beach

(Province of Ravenna) This stretch of public beach, which is about 450m long, is found in the municipality of Marina di Ravenna and is of extreme naturalistic interest due to its dunes which reach heights of 2-3m and are covered in dense vegetation. There are various points of access, both opposite the former CRI (Italian Red Cross) summer camp and near the adjacent private beach. Along the stretch of public beach the sandy shore is 70-80m wide on average. Along the seashore, the pinewood is 70-80m wide. The vegetation consists mainly of tamarisks with some fine examples of spurge laurels.

x Colonia Varese Beach and Park

(Province of Ravenna) In Milano Marittima holidays center on two things - the beach and the pinewood - and there are still some areas that have not been developed. This former summer camp is a wonderful example of 1930s architecture. The surrounding park and beach have been left to grow wild. In the dunes opposite, you can find dropwort, wormwood, sea rocket, soldanella, sea fennel, salwort, common evening primrose and a strong-smelling grass: the cocklebur, once found on all the dunes along the coast of Cervia. Conservation has enabled this area to be restored to its former glory.

Bassona Beach

(Province of Ravenna) Bassona beach, at Fosso Ghiaia, between Ravenna and Cervia, is part of the Riserva Naturale della Foce del Bevano and protected to the rear by a large pinewood. Just a few metres from the sandy shore, there is a 1km-long dune belt, partly shaded by pine trees.

There are no facilities or organised entertainment. To reach the area follow the gravel road which, after the SS 16 road at Fosso Ghiaia, turns east towards the mouth of the Bevano. Continue to the end, following the river, and you come to the sea. To get there from the north, follow the signs for Lido di Dante.

Pinarella di Cervia Beach

(Province of Ravenna) The beach stretches for about 2,600m with a lovely pinewood to the rear with fossil dunes. From the naturalistic point of view we recommend the salt marshes of Cervia, beyond the SS 16 road. The salt marshes, in the heart of the southern part of the Parco del Delta del Po are European Union conservation sites and home to numerous and important bird species such as herons, pink flamingos and spoonbills.

The canal through the salt marshes in Cervia

Cesenatico Public Beach

(Province of Forlì-Cesena) In the home of beach resorts, discos, water parks and beach hotels, you can still find a few grains of sand which are unspoilt and some short stretches of semi-natural coast. In Cesenatico for example there is about 1km of public beach where you can treat yourself to a few hours of leisure, much better if it is in low season. Avoid July and August when the shore is crowded with kids on organised holidays. Instead, at the end of May or the beginning of June or September the area is quiet and pleasant with its wide sandy beach and shallow waters. To reach the beach exit the A14 highway at Cesena Sud and then follow the signs.

Beach life

Since the first seaside resorts dating back to 1843, principally conceived to offer spa treatments exploiting the thalasso-therapeutic properties of the Adriatic Sea, the Rimini Riviera has been a testing ground for every new idea that has been dreamt up to improve the quality of "beach life". Such attention, with the intent to offer tourists the best possible welcome, is the result of a veritable philosophy of life, which sees in hospitality and entertainment two of the cornerstones on which to base a professional approach brimful of surprises.

The highest concentration of hotels in the world. The highest number of workers in the hotel industry per number of inhabitants. The city most visited by Italian tourists. These impressive figures are partly the result of 40km of fine sandy beach, which in some places reaches a width of 200m. This natural heritage has produced a fair number of public beaches as well as 700 bathing resorts. A paradise of entertainment and efficiency, a place to relax where the facilities on offer cleverly combine tradition and technology.

And so here we have "technological" beaches alongside the inevitable sun loungers and parasols. In some resorts the tourist can use high tech sun loungers which unfold by remote control, king sized sun loungers and sun loungers with panels that protect you from ultraviolet rays, but also sun loungers and deckchairs equipped with panels that intensify your tan. For complete relaxation there are comfortable massage armchairs with adjustable vibration, perhaps equipped with fans and gentle jets of mist, a refreshing device for resisting the heat without foregoing a tan.

The marriage of technology and beach is seen in the increasingly numerous internet points, in web-cams and in text message services sent to yachtsmen to warn them of changing weather conditions or sudden squalls. Here we have environmentally friendly beach resorts where technology goes hand in hand with nature. In recent years ad hoc resorts have sprung up. Their plans for the environment, beginning with recycling waste, aim to make the impact on the environment of the huge mass of tourists who crowd the beaches less burdensome. The resorts, built from environmentally friendly materials, are equipped with technologies for saving water and energy as well as sound proof structures for reducing noise pollution.

As well as protecting nature, the novelty of beaches aimed at improving well-being has been successfully launched in recent years. On the seashore you can get into physical and spiritual shape through art, gymnastics, dance, song, martial arts and health food. There is also space for books. For people who love reading, be it magazines or novels, there are resorts with small libraries. Libraries and toy libraries. As ever a great deal of attention is given to families with small children. Every bathing resort has a play area for kids that is often fenced off, with swings, roundabouts and inflatable toys. Some have beach huts with facilities for warming babies' bottles and nappy changing. On many beaches professional entertainers entertain the whole family with mini Olympics and all kinds of games and workshops where you can make kites and puppets. If the family also has a pet there are specially

one of the legs of the Italian championships). You can also play bowls, Frisbee and basketball. There are many open air gyms for body building enthusiasts. Not to mention pleasure-boating and pedalo-rides, surfing, canoeing or jet-skiing. The Riviera is a veritable breeding ground of new fashions in sports and beach games. And so we have cheecoting (dear old marbles; the first championship on giant tracks made by a sand artist was held in Rimini), tchoukball (a combination of handball and Basque pelota), beach polo, beach boxing (where qualified instructors reveal the secrets of boxing and kick boxing), kite surf (the board is pulled along by the kite which flies over the waves). After so much effort why not treat yourself to something naughty but nice? There are lifeguards who regularly bring down local specialities for you to try on the sea shore. And beach life doesn't stop when the sun goes down. Dusk makes the atmosphere even more pleasant and picturesque. Numerous bathing resorts become the ideal spot for happy hours, aperitifs, dinners on the beach, or open air cinema. And the latest craze is dancing barefoot on the sand, turning the beach into an open air disco.

equipped areas (beaches are, generally speaking, strictly off limits to animals). As well as being a great place for kids (there are numerous swimming, windsurf and canoe lessons designed for little ones) the beach is the ideal setting for all sports enthusiasts. Everywhere beaches are equipped for beach tennis (the old jumbo-sized rackets), and often have beach soccer and beach volleyball courts now that Olympic sports are very much in vogue in Rimini (the city hosts

HISTORICAL CENTER OF BOLOGNA AND FERRARA

NATIONAL PARK OF THE FORESTS OF CASENTINA, MONTE FALTERONE AND CAMPIGNA

CENTRO RISORSE HANDICAP DEL COMUNE DI BOLOGNA (RESOURCES IN BOLOGNA FOR DISABLED PEOPLE), TEL. 051204353
WWW.HANDYBO.IT

IAT CASTELLO ESTENSE FERRARA
TEL. 0532209370 WWW.FERRARAINFO.COM

GETTING THERE

BY CAR: ATC (BOLOGNA PUBLIC TRANSPORT)
TEL. 051290290, WWW.ATC.BO.IT

COTABO - BOLOGNA TAXI COOPERATIVE
TEL. 051372727, WWW.COTABO.IT

BY TRAIN: BOLOGNA STATION

VISITOR CENTER LA FAUNA, VIA ROMA 34, PREMILCUORE (FORLÌ-CESENA)
TEL. 0543956540
WWW.PARCOFORESTECASENTINESI.IT

OPEN MAY TO SEPTEMBER

GETTING THERE

BY CAR: A14 HIGHWAY, FORLÌ EXIT THEN THE SS 310 ROAD TO PREMILCUORE

BY TRAIN: FORLÌ STATION

Bologna boasts a historical center which is wheelchair-friendly thanks to the work which has been carried out there and the capacity of the Bologna disabled to provide reliable information. In Piazza Maggiore you can visit the Basilica of S. Petronio. The main entrance is not fit for use and you have to enter from Piazza Galvani. Inside the floor is on one level. At the entrance of Palazzo Comunale you can take a lift which is suitable for wheelchairs. Toilet facilities are on the ground floor. Detailed information about wheelchair accessibility of Bologna's museums, churches and monuments is contained in the publication Guida a una Bologna accessibile, which can be ordered from Bologna City Council.
Ferrara is "Bicycle City". Its high degree of wheelchair accessibility is partly due to this. In 2001 it was awarded a prize by the organisation of the associations of German disabled persons for being the best holiday destination in Europe. The Centro Storico car park, near Piazzale Kennedy (8 reserved spaces) is next to the Mobility Center, where you can buy the Mobility Card which entitles you to hire, though you must book in advance, electric scooters, (electrical or manual) wheelchairs and strollers, free entry to the Municipal Museums and discounts in restaurants and hotels which have a special agreement. On the city map, which is free to all visitors, you will find information regarding wheelchair access to buildings, museums, monuments and churches. This information can also be found on the Council's website.

Those sections of the park which are wheelchair accessible are the result of listening carefully to the needs of visitors with disabilities. The park, which was established in 1993, covers an area belonging to the Tuscan and Romagna Apennines which has dense forests which are some of the best preserved in Europe. This ancient park, centred on the forest of Casentina with its beeches and silver firs, is characterised by a wealth of flora and fauna. It includes the Riserva Naturale di Sasso Fratino, the first in Italy (1959), the Riserva Naturale di Pietra and other bio-energetic reserves, run by the Foresters Corps. Numerous trails criss-cross the woods. The 11 visitors' centers are all wheelchair-friendly, except that of S. Benedetto (Forlì-Cesena).

Vitality and black humor: two faces, one soul

The triangle comprising the Po, the Adriatic and the Apennines has, since the dawn of moving pictures, been home to numerous famous directors, such as Michelangelo Antonioni, Federico Fellini, Pier Paolo Pasolini, Pupi Avati and Bernardo Bertolucci. Ferrara has also been a part of this trend, although it has often remained a little in the background. The local character, full of exuberant vitality, ironic verve and taste for rebellion, is found in the poetics of every one of them and Avati even makes these traits his distinguishing feature. Ferrara, whose best known movie-maker is Antonioni, instead gives an overriding sense of sadness, fear and death, with silences and suspicion being defining features. After the heyday of cinema, a more reflective and brooding side of cinematographers started to become evident. This has now become the dominant force, imbued with a melancholic sense of memory and critical reappraisal of the past.

Parma and the Po, on the trail of Bertolucci

Parma claims it is independent, and not just intellectually so. It is a small capital, a self-contained town where the working class soul and the bourgeois town live side by side, observing each other and asking each other questions. Parma was also used as a location for some films by Bernardo Bertolucci, the famous director whose film The Last Emperor, won nine Oscars in 1987.The contrasts between bourgeois spirit and working class soul center on the figure of Fabrizio in Before the Revolution (1964). Locations included Fidenza, Rocca di Fontanellato and the town square. Another setting was the Po, because "you always carry the Po within you". Bernardo Bertolucci returned to Parma fifteen years later with Luna (1979) using the same locations for the wanderings of soprano Caterina Silveri (Jill Clayburgh), accompanied by her son Joe (Matthew Barry). She wants to wean him off heroin but her protective love is transformed into something physical. The film embraces the passage to the north-east of the city and then immerses itself in a Verdi landscape: Casa Verdi in Roncole, the farm, the trattoria La Buca di Zibello, the level crossing between Sant'Agata and Gramignazzo. The same locations where 1900 was filmed three years earlier. 1900 is an epic film in which characters are emotionally linked to places. Alfredo Berlighieri (Robert De Niro) and Olmo Dalcò (Gérad Depardieu) are born on the same day in 1900 on the farm called Le Piacentine at Roncole Verdi, a corner of the countryside near Parma which becomes the setting for the monumental saga of 1900. A social tapestry with an extraordinary reach in which the separate fates of the two protagonists are mixed up with the historical destinies of the class they belong to: the great landowners and the agricultural laborers who work the land. On the farm Le Piacentine at Roncole Verdi, with its beautiful traditional

architecture, you can still hear the echoes of the voices of the farm laborers and landowners in an epic marked by strong symbolism and contrasts. Actors include Burt Lancaster (Alfredo Berlighieri), Sterling Hayden (Leo Dalcò), Robert De Niro and Gérard Depardieu. The village, the Renaissance Palazzo del Comune and the neo-Gothic towers of the Rocca also played an important part in the work of cinematographer Vittorio Storaro.

Bologna and the cinema

One angle is used again and again in many films about Bologna. It is the roofs. The city seen from above, with the towers in the background, is a classic image. But entering the streets the eye is bewildered by the multitude of perspectives. Bologna, the birthplace of Pier Paolo Pasolini, is in at least three of his films. Some interviews on the relationship Italians have with sex in Assembly of Love (1964) were filmed using the Dall'Ara municipal stadium as a backdrop. The portico of the church of the Servi and Piazza Maggiore provide settings for Oedipus Rex (1967), a psychoanalytical transposition of Sophocles's famous tragedy. The facade and gardens of Villa Aldini were the setting for Salò or the 120 Days of Sodomy (1975), Pasolini's last film. Gabriele Salvatores also, who won an Oscar for Mediterraneo (1990), uses Bologna as a backdrop for his noir Quo Vadis, baby? (2005). Private investigator Giorgia Cantini (Angela Baraldi), dealing with the most difficult and dangerous investigation of her career, involving the secrets and dramas of her own family, wanders restlessly through the porticoes of the old city center. But Bologna, cinematographically speaking, is, above all, the city of Pupi Avati who uses it as a setting for: Blood Relations (1968), a film about a dwarf believed to be able to perform miracles; Revenge of the Dead (1983), a graveyard horror film with Gabriele Lavia; The Three of Us (1984), on the sexual awakenings of the fourteen year old Mozart on a mission

to Bologna; Impiegati (1984), bitter portrait of office life; The Story of Boys and Girls (1989), an engagement party celebrating the engagement of two young people from different social backgrounds, inspired by the director's own parents; Declarations of Love (1994), a chronicle of a love lasting from 1948 to today...Avati incessantly returns to the old city center. In the film The Heart is Elsewhere (2003) he tells of the delicate and impossible love of the naive Nello Baiocchi (Neri Marcoré) for the young blind woman Angela (Vanessa Incontrada). The story begins at Lyceum Galvani (a recurring location for Pupi Avati) and crosses historical Bologna taking in the church of S. Francesco, the towers, Piazza Santo Stefano, the tombs of the commentators in Piazza S. Domencio and Giardini Margherita. Avati proposes a trip into the countryside up in the Apennines in a slightly dreamlike film which tells how a whole class discovers what it is liketo fall in love. This is A School Outing (1983) which heads south into the hills taking in Vergato, Porretta Terme, the chestnut woods, the walls and keep of Castel di Casio. The route through the countryside is the road which takes you from Sasso Marconi towards Pistoia.

THE "SMALL WORLD" OF GIOVANNI GUARESCHI

That "ugly slice of land between the Po and the Apennines" is the "small world", circumscribed by a church, a school, a few farmhouses "drowning in the middle of maize and hemp", the tavern and the inevitable Casa del Popolo. This is the setting for the uneasy cohabitation of Don Camillo (Father Camillo), the short-tempered parish priest, and Peppone, the communist mayor hostile to the church, created by the pen of Guareschi. The two characters represent the Bassa area and more generally post-war Italy, a provincial Italy divided by ideologies but united by "good sense and practical matters". The protagonists often scuffle but, when in need, help each other out for the common good. The film version, set in Brescello, became a long and successful series. Archivio Guareschi, owned by his heirs, was declared by the Ministry for Cultural Heritage to be "of considerable historical interest" and contains almost 200,000 documents. The study center of the same name makes paper and electronic documentary material available to students and specialists and is a primary source of interest for the political, social and cultural history of contemporary Italy.

Ferrara and the Po Delta

Vittorio De Sica, actor and director, winner of four Oscars for best foreign film for Shoeshine (1946), The Bicycle Thief (1948), Yesterday, Today and Tomorrow (1963),and The Garden of the Finzi Continis (1970), and an Oscar for lifetime achievement. WithThe Garden of the Finzi Continis he enters the Jewish community of Ferrara, where youngsters are facing the tragedy of the racial laws. In this film, starring Dominique Sanda, Fabio Testi, Romolo Valli, Lino Capolicchio and Helmut Berger, the Ferrara of the years between 1938 and 1943 is reconstructed with a meticulousness which resembles oil painting. The lean style of the golden age is just a memory and a climate of forced decadence impregnates the streets, the squares and the villas of the city, populated by rich and fatuous youth, still ignorant of the catastrophe which is about to blow away their golden nests.

Distinguished director Michelangelo Antonioni, awarded an Oscar for lifetime achievement in 1995 sets many of his films outside the city limits, towards the Po Delta and the Adriatic. "It was in '43...on the banks of the Po. I was

UN FILM DI **VITTORIO DE SICA**

IL **GIARDINO**
DEI
FINZI CONTINI

making my first documentary. The Po di Volano belongs to the landscape of my childhood, the Po di Goro belongs to my youth" Antonioni recalls in 1967. "That landscape which until then had been a landscape made up of still and solitary things: the muddy water full of eddies, the lines of poplar trees which fade into the fog, the white island in the middle of the river at Pontelagoscuro which split the current in two. That landscape moved, filled with people and came to life".The director initially concentrated on the river. His documentary debut, People of the Po River (1947) is filmed on the barges and in the shacks of the poor, "beleaguered by the freshwater of the river and the bitter sea water". The Po Delta, leaden, stark and foggy, reflects the state of mind of factory worker Aldo (Steve Cochran) who struggles with anxiety and unhappiness in The Cry (1957), probably the masterpiece of Antonioni's early career. The sorrowful Po Valley pilgrimage also takes in Comacchio, Bondeno and Ravenna, landscapes which are first rural and then industrial and which, with their monotonous imperturbability, emphasize the irreversible crisis into which the protagonist is plunged. In the Italy of the late fifties the film was heavily criticised: the idea that a working

STEVE COCHRAN in

IL GRIDO

UN FILM DI
MICHELANGELO **ANTONIONI**

class man could conceive of suicide, considered to be the prerogative of a certain type of bored bourgeoisie, was held to be unacceptable and offensive. In the film river banks and fog are symbols of the distress felt by Aldo (Steve Cochran), abandoned by Irma (Alida Valli). Aldo runs away with his small daughter, who in the end will be returned to her mother, and aimlessly wanders along the roads between Comacchio and Bondeno. He looks up his ex girlfriend Elvia (Betsy Blair), finds some solace for his loneliness in Cervia with Virginia (Dorian Gray), who lives with her elderly father who is then taken to a hospital in Ravenna, and runs a petrol station. In Antonioni's cinema Ravenna also has the acid colors of The Red Desert, which won the Leone d'Oro at the Venice Film Festival in 1964. In this case it is Giuliana (Monica Vitti) who is a depressed and frustrated wife whose affair with Corrado (Richard Harris) does little to console her. The setting is industrial bourgeoisie. In this alienated world of refineries, we hear dialogues of a banality which verge on cynicism, evidence of the void of thought and feeling in which the bourgeoisie flounder: "The discharges of all these factories have to end up somewhere..." "He was complaining because the eel tasted of petrol..." The movie was filmed on the SS 67 road, in the port of Ravenna, in former Sarom shipyards in Marina di Ravenna, the pinewood of San Vitale, and the huts and river banks of Porto Corsini. It is worth tracing this route to see the enchanting beauty of the pinewood. Pupi Avati filmed Graduation Party (1985) at Codigoro and the lidos. Once again this film explores memory and nostalgia, evoking a student party in the 1950s.

Somewhere between the Po and Marina di Ravenna, Pupi Avati made the shocking horror film The House with Laughing Windows (1976), filmed in Via Cappuccini and in the old city center of Tre Ponti, at Lido degli Estensi, at Casa Parmeggiani at Cento and at the Porto Tolle ferry. The film is about the disturbing finds of a restorer (Lino Capolicchio) made while working on a fresco of St Sebastian painted by a mysterious and cursed local artist.

Fellini's places

Looking at the streets of Rimini through Fellini's eyes (1920-1993) transforms real places into visions of places half-recalled. In this way, Piazza Cavour and Piazza Tre Martiri become the piazza in Amarcord (1974, winner of the Oscar for best foreign film), where public and social life converge, under porticoes and in buildings, in shops and on benches. However, it is also the place where I Vitelloni (1953) are seen loafing around.

Rarely in movie history has a film connoted a place with such sociological accuracy and with such evocative power as I Vitelloni did with Rimini and the Romagna Riviera. The idleness of the five protagonists, the repetitiveness and the self-referential nature of provincial life, the schemes dreamed up in the bar without the slightest desire to put them into practice are at one with the streets, the piazzas, the desolate beaches and the rough sea of the coast out of season. Never had Rimini, stripped of its seaside resort clichés and at times dreamlike appearance, seemed so grey.

And yet, just as Fellini tainted the elegy of provincial life with his critical and bitter realism, he made it immortal in the collective imagination, aided by the extraordinary performances of his leading actors.

along Corso Augusto, a short distance from Piazza Cavour, looms the Fulgor cinema, portrayed in Amarcord, as a place of dreams and desires. It is an image which belongs to a bygone era. Cross the Ponte di Tiberio bridge and continue as far as the ancient hamlet of S. Giuliano, which seems secluded from the chaos of the rest of the city. Here you will find Gradisca, Volpina, Saraghina, Ronald Coleman, Don

Balosa, Pataca, the crazy uncle, Titta, the lady tobacconist, Mastroianni and Ekberg, the characters and the actors from Fellini's best-known films, reproduced on the walls of the houses. Leaving the hamlet you reach Marina Centro and the Grand Hotel, which in Amarcord was the symbol of unattainable, exotic, prohibited worldliness.

The music of its orchestra accompanies you as far as the wharf, the winter haunt of I Vitelloni and the setting for the stunts of Scureza, the motorcyclist in Amarcord. And then the beach, where the mysteries of sex are revealed. Here women's bodies are glimpsed for the first time, spied on in secret while they strip off, in City of Women (1979); here young lads look for the wild sensuality of Saraghina with a mixture of excitement and fear, in 8¹/₂. Three years after Fellini created his most famous work, La Dolce Vita, he made 8¹/₂, another surreal and visually outstanding masterpiece, adding even more autobiographical elements, starting with the setting. The esplanade of Rimini, the coast between Cesena and Savignano and his parents' home at Gambettola (a village of less than 10,000 people not far from Cesena) are the haunts of Fellini's childhood and youth, destined to remain the landscape of his soul even after he moved to the Italian capital just before the outbreak of the World War II.

The existential, sentimental and professional crisis of Marcello Mastroianni, Fellini's faithful alter ego, mirrors the growth of an artist in search of new means of expression and the sense of life. Symbolism and metaphor are the vehicles he uses to go to the heart of people and absolute themes such as love, art and death. The end, with the leading characters reunited on the film set dancing to the tune of Nino Rota's circus march, has entered the annals of cinema history. The film was awarded two Oscars in 1964: best foreign film and best costumes (Pietro Gherardi).

Finally, the vast ocean where the marvellous transatlantic liner Rex materialises in front of a crowd of incredulous, enchanted local people: the chance of a dream, a faraway life overseas (Amarcord). All with that down-to-earth hospitality which is part of the people of Rimini and sojourns there. "... I left Rimini in '37. I returned in '46. I came to a sea of ruined houses. There was nothing left. The only thing to emerge from the rubble was the dialect, the familiar cadence, a Siren's call: Duilio, Severino! Those strange, curious names... I was struck by the industriousness of the people, holed up in wooden shacks, who were already talking about building hotels, hotels, hotels, this desire to build houses". You might pay homage to the great maestro, recognised in 1993 with an Oscar for lifetime achievement, in addition to two other Oscars for best foreign film for The Road (1954) and Nights of Cabiria (1957), in the Municipal Cemetery, at the monumental tomb designed by Arnaldo Pomodoro.

The quotations used above are from Federico Fellini's La Mia Rimini 2003 (translated into English as My Rimini).

DUCATI MUSEUM

GENERAL INFORMATION
Via Cavalieri Ducati 3, Bologna
Tel. 0516413343 www.ducati.com
HOW TO GET THERE
Bologna beltway, exit at Borgo Panigale
OPENING HOURS
Open Mondays to Fridays: guided tours include the production plant (by prior arrangement), 11.00 and 16.00; Saturdays, 9.30-13.00; closed Sundays and holidays. No entrance fee.

How the museum was founded
Inaugurated in 1998 to symbolically ratify the transfer of ownership of Ducati from the Cagiva group to the American Texas Pacific Group in 1996, the museum explores the company's glorious manufacturing past, illustrating some of its social and cultural links with Bologna and the surrounding area from 1926 on.

What it contains
The museum contains approximately thirty historical and present-day Ducati racing bikes, an exhibition of pre-motor-racing artefacts, advertising brochures, archive pictures, historical videos, racing outfits which belonged to Ducati pilots, technical drawings exhibited in the large central hall and in six themed rooms, and an auditorium.

Aims
Intended to be an important marketing and public relations tool for the company, the museum's purpose is to showcase and spread the story of Ducati. It was conceived to be flexible and practical (it has a conference room with state-of-the art technology), incorporating all the features of a proper modern museum and recognised as such by the European Museum Forum in 2000. The exhibition, centring on the competitive history of Ducati, which has always run parallel to the manufacturing side, tells of the victories of the "Borgo Panigale reds" using motorbikes, videos, objects and images. The museum was conceived to be a dynamic instrument, with a "light" structure so that the motorbikes and exhibits could be transported overseas to spread the "Ducati legend" world-wide.

Activity
The Ducati Museum organises numerous activities in academic environments and at Expos and conferences in Italy and abroad. It organises talks at Italian and overseas universities on the history of Ducati and its technological evolution and takes part in the most important international motor shows. These initiatives are flanked by the restoration of vintage vehicles – which are then exhibited –, calling on the talents of former racing team mechanics. A school for motorcycle restorers is in the pipeline. Internally, the museum provides a back-up for all sectors of the company which require historical information, pictures and materials. Externally, through telephone and internet contacts, it provides useful information for any enthusiast who wishes to know more about their motorcycle or the history of the company. The museum's historical archive is continually being added to as the history of Ducati is researched with the aim of salvaging and exploring the company's heritage.

FERRARI GALLERY

GENERAL INFORMATION
Via Dino Ferrari 43, Maranello (Modena) Tel. 0536949713, §
www.ferrariworld.com
HOW TO GET THERE
A1 Milan-Bologna highway, Modena Nord exit, then follow the signs for Maranello
OPENING HOURS
Open every day, 9.30-18.00. Entrance fee.

GALLERIA FERRARI

How the museum was established

Galleria Ferrari, inaugurated in February 1990 and recently extended, is housed in a modern and functional building. The organisation of the exhibition space mirrors the company spirit: to make progress, improve oneself and deal with new challenges, conscious that the best vehicle is yet to be built, as Enzo Ferrari maintained.

What it contains

Galleria Ferrari is divided into various rooms, designed for exhibiting historical automobiles, Formula 1 single-seaters and modern sports-cars, innovative technologies, trophies, technical drawings, films and photographs. There is also the Ferrari shop selling original Ferrari merchandise. The visit begins with the section dedicated to Enzo Ferrari and the legend he created and reaches its climax with the sports and business successes achieved by Chairman Luca di Montezemolo. The second part is dedicated to Formula One single-seaters of the past and present, to the cups and trophies won on racing circuits around the world. The third section includes the modern road vehicles, sophisticated mechanical and electronic components designed for competitions and the "wind tunnel" with relative scale models. At the end there is an amphitheatre laid out for themed exhibitions.

Aims

An illustration of the company's history is accompanied and interwoven with the main events of the Italian automobile industry, which Ferrari, over the past 58 years, has contributed to in terms of innovative technology and safety.

Activity

Themed exhibitions and cultural activities, as well as the organisation of conferences and meetings in the "Enzo Ferrari" Auditorium.

BARILLA HISTORICAL ARCHIVE

GENERAL INFORMATION

VIA MANTOVA 166, PARMA, TEL. 0521262944
WWW.BARILLAGROUP.IT

HOW TO GET THERE

A1 MILAN-BOLOGNA HIGHWAY, EXIT AT PARMA, TANGENZIALE NORD TOWARDS BOLOGNA, MANTOVA SORBOLO EXIT.

OPENING HOURS

BY ARRANGEMENT ONLY. NO ENTRANCE FEE.

How the archive was conceived

The Barilla Historical Archive was conceived in 1987 on the initiative of Chairman Pietro Barilla. The company grew from the Forno (or Oven) which Pietro senior, a descendant of a baking family with records going back to 1576, opened in Via Vittorio Emanuele in Parma in 1877. It slowly grew until now the company is a world leader in pasta and an European leader in baked goods. The archive, with over 30,000 documents, was declared by the Ministry of Cultural Heritage to be of "considerable historical interest" in so much as it "witnesses the development of the food industry in Parma and the development of the tradition in Italy".

What it contains

Photographs, artwork, adverts, brochures, commercials, machinery, objects and documents on the history of the company, pasta, advertising and Barilla trademarks.

Aims

The Barilla Historical Archive was created to collect, preserve and showcase papers relative to the company's history, products, old advertising and trademarks (Barilla, Braibanti, Mulino Bianco, Pavesi, Voiello).

Activity

It plays a role in exhibitions and events, organising travelling exhibitions (history of pasta and advertising), aiding research, producing videos and books, and organising conferences.

FERRARA, THE BICYCLE CITY

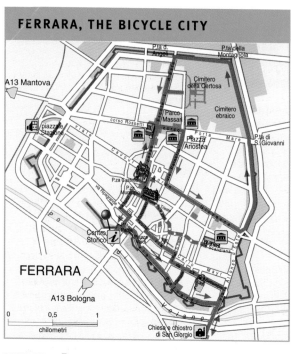

Key to symbols

- Point of departure and arrival
- Stop en route
- ℹ️ Tourist Information Office
- Train station
- Tower
- Church
- Museum
- Monastery, Abbey
- Farm
- Viewpoint
- Spring
- Beach

ROUTE KM 12: THE ROUTE FIRST TAKES YOU THROUGH THE MEDIEVAL PART AND THEN THROUGH THE RENAISSANCE PART OF THE CITY, MOSTLY FOLLOWING THE CITY WALLS.

DIFFICULTY: NONE WHATSOEVER. BEST TO STUDY THE ROUTE ON THE MAP BEFORE YOU SET OFF SO YOU CAN FIND YOUR WAY THROUGH THE CITY.

BIKE+ TRAIN: VARIOUS INTERREGIONAL TRAINS CONNECT FERRARA WITH BOLOGNA, VENICE, FLORENCE, ROME AND TRIESTE.

ITINERANDO, VIA VOLTAPALETTO 33 TEL. 0532202003, OFFERS HIRE OF BICYCLES, BABY CHAIRS AND CARRIAGES, GUIDED VISITS.

The office provides information on cycle paths, bicycle rental and repair. From the old city center car park head towards Porta Paola. Turn left into Via Baluardi and, after 1.4km, turn right where the road widens towards the bridge over the Po di Volano which leads to the church and cloisters of S. Giorgio, the spot where the city was founded. Go back across the bridge and continue for 350m on Viale Alfonso d'Este until you reach the crossroads with Via XX Settembre where you turn left. On your left, in rapid succession, you will see the Museo dell'Architettura (Museum of Architecture, 100m) and Palazzo Costabili (300m). 700m along Via XX Settembre turn left into Via Porta San Pietro which leads

to Via Carlo Mayr where you must keep to the left. Once you have reached Piazza Verde (the car park) turn right and then left again by Palazzo Paradiso. Then continue along the picturesque Via Volte until you reach the junction with Via San Romano, the business heart of the old city. Turn right towards Piazza Trento e Trieste before the cathedral. Keep to the left until you reach the Town Hall and its square facing the front of the cathedral. Returning towards the cathedral turn left and go around the castle. You will come out in Corso Giovecca-Viale Cavour, an axis which divides the medieval city from the Renaissance one. Leaving the castle behind you continue down Corso Ercole I d'Este, a monumental street designed at the end of the 1400s. Cycle to the unmistakable facade of Palazzo dei Diamante, in front of Palazzo Turchi di Bagno, while beyond Corso Rossetti-Corso Porta Mare, you will glimpse Palazzo Prosperi Sacrati with its lovely doorway. Turn right at the traffic lights into Corso Porta Mare, skirting the fence of the Botanical Garden on your right. Cycle as far as Piazza Ariostea and along Via Palestro until you reach the junction with Corso della Giovecca. Cycle to the end of this street (1.1km) where you will find the

18th century arch known as Prospettiva. Get off your bicycle here and climb the steps on the left to the city embankment, the city's green belt. Cycle along the city walls for almost 3km until you reach Porta degli Angeli and then turn left on Corso Ercole I d'Este close to the Certosa and church of San Cristoforo. Continue along the main axis until you reach the castle, turn right at the cathedral square into Via Cortevecchia and then left into Via del Turco crossing Via Volte and Via Ripagrande. Turn left to go back to Porta Paola and the old city center car park.

FORLÌ-CESENA, HILLY ROMAGNA

ROUTE KM 49: FORLÌ - GRISIGNANO - ROCCA DELLE CAMINATE - SANTA MARIA DI FIORDINANO SAN DOMENICO - FRATTA TERME - POLENTA - MONTE FERITI - SAN VITTORE - SAN CARLO - CESENA. ON QUIET SECONDARY ROADS.

DIFFICULTY: THIS IS AN INTERESTING BUT NOT TERRIBLY DIFFICULT ROUTE. THERE ARE TWO STEEP CLIMBS. THE FIRST COMES AFTER 6KM (GRISIGNANO). IT HAS AN AVERAGE GRADIENT OF 7% AND A MAXIMUM GRADIENT OF 10%. THE SECOND COMES AFTER 24KM (FRATTA). IT HAS AN AVERAGE GRADIENT OF 7%, BUT WITH AN INITIAL PEAK OF 14% IT IS CERTAINLY THE MOST CHALLENGING BIT OF THE ROUTE. THE OVERALL DIFFERENCE IN GRADIENT IS APPROXIMATELY 700M. IT IS ESSENTIAL TO HAVE A BICYCLE WITH GEARS AND, IF YOU ARE UNFIT, A GREAT DEAL OF PATIENCE FOR TACKLING THE TOUGHEST BITS.

BIKE + TRAIN: YOU RETURN TO WHERE YOU SET OFF BY TRAIN. THE CESENA-FORLÌ LINE IS SHORT (10-15 MINUTES), DIRECT AND SERVED BY VARIOUS REGIONAL AND INTERREGIONAL TRAINS ADAPTED TO TRANSPORT BICYCLES.

This is a pleasant route on secondary roads through the hilly countryside of Romagna. Start cycling along the cycle path parallel to Viale della Libertà near Forlì train station. Once in Piazza della Vittoria follow signs for Predappio. When you reach Rocca di Rivaldino take the Viale dell'Appennino cycle path leaving Forlì behind you. The route continues along the SS 9Ter del Rabbi road as far as Grisignano where you turn left onto the SP 125 road following the signs for Rocca delle Caminate. The road begins to rise until it reaches the crest between the Rabbi and Para rivers. Here you proceed by fits and starts, alternating short, uphill stretches with long, apparently flat stretches. Once you have left Parco della Rocca behind turn left towards Meldola on the SP 126 road. Leave the main road and take the Sentiero degli Alpini secondary road towards the church of Santa Maria di Fiordinano. Here you crest the hill and turn left towards Monteguzzo cycling downhill to Meldola. From Meldola follow the SP 99 road to Fratta Terme and then follow the signs to Polenta on the SP 83 road where you will begin the second climb of the day. At first it is rather difficult but then it turns into a pleasant ride affording a lovely view of Bertinoro and ending with a difficult stretch near the church of Polenta after cycling along an avenue lined with cypresses. You will soon be enjoying freewheeling downhill. 800m after Polenta turn right onto the SP 116 road and head towards San Mamante. After some ups and downs the real descent begins

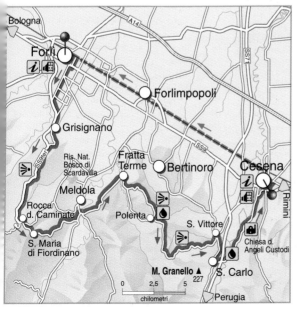

when you reach the road overlooking the Savio Valley. Cycle down to San Vittore and, at the roundabout, ignoring the signs for Cesena but following the ones for Rome, cycle to the village of San Carlo. Turn right into Via Castiglione in front of the church and cycle through the underpass to the other side of the highway and the Savio River. Then cycle down Via Roversano on the right bank of the river. After cycling around the Parco Naturale del Savio, you come the center of Cesena without any particular difficulty.

THE HILLS OF BOLOGNA

ROUTE KM 52: Monteveglio - Montemaggiore - Monte San Pietro - Isola - Mongiorgio - Badia - Gavignano - Savigno - Tiola - Castello di Serravalle - Monteveglio. On tarmac roads.

DIFFICULTY: The route is hilly. There are 7 uphill bits. None of them are very long but some are difficult. 2 of them (Montemaggiore and Monte San Pietro) can be avoided by taking the Fagnano alternative route. This excursion is good fun if you are fit.

Itinerary rich in history, nature and local products.

Start from the Centro Parco San Teodoro in Monteveglio. Go down Via Abbazia towards the village and, at the end, turn

right into Piazza della Libertà. Turn left at the traffic lights into Via Ponti and, once past the bridge which crosses the Samoggia River, turn right onto the SP 76 road following the stream as far as Stiore. At the fork at the end of the village turn right and continue along the SP 76 road through orchards and vineyards. At the next fork where SS 75 and 76 roads meet, turn left to Montemaggiore along the uphill SP 75 road towards the village (to avoid the climb you can go straight on to Fagnano) and then cycle downhill to Loghetto, where you turn right and follow the Landa River. The road now goes uphill again in the direction of Monte San Pietro and takes you to the highest part of the ridge along Via Castello. Cycle downhill and then, after a brief uphill bit, descend towards Ca' Silvestri and the bottom of the valley and turn left onto Via Sant'Andrea cycling by the Samoggia River and the hamlet of Stella.

Continue along the Samoggia and, just after the island, cycle uphill in the direction of Mongiorgio and then down to Badia. Turn right onto the SP 26 road (Via Lavino), which runs along the bottom of the valley as far as the bridge across the Lavino at Pilastrino, where you turn right towards Gavignano. The road rises between chestnut trees until it reaches the crest before Merlano. At the end of the road cycle down Via Merlano as far as Savigno and the old town center.

Turn right onto the SP 27 road (Via della Libertà) which crosses the Samoggia and then runs alongside it. After a while turn left onto Via Tiola where the first section is quite steep, followed by a gentle undulating stretch which takes you to Tiola. At the fork go straight on downhill and then turn right onto the SP 70 Serravalle road, continuing to Castelletto where you turn left onto Via Castello. The church of

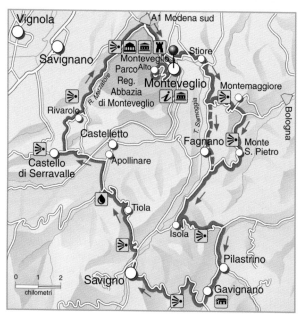

Sant'Apollinare stands at the fork. Once back on the SS road head towards Mercatello where the switchback begins which takes you to Castello di Serravalle. Turn back on the SS road and cycle for about 500m and then turn left into Via San Michele. Cycle along the ridge until you reach Cascine di Rivarolo Vecchio. Turn left and cycle down to the bottom of the Marzatore Valley on the road with the same name. Skirt the Parco Regionale dell' Abbazia di Monteveglio until you reach the SP 28 road and then turn right towards Monteveglio. Turn right at the traffic lights into Via Abbazia and cycle uphill towards the village.

THE SOUTHERN SECTION

ROUTE KM 74: REGGIO EMILIA - CADELBOSCO DI SOPRA - VILLA SETA - VALLI DI NOVELLARA - GUASTALLA - LIDO PO - GUALTIERI - BRESCELLO INCLUDING THE DETOUR AT NOVELLARA).ON TARMAC ROADS, EXCEPT FOR A BRIEF 1.3KM STRETCH.

DIFFICULTY: NONE IN PARTICULAR GIVEN THE GENTLE GRADIENT. HOWEVER, 74KM IS NOT TO BE UNDERTAKEN LIGHTLY SO IT IS BEST TO BEGIN THE ROUTE WITH A LITTLE TRAINING UNDER YOUR BELT.

BIKE + TRAIN: REGGIO EMILIA IS ON THE PARMA-BOLOGNA RAILWAY LINE. TAKE THE TRAIN BACK FROM BRESCELLO TO PARMA (A LITTLE UNDER HALF AN HOUR) AND THEN CHANGE TRAINS FOR REGGIO EMILIA (ABOUT 40 MINUTES).

A cycle ride through the southern part of the province of Reggio taking in poplar woods, fortresses and palaces. Start from Reggio Emilia's inner circular road and then turn right into Via Fogliani. The road turns left into Via Cisalpina and continues for about 2.5km until it reaches a crossroads with a set of traffic lights where you turn right towards the village of Sesso. An underpass with a cycle lane takes you to a crossroads (after 4km) where you turn left towards Cavazzoli and Roncocesi. Once you are in Cadelbosco di Sopra (after 12km), avoid the busy SS 63 road by taking Via Prampolini as far as the crossroads with the trunk road at Zurco. Turn left and cycle as far as the turning for Bagnolo on the right.

Turn left at the next crossroads and then head straight out into the countryside. Cross an irrigation canal and then continue along a dirt track towards the station of San Bernardino (avoiding Via Levata) for 1.3km. Cross the main road and enter the farm of Agricola Riviera. A variety of birds of passage can be seen in the nearby valleys of Novellara, easily reached by taking the SS road and then the dirt track which enters the protected area, heading towards Novellara. Once back on the road continue as far as the dusty Via Spino Viazza and then on to Guastalla, through the hamlets of San Giacomo and Pieve. 3km after the village of Guastalla you will reach Gualtieri and here it is advisable to leave the road on the embankment and opt for the road below which, after Boretto and Santa Croce, eventually reaches Brescello (12km from Guastalla). Take the train to Parma, where you will need to change to get a connection back to Reggio Emilia.

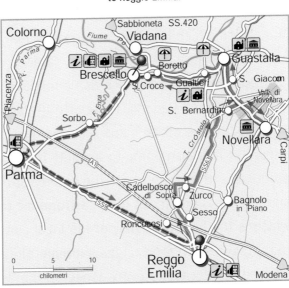

🥫	PASTA	🍾	OIL
🍖	HAMS AND SALAMIS	🍇	WINE
🧀	CHEESE	🍰	CAKE

Emilia-Romagna is the land of good food par
excellence. The area's resources and the local
people's innate propensity to enjoy life have resulted
in a region which is a treasure-trove of real, genuine
flavors. This area is home to many famous
gastronomic traditions, such as Parmigiano
Reggiano, Grana Padano, Prosciutto di Parma and
Brisighella olive oil, to name only the most common
ones. But it is also home to a whole host of local
products and recipes where the quality of the
ingredients is enhanced by a gastronomic tradition
which is the historic legacy of the local culture.
Here, really good food reigns supreme and is
integrated into nearly every aspect of life. It is the

Food

cradle of Italy's most famous hams and cheeses and even the wines, which might be slightly less well-known, have a very distinctive flavor. It's a region worth visiting with the spirit and curiosity of a real food connoisseur.

Highlights

- Your taste-buds will tingle as you discover the traditions of Grana Padano, Parmigiano Reggiano and Formaggio di Fossa
- Jolly conversation at table as you sample home-made cakes and traditional sweets and sip the excellent local wine
- The cured pork meats of Parma and Piacenza: a treat not to be missed
- Brisighella's excellent olive oil

Inside

140 **Pasta**
144 **Hams and Salami**
150 **Cheese**
154 **Oil**
155 **Wine**
161 **Liqueurs**
162 **Cake**
167 **Festivals**

Emilia-Romagna, the two sides of good food

There is no actual boundary marked on maps separating Emilia with its appealing dishes, the fried "gnocchi" (an Emilia specialty obtained by mixing flour, water, yeast, lard and salt, then rolling it out in a sheet of pasta dough, cutting it into small square pieces and frying them in boiling hot oil), from Romagna with its zesty flavors and its "piadina" (a tortilla shaped focaccia with a filling, see box on page 142). It is rather the meeting point of the two souls of the same land.

The trapeze formed by the territory between the Po River, the Adriatic Sea and the Apennines is undoubtedly the richest gastronomical area in Italy. Its inhabitants are known to be good eaters and fond of hearty food. The cult for a well-garnished table is found all over, fueled by a dual spirit. From Piacenza to Bologna lies Emilia, from Ravenna to Rimini it is Romagna, separated at the fall of the Roman Empire by a geographic and cultural frontier with the Lombards on one side, the Byzantines on the other. The former favoured pork, beef and iron pan cooking, the latter wheat, lamb, mutton and terracotta hotplate cooking; on one side cured pork meats, cheeses and fried gnocchi, on the other, "castrato" (male sheep meat) and "piadina".

The region includes the entire area from the Po River, to the Apennines and the sea. The dominant lines enclosing the landscape are the Po riverbed and the ridge of the Apennines. The horizon rises from the river stretching across lowlands with poplars, plowed stretches of land, and the great courtyard farmhouses. From the west to the east, first there is the corn and alfalfa of the Parmigiano-Reggiano land, then the great Lambrusco vineyards, market gardens, orchards, and finally the reclaimed lands and Comacchio fishing marshes. From the opposite side, the rivers descend fashioning a bright green, unexpected mountainous zone; mushrooms and chestnuts from the woods; meat, cured pork and cheeses from the pastures. Lower down, the hillside belt swarms with busy districts and productive activities: between the Trebbia and the Marecchia rivers there are the vineyards - Gutturnio to Albana - alternating with cherry and plum orchards. Then the narrow strip of pinewoods and beach heralding the flavors of the sea.

As far as farming and foods are concerned, the Emilia-Romagna region is a leader in many ways. Statistics set it highest in the production of soft wheat, in the top positions in the fruit, brandy and wine sectors; the same can be said as concerns the manufacture of cheese, cured pork meats and vegetables in general. In fact several of the major Italian food production firms are from this region. What is even more remarkable, however, is its reputation as a culinary paradise according to the collective image. "Alla bolognese" (Bologna style) is a term that is used (and abused) on a worldwide level, and two typical products such as Parmigiano-Reggiano and Prosciutto di Parma, the industrial production of which has managed to combine tradition and organic excellence.

ve equal worldwide reputations. A more recent and exclusive achievement is the
ernational renown of traditional balsamic vinegar, representing the last word in resistance
mass produced food: a magic, dream-evoking potion sold in small quantities in precious
sks, proof of the potential of a typical Italian product.

astronomy and tradition

already mentioned, the gastronomy is divided between two contrasting cultures: that of
ilia, based softly and appealingly on the general idea of butter and mellow sauces, and the
magna tradition which is more sanguine and inspired by the avant-garde strong flavors of
ntral Italy. The gastronomic differences that develop when moving from one to the other
ea are extremely varied. It is enough to mention pasta, the regional symbol: the center of
avity is held by the "tortellino" for which Bologna and Modena both claim parenthood, but
Piacenza and Parma with only slight variations we find the "anolino", in Reggio Emilia the
appelletto", in Ferrara pumpkin "tortelli"; while going down into the Romagna area,
uffed pasta gives way to "garganelli" or "cappelletti" with only a cheese filling. Left to itself,
ilia, where pork holds sway, has a great number of specialties such as horse meat in
acenza, pigeon in Parma, rabbit in Modena. In the mountains the scenario is enhanced by
ements originating from the other side: traditions of the Liguria region found in the upper
acenza area, Florentine customs descending the Parma river valley and the Tuscan-Emilian
pennines, Montefeltro customs along the southern border. The same goes for the coast where
e "brodetto" (fish soup) alternates with fried "seppie" and "calamari" and grilled fish, empha-
zing different flavors according to whether the focal point is towards Rovigo or Pesaro.
he Emilia-Romagna region offers opportunities for gastronomic tourism for all
stes and all incomes. The number of restaurants as a whole is conspicuous in the
ties that are art centers, extremely rich on the Romagna coast, surprisingly so also
the Apennine mountains, offering a large choice of top quality settings, plus a
eries of "trattorie", "osterie", wine bars with kitchen service, even back
hops with chairs and tables for a snack. The most remarkable
eature, however, is the myriad of kiosks located ever-
where along the Romagna coast: the fast foods of
piadina" with its many delicious fillings, the cured pork
eats, the "squacquerone", the greens...

he Po River, leading character
f the landscape and cooking
f the Emilia-Romagna
egion

FOOD

PASTA

The Emilia-Romagna region is the home of egg pasta, where the preparation of pas[ta] is still practically a ritual. Production includes a wide range of varieties, also in t[...] many stuffed versions: every town and almost every family has its own secrets [...] kneading pasta. The eggs are selected from those with a darker shell, guaranteei[ng] brightly colored yolks that will give the pasta a golden hue; the sheet of dough [...] stretched and skillfully cut according to its intended use: a thin sheet cut in wider stri[ps] for pasta with sauce, a thicker sheet of dough cut narrow for pasta served in broth. T[he] fillings are vegetables and cheese for vegetarian tortelli, meat for the cappelle[tti] Reggiani and for the anolini of Piacenza. They are all served preferably in broth, like t[he] queen of stuffed pasta, tortellini, the emblem of Bologna, which according to legend wa[s] inspired by the perfect shape of Venus' navel. Among the sauces used for pasta, t[he] place of honor is taken by ragu (meat sauce) which originated in this area; rich and tas[ty] it requires long, careful cooking to enhance its flavors.

Cappelletti are one of the symbols of Emilia-Romagna's gastronomic tradition

Anolini

Fresh stuffed pasta shaped like a half moon or circle.
Typical of the provinces of Parma and Piacenza it has a filling of lean beef, butter, grana cheese, breadcrumbs and eggs, or grated cheese, breadcrumbs scalded in stock, eggs, salt, "stracotto" (a traditional meat dish: the main ingredient is meat cooked for a long time in stock, wine or tomato sauce). Anolini are a classic winter dish and are served in broth.

Cappellacci

Fresh stuffed pasta.
Typical of the province of Ferrrara, cappellacci have a filling of yellow pumpkin baked in the oven, strained through a sieve and mixed with Parmigiano-Reggiano, breadcrumbs, eggs and nutmeg.

Cappelletti

Fresh stuffed pasta.
Cappelletti are one of the most typical symbols of the gastronomic tradition of Emilia-Romagna: there are several versions, differing mainly in the filling.

They owe their name to their hat shape. The cappelletto of Reggio is traditionally filled with just beef "stracotto", although through the years the filling has been enriched with other kinds of meat, such as pork, chicken and mortadella.
In the Ferrara area cappelletti are filled with a mixture of chicken breast, pork meat, veal, cooking salami or sausage, Parmigiano-Reggiano, eggs, nutmeg and salt.
Cappelletti are traditionally served in capon bouillon.

Garganelli

Short fresh pasta, garganelli derive their name from the gullet of the chicken, which in the Romagna dialect is called "garganel". They are short ridged maccheroni, with the ends cut at an angle using a utensil called a "comb", similar to a loom, made of two small parallel boards connected by bamboo strips. The egg and flour dough, enriched with grated grana cheese and nutmeg is stretched thinly and cut into squares that are set on the "comb" and rolled around a stick:

this produces small cylinders with a ridged outer surface. The size of the garganelli varies according to their use: those served in broth are small, while those with sauce are usually obtained from squares with 3-4 cm. side. Garganelli are served with delicate sauces (e.g. peas cooked in butter with the addition of tomato sauce) or simply with butter and Parmesan cheese.

ramigna

Hollow, thick spaghetti, curved in a curl shape; the smaller size is for soup, while the larger one is traditionally seasoned with meat sauce or with sausage.

asagne

Large dough rectangles (10-12 cm. sides) stretched not too thinly, usually baked in the oven, after boiling, and with layers of meat sauce, bechamel and a sprinkling of grated cheese. The dough for lasagne can be enriched with chopped spinach, in which case they are called green lasagne.

Maccheroni Bobbiesi

This is a typical specialty of the town of Bobbio (Piacenza): the dough is made of durum wheat and water (or half semolina, half white durum wheat flour, kneaded in this case with both egg white and yolk), it is cut into pieces 6 cm. in length that are rolled around a small iron rod, obtaining a sort of large hollow spaghetti. They are usually seasoned with mushroom meat or "stracotto" sauce.

Maltagliati

Strips of egg dough of irregular shape, or unevenly shaped and sized rectangles made from leftover dough for anolini, cappelletti, etc. Maltagliati come in different sizes according to their use: the smaller size is used in soups, particularly bean and chickpea, while the bigger pieces are served with sauce.

Pisarei

Small gnocchi made of flour kneaded with water and/or milk, typical of the Piacenza area: they are the size of kidney beans and are served with a tomato and bean sauce.

Tagliatelle

Ribbon-shaped fresh egg pasta. The blond head of hair of the noblewoman Lucrezia Borgia was, according to legend, the original inspiration for tagliatelle: they were supposed to have been created by the Court chef of Giovanni Il Bentivoglio, Lord of Bologna between 1463 and 1506, to reproduce the lady's hair, when she arrived in Bologna to marry the Duke of Ferrara, Alfonso d'Este. It is practically impossible to make a complete list of all the sauces and seasonings for tagliatelle; among them, the two most typical are the rich Bologna meat sauce, and "stridoli", wild greens and herbs from Romagna.

Tortelli

Fresh pasta with a vegetarian filling. There are a large number of tortelli in the Emilia-Romagna region with a similar filling of greens and cheese; they are prepared with dough made with soft wheat flour and eggs. The most characteristic definitely include "tortelli con la coda": the dough is knotted at the two ends around the filling of spinach or chard, ricotta, grana cheese, and nutmeg in such a way as to recall the tail of a fish or a butterfly. In the Parma lowlands "tortelli di erbette" are shaped like a half moon and filled with cow's milk ricotta, grated cheese and "erba bieta" (chard) known as "erbetta". In the Parma area there are also potato tortelli, filled with potatoes, ricotta, bacon or with potatoes, stracchino cheese and eggs. In the Romagna area vegetarian tortelli (with a filling of ricotta, Parmesan cheese, parsley, egg and nutmeg flavoring) have the shape of a half moon

In Emilia-Romagna, fresh pasta has numerous shapes and sizes

FOOD

141

and the closed ends are marked with the prongs of a fork and are called "orecchioni". Bologna has what is known as "turtlò", tortelli for Christmas Eve feasting, in a half-moon shape, filled with ricotta, Parmesan cheese, parsley, egg and the usual nutmeg flavor.

Tortellini

A kind of egg pasta with filling, typical of Bologna and symbolic of this city. Originally meant to be served in broth, on all the major holidays of the year, they are now often served in a cream sauce or in bean broth. They are very popular across the entire region, although there are slight variants in which they are prepared.

BOLOGNA

Come una Volta
Via della Crocetta 15,
Tel. 0516142378
The name means "as in olden times", and promises a return to the traditions of Bologna and the Emilia region: tortellini, tagliatelle and traditional or spinach lasagne.

Pastificio Dolce Sana
Via Ercole Nani 11,
Tel. 051402156
A pasta factory that makes and sells its own fresh pasta products according to the Bologna tradition (e.g. tortellini, tagliatelle, garganelli and gramigna).

FERRARA

Pasticio Ricci
Via Pomposa 135,
Tel. 0532740600
This pasta factory produces various different varieties of pasta: durum-wheat pasta, egg pasta and special pasta made with spinach or tomato. The pasta is dried at a low temperature.

MODENA

La Divina Pastella
San Damaso,
Stradello Scartazzetta 33, Tel. 059469896
A pasta factory producing tortelli in the Modena style, with filling of pork meat, sausage, prosciutto from Modena, mortadella, Parmesan cheese, egg and nutmeg. They also make tortelli with fillings of ricotta and greens or pumpkin.

Pastificio Chicco d'Oro
Via Francesco Selmi 27,
Tel. 059218216
This pasta factory offers the pasta and flavors of traditional cooking in Emilia besides fresh pasta, there are also prepared foods for sale. There is a wide choice of local tortelli, "tortellaccio" (100 gram tortello with traditional filling or with a filling of pumpkin, Parmesan cheese, amaretto biscuits and Sassolino liqueur), or meat and cheese ravioli.

THE "PIADA", TRADITIONAL FOOD OF THE ROMAGNA

The piada (plural piade or piadas) started out life as humble, traditional food of people living in the Romagna countryside, but today it has become a leading example of Italian fast food that can be found in bars and similar outlets across the country. The piada (or piadina as it is frequently called) is unleavened bread and has a history going back in time and mingling with peasant tradition. The ingredients are simple: water, flour and lard. These are then combined and kneaded together before, according to tradition, being rolled out by housewives using rolling pins. Once upon a time the piada, made with country herbs and boiled or cooked in salt, was a stock dish of the populace. Nowadays it is folded in half and filled in various ways: with cured ham, roast fish, salad, roast sausage or squacquerone (a soft local cheese).

In the past, it was cooked on round, flat brick stones, but today it is baked on iron or cast iron hotplates. Piade come in a great variety of sizes and thicknesses, however, the traditional one from Rimini is large and thin... and highly appetizing.

There are also Modena tortellini and tagliatelle, plain or colored: green with spinach, red with beet and peppers, or whole wheat.

stificio La Credenza
Viale Gaetano Storchi, 10/B/C,
Tel. 059225957
This pasta factory specializes exclusively in egg pasta handmade with 'oo' flour (i.e. highly refined), and fresh eggs. The types of pasta are tortelli with ricotta and spinach or with pumpkin, tortellini Bologna style, and lasagne with meat sauce. One of their specialties is green spinach pasta, although this is only available to order.

PARMA

glia di Pasta
Via Imbriani 55/E,
Tel. 0521237650
They have fresh or normal pasta, egg pasta, durum wheat pasta or pasta made with special flour such as wholemeal, barley, rice, spelt or chestnut. The eggs used are either fresh or pasteurized. The varieties of pasta are traditional: tortelli and cappelletti filled with meat or radicchio, artichoke and asparagus, according to the season.
Of the plain pasta without filling, tagliatelle and maltagliati are recommended.

PIACENZA

IORENZUOLA D'ARDA
a Buona Tavola
Via Kennedy 2,
Tel. 0523981233
A pasta factory producing its own fresh, hand-rolled egg pasta. Anolini, tortelli and pisarei are available.

RAVENNA

BRISIGHELLA
Pastificio Arte del Mattarello
Via Alberto Baccarini 21,
Tel. 054681330
This pasta factory offers its own production of cappelletti, tagliatelle, garganelli and tortelli.

CERVIA
Il Matterello
Viale Nazario Sauro 142,
Tel. 0544973482
A pasta factory producing its own hand-rolled, fresh pasta: cappelletti with a cheese filling, tortelli with spinach and cheese, as well as the other typical varieties found in Emilia and Romagna.

FAENZA
Bottega della Pasta Fresca
Corso G. Garibaldi 32/B,
Tel. 054628510
The varieties of pasta on sale all come from the regional culinary tradition: tortelli with ricotta, spinach and Parmesan cheese, Romagna cappelletti with Parmesan cheese and nutmeg, and garganelli.

REGGIO EMILIA

La Forchetta
Via Francesco Cassoli 34/A,
Tel. 0522285185
The local products sold in this store include cappelletti and tortelli with a filling of greens or pumpkin.

MONTECCHIO EMILIA
La Bottega dei Sapori
Viale Camillo Prampolini 21/C,
Tel. 0522865811
A pasta factory making its own fresh egg pasta: tagliatelle "paglia e fieno", so called because they are yellow like straw (paglia) and green like freshly cut hay (fieno), tortelli, tortellini Bologna style and cappelletti Romagna style.

RIMINI

Non Solo Pasta
Via Marecchiese, 125/A,
Tel. 0541791866
A pasta factory making its own fresh pasta, with a food store on the premises, selling all the varieties of pasta from the Romagna tradition, made with local flour and fresh eggs: cappelletti, tagliatelle, and maltagliati. The store also has sauces such as Bologna style meat sauce.

FOOD

When considering the pork curing business of the Emilia-Romagna region, names products come to mind that represent truly sumptuous food: "salama da sugo", "ca pello del prete", "Bell e cott", "prosciutto di Parma" and "mortadella di Bologna". T culinary tradition of the region shows that preparing food and sitting down to a meal a rituals with special rules: fully enjoy your food and leave your worries behind. At the fc of the hills around Parma and Bologna, sliced prosciutto crudo and culatello can be co sidered a main course with piadina and fried gnocchi. In the other, more mountainous h of the region, salami, mountain hams and wild boar hams are served. In the fall, the cured pork meats are served with chestnuts boiled with bay leaves, sautéd, or turned flour to make fritters.

Bell e cott

This sausage is similar to cotechino and is produced in limited quantities by small firms in the province of Ravenna. It is made using second or third choice pork cuts that are ground into a fine mixture, seasoned with salt, pepper, garlic and cinnamon, and then put into sausage skins and tied with string into medium size sausages. Once prepared, they need about 10 to 15 days to mature and then they are ready to be eaten after being boiled in water.

Bondiola

This sausage is eaten cooked. It is made of 100% pork, and prepared in limited quantities in the provinces of Parma and Piacenza. Lean pork meat is used, along with pork fat, tender rinds and "guanciale" (the fleshy part of the head). The ingredients are ground and seasoned with salt, pepper, spices, garlic and red wine, then the mixture is put into natural cow gut and aged for 1-3 months.

Cappello del prete

A cured pork meat sausage that has a distinctive triangular or three-cornered shape stitched by hand. It is a typical product of northern Emilia.
Shoulder meat, rinds from the back, meat from the throat and fat are medium ground and seasoned with salt, pepper, various spices and garlic marinated in white wine and crushed. The mix is then put into skin from the end of the pig's trotter and stitched in a special way to give

it its particular shape (the name translates as priest's hat). Ageing lasts 2-4 months. It should be boiled before eating.

Coppa Parma

A large, cylindrical piece of cured pork meat with one end slightly more tapered than the other, produced all over the province of Parma.
Coppa is made using a single piece from the neck muscle. The meat is sprinkled with a blend of salt, crushed pepper grains, various spices, preservants and sometimes wine. Coppa is matured for 7-10 days during which time it is massaged by hand or mechanically, then put into sausage skin and tied with string in a tight knot. When cut, it is compact, bright red with some fat veining.

Coppa Piacentina DOP

A large, cylindrical piece of cured pork with slightly tapered ends produced in the province of Piacenza. When cut, it is compact, uniform and bright red in color, veined with white and pinkish fat. The taste is best described as mellow.

Cotechino di Modena IGP

This 100% pork meat sausage has a distinctive cylindrical shape and is eaten cooked. It is made in many provinces in the region, namely Modena, Ferrara, Ravenna, Rimini, Forlì, Bologna, Reggio Emilia, Parma and Piacenza. When cut, the meat of the cotechino di Modena should be compact and not crumble; the color is rosy pink.

entils and cotechino form a typical and much loved
milia dish that is normally eaten in winter

ulatello di Zibello DOP

This sausage is only made in the
province of Parma in the towns of
Busseto, Polesine Parmense, Zibello,
Soragna, Roccabianca, San Secondo,
Sissa and Colorno. It has a distinctive
pear-shape and weighs about 3-5 kg.
The meat is bright red with limited fat
veining.

iocchetto

This is a cured pork meat that has a
distinctive rounded pear-shape
and is produced all over the Parma
area and also in some parts of the
province of Piacenza.
A fairly lean meat prepared with the
part of the leg remaining after removal
of the culatello, that is, the rump of the
shoulder or the part under the bone.
The meat is carefully trimmed of fat
and nerves, then cured with a mixture
of salt, pepper and garlic, and left to
season for 15 days. It is then soaked
in dry white wine or vinegar for 3
more days, after which it is drained,
carefully rubbed, put into sausage
skin and tied. The drying stage takes
a further 8-10 days and is done in
an airy space. Finally, it is matured
for between 6 and 8 months.

Mortadella di Bologna

A 100% pork meat sausage that is
ovoid or cylindrical in shape. It is
made with choice cuts of lean and fat
meat that are ground three times to
produce a very fine mix. Added to the
mix are small cubes of fat from the
throat, previously heated, washed in

water and drained. It is then cured
with salt, pepper in whole or crushed
grains, and sometimes herbs and
spices, sugar and shelled pistachio
nuts. It is put into natural or synthetic
sausage skins of varying sizes. The
product is cooked in dry-air stoves
and cooled. When cut, mortadella
di Bologna displays a compact not
elastic texture with an even bright pink
color with conspicuous white fat
spots in an amount which should be
no less than 15% of the whole.
The taste is mellow, never acid.

Pancetta Piacentina DOP

A 100% pork sausage that is large and
cylindrical in shape. It is prepared in
the Piacenza area using cuts of meat
from stock farms in Emilia and
Lombardy that have been certified
for the production of prosciutto di
Parma. When cut, pancetta piacentina
is bright red in color with white parts.
The taste is sweet and spicy.

Prosciutto di Modena DOP

This is a typical prosciutto crudo
(cured ham) from the valleys
and hills around the Panaro River,
including the towns in the provinces
of Modena, Bologna and Reggio Emilia.
It is prepared with fresh pork legs
and when cut it is bright red with a
mellow taste.

Prosciutto di Parma DOP

This is a prosciutto crudo (cured ham)
prepared in an area restricted to the
territory of the province of Parma,
south of the Via Emilia, bordering to the
east with the Enza River and to the west
with the Stirone River. Its flavor stems
from the balance between the fat and
lean parts of the pork legs and from
maturing that lasts over 12 months.
If the final product presents the proper
requirements it is awarded the
much sought after mark of the duke's
crown. This is the true Parma ham.

Salama da sugo di Ferrara

A sausage in a distinctive round shape,
eaten cooked and
made of pork meat
only: coppa di
collo, pancetta,
fat, liver and tongue.

PARMA

FOOD

145

The ingredients are ground and seasoned with salt, pepper, red wine (usually Sangiovese or Barbera), sometimes cloves and cinnamon. The mix is put into a pig's bladder, then the sausage is tied with string into 8 segments and left to season in a warm, ventilated room for a few days, and is then matured for 6-12 months in well-aired, dark premises.

Salame Felino

A large, tapered salami of 100% pork meat, prepared using first-choice lean cuts. The meat is cleaned and trimmed of any nerves, connecting tissue and fatty tissue and is then left to rest for some time in cold store to dry out. It is then thinly ground together with prosciutto and pancetta trimmings. The mixture must be thoroughly blended and cured with salt, pepper (whole or ground), and a limited amount of crushed garlic dissolved in a small amount of wine. The mixture must be left to rest at a low temperature to dry out further, and is finally put into natural pig gut, which gives this sausage its distinctive irregular shape. It is tied with string and moved for a few days into special maturing rooms.

The bright red coloring of the meat is one indication of correctly preserved sausages

This is followed by maturing in ventilated premises for 2-4 months. When cut, salame felino is bright red i color and has a fairly coarse grain.

Salame Fiorettino

Sausage made by small, family firms all over the province of Reggio Emilia with top quality finely ground pork cuts to which small cubes of pork fat are added. The mixture is flavored with salt, pepper, natural herbs and spices, and put into gut. It is left to dry for 12 hours in a cool room, then moved into cellars for no less than 60 days.

Salame piacentino DOP

Also known by its dialect name of "salame cu la güssa" because it runs when cut, this sausage has an intense aroma and is produced in the Piacenza area. It is made with lean cuts and small pieces of lard, throat and pancetta with the soft fat removec Everything is minced into a coarse mix, cured with sea salt, pepper in whole or chopped grains, sugar, wine in which garlic has been steeped, and additives. The mixture is then made into sausages in pork gut and tied in a thick string mesh into a cylinder shape. It is bright red in color with grains of white fat.

Spalla di San Secondo

The area producing this sausage is San Secondo and the entire Parma area between the towns of Fontanellat and Roccabianca. It is prepared with pork shoulder with the bone left in. After it is trimmed of part of the fat and nerves, it is cured with a mixture of salt, pepper, herbs, cinnamon, garlic and nutmeg, and then dipped in a marinade of white or red wine. Following this, it is left in col store for 15 days. After draining, the meat is rolled, tied with string, put intc pork gut and tied again to form a large rounded sausage. At this point the shoulder is left to drain for several hours, then moved to cold storage for maturing for about 30 days. It is then cooked in water and wine. If conditions so permit, the shoulder can also be preserved raw for two years, or even longer.

Zampone di Modena

This is a 100% pork meat sausage that is traditionally produced in the Modena area as well as the surrounding Emilia and Lombardy provinces.

The mixture is based on coarsely ground striped muscle and fat with the addition of finely ground pigskin, which is then flavored with salt, pepper (whole or ground), and various ingredients including wine, water, sugar, spices and natural fragrances (any products obtained chemically or from smoking are prohibited). It is then made into a sausage in the skin of the pig's front leg including the toes, and tied at the top with string. The product thus obtained may be left to dry in special hot air stoves and sold fresh, or alternatively placed in special containers with a hermetic seal and sold already cooked.

BOLOGNA

La Cotica
Via Farini 37/A,
Tel. 051220749
This shop is like a paradise of prosciutto crudo, with over 40 hams available for slicing. In a way, it is like taking a gourmet trip through the best productions of Emilia and, indeeed, the whole of Italy.

Salumeria Pasquini & Brusiani
Via delle Tofane 38,
Tel. 0516143697
www.pasquiniebrusiani.com
A small artisan establishment where, among other interesting products, mortadella is available in both the standard and traditional versions.

FERRARA

Antica Salumeria Marchetti
Via Corte Vecchia 35/37
Tel. 0532204800
An old-time shop in the very center of town. Its specialties include interesting garlic flavored sausages, the round salama dasugo di Ferrara and, although not a ham or salami, its own home-made fresh pasta.

Salumeria Mario
Via Aria Nuova 51 A/B,
Tel. 0532209476
For the past 40 years the same people have been making their own salama da sugo in this shop, where it is sold, if ordered in advance, with the typical side dish of mashed potatoes.

FORLÌ-CESENA

FORLÌ
Salumeria Tomba
Via Bella 1,
Tel. 054320054
A traditional delicatessen, founded in 1906, and practically unchanged in its pre-war décor. The cured pork meats are selected from the best private producers in the area or self-produced, like the cotechino and salama da sugo.

CESENA
Salumificio Faggioli
Via Q. Bucci 237,
Tel. 0547384733
The pigs utilized in this firm's production are all from reliable stock farms in the Romagna area. Do not miss their salami, coppa, prosciutto, sausages and cotechino.

MODENA

Premiata Salumeria Giusti
Via Farini 75,
Tel. 059222533
This is an old Modena delicatessen offering the best of private production, among which its home-produced succulent salami, as well as salami Felino, coppa and pancetta piacentina.

Premiata Salumeria San Francesco - Ristorante Fini
Corso Canalchiaro 139,
Tel. 059223320
A well-deserving dinasty of Emilia's regional gastronomy, which has been in business since 1912. Besides cured pork meats and cheeses, there are a wide choice of take-away dishes and a "deli" section in which to have lunch.

FOOD

PARMA

Agrinascente
A4 highway, Fidenza exit
Tel. 0524522334
Just a few yards off the highway from
the Fidenza toll-booth, production and
sale of Parmigiano-Reggiano DOP and
the cured pork meats of the Emilia
region, such as culatello di Zibello
DOP and salame Felino.

Salumeria Sorelle Picchi
Via Farini 27,
Tel. 0521233528
For over 30 years this shop has been
a "must" for the purchase of Parma
specialties of cheese and cured pork
meat. Try also the fresh pasta and
take-away foods.

BUSSETO
Salsamenteria Storica Verdiana Baratta
Via Roma 76,
Tel. 052491066
www.salsamenteriabaratta.it
A warm and welcoming environment
in which to buy and also to sample
privately produced cured pork meats:
culatello, spalla cruda and cotta
(raw and cooked shoulder of pork),
mortadella di Bologna, coppa and
prosciutto.

FONTANELLATO
Salumificio Rossi Ca' di Parma
Sanguinaro, Via Emilia 129
Tel. 0521825107
www.culaccia.it
"Culaccia" was launched on the
market by this producer; it is
obtained from the best parts of the
hind legs of Italian bred pigs,
according to a technique that places
it, so to speak, halfway between
prosciutto and culatello, with the
flavor and consistency of both.
It is definitely worth trying it.

FORNOVO DI TARO
Salumificio Bocchi Lucedio
Piazza I. Pizzi 6,
Tel. 05252484
A small private manufacturer of
cured pork meat with its own shop,
which continues the family tradition
of limited, careful production.
Certain types of treatment and
processing are avoided to
make sure the natural flavors
of the selected raw materials
come to the fore.

CONTROLLED ORIGIN, ORGANIC CURED PORK MEATS

Organic cured pork meats are manufactured with raw materials from stock farms
that are subjected to strict controls, from feed production to the selection
and treatment of the meats, according to European Union and Italian
regulations on organic technology. The pigs are raised in their natural state, and fed
with special organic feeds that increase their physical endurance.
They are not given whey (the primary food of conventional stock farms), but only
cereals and organic fruit. With this treatment, pigs grow with their natural life cycle,
and only healthy, genuine and flavorful cured pork meats are produced,
such as prosciutto crudo, salami, pancetta, coppa and mortadella.
The processing of organic products is regulated in the European Union by European
Community Regulations 2092/91,
primarily regarding guidelines for
production, labeling, control system and
import from countries not belonging to the
European Union, prohibiting the use
of GM (genetically modified).
Organic products are easily recognizable
because the packaging must bear the
wording "produced from organic
agriculture", followed by the indications
required by law and a series of codes and
figures identifying the controlling
organization.

Salame Felino is a high-quality sausage with a distinctive and irregular elongated shape.

SAN SECONDO PARMENSE

Salumificio Emanuele Cavalli
Via Verdi 31,
Tel. 0521874434
The owner of this cured pork meat factory is a true "philologist of sausage production". In a constant search for old recipes, he learned the skills of his job from childhood by going out to the country to watch when pigs were butchered.
A connoisseur, he is able to repropose the flavors of times gone by.

SORAGNA

Salumeria Crocedelizia
Via Emilia 1,
Tel. 0524596061
The privately produced sausages and cured pork meats are free from any chemical additives or preservatives; the skill of the pork butchers and the area's exceptional climate guarantee first-rate taste and aroma.

ZIBELLO

La Boutique delle Carni e dei Salumi
Piazza Garibaldi 40,
Tel. 052499676
Privately produced sausages and pork meats are cured by hand and matured naturally, only with the aid of the mists of the Parma lowlands along the right bank of the Po River.

PIACENZA

Salumeria Garetti
Piazza Duomo 44,
Tel. 0523322747
During the winter months this well-known delicatessen offers its own private production of cured pork meats, and also products from other, carefully selected pork butchers.

BOBBIO

Salumificio Bobbiese
Via IV Novembre 23,
Tel. 0523936548
www.salumificiobobbiese.it
A small establishment in the Piacenza pork meat curing tradition.
The culatello is superb, and also coppa, pancetta, salami and cotechino.

CARPANETO

Giordano
Case Draghi, Via Provinciale 28
Tel. 0523859083
The products of this small private manufacturer of cured pork meats all carry the Piacenza DOP marks, and the selection of raw materials is standard. Pork butchers for generations, the Giordano's operate in the special environment of Carpaneto, in the heart of the Emilia pork-curing area.

REGGIO EMILIA

Antica Salumeria Giorgio Pancaldi
Via Broletto 1/P,
Tel. 0522432795
The owners of this shop buy the meat fresh from reliable butchers and commission its processing, keeping close control of production. They carry also prosciutto, culatello, coppa, and salami of their own production.

CORREGGIO

Salumificio Bidinelli
Via Circondario 17,
Tel. 0522692527
Mortadella is made by hand from high-quality cuts, without using polyphosphates, milk powder or dextrose, and offered in sized cuts, also in tasty versions with truffle and pistachios

FOOD

CHEESE

The sea, great river, plain and Apennines are its borders, and they account for all the diversity. But as if this were not enough, there seem to be more differences defining the personality of the inhabitants: supposedly, the people of Emilia are more easy going and the Romagna people more highly-strung. However, one aspect they have in common is their love of food, originating from and inspired by the extremely varied range of gastronomic products such a rich variety that is found in no other region in Italy. Foremost is Parmigiano-Reggiano cheese, famous, international, imitated, but unique. Linked to peasant shrewdness and originating from the hills is the "formaggio di fossa" of Sogliano. Pecorino cheeses come from the Apennines. From Romagna, "robiola" and "squacquerone" are soft blends for "piadine".

Grana Padano DOP

The production of this traditional cheese for grating, shared by other northern regions, is mainly connected to the province of Piacenza with lesser locations in the Bologna, Ferrara, Forlì-Cesena and Ravenna areas. It is a product with similarities, both historically and in the way it is processed, with Parmigiano-Reggiano DOP, the most typical and well-known of Emilia's cheeses.

Fossa di Sogliano al Rubicone

The center of the Romagna hinterland upholds the traditions of this production, the area of interest covering the territory of the provinces of Forlì-Cesena, Rimini and, in the Marche region, that of Pesaro and Urbino. This sheep's milk or mixed cow's and sheep's milk product is made in round cheeses with a distinctive seasoning procedure, which takes place in canvas bags in hermetically sealed tufa pits. The cheeses take on uneven shapes, the rind becomes damp and greasy, with condensed fat and mold. The cheese becomes a variable color between white and rich yellow, and takes on a slightly bitter taste with a distinctive fragrance of woodland undergrowth. PGI recognition is being investigated.

Parmigiano-Reggiano DOP

The origin of this celebrated cheese has an exact location in place and time: the place is the valley of the Enza River which separates today's provinces of Parma and Reggio Emilia; the time is the Middle Ages when this land prospered thanks to the agricultural activity started by the Benedictine and Cistercian monks, in particular cattle breeding and cheese production. The ambition of reaching beyond the local market was an incentive to creating a long-life product that could travel without problems, and these requirements resulted in the cheese we know today: finely granular and tending towards a flaky quality, a sharp taste, though never spicy. Today the production area includes the provinces of Parma, Reggio Emilia, Modena and Bologna, on the left bank of the Reno River, with an offshoot into the Lombardy region on the northern side of the Po in the Mantua area. The procedure has remained practically the same, requiring two milkings: the evening one semi-skimmed from the surface, and the morning one of whole milk. The milk is worked raw to maintain the bacterial flora, only with the addition of whey from the previous day, rich in lactic cultures, facilitating

The milk from the red cows of Reggio is used for a particularly fine variety of Parmigiano-ReggianoV

its transformation. The formation of the cheesy mass is obtained by using calf rennet, followed by a slow cooking process; the curd is finally removed to cylinder shaped molds bearing the dotted inscription "Parmigiano-Reggiano" on the side and a plaque identifying the round of cheese. These rounds (weighing 25 to 40 kg) are then submitted to the salting procedure and to seasoning with a minimum duration of 12 months, but may remain for as much as 36 months for top quality products.

Pecorino del Pastore
From the hills and mountains of old Romagna. A whole sheep's milk cheese, raw or pasteurized, offered in different sizes, both fresh and mature, abiding by the manufacturing process followed in the Romagna hinterland since the 16th century. The production of Castel San Pietro and Palesio (Bologna) are very well known.

Pecorino dell' Appennino Reggiano
An Apennine cheese typical of the mountains of the Reggio province made of whole sheep'smilk coagulated with lamb rennet and then cooked. When cut, after 60 days, the cheese mass is light in color, compact, with no holes, and a strong flavor.

Ravaggiolo
Produced in a few Apennine townships in the province of Forlì-Cesena: Tredozio, Modigliana, Portico di Romagna, San Benedetto in Alpe as well as Sogliano al Rubicone. It is a fresh cheese made of freshly milked cow's milk, which used to be mixed with goat's milk. The curd, placed on cabbage, fig or fern leaves is ready to be eaten in just a few days, soft and mild in taste.

Fresh cow's milk ricotta traditional of the Emilia-Romagna region
This production is linked to that of Parmigiano-Reggiano and it is from the same territory.
The raw material is the whey from the primary processing, with the possible addition of milk or cream. The term "ricotta" (in other words cooked twice) refers to the heating of the whey, followed by the curdling caused by the addition of an acidification agent.

Robiola
A product typical of the Tidone Valley in the Piacenza area. It is a fresh, creamy sheep's cheese with milk, sugar, dry white wine or even grappa or cognac, put in small glass jars, covered with oil and left to mature until it becomes strong. Among the places where it is produced are the townships of Castel San Giovanni and Morfasso.

Squacquerone di Romagna
This is a fresh cheese with a soft, almost fluid, consistency. It is made from cow's milk and is identified by the absence of rind, a pearly colour, and a pleasant, slightly sour taste. The production area includes the provinces of Bologna, Ravenna, Forlì-Cesena and Rimini; Squacquerone from Castel San Pietro (Bologna) is extremely well known. It is a product that has humble origins, but ever since the early 19th century has been acknowledged by sophisticated consumers.

BOLOGNA

Antica Formaggeria Zaratini
Via Guerrazzi 10/B, Tel. 051220544
Top quality cheeses in this shop which has been operating for over 50 years. In season there may be a selection of as many as 200-300 different types, originating from all over Italy and abroad.

The fire brand puts the permanent seal on Parmigiano-Reggiano

Bonacorsi
Via Maestri del Lavoro 34/34
Tel. 0516013965, www.bonacorsi.it
They age their cheeses in Castelfranco Emilia, notably Parmigiano-Reggiano and Grana Padano.

FERRARA

Goloseria
Via Garibaldi 27,
Tel. 0532206636
A wide range of national and foreign cheeses in this shop where other local products can be found.

CENTO
Al Furmai
Via Ugo Bassi 21,
Tel. 051902295
The owner personally selects and researches the best available local products, such as Fossa di Sogliano al Rubicone, along with a rich selection of fresh and matured cheeses produced throughout the rest of the country.

FORLÌ-CESENA

SAVIGNANO SUL RUBICONE
Caseificio Pascoli
Via Rubicone Destra 220
Tel. 0541945732
www.caseificiopascoli.it
For over 30 years they have produced sheep and goat cheeses, squacquerone and fossa cheeses: besides its own products it also sells Pecorino cheeses and various ripened cheeses.
It belongs to the Strada dei Vini e dei Sapori (food and wine itineraries) organized locally by public companies and retailers, and it can be visited by appointment.

SOGLIANO AL RUBICONE
Formaggio di Fossa
Via Pascoli 8,
Tel. 0541948687
www.formaggiodifossa.net
Producer of Fossa di Sogliano cheese. The pits date back to the period

between the 14th and 15th centuries. They can be seen, on request, only during the week in which they are emptied.

Fossa Pellegrini
Via Le Greppe 14,
Tel. 0541948542
www.formaggiodifossa.it
This cheese factory, dating from the Malatesta period, produces 10 types of the Fossa di Sogliano. The pits can be seen, on request, during the Formaggio di Fossa Fair; besides making purchases, it is possible by reservation to have your own cheese matured i the firm's pits.

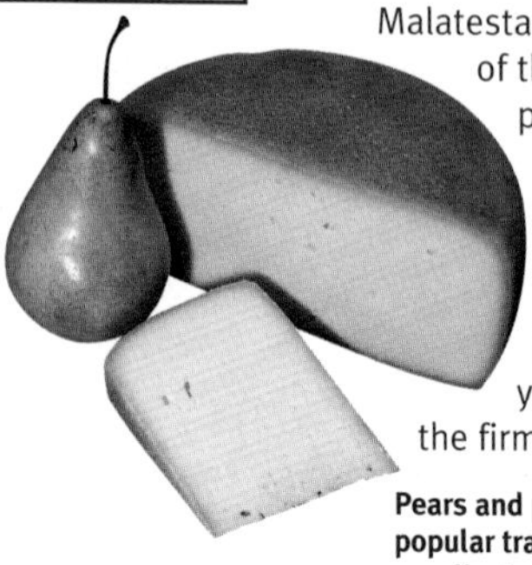

Pears and pecorino is a classic dish. Even popular tradition has a proverb recalling th excellent combination of this cheese with

Fosse Venturi
Via Roma 67, Tel. 0541948521
This cheese manufacturer produces 10 different kinds of pit-ripened cheese, mixed sheep, cow and buffalo cheeses, and organic goat and sheep cheeses. The pits are dug under the house; they were rediscovered and restructured about 10 years ago and are open, on request, whe the cheeses are taken out or put in.

MODENA

Azienda Agricola Hombre
Via Corletto Sud 320,
Tel. 059510660
www.hombre.it
This firm sells its own products, butter and ricotta. ISO 9002 certifies Parmigiano-Reggiano produced organically with methods attested by AIAB (The Italian Association for Organic Agriculture); guided tours must be booked.

PARMA

Casa del Formaggio
Via Bixio 106,
Tel. 0521230243
An outstanding shop: in winter there may be as many as 500 different types

of cheese; also extra-virgin olive oil from Brisighella and balsamic vinegar from Modena and Reggio-Emilia.

aseificio Ottorino Barani
San Prospero, Via E. Lepido 291
Tel. 0521645148
Besides its own Parmigiano-Reggiano matured up to 30 months, there are other locally produced cheeses.

SALSOMAGGIORE TERME
San Nicomede
San Nicomede, Via Maestà 28/A
Tel. 0524572089
The firm is in the area of the Parco dello Stirone, and produces ripe and fresh Parmigiano-Reggiano.

RAVENNA

CASOLA VALSENIO
attoria Rio Stella
Zattaglia, Via Monte Mauro 17
Tel. 054671470
Sale of local certified organic cheeses of the Romagna Apennines: from raw whole sheep's, goat's or brown cow's milk; from raw whole mixed milk (Caprino-Vaccino, Montemauro, Tomino, Speziato); Favoloso cheese and Ricotta Montemauro. This cheese manufacturer uses only milk produced from organic breeding farms under ANFOSC (Assoc. Naz. Formaggi Sotto il Cielo, Nat. Assoc. for Cheeses under the sky); visits on request.

REGGIO EMILIA

Consorzio per la Valorizzazione Prodotti Antica Razza Reggiana Caseificio Notari
Coviolo, c/o Istituto Agrario Zanelli,
Via F.lli Rosselli 41/2,
Tel. 0522294655
An annex of the Zanelli Agricultural Institute, this cheese manufacturer produces an exclusive Parmigiano-Reggiano with milk from red cows, an old, native breed well known for the high quality of its milk.

CAMPEGINE
Latteria Sociale Case Cocconi
Via della Fornace 4/A,
Tel. 0522677490
www.ilparmigiano.com

This old, renowned cheese manufacturer, which may be visited on request, has since 1940 been producing and selling butter and the real Parmigiano-Reggiano DOP, matured from 12 to 26 months.

CANOSSA
La Corte di Matilde
Ciano d'Enza, Via Val d'Enza Nord 167
Tel. 0522872225
The farm annexed to the IAT office (tourist Information) is the shop of the Consorzio Buonappennino, operating in the Parco del Gigante (Giant's Park) and offers organic products: branded, mountain quality Parmigiano-Reggiano.

RIMINI

Ai Sapori Felici
Via Castelfidardo 52,
Tel. 054127972
This major Rimini food store offers Fossa, Squacquerone, Parmigiano-Reggiano and Grana Padano cheeses, plus fresh and ripened goat cheeses.

FOOD

Steel milk containers and copper processing boilers are an indication of the careful attention to hygiene in modern production.

OIL

Olive oil from Emilia Romagna tends to be full-bodied, deep in colour and aromatic. It is produced both in the coastal zones, where the climate is mild, and sections of the Apennines, where it is colder. Although farming in this region remains largely traditional, favouring mixed crops rather than specialisation, the last 30 years have seen a definite move towards more olive groves. Nowadays, the majority of olive oil produced in Emilia-Romagna comes from the Romagna section, where olive cultivation is expanding. By contrast, the olive oil produced in Emilia tends to be for home consumption. There are about 30 active olive oil producing plants in the region, with roughly half still using traditional pressing methods and the other half using more modern techniques.

The advantages of small scale production

Although the olive oil produced in Emilia Romagna only accounts for a small part of the regional agricultural economy, it has caught the attention of the market, receiving the EU's Protected Designation of Origin seal for Brisighella in 1998. The name comes from a delightful little town near Faenza, nestled in the shadow of three chalky hills dotted with many sites of historical and artistic interest. This olive oil production area extends into the provinces of Ravenna and Forlì-Cesena, and includes part or all of the Brisighella, Faenza, Riolo Terme, Casola Valsenio and Modigliana municipal districts.

In this area, on the left bank of the Lamone, the unusual soil and climate, partly due to the Vena del Gesso hills, give the olives some distinct characteristics. Indeed, some cultivars thrive here, such as Nostrana di Brisighella, which originated in this area thousands of years ago. Closer to Forlì, there is also another local variety, Selvatico. The Rimini area also produces a fair amount of oil, although most of it is either consumed by local families or sold to wholesalers. Aside from a local variety, Rossina, the cultivars found here are the same as those in Tuscany and the nearby Marche region, namely Frantoio, Moraiolo, Pendolino, and Correggiolo.

THE EXTRA-VIRGIN OLIVE OILS OF BRISIGHELLA

There are 4 classifications, all "extra-virgin oilve oils": Pieve Tho, Brisighella DOP, Cru Brisighello, Nobil Drupa selection. These oils produced in the hills surrounding the town of Brisighella display the best and most pleasing sensory characteristcs, in particular the fruity element, typical of green oil, as well as the distinctive flavor of green artichoke, a sensation of fluidity on the palate, and no feeling of stagnation. The olives are mainly of the local Brisighella variety, and only the "ghiacciolo" variety for the Nobil Drupa olive oil. Brisighella olive oils are suitable in many cooking uses. Proof of good quality is the yield of olives in oil which is around 11-15%. Olive pressing in real time is within 24 hours, as determined by the associated olive pressing mill. Processing is by cold-olive pressing using the "Sinolea" filtering system of oil-must, separating the components and catching the oil as it surfaces, with due consideration for the intact and natural state of the oils, which are not compressed, centrifuged, beaten, or mechanically treated. These olive oils are produced and sold by the Brisighella Agricultural Cooperative.

WINE

A huge vineyard extends from the Apennine hills to the shores of the Po River and the Adriatic Sea, offering well-known wines that have come to symbolize this region where good food and company are at the center of everyday life. The Via Aemilia (the ancient Roman road whose construction began in 187 BC) runs through the whole region along a string of cities from Piacenza to Rimini, and divides it in half: on one side, the Apennines whose gentle hills are favorable for vines for their position and climate; on the other, the plain descending to the Po River and the Adriatic coast, revealing a wine-making vocation that is far above expectations. This geographic area consists of four production districts that are consistent by tradition and ampelographic composition. The first is located on the hills of Piacenza and Parma, where the red Barbera, Gutturnio, and Bonarda prevail, demonstrating the evident influence of the neighboring Oltrepò Pavese area, but the white Ortugo and Malvasia di Candia are also present. Then there are the lands of Lambrusco, emblematic of Emilia's wine production, extending from the hills to the banks of the Po in the provinces of Reggio Emilia and Modena. These are followed by the Bologna hills and the lower valley of the River Reno, where traditional white wines prevail, such as Pignoletto and Montù. Finally comes the vast vineyard of Romagna, with Sangiovese, Trebbiano, Pagadebit and Albana dominating the scene. The regional scenario closes at the Ferrara end, with the vineyards planted at Fortana on the sands of the Po Delta. Other DOC (controlled denomination of origin) recognized areas are Bosco Eliceo, and the hills of Faenza, Imola, Rimini, Scandiano and Canossa.

One DOCG wine, Albana di Romagna, and 20 DOC

The composition of the Emilia-Romagna vineyards, extending two thirds on the plain and the remainder on the hills, is clearly outlined. Only two vines cover almost half of the region: they are the white Trebbiano Romagnolo and the red Sangiovese, both characteristic of the Romagna production in particular. Reinforcing the position of the slightly predominating reds, there are the Lambrusco wines, the Ancellotta, and the coupled Barbera and Bonarda. Among the whites, the Albana is foremost, as the only DOCG wine of the region. Also worthy of mention are some interesting local wines such as the Montù of the lower Reno River area, and Malvasia Bianca di Candia from Parma and Piacenza. Pride of the region is the DOCG attributed to Albana di Romagna, followed by 20 DOC and 10 IGT areas. The DOC production places Emilia-Romagna in fifth position in Italy with two wines, Colli Piacentini and Reggiano, among the top 20 Italian DOC wines; in this sector red wines are more than twice as many as whites but the production is only partially DOC (25%) or IGT (40%). However, since the region is particularly alert in evaluating its wine and food resources, there are prospects pointing to a prompt extension of such protective measures. The vitality of this sector is unquestionable and mention should be made of the wine tours, on fertile ground in the Emilia-Romagna region due to the beauty of the landscape, its art treasures, and traditions for reception and welcome. There are as many as 11 food and wine routes (promoted and supported by local organizations and retailers) significantly present in the area and backed by a network of hotel and restaurant hospitality unequaled in the entire country.

Albana di Romagna DOCG

A wine produced in the provinces of Bologna, Forlì-Cesena and Ravenna. Unmistakable on the vine for its elongated bunches of golden yellow grapes, Albana stands out for its sugar content which is the basis for exceptional vinification. It is the first Italian white wine to have obtained the DOCG recognition and offers a production code covering several different types: dry, straw-yellow in color tending to golden with aging, a

FOOD

155

characteristic bouquet and a dry, slightly tannic, warm, harmonious flavor; Amabile and Dolce differ in the intensity of fruity hints and rounded flavor; Passito, amber in color, intense bouquet and velvety, full flavor. Its ageing capacity increases in proportion to its alcoholic content, from 2 to 3 years for the dry wine, 10 or more for passito. The dry type goes well with seafood in general, especially shellfish and fish soups; it can also accompany white meats. The Amabile and Dolce are dessert wines accompanying a wide range of combinations, and traditionally Ciambella, the local cake. Passito is usually served with pastry and dried fruit, but also with herbed or spiced cheeses.

Gutturnio, a Roman wine jug

Bonarda Colli Piacentini DOC

Obtained from the vine with the same name, this is a ruby red, at times intense table wine, very suitable for the products of local gastronomy such as Coppa Piacentina. It is produced in Frizzante or Spumante types and has a flavor that can be dry, abboccato (sweetish), amabile (semi-sweet), or dolce (sweet), slightly tannic, fresh, still or fizzy; ageing can last up to 3 years.

Gutturnio Colli Piacentini DOC

This derives its name from a silver Roman goblet recovered from the Po River in 1878. It is the best known of the Colli Piacentini DOCs and has a distinctive blend of Barbera and Croatina grapes typical of the area. A wine with a wide spectrum, dry or semi-sweet, still or sparkling, it also comes in the Novello, Superiore and Riserva types. The label can indicate the "Classico" qualification if produced in the area of the oldest tradition. It is particularly suitable in a combination with "Coppa" or with the tasty local first courses such as "Pisarei con Fagioli".

Lambrusco DOC

A denomination that refers to a large family of red grape vines and several different DOC productions in the area of Reggio Emilia and Modena. Three of them, Lambrusco Grasparossa di Castelvetro, grown in the hills, Lambrusco Salamino di Santa Croce and Lambrusco di Sorbara, widespread in the plain, have acquired autonomous denomination. These sparkling wines share the fragrance of bouquets with marked hints of violets, their slightly acidulous flavor and freshness making them ideal companions for cured pork meats, especially the cooked ones, and for the rich Emilia cuisine in general. Castelvetro di Modena lends its name to Lambrusco Grasparossa di Castelvetro, typical of the Emilia tradition but now widespread thanks to its relatively low alcohol content and slight sparkle, making it agreeable and easy to drink. Compared to the other types of Lambrusco, it is firm in structure, intense in color

Travo, a farm and rows of vines in the Piacenza area

Countryside with vineyards between Reggio Emilia and Modena

and bouquet and full-bodied. By local custom it is drunk throughout the entire meal.

Lambrusco Salamino di Santa Croce comes in two types, Frizzante Rosso (sparkling red) and Frizzante Rosato (sparkling rosé) and can be Secco, Abboccato, Amabile or Dolce. Ideal for first courses and cured pork meats, it is also an agreeable end-of-meal wine in the Amabile version.

Lambrusco di Sorbara is the most valued of the Emilia Lambrusco wines; it is a red or rosé sparkling wine, owing its reputation to its preservation capacities, which have favored its export. Light ruby red in color, a rosy froth, it has a fresh, fine bouquet with hints of violets, slightly aromatic and fruity. The typical combination is with cured pork meats, Parmesan cheese and pasta courses.

Malvasia Colli di Parma DOC

White wine produced from the Malvasia di Candia Aromatica vine. Straw-yellow in color and dry in taste, still or sparkling. It comes in the Amabile, Spumante and Frizzante types and is ideal for seafood dishes.

Ortrugo Colli Piacentini DOC

A local white wine produced from a rare, native vine of the same name – Ortrugo – straw-yellow in color tending towards greenish. Delicate, aromatic bouquet, dry flavor with a slightly bitter

aftertaste, it accompanies omelets, soft cheeses and tortelli with herbs. It comes in Secco, Frizzante and Spumante types.

Pagadebit di Romagna DOC

Amabile white wine (also Frizzante), produced from the Bombino Bianco vine, a type of high-yield grape guaranteeing a good harvest even in difficult years. It is straw-yellow in color, with a characteristic bouquet of hawthorn and a delicate flavor that is dry, grassy and harmonious. It qualifies as Bertinoro if produced in the limited area of this township. (Secco or Amabile, also Frizzante).

Sangiovese di Romagna DOC

This is the most widely cultivated vine in Italy. It crossed the Apennines from its native Tuscany to become the vine that is the symbol of Romagna, grown predominantly on the hills. The earliest evidence of its presence dates from the 17th century, and since then its reputation has constantly grown. In the valleys between Imola and Rimini the climate and the evolution of the vine through the centuries have produced a ruby red wine with possible purple hues, delicate bouquet with hints of violets, dry and harmonious with slightly bitter undertones. It is made in the Novello, Superiore and Riserva versions, as well as geographic denomination of the best known areas (Faenza, Forlì,

FOOD

157

The appealing interior of a winery

Cesena, Imola and Rimini).
It goes well with roast meats, but can also accompany tagliatelle with meat sauce.

Trebbiano di Romagna DOC

This is the other record-holder among regional wines, as well as being the most-produced white wine in the world. A highly productive vine, it is traditionally converted into easy-to-drink wines. This is a good feature in particular if the producer is able to bring out the characteristic bouquet of apple and fresh grass with a dominating acidulous hint. Its straw-yellow color, floral bouquet and delicate flavor make it suitable for combinations with tortelli alle erbette and with the Adriatic coastal seafood cuisine.

TRADITIONAL DOP BALSAMIC VINEGAR

Another offshoot of the vineyards is traditional DOP balsamic vinegar, uniting Reggio Emilia and Modena in a production that is unique. A tour of a vinegar plant is an experience not to be missed: there is an amazing assortment of casks used for ageing. In order to qualify as traditional, balsamic vinegar must originate from grape-must concentrated through boiling over a direct flame (not from wine, as in the standard versions). The grapes most commonly used are Trebbiano, therefore white, although there are additions of red grapes, Lambrusco and others. The liquid resulting from this processing then has to mature by slow, natural acetification and finally undergo refining requiring at least 12 annual decantings into kegs of different types of wood (oak, chestnut, cherry, juniper and mulberry) exposed in attic storerooms to temperature variations that favor the assimilation of the noble tannins of the different woods. Aceto Balsamico Tradizionale of Reggio Emilia (www.acetobalsamicotradizionale.it) comes in three varieties: Aragosta (lobster red), Argento (silver) and Oro (gold) – Extravecchio (aged for over 25 years), according to the color of the corresponding label; with increasing age they acquire a higher sugar content passing from general use as a condiment for meat and cheese to a garnish for desserts. Aceto Balsamico Tradizionale di Modena (www.balsamico.it), bottled in the exclusive globe-shaped vial with a rectangular base, also has the denomination Extravecchio (gold capsule). For vinegars that have been thus aged there is also the term "balsamic for tasting".

BOLOGNA

IMOLA

e Monti
Bergullo, Via Lola 3, Tel. 0542657116
www.tremonti.it
- Colli di Imola Rosso Boldo - DOC
- Sangiovese di Romagna Superiore
  Thea - DOC
- ○ Albana di Romagna Secco Vigna della
  Rocca - DOCG
- ○ Trebbiano di Romagna Vigna del Rio -
  DOC
- ☾ Albana di Romagna Passito - DOCG

FORLÌ

alonga
Via Castel Leone 8, Tel. 0543753044
- Sangiovese di Romagna Superiore Il
  Bruno - DOC
- Sangiovese di Romagna Superiore
  Riserva Michelangiolo - DOC
- Castellione Cabernet Sauvignon Forlì
  - IGT

BERTINORO

Madonia Giovanna
Via Cappuccini 130,
Tel. 0543444361
- Sangiovese di Romagna Superiore
  Fermavento - DOC
- Sangiovese di Romagna Superiore
  Riserva Ombroso - DOC
- Sterpigno Merlot Forlì - IGT
- ○ Albana di Romagna Passito Chimera -
  DOCG
- ☾ Albana di Romagna Passito Remoto -
  DOCG

MODIGLIANA

Castelluccio
Via Tramonto 15, Tel. 0546942486
www.ronchidicastelluccio.it
- Sangiovese di Romagna Le More - DOC
- Ronco dei Ciliegi Forlì Rosso - IGT
- Ronco delle Ginestre Forlì Rosso - IGT
- ○ Lunaria Forlì Bianco - IGT
- ○ Ronco del Re Forlì Bianco - IGT

SAVIGLIANO SUL RUBICONE

Colonna Giovanni - Spalletti Vini
Via Matteotti 62, Tel. 0541945111
- Sangiovese di Romagna Superiore
  Rocca di Ribano - DOC
- ○ Albana di Romagna Secco - DOCG
- ☾ Albana di Romagna Passito Maolù -
  DOCG

MODENA

BRISIGHELLA

La Berta
Via Berta 13, Tel. 054684998
- Colli di Faenza Rosso Ca' di Berta -
  DOC
- Sangiovese di Romagna Superiore
  Riserva Olmatello - DOC
- Sangiovese di Romagna Superiore
  Solano - DOC
- Almante - IGT
- ☾ Infavato - VDT

CASTELVETRO DI MODENA

Tenuta Pederzana
Via Cavalliera 8, Tel. 059748072
- Lambrusco Grasparossa di
  Castelvetro Semisecco - DOC
- Puntamora Rosso Amabile - VDT
- Ronchigliano - VDT

Pomposa, large buildings and vineyards; in the background, the abbey bell tower

FOOD

Wine Categories

Three labels define Italian wines according to quality. IGT (Typical Geographic Indication) guarantees vine cultivation according to certain regulations. DOC (Controlled Origin Denomination) indicates conformity to regulations on area of origin, and production and maturation procedures. The top label is DOCG (Guaranteed and Controlled Origin Denomination); there are around 20 DOCG wines in Italy, 6 in Tuscany. VDT is for table wine with an alcohol content of at least 10%.

RAVENNA

FAENZA
Fattoria Zerbina
Marzeno, Via Vicchio 11, Tel. 054640022
- ● Sangiovese di Romagna Riserva Pietramora - DOC
- ● Sangiovese di Romagna Superiore Torre di Ceparano - DOC
- ● Marzieno Ravenna Rosso - IGT
- ◐ Albana di Romagna Passito Arrocco - DOCG
- ◐ Albana di Romagna Passito Scacco Matto - DOCG

LUGO
Cantina Ronchi
Via Paurosa 15, Tel. 054523041, www.ronchivini.it
- ● Sangiovese di Romagna Superiore Riserva Borsignolo - DOC

REGGIO EMILIA

Castelli del Duca
Gaida, Via Newton 13/A Tel. 0522942135
- ● Colli Piacentini Gutturnio Riserva Sigillum - DOC
- ● Colli Piacentini Gutturnio Superiore - DOC
- ◐ Colli Piacentini Malvasia Passito Soleste - DOC

WINE LEGEND

Wines are listed with symbols which indicate their type
- ● red
- ○ white
- ● rosé
- ◐ sweet or dessert

Bertinoro, a farm surrounded by vineyards

LIQUEURS

n Emilia-Romagna the production of liqueurs and distillates comes from both small manufacturing workshops where methods follow age-old traditions and the quantities of finished
`oduct are small but high in quality, and a brandy industry that respects traditional methods
ut produces large quantities, putting this region in first place in national production. There is
so the monastery liqueur distillery which is a treasure chest of the region's wine and gastron-
my culture and a stronghold of local tradition.

Marsala all'Uovo

This is produced using fine Marsala wine at least one year old, blended with caster sugar, eggs, and flavoring. It is aged in casks for at least one year.

Nocino

A local liqueur produced in Noceto (Parma) and in neighboring towns, based on a blend of walnuts, from which it takes its name. Its origins stem from medieval times. To prepare this liqueur the hand-gathered, green husks of the walnuts are used, chopped, and put into an alcohol infusion in tanks, where the mixture is left to rest for a period of two to four years and then filtered and bottled. Some variations allow for the use of sugar and natural flavors, such as cloves, cinnamon, lemon zest or coriander seeds, resulting in a dense, amber colored liqueur with a rich and agreeable nut fragrance. It should be savored straight, cold or at room temperature as an after-dinner liqueur; it can also be used to flavor vanilla ice cream or plain cream, and in the preparation of desserts.

Sassolino

A liqueur obtained from distilling anise with sugar and alcohol. Served cold or at room temperature with a grain of roasted coffee, it is an excellent after-dinner liqueur. It is also used in the preparation of several local desserts.

Brandy

The term brandy indicates the spirit obtained from the distillation of wine followed by aging. The name derives from the Dutch brandewin, which means burnt wine. The earliest evidence of its existence dates from the 16th century. The minimum alcoholic content cannot be less than 38%, but it is normally marketed with 40%. Aging, which is rigorously a minimum of one year, usually in oak casks, is a delicate and important stage because it is necessary to refine its taste and flavor which is affected by the type of wood the casks are made of. The taste, dry or mellow, depends on the skill of the wine cellar experts who blend different lots of distilled and aged product. The coloring is determined by the caramel added to it, and to a lesser degree by the effect of the substances contained in the wood of the casks. The area of the Romagna hills and the Trebbiano grapes lend themselves to the manufacture of an excellent brandy, which is here obtained without any oenological additive and is aged for no less than 30 months in small oak casks, with no addition of flavoring or caramel. Italy features a great brandy tradition, with a large number of excellent producers, including Fabbri, Landy Freres, Oro Pilla and Vecchia Romagna. The proper glass for tasting it is the classic "balloon": the brandy should be aired and warmed with a slight rotating motion in order to exalt the aroma and flavor as much as possible. Brandy is also much used in the kitchen where it lends a touch of style to beef fillets, lobster, chocolate pudding and ice cream.

FOOD

CAKE

Emilia-Romagna is a region with a multi-faceted gastronomy. The first aspect of the diversity is found in the historical differentiation between Emilia and Romagna: the former, a land of Lombard settlements, then independent states in contact with the European nations; the latter passing from the Byzantines to the Church State and remaining traditionally Latin; the former with the Po Valley traditional cooking, relying heavily on butter and cream in pastry; the latter of Adriatic tradition, including everything that maritime interchange has brought to cooking through the centuries, as well as Latin tradition of more archaic tendency. In the confectionery sector the main cities keep alive the tradition of the medieval courts (such is the "pan speziale" of Bologna), and of the Este family, lords of Ferrara in the Renaissance period, who are credited with complex dishes such as "torta ricciolina" and "zuppa inglese" (liqueur soaked sponge cake with a filling of cream and chocolate). In the smaller towns instead, the peasant tradition prevails: in the lowlands there are the leavened ring-shaped cakes, in the mountains the desserts prepared with chestnut flour and ricotta.

Biscione Reggiano (Reggio Emilia)

A Christmas cake. In spite of its simple appearance, it requires lengthy preparation. The basis is almond pastry covered with meringue, in the shape of a snake, which gives it its name.

Ciambella (ring-shaped cake) Ferrarese or "Brazadela"

This Ferrara Easter cake, partly for its ring-shape, is linked to the archaic tradition of propitiatory sweets. The pastry is soft and fragrant, made from white flour, sugar, eggs, milk, butter, yeast, anise, lemon zest and salt. By tradition, it is eaten dipped in wine.

Ciambella Reggiana or "Bresadela" or "Busilan"

The ingredients are white flour, eggs, butter, sugar, lemon zest, Sassolino liqueur and yeast. It is made in different shapes, like a ring or a loaf. The pastry is brushed with beaten egg and granular sugar and baked in the oven.

Ciambelline or "Buslanein"

Oven-baked, ring-shaped cookies typical of the Piacenza area, kneaded with white flour, eggs, sugar and milk. They are sold loose or tied like a necklace. In the 14th century they were the ritual gift to the priests of the cathedral.

Dolce di San Michele

Prepared on the feast of the patron saint of the town of Bagnacavallo (Ravenna), September 29th, this is a shortcrust pastry cake with "panna cotta", garnished with nuts, almonds and pine nuts. It is prepared to a recipe taken from a text of the 16th century which is kept in the town records.

Mandorline del Ponte

The reference is to Pontelagoscuro, a suburb of the city of Ferrara, overlooking the Po River. Rose colored "spumiglie" (puffs) made of whole or broken almonds mixed with egg white whisked until stiff, and honey, then baked in the oven.

Miacetto

From the town of Cattolica (Rimini), a Christmas sweet, made with ingredients that are compatible with penitence fasting of the Roman Catholic tradition: flour, nuts, toasted almonds, pine nuts, sultana raisins,

The classic Ferrara Easter cake is flavored with anise and leon

honey, sugar, lemon and orange zest, cocoa, cinnamon, salt, olive oil, water.

istuchina

An old-time traditional baked product that was originally connected with penitence fasting in the Romagna lowlands, particularly Bagnacavallo (Ravenna). It is created using dough made of chestnut flour and water, adding "saba", aniseed, orange and lemon peel, and is garnished with confectioner's sugar.

ampapato

A 17th-century recipe from Ferrara, traditionally prepared by the nuns of the Convent of Corpus Domini as a Christmas tribute to the top dignitaries of the city's church; the name means the Pope's bread, and the shape happens to recall the shape of the high prelates' skull-cap. The mixture is made of flour, water, cocoa, sugar, honey, almonds, hazelnuts, candied orange peel, a few drops of ammonia and natural flavoring. After baking, it is

ampapato were invented in the 17th century in Ferrara

sprayed with orange water. The top glazing, which was added in recent times, is bitter chocolate.

'an speziale or Certosino

The Bologna Christmas cake (a compact, long-lasting fruitcake based on dried and candied fruit) probably derives its name from the fact that in Medieval times the first to prepare it were the pharmacists, called "speziali" at the time, with ingredients then considered "exotic", such as the almonds which they traded. Later the Carthusian monks of Bologna became

the producers par excellence of this cake, which consequently gained the name Certosino. The ingredients: the finest flour, sweet and bitter almonds, pine nuts, raisins, candied citron or orange, anise seeds, honey, rum, chocolate and sugar.

Pattona

A specialty of the upper valley of the Taro River (Parma), this cake is made with a base of chestnut flour kneaded with water, oil and salt, covered with ricotta (soft white unsalted sheep's milk cheese) and baked in the oven. It is a humble dessert, making use of the few ingredients available in times of shortage and poverty.

Pinza Bolognese

A cake of peasant origin, oblong in shape, consisting in an outer shell of puff pastry with orange flavor, and a filling of "mostarda" (spiced fruit) traditional of Bologna, sultana raisins and pine nuts, with the occasional addition of nuts and almonds. Its characteristic taste is of quince which is the basis of mostarda.

Spongata

A flat round pie, consisting in an outer shell of thin crisp pastry, covered with confectioner's sugar, and a soft, light brown filling with a spicy taste. The traditional recipe is recorded from the 14th century. The ingredients: toasted bread, amaretto biscuits, nuts, honey, sugar, pine nuts, sultana raisins, cloves, nutmeg, cinnamon, orange peel, white wine. The name refers to the sponge-like consistency of the filling and to the surface of the outer shell which is riddled with holes. The geographic area of Spongata has its center in Reggio Emilia, with specific tradition in the town of Brescello, and extends to the adjoining provinces of Parma and Modena.

Recently it has also become available in a chocolate version.

Spongata of Busseto

An oven baked cake, typical of the

FOOD

163

central Parma lowlands. The outer shell is puff pastry kneaded with flour and butter; the filling is a mixture of apples, almonds, pine nuts, candied fruit and raisins, finely chopped with the addition of crumbled rusks, and bound together with honey previously heated in white wine.

Spongata di Reggio Emilia

An oven-baked cake of medieval origin, it was first made in Brescello, a town in the Po Valley. The outer shell is short-crust pastry with a filling of honey, almonds, pine nuts and sultana raisins, of soft consistency and spicy in flavor.

Sugali

Typical of the Romagna area, in particular Bagnacavallo, this was the dessert of the peasants after the grape harvest, made with grape must, corn flour, white flour, breadcrumbs, semolina, lemon zest and anise seeds.

Sugo d'Uva Reggiano

Made in the province of Reggio Emilia and in the areas of the Lancellotta grapes. It is a pudding made by

thickening grape must with sugar an flour.

Topino d'Ognissanti or "Punghe or "Puntech"

A dessert from Comacchio (Ferrara) i the shape of a mouse, a blend of flo eggs, milk, butter, yeast, herbs and spices, and two grape seeds for the eyes. The name is a reference to a memorable invasion of rats in the cit cemetery, which was ended with the help of the Virgin Mary.

Torta di Riso Reggiana

A round or rectangular baked cake consisting of rice, flour, eggs and sugar; on the surface the typical swee layer due to the deposit of rice on th bottom of the mold. The original recip came from the custom of Reggio Emil women to participate in the rice harvest, obtaining part of their pay in kind.

Torta ricciolina or Torta di Tagliatelle or Taiadela

The recipe originated at the Este cour in Ferrara and its neighboring towns. is short-crust pastry filled with egg

BOLOGNA CHOCOLATE

The Laboratorio delle Cose Dolci (confectioner's workshop) was established in Bologna in 1796. Originally dedicated to the production of the hot chocolate drink, in 1832 it introduced the first solid chocolate to Italy, known as "Scorza", still produced to the original recipe. Then the Majani pastry shop in Via de' Carbonesi opened in 1834, and it is still active and filled with atmosphere. The business gradually extended its range, until Giuseppe Majani went personally to Turin, crossing the borders of three states, to purchase the most innovative machinery for the production of chocolate, activated by a portable steam engine. Recognition and praise soon

followed: Aldo Majani was awarded the cross of Grand Master of the order of the Italian Crown; in 1878 the King of Italy conferred the title of Royal Supplier to the chocolate factory and granted it the use of the coat-of-arms of the House of Savoy; that same year the Paris Universal Exhibition awarded it the silver medal... But the golden age for Majani was the dawning of the new century. The chocolate factory was extremely popular in artistic and university circles, and in 1911 it conceived its lead product, "Cremino Fiat", ordered by the Turin automobile firm as its promotional gift for the launching of the new Fiat model 4. In those years it also built the magnifi-

cent Art Nouveau style villa i the city center in Via Indipen denza, which soon became a meeting point for artists and scholars. The firm, still held by the same family, re-launched production in 1980, opening a new hi-tech plant in Crespellano.
Along with its traditional "Scorza" and "Cremino" products, which today come also in a Noir version with bitter chocolate, it offers a Majani Line, including remakes of the chocolate bars, the "Cannellini" and wafers with a Cremino Fiat filling. Decorated Easter eggs are also produced.

Majani Fabbrica di Cioccolato
Via de' Carbonesi 5,
Tel. 051234302V

ppa inglese

tagliatelle mixed with almonds and candied fruit, soaked in liqueur and dusted with confectioner's sugar. By tradition it is made at Christmas and Easter.

rtelli di Carnevale or Frittelle piene
A kind of biscuit with a filling, fried in oil or lard, typical of Piacenza. The outer shell of puff pastry is made with flour, sugar, butter, eggs and white wine. The filling is "mostarda" (spiced fruit), amaretto biscuits, chocolate powder, boiled dried chestnuts and rum. Garnished with confectioner's sugar.

uccherino Montanaro Bolognese
This is produced in several townships of the Bologna Apennines, including Grizzana Morandi, where on the Feast of the Assumption, August 15th, a specific festival is held in its name. It is a small ring-shaped cake with icing, flavored with anise, made with wheat flour, olive oil, eggs, lard, sugar and yeast.

uppa Inglese
The Este court in Ferrara in the 16th century had a friendly diplomatic relationship with Elizabethan England. An English ambassador happened to sing the praises of "Trifle", a dessert of English working-class tradition, consisting of a base of soft whipped pastry, soaked in sweet wine and then enriched with cream, jam and amaretto biscuits. The Po Valley version known as "zuppa inglese", originated from this source, with sponge cake soaked

in Alkermes liqueur and rum, alternating with layers of plain or chocolate confectioner's custard. A dessert destined to become a specialty of the culinary art of Bologna and of the entire Emilia-Romagna region.

BOLOGNA

PIEVE DI CENTO
Omar
Via L. Campanini 14, Tel. 051975510
A stylish pastry shop in a good location near the old gate to the town. A wide variety of excellent traditional sweets as well as attractively decorated, good quality modern cakes and pies.

ZOLA PREDOSA
Pasticceria dei Castelli
Via Risorgimento 151/1, Tel. 051755590
Fresh pastry, chocolate cakes, "torrone" (nougat), sweet and salt "panettone", and "torta di riso" rice cake.

FERRARA

Leon d'Oro
Piazza Cattedrale 2/10, Tel. 0532209318
Spacious, bright premises with whole counters filled with the typical Ferrara sweets: "pampapato", "ciambelle", and an unusual flan of maccheroni covered with sweet pastry.

CENTO
Pasticceria del Guercino
Via Cremonino 58, Tel. 0516832244
This small attractive shop resembles a sweet tin and its inviting fragrances fill the entire street. Its own production of "panettone", "pandoro", "pampapato", and the traditional "torta di tagliatelle".

FORLÌ

Pasticceria e Caffeteria La Loggia
Corso Garibaldi 125, Tel. 054333075
An elegant pastry shop, with mosaics and pictures on the walls. It produces its own sweet and savory pastry; among the

FOOD

specialties are ciambella Romagnola and torrone.

CESENATICO
Il Giardino dei Sapori Perduti
Piazza Fiorentini 10,
Tel. 054782507
www.ilgiardinodei
saporiperduti.com
Located in the old town center, a pastry shop that is worth a visit: all the sweets are hand-made, with the aid of rolling pins and pastry cutters. The cookies and pies coming out of the adjoining ovens are irresistible.

MODENA

Pasticceria Artigiana
Viale Don Minzoni 183, Tel. 059302141
Own production and sale of candy and traditional cakes such as "ciambellone" and fresh fruit pies.

PARMA

Pasticceria San Biagio
Via Garibaldi 41, Tel. 0521286057
This shop displays a wide variety of sweets, from that dedicated to Maria Luigia, to the "dolce San Biagio" after which it is named.

PIACENZA

Galletti
Corso Vittorio Emanuele II 62
Tel. 0523324758
A traditional shop that has been managed for years by the same family. The premises are small, but well run and pleasant and the pastries are good quality.

RAVENNA

Pasticceria Cacao
Punta Marina Terme
Via della Conchiglia 15,
Tel. 0544437523
Tiny and cosy, this is filled with

delicious fragrances; on summer evenings the cream "krapfen" are definitely something to try.

FAENZA
Pasticceria C&P
Via A. Murri 28,
Tel. 0546621317
Own production and reta outlet: traditional products, foremost amor which the typical ciambell. to be accompanied with swee or Amabile wines such as Sangiovese and Cagnine.

LUGO
Caffetteria Pasticceria Tiffany
Via Tellarini 1, Tel. 054522517
A typical family meeting place, with a good coffee-shop service: the ciambella with preserved quince fillin; is outstanding.

REGGIO EMILIA

Torinese
Via Fornaciari 3/A, Tel. 0522541729
An early 19th-century setting for one o Reggio's oldest pastry shops. The assortment is excellent from breakfast pastries to jams, chocolate and local cakes.

RIMINI

Pasticceria Rinaldini
Via Coletti 131, Tel. 054127146
www.rinaldinipastry.com
An elegant setting with a first-rate production of pastry and chocolate; specialties not to be missed are "Venere nera" and lemon plumcake.

CATTOLICA
Bar Pasticceria Canasta
Via Risorgimento 22, Tel. 0541961101
www.pasticceriacanasta.it
This is definitely one of the best places in town, for its style and wide assortment of pastry and chocolate. The pastry chef offers a traditional line and also a more up-to-date one with extremely interesting creations; try the "miacetto", which is the local sweetmeat.

JANUARY

5th January
OTT DE BISÒ
enza (Ravenna)
Pro Loco
Tel. 0422549648
(www.prolocofaenza.it)
The name means the Night
of Mulled Wine. While they
wait for the Befana (the witch
who traditionally arrives
on the night of January 6th
with gifts for good kids and
coal for bad), the locals taste
local specialties,
such as piadinas, sausages
and polenta, accompanied
by mulled wine (bisò),
served in small decorated
goblets called gotti.
At midnight, a propitiatory
bonfire sweeps away
all the tragedies and evils
of the previous year.

MARCH

End of March
FIERA DEL BUE GRASSO
avriago (Reggio Emilia)
Town Hall
Tel. 0522373429
(www.comune.cavriago.re.it)
This traditional show focuses
on the old reggiana breed
of cow and is accompanied
by stalls where craftsmen
practise traditional skills
and food stalls offering free
samples of cheese, balsamic
vinegar, mortadella and
excellent local wines.

Week of 19th March
FIERA DI SAN GIUSEPPE
AND SAGRA DELLA SEPPIA
iranella di Cervia (Ravenna)
*IAT (Tourist Information
Office)*
Tel. 0544993435
*(www.comunecervia.it/
turismo)*
This festival takes place
every year during the week
including March 19th (the
festival of St Joseph) and
lasts for five days until the
Sunday. During the festival, a
food stall offers dishes based
on cuttlefish, such as lasagne
al nero (lasagne baked with
black cuttlefish ink) and the
traditional dish of seppie con
piselli (cuttlefish and peas).
The arrival of spring is
celebrated on the beach with
a huge bonfire 20m high and
a fire-work display. Here, too,
food stalls serve dishes
typically associated with the
festival.

MAY

Last week-end of May, every three years (next in 2008)
GNOCCATA
Guastalla (Reggio Emilia)
*IAT (Tourist Information
Office) Tel. 0522219812*
(www.comune.guastalla.re.it)
At this festival, when the
locals dress in historic
costumes, food stalls
distribute gnocchi (rounded
lumps of pasta which are
boiled) cooked in various
ways: with mushrooms,
chestnut flour or classic
gnocchi made with potatoes
and flour.

AUGUST

15th August
SAGRA DELLO ZUCCHERINO MONTANARO
Grizzana Morandi (Bologna)
Town Hall
Tel. 0516730311
*(www.comune.
grizzanamorandi.bo.it)*
This festival gets its name
from a local kind of aniseed
cake. The actual event
involves a historical re-
enactment filled with
dancing, demonstrations,
spectacles and processions
in medieval costume.
During the festival, aniseed
cakes are distributed free
to the populus and other
stands sell the typical
sweets of the area
"zuccherino montanaro"
(see photo).

SEPTEMBER

Second Sunday of September
SAGRA CASTELLANA DELLA BRACIOLA
Castel San Pietro Terme (Bologna)
Pro Loco
Tel. 0516954124
*(www.comune.castelsanpietr
oterme.bo.it/proloco)*
This festival includes a
competition for vehicles
pushed by hand.
The gastronomic side of the
festival is devoted to the
humble lamb chop,
in particular, the meat
of castrated animals
produced locally and other
specialties of Castel San
Pietro Terme. The festival
ends at midnight with
a fire-work display.

NOVEMBER

Last two Sundays of November
FIERA DELL'OLIVA E DEI PRODOTTI AUTUNNALI
Coriano (Rimini)
Pro Loco
Tel. 0541656255
(www.prolococoriano.it)
This festival is an excellent
opportunity to taste the
delicious olives produced in
the hills around Rimini.
They go particularly well with
the traditional dishes of
Romagna cuisine and are also
used to make an excellent
extra-virgin olive oil.
The event includes an
exhibition of wine and oil
where the products are also
for sale.

Last two Sundays of November and first Sunday of December
FIERA DEL FORMAGGIO DI FOSSA
Sogliano al Rubicone (Forlì-Cesena)
Fossa Pellegrini
Tel. 0541948542
(www.formaggiodifossa.it)
At the Fiera del Formaggio di
Fossa, producers offer free
samples of the typical local
cheese and the products of
many other traditional cheese
factories. During the three
Sundays of the fair, visitors
can purchase cheese and visit
the pits (fosse) where the
cheese is matured.

FOOD

- 🦢 **CERAMICS**
- 🧣 **FABRICS AND EMBROIDERY**
- 🧺 **WOOD**
- 🎼 **WOVEN BASKETWARE**
- ⛵ **MUSIC**
- 🛶 **BOATS**
- ⚫ **WROUGHT IRON**
- 🔵 **MOSAICS**
- 👤 **FASHION**

Quality, elegance and unmistakable Italian style distinguish the products of this region. Along with the products of modern industries and new technologies, these include a vast range of hand-made articles which are quite unique. Strolling through the streets of Ravenna and Faenza you will encounter many craft workshops which are highly specialized in mosaics and ceramic production by hand. In these workshops, which we would strongly encourage you to visit and spend some time looking around, the traditions which have made these two cities famous the world over are alive and well, and, what's more, are being constantly

Shopping

renewed. There are also many special products which are peculiar to this region, again the result of a purely local culture which has taken advantage of the typical raw materials available, like the boats used in the Po Delta.

Highlights

- At the lively local markets you will find rare antiques and unique craft products made locally
- The art of mosaic: linking the past and the present
- Home to the famous ceramicists of Faenza
- Traditional production of the boats used on the lagoon

Inside

170 **Arts and Crafts**
176 **Markets**
178 **Fashion**

The rich fertility of the planes of Emilia-Romagna meant that for a very long time he life revolved around agriculture, while this generous resource also led to the flourishing of crafts. When the economy came to rely on industry the people of this regic remembered why they had prospered in the first place and made sure to conserve the foundations of their well-being. As well as the cornerstones of popular culture (tradition music, gastronomy etc) these included the many forms of a craft tradition which, fro being revered and fossilized like some sort of museum piece, is brought to life on a dai basis. In some cases its most traditional forms have been given a new lease of life, others it has been revamped and made into the driving force of a radical transformatic which has turned a land which was designated for farming into one of the most advance regions for industrial innovation. In Emilia Romagna we find traditional crafts such a boats, wood and embroidery and other more unusual crafts such as bells, potter mosaics and embroidery.

Bells

Of all the various metal arts, the casting of bronze bells is unique. In Emilia the nucleus of this unusual specialization is in Castelnovo ne' Monti (Reggio Emilia) where records can be traced back as far as the sixteenth century. Indeed, there is a bell which bears the date 1565 and the name Betalli, a local family of master casters.

This traditional craft has, over the last few centuries, become tied up with the affairs of a single family, the Capanni family, have handed down the craft from father to son right up to the present day, preserving

The bell made by Campane Capanni for the Sanctuary of Lichen in Poland.

traditional techniques and combining them with various technological advances which have allowed their bells to compete with those produced using modern industrial methods. This handing down from generation to generation has enabled them to make and export bells, using the techniques of the master craftsmen of the Middle Ages and Renaissance, all over the world.

Various skills are brought to bear during the making of the bells as they are not made purely for ornament but must, first and foremos ring with a mighty sound that is rich in personality. Breadth, weight, circumference and height are important factors which give each bell a distinctive note. Every single bell is a piece made unique by lost wax smelting, essential for producing the finest inscriptions and decorations.

Pottery

Pottery is one of the most important industries in Emilia-Romagna. There is no country in the world which does not import the tiles produced in Sassuolo (Modena) and Casalgrande (Reggio Emilia).

The current industry represents the successful fusion of a mixture of elements, techniques, cultures, traditions, manual skills, which have developed over the centuries in the crafting of both ordinary and decorative artefacts. Here the transition from craft to industry did not lead to the former succumbing to the latter and the two sectors prosper in different sized markets.

Historically, everything began in the interesting town of Faenza where the craft of pottery is so time-honoured and established that in the languages of half of Europe the name of the city is synonymous with majolica. Suffice it to say that, in potters' jargon, wherever faenze are produced, the name means white enamelled earthenware pottery decorated with bright colours. Back in the Middle Ages the city was already famous for its pottery but the real boom arrived at the end of the 16th and beginning of the 17th century, when the style changed from Gothic and oriental to something more Italian.

At first decorations were heraldic and ornamental but these were eventually replaced by a series where the human figure began to appear increasingly often. In the second half of the 19th century, a further evolution led to white pottery, characterised by soft and whimsical shapes, simply decorated with almost sketched designs. While the artistic evolution was taking place Faenza potters fine-tuned new technologies and introduced other materials which gave their studios fresh impetus and made them the absolute leaders in the 17th century. Towards the end of this century came the last great revolution with new, dainty decorations such as the vine leaf, the festoon and the acorn, used on shapes whose simplicity and clean lines were forerunners of the advent of neo-classical taste.

This industry is commemorated in the Museo Internazionale delle Ceramiche di Faenza, where local pottery is displayed along with pieces from all over the world. In the environs, the streets of the old city

Above Faenza pottery

centre teem with studios producing hand decorated vases fired using traditional techniques. As well as Faenza there is also Noceto (Parma) famous for its medicine jars and the villa Il Ferlaro in Collecchio (Parma), where we find a style characterised by white bases with decorations which range in colour from rust to deep blue. We must not neglect to mention the traditional tankards, once found in inns and taverns everywhere, which are now the major product of various studios in Imola (Bologna).

Wrought iron

In the Emilia-Romagna region, the majority of smithies became small but dynamic firms, mostly focusing on the production of metalwork and fixtures. The wrought iron craftsman, who comes from a long tradition in these parts, continues to work in tandem with this industry.

The most typical expressions of this ancient art survive, more for the sake of tourists than anything else, in the lanes, streets and alleys of Grazzano Visconti (Piacenza). This picturesque village is an unusual and rare example of a neo-Medieval setting. It was created by the Milanese entrepreneur Giuseppe Visconti di Modrone at the beginning of the 20th century, which provides a setting for the lovely 14th century castle. Here, as well as adding to the picturesque effect, smithies continue to hammer iron.

The decorative working of iron is widespread throughout the entire region, although some towns favor one process over another. For example, in Ciano d'Enza (Reggio Emilia) beds and other items of furniture are produced, Brisighella (Ravenna) specializes in antique lamps and fire-irons, and in Ferrara, craftsmen produce gates, fences and balustrades.

Known as 'batane', these typical flat bottomed boats are found all over the Po Delta.

Boats

The Po Delta microcosm has always attracted people from surrounding areas who, in order to settle there and make it their home, have built simple and efficient boats that are easy to manoeuvre and can been taken everywhere.

The river's constant supply of materials (namely, sand and lime) creates sandbars or mounds at the mouths and along the *buse* (smaller secondary branches, the size of a canals) which, as a result of the currents and wave motion of the river, shift continuously. All of this creates a changing river, making flat bottomed rowing boats necessary for moving through the shallow waters. The water is also extremely shallow in the maze of *paradelli*, the narrow canals which wind between the reed-beds. The first flat-bottomed boats were followed by specialised models, such as the *mammalucco*, which has a 5m hull making it suitable for hunting, the longer and wider *batana* used for fishing and the *velocipede*, with its long and tapering hull, used for regattas. The most popular of these is the *batana* (plural *batane*), from 5 to 7 metres long and almost a quarter of that length in width. It is used by fishermen, reed cutters, hunters or anybody else who needs to move about in the Delta. Despite the competition from plastic hulls, local boatbuilders continue to build their boats forced, due to the scarcity of orders, to do so by hand and to use, as in the past, local timber: poplars for the bottom and sides, walnut, cherry and other fruit trees for the ribs.

Weaving

The marshy areas of the Po Delta have always teemed with human, animal and plant life. The union of land and water, which appear to literally run in to one another, has produced lush vegetation which hosts numerous different and populous colonies of animals. Man has braved this unwholesome environment, attracted by the riches it offers, striving to exploit each and every aspect. He has even managed to cherish the most apparently insignificant resources, such as the typical common reed, here known as *pavera*, used for making mats, bags and hats, or *bosmarola*, a weed which grows in wet zones, used for making brooms and brushes. These crafts survive in the Delta in their traditional forms, above all in the area around Bagnacavallo (Ravenna) Elsewhere they have become more industrialised, especiall in Ciano d'Enza (Reggio Emilia), and in Roccabianca (Parma), where wicker furniture is now produced. A similar handicraft, which makes use of an unusual material, is the weaving of willow or poplar wood shavings, typical of Carpi (Modena). It began as a cottage industry on farms and consisted of shaving off pieces of wood and weaving them into solid and lightweight hats. In the last few decades of the 19th century, production reached its peak with orders pouring in from all over Europe and America.

Now the activity has been partly industrialised, concentrating on the production of semi-processed goods which then find the most varied applications.

Unfortunately, the consequence of this modernisation is that the number of craft workshops dedicated to producing the finished products and typical hats is on the wane.

Wood

Scattered around the region are numerous cabinet makers' workshops producing finely crafted furniture. The major centres are Ferrara, Colorno (Parma), San Cesario (Modena), where inlay is made, and Ravenna. The best place to find traditional carpentry is Grazzano Visconti in the province of Piacenza. Although the transformation of this ancient rural village, spread around the foot of the castle, into a thriving craft centre only dates back to the early 20th century, it took merely a few decades to spread the fame of this 15th century inspired craft which generated the Grazzano style of furniture. The characteristic features are low relief designs with luxuriant and deep fretwork, where the figures are first drawn on the table and then engraved with embossed edges.

The woodworkers of Grazzano Visconti still produce this style which has made them famous, making solid wood furniture, tallboys, bedsteads and bureaux whose shapes are unmistakable.

Nowadays market forces have spurred them to diversify. Indeed, they also produce furniture in the English or Provencal style, Tuscan or Venetian wardrobes, Provencal style and solid wood kitchen cupboards, just as modern as their mass-produced counterparts but light years away in terms of finish and robustness.

Mosaics

The handing down of a craft from father to son is always seen to be the best way. However, the most tangible results really are produced by colleges of further education, such as the Istituto Statale d'Arte per il Mosaico (State Institute of Art for the Mosaic) in Ravenna. This takes the credit for transforming mosaic into something living, to be designed and produced, not just admired on the town's Byzantine monuments. Mosaic does not begin and end with the creative act. It combines the artist's concept with the craftsman's manual skill.

On the whole, the mosaic workshops of Ravenna represent a truly extraordinary world of crafts in which all possible varieties of mosaic are experimented with. One the one side, you have the reproduction of ancient mosaics, using techniques and coloured vitreous paste like those used in Roman and Byzantine

Detail of the apse of the Basilica of Sant'Apollinare in Classe.

times. On the other, you have experiments with new artistic and technical methods.

Textiles and lace

In the past Rimini was an important town for elegant lace-making. These skills still exist and such lace is still produced, although less than it was in the past.

In this region, the textile industry in general was favoured by the spread of hemp cultivation on the planes of Emila and familiarity with the raw material meant that every farmhouse had a handloom for making cloth for the household and for selling at local markets. The cloth differed from other regions in the abundance and brightness of the decorations that were applied with a simple and original technique, using wooden

SHOPPING

The oldest workshop for the famed Romagna fabric printing is the Pascucci family workshop

stamps and blends of mineral dyes mainly in shades of green, blue and red.

The first records of the stamp being used on cloth in Romagna date from the end of the 18th century, though this craft began to be popular in the early decades of the 19th century when the number of stamps multiplied notably, many of which are still used in the southern part of Romagna. This production was destined for modest families who had to make do with surrogates of rich embroidered fabrics: hemp tablecloths, curtains and bedspreads, embellished with ornamental motifs printed using stamps.

Ironically, it was due to this need to copy that the stamp was modernised and became more sophisticated.

Eventually techniques were invented which meant that not only the decorations but also the texture of the embroidery, the carpets and the brocades, often accompanied by painted braids, ribbons, bows, could be emulated.

This craft has not been entirely substituted by the more modern, economical and efficient (in terms of time and money) digital printing methods. It can still be seen in the areas surrounding Gamettola, in the province of Forlì-Cesena, and Imola, in the province of Bologna, where they heroically combine traditional heritage (using the same stamps they used in the 19th and early 20th century) and technological know-how, above all in mixing the dyes.

THE OCARINA

The people of Emilia and Romagna have an innate predisposition for socialisation and all forms of expression which favour it. This propensity is mirrored in food, wine and, above all, in music. Not just opera music but "liscio" too, a genre of folk music which emerged in Romagna at the end of the 19th century, so-called because once it was danced to in the barnyard where the soles of shoes slid along the floor "lisciandolo" or making it smooth. It is a blend of waltz, mazurka and polka.

One of the elements which make this music that cheers the village fairs so pleasing to the ear is a folk sound which not even the most sophisticated electronic instrument can reproduce. This is the ocarina, a simple clay wind instrument invented in Budrio, in the province of Bologna, by Giuseppe Donati, in around 1860. Its success, due to an

ingenious design which enables you to modulate a diatonic scale together with chromatic notes, has made Budrio a kind of place of pilgrimage, where the art of making and of playing the ocarina in its traditional habitat of traditional folk music, and in tough competitions where local musicians compete by playing well-known classical music pieces, has been encouraged and preserved since the 1800s.

FERRARA

ARGENTA
Grazia Dal Pozzo
Via Garibaldi 12, Tel. 0532804919
Wicker objects

FORLÌ-CESENA

FORLÌ
Arredamenti Perugini
Via Edison 7, Tel. 0543720579
Decorated furniture

CESENA
Carmen Ceccaroni
Via Arenzano 107, Tel. 0547346036
Making wrought iron

MODIGLIANA
Vittorio Laghi
Via dell'Artigianato 8, Tel. 0546941781
Making wrought iron

Cabinet-maker Tacconi in his workshop in
Spilamberto (MO)

MODENA

VIGNOLA
Decor Art
Via Trinità 1/4, Tel. 059772450
Making mosaics

PARMA

COLLECCHIO
Ceramica del Ferlaro
Strada Privata Burbelles 4
Tel. 0521805348
Decorative pottery
Falegnameria Musiari
Via Prampolini 32, Tel. 0521804592
Furniture

NOCETO
Baroni Ceramiche
Via Emilia 102/A, Tel. 0521825148
Decorative pottery

ROCCABIANCA
Giovanni Ferrari
Fontanelle, Via Babilana 10, Tel. 0521870111
Wicker furniture

RAVENNA

Artemosaico
Viale Baracca 5, Tel. 0544213904
Making mosaics
Cooperativa Mosaicisti
Via Fiandrini 13, Tel. 054434799
Making mosaics
Mosaici Antichi e Moderni
Via Mariani 9, Tel. 054435448
Making mosaics

FAENZA
Bottega D'Arte Ceramica Gatti
Via Pompignoli 4, Tel. 0546634301
Decorative pottery
Ceramica Monti
Via Pier Maria Cavina 22, Tel. 054625264
Decorative pottery
Ceramiche Artistiche Vignoli
Via Fermi 30, Tel. 0546621076
Decorative pottery
Le Terre di Faenza
Via Cavina 30, Tel. 054629440
Decorative pottery
Maestri Maiolicari Faentini
Via Granarolo 63, Tel. 0546664139
Decorative pottery

LUGO
Arte della Ceramica
Via Matteotti 27, Tel. 054532397
Decorative pottery

REGGIO EMILIA

Artefer
Via Monti 15/A, Tel. 0522551879
Making wrought iron

RIMINI

Fratelli Leurini
Via Coriano 342, Tel. 0541731393
Making wrought iron

MARKETS

In Emilia-Romagna handicrafts are well rooted in popular culture and their traditions ar[e] preserved and upheld in shops and markets. Small town life is indeed enlivened b[y] picturesque local markets where you can find both rare antiques and unique artefacts.

BOLOGNA

Antiche Pagine
30 April and 1 May
The Basilica of San Francesco and Palazzo Malpighi, Bologna plays host to around fifty antique booksellers selling all kinds of antique volumes: precious 18th century books, art or science books, original comics...
For further information: Tel. 051232173

FERRARA

Mercatino dell'Antiquariato e Cose d'Altri Tempi
First weekend of every month
At the small antiques market in Piazza Trento e Trieste and Piazza Savonarola you can find coins, medals, pottery, porcelain, lace, embroidery, frames and prints, miniatures, manuscripts, books, military items, gramophones and radios. The small craft market instead sells local, individually made handicrafts.
For further information:
Tel. 0532209370

FORLÌ-CESENA

CESENA
Cesena in Fiera
22 to 26 June
Once the Feast of St John, this festival in the heart of Cesena has music, shows and a market with almost 600 stall-holders selling antiques traditional crafts, wines and food.
For further information:
Tel. 0547613419

CESENATICO
Mercatino delle Pulci e dell'Artigianato
Every Tuesday evening from June to September
Located in the old town centre, you can browse and buy antiques, collectibles and handicraft, and hobby items.
For further information:
Tel. 0547673287

MODENA

Fiera Antiquaria Città di Modena
Fourth weekend of every month except July
There are over 300 stalls, side-by-side on the old racecourse and in the picturesque Piazza Grande, selling fancy goods and antiques.
For further information:
Tel. 0592032544

PARMA

FONTANELLATO
Mercatino dell'Antiquariato
Third Sunday of every month except January
Rocca Sanvitale, a medieval castle still surrounded by a moat full of water, provides a backdrop for over 300 stalls set up in the square, along the moat, under the porticoes and in the narrow lanes of the town centre. The market has antiques, collectibles, and second hand and fancy goods. You can find old pottery, prints, records, books, dolls, clocks, paintings, picture-frames, glass and crystal, mirrors, wrought iron, copper objects, coins, accessories and vintage clothing.
For further information:
Tel. 0521823220

PIACENZA

PONTENURE
Mostra Esposizione dell'Antiquariato
Second Sunday of every month except August
Picturesque show and sale of small antiques and objects from bygone eras,

located in Piazza Re Amato and neighbouring streets. There are around 50 stalls.
For further information:
Tel. 0523692041

RAVENNA

BRISIGHELLA
Mercatino Serale del Venerdì
From the second Friday in June to the first Friday in September
Small market located in the old town centre selling antiques, handicrafts, hobby items, collectibles, typical products and gastronomic specialities.
For further information: Tel. 054681166

CASOLA VALSENIO
Festa dei Frutti Dimenticati
Third weekend in October
Some fruits which were once quite common have now all but vanished. This fête brings some of them, such as the quince and the rose apple, back to life. During the fête a jam competition is held, while local restaurants serve Cucina dei Frutti Dimenticati or dishes cooked with these forgotten fruits. The fete includes a show and sale of fruits of bygone days. The Strada dei Frutti Dimenticati also deserves a mention. It is a signed route which winds through 8 oases where 50 of these almost forgotten fruit trees are cultivated.
For further information:
Tel. 054673033
Mercatino Serale delle Erbe Officinali
Every Friday evening in July and August
In Casola Valsenio, the Giardino delle Erbe, open to visitors, is a treasure chest of medicinal and aromatic herbs. Over 400 native and non-native species are preserved here. Opened in 1938 it covers 4 hectares of land and is a permanent exhibition of medicinal, perfumed, cosmetic and melliferous plants. Connected to the garden, the little market is a multi-sensory experience rich in perfumes and colours. You can also try dishes cooked with aromatic herbs by local chefs.

Don't forget the scenic Strada della Lavanda or Lavender Route, which winds between borders and rows of various varieties of lavender.
For further information: Tel. 054673158

FAENZA
Estate Ceramica
From mid-June to the end of October
Palazzo delle Esposizioni is home to various pottery exhibitions, the Galleria Ceramica di Faenza showroom and the gift-shop.
For further information:
Tel. 054621145

Majolica jar, Faenza
(first half of the 16th century)

Martedì Sera
Every Tuesday evening from June to August
The old town centre of Faenza is home to small markets selling traditional handicrafts, antiques, collectibles and ethnic items; painting exhibitions and flower shows; stalls selling typical food and wine; concerts and various performances.
For further information:
Tel. 054621355

RIMINI

Anticovariato
Every Friday evening from June to September
Piazza Cavour is the backdrop for a small market selling crafts, antiques, vintage clothing, collectors' items and ethnic items.
For further information:
Tel. 054151331

SANTARCANGELO DI ROMAGNA
Fiera di San Martino
From 10 to 13 November
San Martino is a fête made cheerful by story-tellers, who meet every year on the feast day dedicated to them. Piazza Marini is the setting for the Casa dell'Autunno, a food and wine market, alongside the traditional street vendors you will find around 550 stalls displaying antiques and handicrafts.
For further information:
Tel. 054153294

FASHION

Outlets are a fresh, modern discount shopping concept. They are "virtual" villages, designed and built exclusively for the purpose of shopping, where the shopper can lose himself or herself in a maze of shops in an atmosphere that resembles an amusement park. Alongside boutiques selling clothes, shoes and accessories, usually exclusive Italian designer labels, are services designed to make the customers' stay more comfortable: large car parks, bars and cafeterias, ice-cream parlours with seating, as well as play areas for kids. In Emilia-Romagna there are veritable shopping citadels, like Castel Guelfo in Bologna, which host outlets selling famous Italian and overseas names, as well as the factory stores which belong to individual companies such as Pollini, Sergio Tacchini and Driade, which sell elegant Italian quality and design at a discount.

BOLOGNA

Bruno Magli Outlet Store
Via Larga 33, Tel. 0516015879
Bruno Magli owns this outlet, originally a shoe factory, where you can buy shoes for men and women, bags and small leather goods items, ties, jackets and shirts made by this well-known designer, with an official discount of 50% on the previous season's recommended retail price.
There are also marked down items from the current season's collections.

Griffes Diffusion
Via Cavalieri Ducati 5, Tel. 0516415873
Outlet owned by the Mariella Burani Fashion Group: men and women's clothes and co-ordinated accessories including belts, bags, shoes, scarves, ties. Discounts of up to 65% on items from the previous season's collections and further discounts during sales periods.

CASTEL GUELFO DI BOLOGNA

Castel Guelfo Outlet
Poggio Piccolo, Via del Commercio 20/D
Tel. 0542670762
www.outletcastelguelfo.it
A veritable shopping town. The 50 shops sell all kinds of clothing for men, women and children, beauty care and leisure items. You will also find some of the biggest designer labels, such as Mila Schön, Renato Balestra, Fiorucci, Guy Laroche, Calzedonia, Parah, Roccobarocco, Bikkembergs

and others, all offering discounts of up to 50%.

Pompea Outlet Castel Guelfo
Poggio Piccolo, Via del Commercio
Tel. 0542670769, www.pompea.com
Vast assortment of stockings, lingerie and beachwear in cotton and microfibre, fashion and sportswear outfits for men and women from the Pompea or Pompea Gym range. Samples, seconds, flawed garments or garments from the previous seasons' collections. Guaranteed discounts from 30 to 70%.

Sergio Tacchini Factory Outlet
Poggio Piccolo

Via del Commercio 12/50
Tel. 0542670592
www.sergiotacchini.com
Casual and sporty clothing for men, women and children. Also shoes, accessories and leather goods. Guaranteed minimum discount of 30% on the recommended retail price and bargains to be had with special offers. Sales throughout the year.

Désirée Ugo Colella Retail s.r.l.
Poggio Piccolo, Via del Commercio 12/F
Tel. 0542670836
Handmade shirts by Ugo Colella and Désirée (made entirely by hand, including "stitched down" neck and cuffs), and the casual Khiurli range. Clothing and accessories, swimwear and towels for men. Shirts, sweaters, trousers, jackets and hats for kids. Various models of blouses for women. Factory prices and end of season discounts; only top quality goods.

FORLÌ-CESENA

GATTEO
Calzaturificio Pollini
Via Erbosa 2/B, Tel. 0541818106
Discounts of 30 to 60% on Pollini,
Moschino and Cheap and
Chic labels. The outlet also sells
leather coats and jackets, small
leather goods items, bags and
shoes for men and women.

SAVIGNANO SUL RUBICONE
Vicini Outlet
Via Oslo 13, Tel. 0541938270
www.vicinioutlet.com
Men and women's clothing from the
Giuseppe Zanotti Design and Vicini
ranges. Clothing from the Roberto
Cavalli collection. The outlet also sells
Vicini Fashion Sport sports clothes
and men and women's shoes.
Accessories include Vicini bags and
sunglasses, belts, purses, watches,
silk scarves, jewellery. Official
discounts range from 50 to 70%.

MODENA

SASSUOLO
Griffes Diffusion
Via Regina Pacis 1, Tel. 0536808413
Outlet owned by the Mariella Burani
Fashion Group: sports, classic and
elegant men and women's clothing:
shirts, sweaters, jackets, trousers,
skirts, duster-coats. Co-ordinated
accessories include belts, bags,
scarves, cravats, glasses, ties. Mila
Schön, Calvin Klein and Thierry Mugler
labels are also present.
Hefty reductions on all items from
previous collections.

PARMA

FIDENZA
Blunauta
Chiusa Ferranda, Via S. Michele in
Campagna, Tel. 0524534221
www.blunauta.it
Vast assortment of clothing and
accessories for men and women from
the Blunauta range, in all sizes and
models.

Items on sale are from previous
seasons' collections. Discounts range
from 30 to 50%
Fidenza Village
Chiusa Ferranda, Via S. Michele in
Campagna, Tel. 052433551
www.fidenzavillage.com
The citadel of the Fidenza Village Outlet
has 36 shops selling the widest range
of goods: clothing, fancy goods,
lingerie, household linen, shoes,
glasses and sports goods. 30 labels are
represented including Phard, Pinko,
Nike, Reebok, Trussardi Jeans, Versace,
Samsonite, Furla, Pancaldi 1888, Frette
and Levi's. Discounts range from 33 to
70%.
There is also an interesting restaurant
called Ristorante Barlumeria which
serves local specialities and where you
can buy local products.

PIACENZA

CAORSO
Da Driade
Fossadello, Via Padana Inferiore 12
Tel. 0523818655, www.driade.com
At this reputable company's outlet you
will find sophisticatedly designed
furnishings and fancy goods. Hefty
discounts.

RIMINI

Calzaturificio Pollini
Viale Vespucci 83, Tel. 0541391724
Men and women's clothing, bags, belts,
bracelets, key-rings, wallets and men's
accessories for the office. Official
discounts from 30 to 60%.

SAN GIOVANNI IN MARIGNANO
Gilmar Company Store
Via delle Rose 15, Tel. 0541959186
Outlet selling the Iceberg Jeans and
Iceberg Primalinea ranges. Men
and women's sweaters and shirts,
skirts, trousers, evening wear
and outfits for special occasions,
beachwear, swimwear and beach
towels. Accessories include belts,
bags, glasses and perfumes.
Shoes from the current year's
collection. Official discount
of 25% on all items.

| 🎼 | MUSIC |
| 🏁 | FOLKLORE |

The rich, varied folk culture of Emilia-Romagna finds expression in numerous folklore events throughout the year, but especially in summer, which liven up the region's lovely towns and cities. In addition to historical re-enactments in costume, there are other events associated with religious festivals or marine activities, as well as the many palios which fuel the friendly rivalry between the various districts of the region's cities. The common ingredient of all these events is the friendly good humor of the participants, which is expressed in folk music of a high standard and ironic eulogies ending with a humorous punch-line. Emilia-Romagna, which has an important, interesting and longstanding musical tradition, is still one of

Events

the most productive regions in Europe in terms of musical output. Spectacular festivals and other musical events, often set in beautiful natural surroundings, animate the warm summer evenings and should not be missed.

Highlights

- ■ Music festivals are often held in delightful settings
- ■ The charming festivals associated with the sea
- ■ The breathtakingly exciting palios of Ferrara and Faenza
- ■ History is re-enacted at Bardi in the form of Gilde et Speziali

Inside

182 **Music**
189 **Folklore**

MUSIC

The remarkable geographical-cultural identity of Emilia and Romagna, expressed as polycentric weave, makes it one of Europe's most musically productive regions. This not a place of outstanding peaks but a cradle of multifarious "experiments" played out in the historic music chapels, opera houses, academies, universities and some of Italy's leading venues: the Teatro Comunale in Bologna and the theaters of the provincial capitals. The many music festivals and concert associations, the way music has taken root in the region universities and in social life all bear witness to the great musicality that is intrinsic to the region. One curious historical note concerns Bologna - it was, from the late 17th century the early decades of the 1800s, the capital of Italian opera production. A city of schools an impresarios, as well as the hub of a blooming theater system, the legacy of which is seen the large number of historic theaters. This music entertainment network is closely linked commercial interests and has sown its seeds all over the fertile region.

BOLOGNA

Accademia Filarmonica
Via Guerrazzi 13, Tel. 051222997
Founded in 1666, the Accademia Filarmonica is housed in the 16th-century Palazzo Carrati; it was a powerful musicians' guild that exercised its control over local ecclesiastical music appointments. Today, the Sala Mozart is the scene of intense concert activity and features excellent acoustics. The Archivio and the Museo dell'Accademia conserve records and instruments of immense value, including manuscripts by Beethoven, Rossini and Puccini.

Angelica
May
An international music festival that flanks representatives from the national and international scene with others from the Bologna area. Also active in and around Modena.
Further information: Tel. 051240310

Bologna Festival
March to October
A classical music appointment programmed in three separate cycles, twice a year. The Stagione di Primavera brings international orchestras, vocal and instrumental groups, famous conductors and a new generation of soloists. In late spring, the Festival presents Nuovi Interpreti, concerts focusing attention on young concert artists. It then returns in fall with Il Nuovo L'Antico, which compares an old vocal and instrumental repertoire, played on

that of the 1900s.
Further information:
Tel. 0516493397

Corti, Chiese e Cortili
May to September
A summer program of cultured, religious and folk music staged in the most charming venues around the province of Bologna.
Further information:
Tel. 051836445

Da Bach a Bartok
July to December
This festival is held in various parts of the province of Bologna with a program that favors the combined presence of symphonic, chamber and vocal repertoires.
Further information:
Tel. 054230802

Festival Internazionale di Santo Stefano
June
This festival is a must for lovers of classical music and it has an admirable objective - to refurbish and promote the monastery of S. Stefano.
Further information:
Tel. 051932718

I Concerti di Musica Insieme
October to May
A major concert with the participation of soloists and chamber music groups. It is held in the Teatro (or Auditorium) Manzoni, in the city center, a few yards from Via Indipendenza.
Further information:
Tel. 051271932

Organi Antichi
March to June
This sees the presence of organs and organists, and focuses principally on

the anniversaries of the great musicians and commemorations.
Further information: Tel. 051248677

...oni dal Mondo
October to December
Concerts exalting the relationship between music research and traditional music, alien to market and consumer dictates.
Further information: Tel. 0512092414

...atro Comunale
Largo Respighi 1, Tel. 051529011
www.comunalebologna.it
Inaugurated in 1763, the theater has hosted Feste Musicali, original themed programs, since the 1960s and Fondazione Musica Insieme events since 1987. The main program runs from October to May and is accompanied by numerous activities, notably collaboration with the University of Bologna in the form of the rich MusicAteneo matinees for students.

...ORRETTA TERME

...orretta Soul Festival
July
Concerts featuring international soul musicians.
Further information: Tel. 053422021

...AN LAZZARO DI SAVENA

...assaggi di Confine
December
Passaggi di Confine explores the crossovers between folk music and other musical expressions containing traces of tradition. It starts from a dialogue with jazz to extend to cultured music and famous songs. The artists come together in research that avoids mere reproduction of tradition, preferring to elaborate on it in a fertile dialogue between past and present.
Further information: Tel. 0516270150

FERRARA

...terforum Festival
May to June
Since the early 1980s Ferrara has been

The tenor Luciano Pavarotti

the home of Aterforum, a showcase for young concert artists promoted by ATER (Emilia-Romagna Theater Association) that has evolved to become one of the most interesting Italian research festivals. Splendid venues include the 15th-century courtyard of Casa Romei.
Further information: Tel. 0532218311

Ferrara Buskers Festival
Last week in August
Since 1988, this medieval city center has been the setting for the Ferrara Buskers Festival, one of the most important events for street musicians worldwide and held in the last week in August. There are two appointments every day, in the afternoon and evening and the artists involved come from all the continents. A great celebration of sound, dancing, joy and color. Scandinavian jazz saxophonists play beneath the portico alongside mimics, jugglers and fire eaters, accompanied by the melancholic notes of American bluesmen. Unlikely musical instruments made out of broom handles, washing boards, utensils and trash cans contrast with the elegant sound of harps and violins. After more than a decade, the fame of the festival has extended beyond the Alps and the streets of the old city center are regularly invaded by tens of thousands of visitors of all ages.
Further information: Tel. 0532249337
www.ferrarabuskers.com

Ferrara sotto le Stelle
June to July
Set in Piazza Castello and Piazza Municipale, this calendar of events spans all contemporary music without exception. The festival combines famous names and young musicians in a musical cross-section that is varied and first rate.
Further information: Tel. 0532241419

Teatro Comunale
Corso Martiri della Libertà 5,
Tel. 0532218311
www.teatrocomunaleferrara.it
Facing Castello Estense, the theater, which is the home of the Ferrara Musica concerts, offers two concert cycles per year, on special occasions with the

EVENTS

participation of the Orchestra Città di Ferrara. There is also a program of dance and opera seasons.

FORLÌ-CESENA

FORLÌ

Emilia-Romagna Festival
July to September
Forlì is the main stage for the Emilia-Romagna Festival, seen mainly in the summer with a number of evening dates all over the province of Romagna. The festival includes classical music concerts with forays into the modern and the contemporary, and also ballet.
Further information: Tel. 054225747

CESENA

I Suoni del tempo
July to August
I Suoni del Tempo is a concert offering several programs of music genres that change every year.
Further information: Tel. 0547355723

Teatro Bonci
Piazza Guidazzi 1, Tel. 0547355714
www.teatrobonci.it
The theater, with its classical facade, horse-show plan and four rows of boxes plus gallery, forms part of the ETI (Italian Teather Body) circuit and hosts opera seasons flanked by dancing and symphonic concert and chamber music. In early summer it is one of the venues of I Suoni del Tempo, which has already celebrated its 20th anniversary.

CESENATICO

Cesenatico Incanto
July to August
A free music event held in the Teatro all'Aperto in Largo Cappuccini and comprising several music genres.
Further information: Tel. 054779274

Concerti all'alba
July to August
Concerti all'Alba is an unusual initiative offering concerts of cultured music, jazz and more. They are held on the beach at sunrise.
Further information: Tel. 0547672888

Notturni alle Conserve
July to August
Free music events in the delightful setting of Piazza delle Conserve.
Further information: Tel. 054779274

Ribalta Marea
July to September
Performances held in the Teatro all'Aperto in Largo Cappuccini bringing together jazz musicians and stars of the tango.
Further information: Tel. 054779274

MODENA

Festival Internazionale delle Bande Militari
July
The streets, squares and courtyard of honor of Palazzo Ducale host the Festival Internazionale delle Bande Militari. This event, unique in Italy, offers concerts, carousels, evolutions and nocturnal parades of military band from various parts of the world.
Further information: Tel. 0592033031

Grandezze & Meraviglie
September to October
Festival of ancient music created to coincide with the historic celebrations of the Este court in Modena. The venues are varied and scattered around Modena and the province.
Further information: Tel. 059214333

L'Altro Suono Festival
March to May
A program of concerts held in the Teatr Comunale exploring structured vocal forms, with special focus on vocals developed for various types of religious and liturgical music. An itinerary visiting several cultural expressions historically and geographically speaking.
Further information: Tel. 059200020

Note di Passaggio
October to April
A music event featuring programs that vary each year and comprise several music genres. Held in several venues around the province. Admission free.
Further information: Tel. 059216233

Teatro Comunale
Via del Teatro 8,
Tel. 0592033010
www.teatrocomunalemodena.it
Inaugurated in 1841, with its 4 rows of boxes and a gallery overlooking an elegant elliptical auditorium, the theater offers a classical repertoire plus new spheres, e.g. L'Altro Suono. L'Altra Danza also offers academic, jazz, ethnic and research contributions.

SSUOLO

ssuolo Musica Festival
June to July
A music event held in Palazzo
Ducale that spans music
and dance.
Further information:
Tel. 0521391320

VIGNOLA

Jazzin' It
June
Held in the vicinity of the Rocca, in
Piazza dei Contrari, this explores the
transversal boundaries of jazz with
artists of international ranking.
Further information: Tel. 059777707

GIUSEPPE VERDI, ART AND PATRIOTISM

e composer Giuseppe Verdi as a sensitive artist attentive the cultural and social mate of his times but also a actical man much loved by s contemporaries. He was orn on 10 October 1813 at ncole, a small district in sseto (Parma). His mother as a spinner and his father an nkeeper and they named him useppe Fortunino Francesco. e young boy's music talent d not pass unnoticed by his ther, who supported it by nding him to study in sseto. In the early 1800s, sseto boasted a mnasium, two libraries, two umanistic academies and a usic chapel. From 1832 to 335 he went to Milan to mplete his music training, anks to the financial support f the Monte di Pietà di sseto, which helped worthy tudents with scholarships. He so received crucial backing om Antonio Barezzi, a ealthy trader and chairman of ne local philharmonic ssociation, whose daughter argherita Verdi married. After ailing his Conservatory ntrance exams, he continued study privately with the embalo master of La Scala nd attended every erformance. Two years later, is first opera was performed t La Scala in Milan: Oberto onte di San Bonifacio. The ears between 1838 and 1840 vere dramatic and distressing s he lost his young children nd his wife Margherita. These

misfortunes and the fiasco of his second opera, Un giorno di regno, cast Verdi into a state of dejection. It was the impresario of La Scala, Bartolomeo Merelli, who convinced him to set Nabucco to music (1842). The opera was a triumph and opened the doors of the great Italian and European theaters to him, marking the beginning of a growing popularity. The female lead of Nabucco was played by the soprano Giuseppina Strepponi, who became Verdi's second wife. In the period leading up to 1858 Verdi was besieged by impresarios and publishers and became what he called his "16 years in jail", during which time he composed frenetically producing about 20 operas. Those were years of the aspirations for national independence and patriotic Risorgimento sentiments, which Verdi transposed into a musical expression of immediate popular resonance, becoming the symbol of Italian Unity. All over Italy the public acclaimed him with the cry "Viva Verdi", which implied "Viva Vittorio Emanuele King of Italy". During the War of Independence, he financed the collection of guns proposed by

the heroic condottiere Garibaldi, was the first to sign a Busseto subscription to help the wounded and families of the fallen and, as the representative of the Province Parmensi, took the announcement of their annexation to Piedmont to Turin. In 1861 he was elected to the first Italian Parliament and in 1874 he became a senator of the Kingdom.
In the meantime, on the Sant'Agata estate outside Busseto, the maestro divided his time between composing and being a careful manager, keeping himself up-to-date on advancements in agricultural science. In 1897 Giuseppina Strepponi died and the musician increasingly abandoned Sant'Agata for Milan. His life ended there on 27 January 1901. It is said that straw was placed beneath the wheels of the carriages and trams to avoid disturbing his final hours. His tomb is in the Casa di Riposo he had built in Milan for destitute retired musicians and to which he left the proceeds from his copyrights. He was also committed to philanthropic work in his hometown and had the lands he owned reclaimed, built a hospital and helped several local institutions.

PARMA

Auditorium Paganini
Viale Barilla 19, Tel. 0521247994
www.fondazione-toscanini.it
An extraordinary osmotic exchange between a building and its environmental context with large picture windows bringing the nature of the surrounding park into the music hall foyer. The Auditorium hosts the concert season of the Teatro Regio, the concerts of the Filarmonica Arturo Toscanini plus other events.

Casa della Musica
Piazza S. Francesco 1, Tel. 0521031170
www.lacasadellamusica.it
Held in the rooms of the splendid Renaissance Palazzo Cusani with concerts.

Estri Armonici
January to May
This is held in the Teatro Cinghio (Largo VIII Marzo 9) with concerts of classical music and crossovers with contemporary and jazz music.
Further information:
Tel. 0521964803

Festival Verdi
April to June
This festival is held in the Teatro Regio (Strada Garibaldi 16/A) and offers opera and concert performances, the culmination of Giuseppe Verdi celebrations in his homeland.
Further information:
Tel. 0521039393

Parmadanza
October to November
The program includes dancing, opera, ballet and folk dancing with the participation of international stars and famous choreographers.
Further information:
Tel. 0521039399

Parmajazz Frontiere
December
An international jazz festival featuring world-famous musicians. Special attention is focused on European music, the young and original productions. Several venues.
Further information:
Tel. 0521200688

Traiettorie
September to October
Local modern and contemporary music

event combining musical and technological research. It is held in the Casa della Musica and Teatro Farnese (Piazza Pilotta 1).
Further information:
Tel. 0521708899

SALSOMAGGIORE TERME

Festival Mozartiano
September to October
Festival of symphonic music with the participation of famous names from the world of symphonic music. It is held in Palazzo dei Congressi (Via Romagnosi 7) and the Terme Berzieri.
Further information:
Tel. 0521391320

THE VOICES OF MUSIC

The search for personal roots in words and music and a cosmopolitan vision are the common traits of music in the Reggio universe. From the Apennines to the low plains, this land is a melting pot of talent, a microcosm of sounds as narrated by the singer Luciano Ligabue in his film Radiofreccia – a snapshot of the experiences that produce the music of the province: the friendships, the sentiments, the loves, the passage from adolescence to adulthood, the arguments and the stories big and small that are played out day after day.

In 1965, the song Dio è Morto marked the beginning of a legend – a group called the Nomadi and their collaboration with singer-songwriter Francesco Guccini, born in Modena in 1940. The singer-songwriter moved to Bologna in the 1960s. Guccini started to play and write songs towards the late 1950s and released his first LP in the mid-1960s. A 30-year career and 19 LPs have brought him fame all over the country, where he is considered a contemporary "poet", a modern troubadour. Guccini flanks his music with teaching in an American university based in Bologna and has written several literary successes, such as Vacca d'un Cane and Questo Sangue che Impasta la Terra.

The founder, soloist and charismatic leader of the Nomadi group was Augusto Daolio, who died a few years ago. He and his group live on after 30 years of music

PIACENZA

Piacenza Jazz Fest
March to April
Not just a music festival but a true cultural event with concerts, exhibitions and conferences involving Piacenza and the surrounding province.
Further information: Tel. 0523606915

Val Tidone Festival
June to October
The festival originated to help maximize the historic, natural, artistic and gastronomic heritage of Val Tidone and is an interesting showcase for young musicians. Several venues scattered around the province of Piacenza.
Further information: Tel. 0385245798

RAVENNA

Ammutinamenti
September
The strong points of this festival are the Incursioni Estreme, daytime performances in symbolic venues around the city and the Danza d'Autore, with performances in the city's theaters. The festival forms part of the international Città che Danzano (CQD) circuit, a network linking several European and American cities with

and concerts in every corner of the world. For many young people of the 1960s and 1970s their unforgettable and still much loved songs raised a banner of simplicity and plain-speaking, the traits of the southern Reggio countryside they came from; always committed to social needs, the Nomadi were dubbed Messengers of Peace.

In the province of Reggio Emilia, just a few kilometers separate Daolio's village Novellara from Correggio, the home of Ligabue – the Italian Elvis, film director and writer. With his fine voice, electric guitar pointing skywards and big boots, he was a star of Italian rock, emerging with the success of the album Buon compleanno Elvis. In blues we trust could be the response of Adelmo Fornaciari, stage name Zucchero, born in Roncocesi, again close to Reggio Emilia. He possesses a remarkable and thrilling ability to relate to the big names in music, as in his deep-rooted human and professional relationship with Sting. Successes such as Blue's, Oro, Incenso e Birra, Miserere e Spirito Divino combine constant research into the emotions and colors of the Po plain with the air and atmosphere of the Mississippi Delta. Another local star is the singer Lucio Dalla, born in Bologna on 4 March 1943. His debut dates from 1964 but not until 1971, after the years of experimentation with beat that produced his first musical compositions, did the Festival di Sanremo sanction his success with the song 4/3/1943, renamed Gesù Bambino by the public. This song was

followed by more successes, such as Piazza Grande, on which theater performances were also based. In 1977, the album Come è Profondo il Mare marked his debut as a singer-songwriter and decreed his entry into the Hall of Fame of the great names of Italian music, as demonstrated by collaboration with famous colleagues such as Morandi and De Gregori. Since then, it has been a succession of albums and growing fame, leading to the song Caruso, famous all over the world and glorified by the interpretation of Pavarotti. The albums Attenti al Lupo (1990) and Canzoni (1996) achieved record sales. Dalla's words are poems and this eclectic and talented artist has embarked on parallel careers: he composes film soundtracks, runs a contemporary art gallery in Bologna, works, sometimes anonymously, on jazz and classical music projects, has written a book of short stories (Bella Lavita, 2001) and lectures on "Advertising language and techniques" at the University of Urbino. In 2003 he wrote an opera, Tosca. Amore Disperato, inspired by Puccini's Tosca.

Luciano Ligabue, the Italian Elvis

Score of I Lombardi alla prima crociata dedicated to Maria Luigia.

festivals relating to the cityscape, with a view to humanizing cities and promoting their artistic and architectural heritage.
Further information: Tel. 3285373819

MEI Meeting delle Etichette Indipendenti
November
A festival dedicated to the most significant new music involving a marathon of music and encounters.
Further information: Tel. 054624647

Ravenna Festival
June to July
Classical music summer program in the select venues of S. Vitale and other churches, the basilicas of S. Apollinare Nuovo and S. Apollinare in Classe, the gardens around S. Vitale and the extraordinary Mausoleo di Galla Placida.
Further information: Tel. 0544249211

Ravenna Jazz
October
This festival features leading names from the international scene and offers original productions.
Further information: Tel. 0544405666

LUGO

Musica Estate
July to August
An event with musicians and composers from all over the world featuring the most diverse proposals that share the common denominator of improvisation. All the concerts are held in the courtyard of the Rocca and are free.
Further information: Tel. 054538542

Opera Festival
March to April
This festival explores the repertoire of 17th and 18th-century theatrical chamber music.
Further information: Tel. 054538542

REGGIO EMILIA

ConFusion&
June to September
Music festival held in various venues the Apennines near Reggio Emilia; several music appointments in village squares and other unusual places.
Further information:
Tel. 059340221

REC Reggio Emilia Contemporanea
September to November
This festival presents the voices of roc and electronic music plus great contemporary composers and new dance proposals.
Further information:
Tel. 0522458811

RED Reggio Emilia Danza
May to June
International dance festival promoted by Aterballetto, the leading dance production and distribution company i Italy. The event often comes out of the theaters bringing events to the city streets and squares.
Further information: Tel. 0522458811

Mundus
June to August
Held in Reggio Emilia but also and above all in the province's towns and villages, this is a festival of sounds anc music from all over the world.
Further information: Tel. 0522444446

RIMINI

Festival Internazionale di Pianoforte Città di Rimini
March to May
The festival presents internationally renowned pianists. All the concerts are free.
Further information:
Tel. 054124321

Sagra Musicale Malatestiana
July to September
Symphonic festival that highlights works that go across the arts, from music to theater dance and the visual arts. Guests of international fame and well-known orchestras. The event comprises Percuotere la Mente, with concerts that combine music research and international Pop.
Further information: Tel. 0541704293

FOLKLORE

The folk traditions of Emilia and Romagna are rustic and genuine, like the inhabitants of this land, who love organizing festivals and having a good time. However, good humor and ʔiality are not the only distinctive features of the social activities of this region. Here, what is usual about traditional events is there is an extra dimension of folk culture with particularly ʔgant musical styles, resulting in performances of a very high standard. Their ability to present ʔetry and literature written in the local dialect in a folk context is also impressive. The festive ʔle of town traditions is expressed particularly well in the great carnival celebrations held in the ʔwns and cities of Emilia-Romagna, for example in Busseto (Parma) and San Giovanni in ʔrsiceto (Bologna). The ceremony of the Segavecchia, held at Forlimpopoli (Forlì) is also held ʔan urban context.

BOLOGNA

ʔN GIOVANNI IN PERSICETO
ʔrnevale
Last two Sundays of carnival
In the centenary of the carnival held at San Giovanni in Persiceto, allegorical floats parade through the streets of the town preceded by the king of the carnival, Bertoldo, his son Bertoldino, his wife Marcolfa and their courtiers. The floats arrive in the main square still camouflaged, but, one by one, they undergo al spel (a transfiguration), revealing the allegorical theme of the float. Each float becomes a stage, the square becomes a theater and the parade turns into a live show. Anything may emerge from the camouflaged float: angels or devils, strange animals, explosions or smoke of various colors. Afterwards a shower of sweets and chocolates rains down onto the crowd.
For further information: Tel. 051826839

FERRARA

ʔalio
May
The "palio" is the name of the cloth or standard which is awarded to the winner of competitions in traditional events. The word has now also come to refer to the actual event. In Ferrara, the Palio consists of a month of merrymaking, parades and competitions between the eight *contrade* (districts) of the town whose representatives endeavor to win the much-prized cloth dedicated to St George, patron saint of Ferrara. The participants parade through the town dressed in 13th-century costumes. The flag-throwing competitions in Piazza del Municipio accompany the

Local girls participating in the Palio delle Putte, Ferrara. Next page: a papier maché float at the Cento carnival

spectators to the horse-race in Piazza Ariostea. There are 4 palios at stake: the green palio dedicated to St Paul is awarded to the winner of the girls' race, the red palio dedicated to St Romanus is awarded to the winner of the boys' race, the white palio dedicated to St Maurelius is awarded to the winner of the donkey race and the yellow one dedicated to St George is awarded to the winner of the horse-race. The festivities are divided into three parts: on the first Saturday of May, the representatives of the 8 districts offer candles in the cathedral, where the palios are blessed. On the third Saturday of the month, late in the evening, there is a historic procession with more than 1,000 of the town's inhabitants dressed in Renaissance costume. The competitions are held on the last Sunday of May.
For further information: Tel. 0532209370

EVENTS

189

NTO

rnevale

Shrove Tuesday and the following Sunday
The carnival at Cento, organized by the 6 *rioni* (districts) of the town, involves an afternoon parade of allegorical floats, huge affairs made of papier maché, from which sweets, chocolates, balloons and soft toys rain down onto the waiting crowd. Each float is surrounded by a merry, colorfully dressed crowd of hundreds of people, including groups of clowns, folk groups, and street artists.
This Carnival ends on the Sunday with the reading of the last will and testament and burning at the stake of the king of the Cento carnival, Tasi, accompanied by a white fox on a lead. He represents a true-life character, Luigi Tasini, who lived in the late 19th century. When faced with the dilemma of having to choose between his wife and a good glass of wine at the local tavern, he opted for the latter. When he has recited his *zirudella* (a typical poem in local dialect), a pretext for describing all the negative things which have happened in the past year, an enormous papier maché Tasi is set alight, symbolizing the end of the carnival. The festival concludes with a spectacular fire-work display at the castle above the town.
For further information:
Tel. 051904257 www.carnevalecento.com

FORLÌ-CESENA

ASTROCARO TERME

a Fugarena

Third Sunday in November
Held in the Terra del Sole district, the Fugarena (bonfire) is a very old folk festival: a large bonfire is erected in the middle of Piazza d'Armi. When lit, it illuminates the monumental buildings overlooking the center of this Renaissance fortress-town. The day of the festival includes the following events: a cross-country race through the lanes around the town; Art'infanzia, a children's art exhibition; musical events; the traditional donation of farm products by local farmers: first they are blessed in the church of S. Reparata and then given to charity; traditional games; a painting session in which children paint a panel measuring 20m x 20m; food and drink stalls where you can sample Romagna gastronomic

specialties and the latest crop of local wine.
For further information: Tel. 0543766766

Palio della Romagna Toscana and Palio di Santa Reparata

July and late August – beginning of September
These two festivals were once a single event involving several towns, each with its own defensive fortifications (fortresses, castles, houses with lookout towers). The Palio della Romagna Toscana takes place in July and the Palio di Santa Reparata is held between the end of August and the beginning of September. In both cases a historic procession parades through the fortress-town of Terra del Sole, consisting of 300 contestants, flag-throwers, musicians and people dressed in medieval costume, ending in Piazza d'Armi, to the sound of medieval trumpets, drum-rolls and the throwing of flags. During the Palio di Santa Reparata, the two districts of Borgo Romano and Borgo Fiorentino compete against each other. The competition, interspersed by flag-throwing performances, involves a cross-bow tournament. After the introduction of fire-arms, cross-bows continued to be used for hunting and for tournaments of this kind. The *veretta* (arrow) is fired towards the target, known as the *tasso*, placed at a distance of 36m. In the Palio della Romagna Toscana, the same kind of competition involves the 17 towns and villages which made up the old province of Romagna Toscana.
For further information:
Tel. 0543766766-0543767273

CESENATICO

Festa di Garibaldi

First weekend of August
This event dates back to 1885 and is a re-enactment of the moment when Garibaldi, hero of Italian independence, set sail from the harbor of Cesenatico, on August 2, 1849. On the Saturday evening, a Palio della Cuccagna is held, disputed by the eight districts of Cesenatico. The contestants have to climb up a pole smeared with grease and hoisted so that it overhangs the port-canal. On the Sunday morning, the festivities continue with a parade of flags and laurel wreaths are placed on the stone marking the place where Garibaldi set sail. After this, a fleet of boats sets off from the harbor to

EVENTS

191

commemorate those who died at sea. The festivities end with a huge fire-work display in Piazza Costa.
For further information: Tel. 0547673287

Palio della Cuccagna dell'Adriatico
23 July
Held at night, at the canal harbor of Cesenatico, the challenge involves the towns on the Romagna coast who compete to win Palio della Cuccagna. The competition consists in climbing a pole 13m long, smeared with grease (the *cuccagna*), erected at an angle so that it overhangs the water. The competitors come from the towns of Casalborsetti, Cervia, Gatteo, San Mauro Pascoli, Goro and Cesenatico.
For further information: Tel. 0547673287

Presepe Galleggiante
From the beginning of December - 6 January
A Christmas atmosphere reigns along the famous canal harbor of Cesenatico, designed by Leonardo da Vinci. The Bragozzo, the Battana, the Bragozzo d'altura, the Lancia, the Trabaccolo da pesca, the Topo, the Paranza and the Barchét, the traditional, brightly-painted boats of the northern and central Adriatic, moored in the harbor, are used as floating stages for life-size wooden statues which form a floating crib. The crib is rendered even more delightful by the lights which play on the crib and are reflected in the water.
For further information:
Tel. 0547673287

FORLIMPOPOLI

La Segavecchia
Sunday half-way through Lent
The old lady who is the star of this particular show is hundreds of years old. She is an enormous papier maché doll who, with the traditional features of an old lady, personifies Lent and all the privations which it used to entail, but also all the evils and ailments of everyday life. The *fantoccio* (doll), which can be up to 5m high, is paraded around the streets on a float followed

by a procession of allegorical floats and clowns which accompany it to the place o execution. The charges against the old la are read out by a voice off-stage. The dea sentence, announced in Piazza Garibaldi, opposite the fortress, is a pretext for listir all the public and private scandals which have taken place in the past year. The *Vecchia* (old lady) is condemned to be sav in two. The hooded executioners pick up enormous woodcutter's saw (*sega*) and, pretending that it is a huge effort, procee to saw the old lady in half. Suddenly, the two parts of the doll fall apart to reveal a cascade of dried fruit (the only delicacy allowed during Lent) and small gifts for th crowd. In the evening, the *Vecchia* is burnt at the stake.
For further information:
Tel. 0543743082-0543749247
www.segavecchia.it

MODENA

Carnevale
Maundy Thursday
For the people of Modena, the arrival of *Carnevale* (Carnival) means the arrival of the Pavironica family. On Maundy Thursda Sandrone, his wife Pulonia and their son Sgroghiguelo, having set off from their home in the town of Bosco di Sotto, arrive

The Vecchia of Forlimpopoli being carried around the town on a huge float.

at Modena's train station to a fanfare of trumpets and a crowd of people in fancy-dress including other *maschere* (carnival clowns). Escorted by two coachmen and valets dressed in 18th-century costume, the Pavironica family is paraded through the streets of the town in a 19th-century carriage drawn by two horses. When they reach the cathedral, they pay homage to the religious, civic and military authorities. Then Sandrone stands on the balcony of the town hall and begins to read his customary *sproloquio*, a speech in local dialect describing the salient events which have happened in the city during the year. He makes criticisms, discusses various situations and suggests how they should be resolved, rubs salt in the wounds of various inhabitants of the town and ends his speech by inviting everyone to keep the peace and work hard. Sandrone represents the peasants of the past, who were simple but cunning. He represents the common people, who were always badly treated and hungry, who always had to struggle to make ends meet.

For further information:
Tel. 059206660-059206659

PARMA

BARDI
Gilde et Speziali
Shrove Tuesday

The *Gilde* (early mutual assistance organizations) and the *Speziali* (spice-sellers) have given their name to a convincing re-enactment of a medieval market. Everyday life in the Middle Ages is played out in one of the most atmospheric settings in the Parma area: inside the solid walls of the Castello di Bardi. The festival is attended by elegant dames, soldiers, busy townspeople, archers, dancers and nobles, all dressed in medieval costume. Entertainment is provided by flag-throwers, jesters, jugglers, people re-enacting scenes of everyday life or practising medieval arts and crafts, and jousting tournaments.
For further information: Tel. 052571626
www.diasprorosso.com

BUSSETO
Carnevale
Sundays during carnival

The Carnevale di Busseto, known as "Lo sballo in maschera" (a pun on the title of one of Verdi's operas), began in 1880 and has kept alive two of its fundamental themes ever since: Verdi's music and good food. The carnival involves the participation of local bands. Traditional brass bands with majorettes walk along between the floats, while more modern bands on board the floats carry on a live and uninterrupted performance of rather different music. The festival takes place in the old town over four consecutive Sundays and, in addition to the floats and the bands, involves processions of groups of people dressed in carnival costumes with a particular theme. In Piazza Verdi, the participants pause for something to eat at the Angolo del Ghiottone (Greedy-guts Corner), where expert chefs offer salami, cured meats and traditional sweets such as the *spongata* (a dry cake made with almonds, pine-nuts and candied fruit). Great effort also goes into entertaining the children of the town who can be made-up, attend kids' shows and participate in team-games.

For further information: Tel. 052492487
www.carnevaledibusseto.com

PIACENZA

GRAZZANO VISCONTI
Corteo Storico
Last Sunday in May

In 1389, Giovanni Anguissola and Beatrice Visconti, sister of the Duke of Milan, Gian Galeazzo, their children and and all the inhabitants of the town, decked out to celebrate the occasion, awaited the arrival of Valentina Visconti, the Lady of Asti, and the allied noble families of Piacenza. As it was then, for the modern historical re-enactment, the whole town is gaily decorated with brightly colored buntings. The town provides a natural stage, its streets throng with dames, knights and damsels, warriors and footmen, squires, troubadours and jugglers who put on improvised shows. There are also demonstrations by flag-throwers, contests between the knights on their war-horses, who compete in tests of strength and riding ability, while armed soldiers wave their pointed weapons in the air. The festivities begin with a procession in medieval costume. There is something happening in every square: jousting tournaments, juggling shows, minstrels, magicians and jesters, archery competitions and medieval games. The grand finale is the Giostra de lo Biscione, a jousting tournament between the noble families of the Piacenza area.

For further information: Tel. 0523870997

RAVENNA

CERVIA
Afferra una Stella
10 August

This festival involves a 5-km walk through the pinewood, the *gioco della cuccagna* (where the contestants have to reach the prize at the top of a pole smeared with grease, hanging over the canal harbor), and brass bands playing jolly music. In the evening of St Laurence's Day, traditionally the best night to see shooting stars, there is a fire-work display.

For further information: Tel. 0544993435

Sapore di Sale
September

Cervia celebrates its tradition of being a salt-town with a festival called Sapore di Sale (Tasting of Salt, coining the title of a famous Italian song of the 'sixties). It involves cultural events, visits to the museum of salt culture, exhibitions and special markets, all on the theme of salt. In particular, during the second weekend of the month, the town celebrates the ancient tradition of delivering the salt. The salt is loaded, as it used to be, into a *burchiella* (a traditional, flat-bottomed boat), and pulled along the canal by two horses to the warehouses. When it reaches its destination, instead of being unloaded and taken into the warehouses as it used to be, it is distributed to the local people. The festival involves guided tours of the salt-pans to see the various phases of salt-processing, production and harvesting using the industrial and old craft methods. The place is rendered even more charming by the pinkish hues of the production tanks and the dazzling white of the piles of salt.

For further information: Tel. 0544993435

Sposalizio del Mare
Ascension Day

The festival was probably initiated in 1445 by Pietro Barbo, who was Bishop of Cervia at a time when the town was part of the Venetian Republic. The story goes that, on returning from Venice, the bishop was caught in a storm at sea. He succeeded in

In the water trying to catch the bishop's ring at Cervia on Ascension Day

calming the swell by praying, blessing the water and committing his pastoral ring to the deep. He then vowed that, every year, on the Ascension Day, he would celebrate the event with a solemn ceremony. From then on, the Sposalizio del Mare (Marriage to the Sea) was repeated every year. The ceremony begins with a historic procession of traditional boats with brightly-colored sails bearing more than 100 locals dressed in 15th-century costume. The procession of boats moves offshore and forms a circle, after which the bishop pronounces the old formula of the blessing of the sea. Then he throws a gold ring, on which the date is engraved, attached to a colored ribbon, into the water. At this point, groups of boys and girls dive into the sea and try to catch the ring. If they succeed, it is a propitious sign not only for the person who catches it but for the town as a whole. Very occasionally the ring has been lost, but mostly it is caught when it is still in the air. On the Saturday before the ceremony there is a historic regatta of traditional boats, called the Regata dell'Ascensione, whereas the week before the festival involves wall-to-wall shows, singing and dancing.

For further information: Tel. 0544993435

FAENZA
L'Oro del Vasaio
July

The Oro del Vasaio (literally, Potter's Gold, a world pot-throwing championship) is an international competition between the world's best potters who meet in the heart of Faenza, in the magnificent square of Piazza Nenni to take up the challenge. The preliminary rounds and the finals of pot-throwing take place over two days. There are two categories: Esthetic and Technical ability. The first category highlights the creativeness of the competitor, while the second assesses his/her technical ability. The contestants have to pass two tests to create the tallest vase and the widest bowl using the same amount of clay.

For further information:
Tel. 054621145 www.enteceramica.it

Palio del Niballo

Last Sunday in June

The Palio is the re-enactment of a medieval tradition. On the Sunday before the festival, the standard-bearers of the five *contrade* (districts) of the town demonstrate their skill in a flag-throwing contest. On the day of the festival, a historic procession commemorates the glories of the town under the Manfredi family, who ruled the town almost continuously from 1313 until 1503. The contest takes place in the municipal football stadium: the contestants are riders representing the five *rioni* of the town, each dressed in different colors. Starting from the same point, the riders, armed with a spear, gallop along a horse-shoe-shaped route in opposite directions until they reach their target: the Niballo, a corruption of the word *Annibale* (Hannibal), the North African king, is represented by a mock half-bust figure holding a metal disk with a diameter of only 8cm at the end of each arm. The first rider to strike one of these targets releases a mechanism which raises the arm which has been struck and blocks the other. Each rider competes against each representative of the other four *rioni*, a total of 20 attempts. Every time a rider wins, he gains the shield of his opponent. The rider who wins the largest number of shields wins the Palio, the much-coveted small piece of green cloth.

For further information:
Tel. 0546691295-0546691499

RIMINI

CATTOLICA

Festa Notturna della Regina del Mare

Last Saturday in August

The festival is held in honor of the Madonna del Carmine (Our Lady of St Carmel), whose 8-meter-high marble statue overlooks the harbor. The festivities start at 8 p.m. with a torch-light procession from the Parish church to the square where the statue stands. There is a mass followed by a blessing. Afterwards, a fire-work display illuminates the harbor, the boat-house and the fishing-boats. The boats are decorated for the occasion and move out to sea to cast a wreath of flowers into the sea in honor of all those who have died at sea. At dawn, the boats return to the harbor one by one and offer delicious grilled fish to the waiting crowd.

For further information: Tel. 0541963341

The Niballo, the target of the Palio di Faenza Palio di Ferrara: the donkey race

I n an area where the quality of life is all-important, it is no surprise to find that it is home to some of Italy's finest spa

<image_icon>	THERMAL SPA
<image_icon>	HEALTH CENTER

establishments and wellness centers. These "havens of well-being", set in beautiful natural environments, are perfect places to relax. From the Apennines near Piacenza to the Romagna coast, the region offers a dense network of spas that use natural spring water for treating a wide range of ailments, diseases and disorders. In many cases, these establishments have interesting histories that are closely linked to the longstanding traditions of the spa culture. However, despite having their origins in the past, they have truly modernised, incorporating the latest

Wellness

technology. These thermal spas offer integrated treatments for wellness and body care, but there are also other interesting options associated with various sports, and cultural or leisure activities.

Highlights

- Salsomaggiore Terme, a haven of health and wellness
- Castrocaro Terme: a blend of culture, art and thermal treatments
- A late-19th century atmosphere pervades Monticelli Terme
- The Terme di Salvarola set among expanses of ancient deciduous trees

Inside

198 Bagno di Romagna
199 Bologna
199 Brisighella
199 Castel San Pietro Terme
200 Castrocaro Terme
201 Cervarezza
201 Cervia
202 Fratta Terme
202 Monticelli Terme
203 Porretta Terme
203 Punta Marina Terme
204 Riccione
205 Rimini
205 Riolo Terme
206 Salsomaggiore Terme
207 Salvarola Terme
207 San Marino
207 Sant'Andrea Bagni
207 Tabiano Bagni

Euroterme

Via Lungosavio 2, Tel. 0543911414
www.euroterme.com
Open April-November

Grand Hotel Terme Roseo

Piazza Ricasoli 2, Tel. 0543911016
www.termeroseo.it
Open year-round

Terme di Sant'Agnese

Via Fiorentina 17, Tel. 0543911555
www.termesantagnese.it
Open April-November

As the archeological remains of the Sant'Agnese baths show, there has been interest in the curative properties of its hot springs since Roman times, when the town was called *Oppidum Balnei*. Today, Bagno di Romagna is a health spa with the following facilities: Sant'Agnese, the first spa complex dating from the 18th century, the Terme Roseo spa and the Euroterme hotel-spa complex. Sant'Agnese offers hydropinic treatments (drinking the spring water), mud- and balneo-therapy, natural caves (for steam therapy), and treatments for vascular diseases and gynecological problems. There is also a wellness center. The Terme Roseo spa has its own spring and, in addition to the main treatments (mud therapy, a steam cave, inhalations, baths and irrigations of various kinds) offers physiokinesitherapy and motory rehabilitation. This spa also has a wellness center. Euroterme has a thermal pool complex, partly indoor and partly open-air, with a solarium, hydro-massage, geyser falls, underwater massage beds, underwater music therapy and a pediatric department with colorful play areas. It also has a sports medical center and a wellness center. The properties of the sulfurous bicarbonate alkaline water are beneficial in the treatment of circulatory diseases, liver and bile-duct complaints, problems of the digestive tract, the motory and respiratory systems, and the urinary tract, metabolism disorders and gynecological problems.

The Grand Hotel Terme Roseo at Bagno di Romagna

Pioggia di Giotto

The water which surfaces at a temperature of 44°C/111°F from the spring at Bagno di Romagna is called Pioggia di Giotto (Giotto's Rain). It takes at least 700 years for the water to complete its underground journey, during which it loses all its impurities and is enriched with precious mineral salts. In other words, the water we see today may have been rain which fell during the famous painter's lifetime.

BOLOGNA ⚕

rme Felsinee
Via Giuseppe Di Vagno 7
tel. 0516198484, www.termefelsinee.it
Open year-round

Bologna's fame as a thermal spa dates back to Roman times, when the Emperor Augustus built some baths below the hill of S. Luca. For a long time, the area was known as Pozzo del Diavolo (the Devil's Well), because the water which surfaces there, and which is rich in sulfur and calcium sulphate, prevented plants from growing. The tradition of hot springs in Bologna has focused on the Terme Felsinee spa complex, set in a vast park. It has five departments (specializing in spa treatments, physical medicine and rehabilitation, medical fitness, special treatments and dermo-cosmetology) and the latest water sports facilities (hydro-machines). The water surfaces at Fonte Alexander (15°C/59°F) and Fonte San Luca (15.5°C/60°F), where the water is sulfurous. The spa water is beneficial for circulatory problems, skin complaints, and problems of the digestive tract, the motory system, the respiratory system, the urinary tract and metabolism disorders.

BRISIGHELLA ⚕

rme di Brisighella
Viale delle Terme 12, tel. 054681068
www.termedibrisighella.it
Open mid-May-mid-November

The salt-rich springs of Brisighella were discovered at the beginning of the 19th century but it was not until 1862 that the first scientific analyses were made of the springs of sulfurous and salt bromine iodic water (15°C/59°F). The spa complex, built in 1962 next to the original establishment built in the mid-19th century, is only 300m from the old town center. It is set in a lovely park with an open-air pool and close to good sports facilities. One department specializes in the treatment of catarrhal deafness, and has a section for treating respiratory problems in children. There is also an active department for treating chronic rheumatoid arthritis and post-operative trauma with mud-bath therapy and massotherapy combined with physiokinesitherapy. The spa offers treatments for circulatory diseases, digestive ailments, and problems associated with the motory system, the respiratory system and gynecological complaints.

CASTEL SAN PIETRO TERME ⚕

rme di Castel San Pietro
Viale Terme 1113, tel. 051941247
www.termedicastelsanpietro.com
Open year-round

The beneficial properties of the spring water at Castel San Pietro were discovered in 1337 when, during a foot-and-mouth epidemic, local people noticed that some cows which had drunk from a spring here were cured of the disease. Studies on the water were conducted the following year, when Castel San Pietro temporarily became the seat of the University of Bologna, which was under a papal interdict. Because of the water's undoubted therapeutic properties, particularly in the treatment of liver complaints, it was called the Fonte della Fegatella (literally Spring of the Little Liver). However, the first spa dates from 1835, when a special company was set up for the purpose. The spa complex was built in 1886 about 1.5 km outside the town, in a beautiful park containing the sulfurous and salt bromine iodic water which surfaces near the source of the Sillaro River. The mud used here is obtained by leaving clay from the quarries at S. Martino in Pedriolo (Bologna) to soak in salt bromine iodic water. The facilities are arranged on three floors. The ground floor has a series of pools, aerosols, and mud therapy; on the first floor is the department of inhalations and another for the treatment of catarrhal deafness, with a special pediatric section, whereas the gym, physical, mud, esthetic and gynecological therapy departments are all on the top floor. The water comes from Fonte Bagni (14.5°C/58°F) and Fonte S. Donato (17.5 °C/68.5°F) and is beneficial in the treatment of circulatory diseases, skin complaints, problems of the digestive tract, the motory system, respiratory problems, urinary tract and metabolism disorders, as well as gynecological and stomatological problems.

CASTROCARO TERME

Terme di Castrocaro

Viale Marconi 14/19, Tel. 0543412711
www.termedicastrocaro.it
Open April-November

There is an unusual story behind the discovery of the hot springs here. In 1829, some customs officers caught a smuggler in the act of stealing a small barrel of salt water from the springs of the Bolga River. The court ordered him to pay a fine since he was found guilty of stealing from the State (since salt was a state monopoly) and ordered that the stolen water should be analyzed. Scientific analysis showed that the water contained not only salt, but also bromine and iodine. This led to the first therapeutic experiments and the erection of spa facilities, as well as the sale of mineral water. The spa complex, founded in 1843, comprises three buildings situated in a park of 8 hectares. They were designed by the Florentine architect Boboli, the same man who created the Boboli Gardens in Florence, and are directly connected to the Jolly Hotel Grande Albergo Terme. The spa is set in a relaxing environment and has excellent facilities for sport and entertainment, including a vast outdoor pool, hydro-massage and trampolines, a mini-golf course and an open-air dance-floor. In addition to traditional spa treatments, there is a specialist health center; a wellness center with pools fed with spring water, hydro-massage, a sauna, a Turkish bath, a steam cave, a Scottish shower, a rehabilitation center (specializing in shoulder complaints); a diagnosis, prevention and rehabilitation center for vascular and lymphatic diseases; departments of esthetic medicine and traditional Chinese medicine, and a homeopathic medicine service. The temperature of the water ranges from 6.5°C/44°F to 15°C/59°F and is beneficial in the treatment of circulatory diseases, skin complaints, problems of the digestive tract, the motory system and the respiratory system and the urinary tract, metabolism, gynecological and stomatological disorders.

Castrocaro Terme: hydro-massage, water-slides and trampolines for a healthy holiday with lots of fun

Jolly Hotel Grande Albergo Terme
Via Roma 2, Tel. 0543767114
www.termedicastrocaro.it
119 rooms, closed from January 6 - mid-February.

Situated in the old park of the spa complex to which it is connected, it has a pool fed with warm spring water, a pool with hydro-massage, a solarium, a sauna, a Turkish bath, a steam cave, vascular water trails and a gym. It offers both manipulative and therapeutic treatments: Ayurvedic massage, holistic massage, anti-stress massage with essential oils, Shiatsu, bio-energetic massage, Californian massage, circulatory foot massage, connective tissue massage, lymph drainage, foot reflexology and acupuncture. The complex also offers esthetic treatments for the face and body and thermal treatments: hydropinic treatments (drinking the spring water), inhalatory treatments, balneo-therapy, mud therapy, thermal rehabilitation, endotympanum insufflations and hydrokinesitherapy.

CERVAREZZA

Terme di Cervarezza
Fonti di S. Lucia 4, Tel. 0522890380
Open April-November

The spa is situated in a park about 2km from Cervarezza. The water flows down from Monte Ventasso (Fonte S. Lucia: the water has a medium mineral content and is alkaline and sulfurous with sodium bicarbonate) and has diuretic properties. The spa complex, which is only open in season, is the only one in the province of Reggio Emilia and offers hydropinic treatments (drinking the spring water), inhalations, mud therapy and balneo-therapy. The water can be used to treat diseases of the motory system, the respiratory system, the urinary tract and metabolism disorders.

CERVIA

Terme di Cervia
Via Forlanini 16, Tel. 0544990111
www.terme.org
Open May-December

It was the salt-workers who worked in the black mud rich with substances such as bromine, iodine, magnesium and calcium who became aware of its therapeutic properties. In fact the first rudimentary spa complex was built in 1930 on the initiative of the Salt-workers Recreation Club.
The current spa complex was built in 1961 and is situated near the sea next to the Riserva Naturale della Salina (part of the Parco Regionale del Delta del Po) and the pinewood of Milano Marittima (province of Ravenna). It is equipped with the latest facilities and exploits the therapeutic properties of the mud at the spring and the mineral water associated with it, which is produced by the slow sedimentation of sea water and the crystallization of the salt in the pools where it collects.
The large indoor pool fed with warm spring water has a constant temperature of 34°C/93°F. Next to it are two pools with vascular water trails, a solarium and a gym for working out. The park surrounding the complex has a fitness trail, a playground for children, a concert hall and cinema. The spa also offers esthetic medicinal treatments.
The water of the salt-pans (20°C/68°F) is beneficial in the treatment of circulatory diseases, skin complaints, motory ailments as well as respiratory and gynecological problems.
The location of the spa, amid the sea, greenery and pinewood, make this site not only a spa center but also a resort where one can combine treatments with real relaxation and enjoyment.

FRATTA TERME

Terme della Fratta
Via Loreta 238, Tel. 0543460911
Open April-November
The Terme di Fratta (from the Latin *urbs fracta*, meaning destroyed town) takes advantage of seven springs which surface close to the Salso River and which can be divided into three categories which are useful for a wide range of cures: Group 1 (12-16°C/54-61°F), salt-iodic; Group 2 (12-16°C/54-61°F), salt sulfurous; Group 3 (12-16°C/54-61°F), sodium chloride (salt). It is situated in a large park with an area of 13 hectares, with a fitness trail and numerous sports facilities. The water has been used for health treatment since the early 19th century, during the Napoleonic period. In 1927, a well was discovered built with curved bricks and river pebbles, which probably dated from a Roman bath complex. Next to the spa built in 1930 is a more recent building which contains a hotel and a wellness center. Thanks to the integration of these facilities, guests can come here to relax and take advantage of massage, esthetic and anti-cellulite treatments. The water here is particularly beneficial in the treatment of liver and bile-duct complaints, skin disorders, problems of the digestive tract, the motory system, the respiratory system, and the urinary tract, metabolism disorders and gynecological problems.

MONTICELLI TERME

Terme di Monticelli
Via Montepelato Nord 4/A
Tel. 0521659190
www.termedimonticelli.com
Open year-round
Although, as the remains of prehistoric pile-dwellings around the modern complex show, the underground river bearing the water of Monticelli Terme has flowed since ancient times, the spa complex is the most recent one to be built in the province of Parma. The salt bromine iodic water was discovered in 1924 by a farmer who was digging a well to irrigate his fields. The spa complex began to operate only three years later. The complex, a unique blend of 19th-century architectural ideas and the simple, elegant lines of Art Deco, is set in an old park of conifers covering an area of 25 hectares, with a keep-fit trail and various sports facilities. The Monticelli spa consists of various specialized centers (for the treatment of vascular diseases, motory rehabilitation, catarrhal deafness, respiratory rehabiltation, dietological medicine, and esthetic medicine), three hotels (Hotel delle Rose and Hotel Terme, each with their own thermal complex, and the meublé Della Quiete) and 3 different pools fed with warm spring water, 2 of which have hydro-massage, deambulation with ozone hydro-massage, water-bikes and a water gym. It is possible to adapt existing programs to personal requirements and any other needs which may emerge from the complete check-up which every guest undergoes at the beginning of his/her stay. The water comes from the following springs: Montirone (14°C/57°F) is sulfurous, and Pozzi 10 and 13 (17°C/63°F) are salt bromine, iodic. The water is beneficial in the treatment of circulatory, respiratory and gynecological problems.

Monticelli Terme has a late 19th-century atmosphere

PORRETTA TERME 🎋 🏃

erme di Porretta

Via Roma 5,
Tel. 053422062
www.termediporretta.it
Open year-round

The growth of the town from the 13th century on is closely tied to the spring water. It became popular with the bourgeoisie and nobility of Emilia and Tuscany. Illustrious visitors to the hot springs of Porretta during the Renaissance include Lorenzo the Magnificent, Cardinal Francesco Gonzaga, and

Elaborate decoration at the Porretta Terme health spa.

the painter, Andrea Mantegna. A legend, which also features in the town's crest, tells that an ailing ox was set free and regained its strength after drinking at the Fonte della Puzzola. The spa draws water from eight springs, located in two distinct areas of Porretta: four of them, known as 'acque alte' (high springs) contain salt bromine iodic water and surface near Rio Maggiore, where the first spa began and where its buildings have now been

abandoned; the other four sulfurous springs, called 'acque basse' (low springs) are about 300m away from the town, near the Reno River. In the 19th century, Porretta Terme became a major Italian spa town. Today the spa complex contains various facilities including nursing and rehabilitation hospitals offering many cures (for circulatory diseases, liver and bile-duct complaints, skin disorders, problems of the digestive tract, the motory system, the respiratory system, the urinary tract, as well as metabolism and gynecological disorders). There is also the Oasi di Benessere wellness center offering esthetic treatments, a solarium, a sauna, a Turkish bath, aromatic hydro-massage, music therapy and chromo-therapy. The indoor pool fed with warm spring water is also open to the public. There is also a gym and a park with a fitness trail and concert area.

PUNTA MARINA TERME 🎋

erme di Punta Marina

Viale C. Colombo 161
Tel. 0544437222
www.termepuntamarina.com
Open year-round

This spa was conceived in 1965 as a thalassotherapy center. Since 1991, it has used the water from a spring discovered, after extensive research, at a depth of 42m and separated from the sea by thick layers of clay. The water of Punta Marina Terme has the rare distinction of containing magnesium. The complex has recently been modernized and now has a pool with a vascular water trail and a gym for rehabilitating patients with neuro-motory problems. The complex is all on one level and the two pavilions of the complex are divided into various departments, with communal areas for relaxation, a solarium, a park with a fitness trail, and direct beach

access. Whereas the thermal treatments (inhalations, balneo-therapy, therapeutic baths, hydro-massage, water trails, humid-hot inhalations, insufflations, irrigations, nebulizations and a pool fed with warm spring water) are offered from April to November, the physical therapy and rehabilitation departments, the pool and the gym are open year-round. It is possible to acquire thermal packages with particular themes (intensive, wellness, anti-stress therapy, anti-cellulite treatment, relaxation therapy, anti-age therapy, concern with self) or customized programs. The water, which contains salt bromine iodine calcium and magnesium, surfaces at a temperature of 17.5°C/63.5°F. It is particularly beneficial in the treatment of circulatory diseases, skin complaints, and motory, respiratory and gynecological problems.

WELLNESS

RICCIONE ♨ 🏊

Terme di Riccione

Viale Torino 4/16
Tel. 0541602201
www.riccioneterme.it
Open year-round

According to tradition, the Blessed Alexius, patron saint of the town, made water spout from a rock to slake the thirst of some pilgrims. Other tales relate that Turkish corsairs used to stop at Riccione during their raids on the coasts of the Adriatic, in order to benefit from the thermal springs here. Historic sources provide evidence that the spring water here was appreciated by the Emperor Diocletian and, in the 17th century, by Queen Christina of Sweden. However, Riccione didn't really become a spa town until the 20th century, when it suddenly became a popular tourist destination. Today, Riccione has a modern spa complex comprising two pavilions (Centrale and Bianco), set in a park of 40,000 m² with a wide range of facilities. The complex is a stone's throw from the sea of Riccione, Italy's leading wellness beach, with a pool fed with spring water, inhalatory treatments and waterfall hydro-massage. The wellness sector is very important here.

Water gym is ideal for physical rehabilitation

The Oasi di Riccione Terme has both a center for thermal medicine and esthetic surgery (with gyms, 4 pools fed with spring water, a humid-hot cave, massage and mud therapy), and the La Marina Bagno 49 wellness beach. There are numerous therapeutic treatments available (for disintoxication, osteoporosis, giving up smoking, backache) and a vast range of thermal and esthetic treatments. The water here is recommended in the treatment of circulatory diseases, liver and bile-duct complaints, skin disorders, problems of the digestive tract, the motory system, the respiratory system, the urinary tract, and metabolism and gynecological disorders.

Des Nations 🏊

Lungomare Costituzione 2
Tel. 0541647878
www.desnations.it
36 rooms, open year-round

The hotel has a small pool with hydro-massage, a sauna with infra-red radiation, a fitness corner and pancafit therapy. It offers manipulative and therapeutic treatments: Chinese medicine, Tibetan medicine, connective tissue massage, Ayurvedic massage, Tuina massage, lymph drainage, cranio-sacral therapy, foot reflexology, kinesiology, Shiatsu massage, posture correction, finger massage, moxibustion, osteopathy, mud therapy and hot-stone massage. There are also treatments to improve psycho-physical well-being: Nature's path therapy, oligotherapy, phytotherapy, homeopathy, aromatherapy, bio-energetic massage, crystal therapy, chromotherapy, Bach flower remedies, iridology, autogenous training, relaxation and meditation techniques, t'ai ch'i ch'uan, qigong, music therapy and chromatic mud therapy. It also offers esthetic face and body treatments.

Milano Helvetia 🏊

Via Milano 2, Tel. 0541605410
www.hotelmilano.net
73 rooms, closed mid-October mid-March

Housed in a historic building, this hotel offers its guests an open-air pool with hydro-massage, a solarium and a Turkish bath. The wellness center offers massotherapy treatments as well as manipulative and therapeutic treatments: Ayurvedic massage, effleurage massage, lymph drainage, polarity therapy, pressotherapy, energetic massage and mesotherapy. It also offers esthetic face and body treatments and thermal treatments: inhalatory therapies, hydropinic treatments (drinking the spring water), electrophoresis, magnet therapy and kinesitherapy.

Promenade 🏊

Viale Milano 67
Tel. 0541600852
www.hotelpromenade.it
48 rooms, open year-round

The hotel has a pool fed with spring water for vascular water trails, a fresh-water pool with hydro-massage, a nudist pool for serious sun-worshippers, and a solarium. The center offers manipulative and therapeutic treatments including Ayurvedic massage, foot and hand reflexology, massotherapy, Watsu massage, holistic full-body massage, Indios stone massage, Lotus flower therapy, Chakra massage and aroma massage. The center also provides esthetic face and body treatments, thermal rehabilitation and treatments for psycho-physical well-being: chromotherapy, aromatherapy, music therapy, oligotherapy and Bach flower remedies.

RIMINI

imini Terme
Miramare,
Viale Principe di Piemonte 56,
Tel. 0541414011
www.riminiterme.com
Open year-round

Rimini Terme arose above the ashes of a previous hydro-therapeutic complex (1870) specializing in thalassotherapy. Thanks to the discovery of the salt bromine iodic Miramare spring (14°C/57°F) in the second half of the 20th century, the complex became a real thermal spa as well as a thalassotherapy center in 1972. Situated right on the sea, it has treatment facilities (departments of mud therapy, inhalations and sand therapy), 4 heated salt-water pools and a wellness center (sauna, Turkish bath, hydro-massage, aromatherapy, esthetic mud treatments and Shiatsu). Around the complex is a park with a fitness trail, a kids' playground and the well-equipped beach of Miramare. The treatments available are recommended for circulatory diseases, and motory, respiratory and gynecological problems.

National
Viale Vespucci 42,
Tel. 0541390944
www.nationalhotel.it
83 rooms, closed over Christmas

Located in the exclusive Marino Centro zone of Rimini, the hotel has a gym, a heated open-air pool, a Finnish sauna, a Scottish shower, a solarium and a Turkish bath. It offers various manipulative and therapeutic treatments: connective tissue massage, lymph drainage, cranio-sacral therapy, foot reflexology and finger massage. Psycho-physical wellness treatments include esthetic face and body treatments, Nature's path therapy, oligotherapy, phytotherapy, aromatherapy and bio-energetic therapy.

RIOLO TERME

Terme di Riolo Bagni
Via Firenze 15, Tel. 054671045
www.termediriolo.it
Open April-November

The cult of the salt sulfurous water of Riolo dates back hundreds of years. People have been coming here since the Renaissance, including such illustrious figures as Lord Byron, the Bonaparte princes and the poet Carducci. The elegant pavilions of the spa of Riolo were built in 1870, with the Oriani pavilion being particularly splendid. The large indoor pool fed with spring water was built comparitively recently. It has three specific areas devoted to vascular water trails, water jets and hydro-massage. It has a special spa for children called Terme Bimbo. There are support therapies available, for giving up smoking and other problems, and natural methodologies including hay and aromatic flower baths, hydro-therapy, oxygen therapy and massage). The center offers various integrated programs combining hotel accommodation and spa treatment thanks to a special arrangement with the historic Grand Hotel Terme, set in the luxuriant park where the spa pavilions are situated.

The therapeutic treatments available are beneficial in the cure of circulatory diseases, liver and bile-duct disorders, skin complaints, and problems of the digestive tract, motory system, urinary tract, metabolism and gynecological disorders.

Heliotherapy: a pleasant interlude during a spa holiday

SALSOMAGGIORE TERME ♒ 🏃

Istituto Termale Ettore Baistrocchi
Viale Matteotti 31, Tel. 0524574411
www.termebaistrocchi.it
Open April-November

Terme di Salsomaggiore
Via Roma 9, Tel. 0524582611
www.termedisalsomaggiore.it
Open year-round

Terme Tommasini
Viale Corridoni 1, Tel. 0524575041
Open May-November

The salt bromine iodic water of Salsomaggiore was already well-known and used in the 8th century, on account of its high salt content. The first public spa complex, which dates from 1858, soon became famous all over Italy. The Terme di Salsomaggiore company operates the Terme Berzieri and Terme Zoia spa establishments. The former was built from 1913-1923 in the Art Nouveau and Art Deco styles. The latter, built in the Parco Mazzini in 1970, has a different style based on simplicity and functionality. The range of treatments offered by the spa is staggering. Terme Berzieri not only has inhalation and mud therapy departments (where the salt bromine iodic water is concentrated into the so-called *acqua madre* - brine - and natural mud), but incorporates the Tempio di Igea wellness center (with a sauna, a Turkish bath, French shower, aromatic treatments, beauty treatments and massage). Terme Zoia offers all the traditional spa treatments and has a modern medical center and various specialized centers (pediatric inhalations, thermal hydro-therapy, osteoporosis analyses, mouth hygiene and esthetic medicine). The Terme di Salsomaggiore company also operates two hotels with in-house treatments: the Grand Hotel Porro and the Hotel Valentini. Both buildings are situated in a park where there is also a large indoor pool (the only one in town fed with thermal spring water). Not far from these buildings, in the town center, is the Istituto Termale Baistrocchi, a historic institution with 300 rooms, which offers its guests a brand new treatment department and weekly programs to improve physical wellness. The water of the Salsomaggiore Terme spring (16°C/61°F) is good for the treatment of circulatory diseases, and problems associated with the motory and respiratory systems, as well as gynecological and stomatological complaints.

G. A. Bolognese 🏃
Viale Cavour 1,
Tel. 0524579141
www.hotelbolognese.it
64 rooms, closed December-March

The hotel has a gym, pools and a sauna. It offers face and body treatments and the thermal treatments include hydropinic treatments (drinking the spring water), inhalation therapies, balneo-therapy, mud therapy and endotympanum insufflations.

G. H. Porro 🏃
Viale Porro 10,
Tel. 0524578221
www.grandhotel-porro.it
85 rooms, open year-round

This spa hotel offers esthetic face and body treatments, treatments for psycho-physical wellness (aromatherapy and phytotherapy) and thermal treatments such as inhalation therapies, balneo-therapy, mud therapy and ultrasound therapy. It also offers the following manipulative and therapeutic treatments: massotherapy, lymph drainage, mesotherapy, underwater massage, a French shower with spring water, pressotherapy and massage with essential oils.

Nazionale 🏃
Viale Matteotti 43
Tel. 0524573757
www.albergonazionalesalsomaggiore.it
42 rooms, closed January 6 – mid-March and December - Christmas

The hotel has a special arrangement with the Terme Berzieri spa establishment and offers esthetic face and body treatments, and treatments to improve psycho-physical wellness: aromatherapy, chromotherapy, yoga and music therapy. Its range of manipulative and therapeutic treatments includes massotherapy, Chinese massage, lymph drainage, finger massage, moxibustion, foot reflexology, pressotherapy and algae treatments.

SALVAROLA TERME

erme della Salvarola
Via Salvarola 137, Tel. 0536871788
www.hoteltermesalvarola.it
Open year-round
The spa uses the sulfurous water with calcium bicarbonate, sulfurous sodic water, and salt bromine iodic water surfacing naturally between the foothills of the Apennines and the bed of the Secchia River. The original spa buildings (1884) are in Belle Epoque style. The 10-hectare park contains the Albergo Salvarola Terme and the Centro Benessere Balnea, housed in a modern building that is over 1,000m². The wellness center has pools at different temperatures with hydro-massage, waterfalls and water features, gyms, saunas and an esthetic center. The treatments available are recommended for skin complaints, problems of the digestive tract, the motory system, the respiratory system and gynecological complaints.

SAN MARINO

. H. San Marino Centro Maurice Mességué
Viale Onofri 31, Tel. 0549992400
www.centromessegue.com
63 rooms, open year-round
This center offers customized treatment programs. Guests are given a medical check-up on arrival so that a special menu can be devised. At the end of their stay, guests are given their clinical file and a personal diet. There are esthetic face and body treatments, yoga sessions for improving psycho-physical wellness, as well as manipulative and therapeutic treatments: mineral salt massage, Ayurvedic massage, Californian massage, connective tissue massage, cranio-sacral therapy, lymph drainage, foot reflexology, Chinese micro-massage, Shiatsu massage, hot-wine massage and hydro-therapy.

SANT'ANDREA BAGNI

Sant'Andrea Bagni Terme
Piazza C. Ponci, Tel. 0525430358
Open June-September
Sant'Andrea Bagni is unusual because its water source provides not only mineral water for drinking but also water suitable for bathing, inhalations and irrigations. The presence of numerous springs with water of differing chemical composition (containing salt bromide iodine, alkaline sodium bicarbonate, chlorine and sodium, iron and potassium, and sulfur and calcium) led to the growth of the town in the late 19th century. The spa forms part of the Terme di Salsomaggiore consortium and offers hydropinic treatments (drinking spring water) and hot-humid inhalations during the summer. Treatments are beneficial for respiratory diseases, and urinary tract and metabolism problems.

TABIANO BAGNI

Terme di Tabiano
Viale delle Terme 32, Tel. 0524564111
www.termeditabiano.it
Open year-round
The curative properties of Tabiano's sulfurous water were noted in 17th century for skin complaints and parasitic ailments. From 1870, it earned a reputation for treating respiratory problems, for which it became famous all over Italy (the water is sold in pharmacies). The modern spa is close to the two springs with sulfurous water with calcium and magnesium sulphate: Pozzo Arvè (15°C/59°F) and Fonte Pergoli (14°C/57°F), set in a lovely park. Recently, a pediatric inhalation center was added, along with a Roman bath complex with a frigidarium (cold room), tepidarium (warm room), calidarium (hot room) and laconicum (hottest of all). The waters are good for liver and bile-duct complaints, skin diseases, and respiratory, gynecological and stomatological problems.

GETTING TO

By plane to Emilia-Romagna

BOLOGNA –G. Marconi Airport
www.bologna-airport.it
Information tel. 051647915
Baggage assistance:
Aviapartner tel. 0516479269
Taxi:
CAT tel. 051534141
Cotabo tel. 051372727
Buses:
to Bologna: Aerobus tel. 051290290
to Modena: ATCM Modena tel. 800111101/059236530

FORLÌ – Forlì Airport
www.forli-airport.it
Information, Lost and Found
tel. 0543474990
Bus tel. 0541646900
E-BUS tel. 199115577 (only in Italy)

PARMA - G. Verdi Parma Airport
www.aeroportoparma.it
Ticket office/Information:
Main desk tel. 05219515
Telephone check-in
tel. 0521951595

Radio Taxi:
Contap tel. 0521252562

RIMINI - F. Fellini International Airport
www.riminiairport.com
Information tel. 0541715711

By train

The regional train network covers the entire region, running from north-west to south-east and connecting the main towns and cities. There are also good connections to the rest of Italy with the Bologna-Padua and Florence-Bologna-Verona lines, as well as other lines going to Ravenna and the surrounding regions (Liguria, Tuscany, Lombardy and Veneto).
For timetables and fares: Trenitalia, tel. 892021, every day from 7 to 21, only in Italy; telephonic ticket office 199166177, every day from 7 to 21; www.trenitalia.com
Ferrovie Emilia Romagna
www.fer-online.it
tel. 800915030 (Monday to Friday 7 to 19; Saturday 7 to 14.30)
Servizio Ferroviario Regionale

tel. 800388988
www.ferroviaer.it

By car

The main highway is the A1 Milano-Piacenza-Parma-Reggio Modena-Bologna-Firenze-Roma running near the main centers in the region. The other highways running to the surrounding regions are: A13 Bologna-Ferrara-Padova (Veneto), A14 Bologna-Forlì-Ancona (Marche), A15 Parma-La Spezia (Liguria), A22 Modena-Verona-Brennero (Veneto-Trentino-Austria) and the E45 Roma-Viterbo-Terni-Perugia-Bagno di Romagna-Cesena-Ravenna.
Autostrade spa, Motorway information center:
tel. 0643632121, 24 hours a day; Freephone 800269269; www.autostrade.it
Radio information:
Isoradio FM 103,3 and Viaradio FM 102,5

By bus

There are bus links from Bologna to various other Italian regions (Basilicata, Calabria, Campania, Molise, Puglia,

TRANSPORT

Public Transport

BOLOGNA – ATC
Call Center 051290290
(everyday 7 to 20)
www.atc.bo.it
FERRARA – ACFT
www.acft.it
Punto Bus (information)
Atrio Train Station
everyday incl. holidays 7.15 to 19.15
tel. 0532599490
Ufficio Biciclette (Bicycle Office)
Via Boccaleone 19
tel. 0532419971
FORLÌ-CESENA – ATR
www.atr-online.it
Modena – ATCM
Information Office
tel. 800111101
www.atcm.mo.it
PARMA – TEP
www.tep.pr.it
Punto Tep (information)

Piazza Ghiaia
Monday to Saturday
7.45 to 19.10
tel. 0521282657/800977966
Prontobus
Bus service by phone request
everyday 20 to 1
tel. 800977900
PIACENZA – Tempi
www.tempi.piacenza.it
Public Relations Office at
Piazzale Marconi 34/q
tel. 0523390623
800-211173
RAVENNA – Mete
tel. 0544689911
www.mete.ra.it
Punto Bus (information) -
Piazza Farini (Train Station)
tel. 0544689900
Radiotaxi tel. 054433888
REGGIO EMILIA – ACT
www.actre.it
Information Office c/o
Autostazione Caserma Zucchi,
Viale Allegri tel. 0522431667
c/o Ticket Office at the Piazzale
Marconi Train Station

tel. 0522435728
Public Relations Office
Viale Trento Trieste 11
tel. 0522927611
Disabled Transport Service
Transport service by phone
request tel. 0522927654
Radiotaxi tel. 0522452545
(every day 6.30 to 20.30) except
in the station area, which
operates around the clock.
RIMINI – Tram
Client Services
Via Dante 42, tel. 0541300533
(every day except Sundays and
holidays 7.30 to 19)
www.tram.rimini.it

Car Hire

AVIS
Bologna, tel. 0516472032
Forlì, tel. 0543781835
Parma, tel. 0521291238
Rimini, tel. 0541370721
HERTZ
Bologna, tel. 0516472015

Practical info

cily, Tuscany) and some
other nations (Austria,
Belgium, Bulgaria, Croatia, the
Czech Republic, Denmark,
Estonia, France, Germany,
Great Britain and Ireland,
Greece, Holland, Hungary,
Latvia, Lithuania, Morocco,
Poland, Romania, Serbia and
Montenegro, Slovenia, Spain
and Portugal, Sweden, the
Ukraine).

TerminalBus, Piazza XX
Settembre, tel. 051242150,
www.terminalbus.it

TOURIST INFORMATION

Website of Regione Emilia-
Romagna:
www.regione.emilia-
romagna.it
Tel. 800662200

CLIMATE

The climate in Emilia-
Romagna can be described as
continental, with hot summers
and relatively cold winters,
especially in the Apennines.
Along the coast, the
temperatures tend to be
milder. The area falls within
three different geographic
zones, namely the Adriatic
coast, the plain and the
Apennines, resulting in local
differences in weather. In
addition, the Po delta and
Valli di Comacchio area has a
unique, lagoon microclimate.

Forlì, tel. 0543782637
Parma, tel. 0521295032
Europcar
Bologna, tel. 0516472111
Forlì, tel. 0543473241
Parma, tel. 0521293035
Rimini, tel. 0541374606

Po Delta Park in Emilia-Romagna

Noi Per Voi (information)
Comacchio, Via Cavour 11
tel. 0533314003
www.parcodeltapo.it

Boat outings

There are different options
for boat outings, especially
in summer: Boretto port is the
starting point for excursions
along the Reggio section
of the Po (tel. 0522963015);
other river journeys take in the
Bassa Parmense (section of the
river north of Parma) and the
stretch around Piacenza

(tel. 0524917008); the
Cesenatico, Ravenna and Rimini
ports have services to Croatia
(Emilia Romagna Lines,
tel. 0547675157, www.emilia
romagnalines.it); from Bellaria
Igea Marina, Cattolica, Cervia,
Cesenatico, Ravenna, Riccione
and Rimini, it is possible to take
boat rides along the coast or
into the open sea; on Friday and
Saturday, the Port Canals of
Cervia and Cesenatico are the
departure points for the Nave
del Blues and the Nave del Jazz
(Blues and Jazz ships,
respectively), where one can
enjoy a dinner on the sea with a
live band (tel. 335314568,
www.naimaclub.it); other
itineraries explore the Po delta,
starting from Gorino, Goro and
Porto Garibaldi, the Valli di
Comacchio (tel. 3402534267),
the Saline di Cervia
(tel. 0544973040, www.salinadi
cervia.it) and the waterways
from Ferrara to the delta: Po di
Primaro, Po di Volano and Po
Grande (tel. 0532205681,
www.lepagine.com).

Inside

Tourist Information:
IAT - URP
Hotels and Restaurants
At night
Museums and Monuments

EMERGENCY NUMBERS

112	Military Police (Carabinieri)
113	State Police (Polizia)
115	Fire Department
117	Financial Police
118	Medical Emergencies
1515	Fire-watch
1530	Coastguard
803116	Road Assistance

ÀBBAZIA DI POMPOSA

> IAT Abbazia di Pomposa
> SS 309 Romea,
> tel. 0533719110

Museums, Monuments and Churches

Museo Pomposiano
SS Romea 309,
Abbazia di Pomposa,
tel. 0533719084
Open every day 9.00-17.00

BAGNACAVALLO

> IAT Bagnacavallo
> Piazza Libertà 13,
> tel. 0545280898

Rural Lodgings

Celti Centurioni
Via Crocetta 10, tel. 0545937382
www.celticenturioni.it
Located 1 km from the Oasi
Naturalistica Podere Pantaleone,
it has 4 comfortable rooms and
a restaurant (only open Friday,
Saturday and Sunday evening).
regional cuisine made with their
own organic products. Sale of
wine and jam.

Restaurants

Il Giardino dei Semplici ⫪
Via Manzoni 28,
tel. 054561156
Closed Thursday
Credit cards: American Express,
Diners Club, Mastercard, Visa
Located in a lovely, spacious old
carriage-house; traditional
regional cuisine with modern,
seasonal touches.

Osteria di Piazza Nuova ⫪ ★
Piazza Nuova 22,
tel. 054563647
Closed midday Saturday
Credit cards: American Express,
Diners Club, Mastercard, Visa
Regional cuisine with innovative
modern touches (meals also
served after 22.00).

Museums, Monuments and Churches

Centro Culturale Le Cappuccine
Via Vittorio Veneto 1,
tel. 0545280913
www.centrolecappuccine.it
Summer: Tuesday-Sunday
10.00-12.00, 16.00-19.00.
Winter: Tuesday-Sunday,
holidays 10.00-12.00,
15.00-18.00.

BAGNO DI ROMAGNA

> IAT Bagno di Romagna
> Via Fiorentina 38
> c/o Palazzo Capitano,
> tel. 0543911046

Restaurants

Paolo Teverini ⫪⫪⫪
Via del Popolo 2,
tel. 0543911260
Closed Monday and Tuesday
except in July and August
Credit cards: American Express,
Diners Club, Mastercard, Visa
The cuisine makes good use of
local traditions, which have
numerous culinary delights.

Locanda al gambero Rosso ⫪⫪ ★
San Pietro in Bagno, Via Verdi 5,
tel. 0543903405
Closed Sunday evening and
Monday (January-March Tuesday
evening and Wednesday)
Credit cards: American Express,
Diners Club, Mastercard, Visa
Regional cuisine in a refined
setting with local craft touches.

BELLARIA IGEA MARINA

> IAT Bellaria Igea Marina
> Via L. da Vinci 2,
> Tel. 0541344108

Hotels

Elios ★★★ ★
Igea Marina, Viale Pinzon 116,
tel. 0541331300
40 rooms. Restaurant
A comfortable and welcoming
hotel with a lovely terrace right
on the beach.

Excelsior ★★★ ★
Bellaria, Via Colombo 55,
tel. 0541347550
www.hotelexcelsiorbellaria.it
24 rooms. Restaurant
Credit cards: Mastercard, Visa
Sea-facing, it offers guests
various good quality services
and facilities, including evening
excursions.

Giorgetti Palace Hotel ★★★ ★
Bellaria, Via Colombo 39,
tel. 0541349121
65 rooms. Parking, gym,
restaurant
Credit cards: American Express,
Diners Club, Mastercard, Visa
Situated right by the sea,
it has some suites and a lovely
terrace bar.

BERTINORO

> IAT Bertinoro
> Piazza della Libertà 3,
> tel. 0543469213

Hotels

Panorama ★★★
Piazza Libertà 11,
tel. 0543445465
16 rooms.
Credit cards: American Express,
Diners Club, Mastercard, Visa
Set in a medieval building, the
rooms are quiet and equipped
with modern comforts.

Rural Lodgings

Fattoria Paradiso ♿ ★
Via Palmeggiana 285,
tel. 0543445044
www.fattoriaparadiso.com
Bicycle hire, pool, restaurant
Credit cards: American Express,
Diners Club, Mastercard, Visa
Situated at the edge of some
vineyards not far from the sea,
these two 18th-century building
are used as rural lodgings.
There are also the wine and
peasant culture museums as
well as a collection of vintage
cars and motorbikes.

Restaurants

Belvedere ⫪⫪
Via Mazzini 7,
tel. 0543445127
www.belvedere-ristorante.com
Closed Wednesday
Credit cards: American Express,
Diners Club, Mastercard, Visa
Two cosy rooms with 16th-
century coffered ceilings and a
terrace veranda used in summer
Regional cuisine with plenty of
hams, salami and local cheeses.

BOBBIO

> IAT Bobbio
> Piazzetta S. Francesco,
> Tel. 0523962815

Hotels

Il Filietto ★★★
Costa di Mezzano Scotti,
tel. 0523937104
www.filietto.it
12 rooms. Restaurant
Credit cards: American Express,
Mastercard, Visa
Ideal for a simple holiday
surrounded by nature. The
restaurant serves local cuisine.

Piacentino ★★★
Piazza S. Francesco 19/A,

⚞ ⚟ ⚟ ★★★ ★★ ★ Hotels ⫪⫪⫪⫪ ⫪⫪⫪ ⫪⫪ ⫪ Restaurants ♿ Disabled ★ Special TCI Rates

0523936563
v.hotelpiacentino.it
ooms. Restaurant, parking,
nming pool, sauna, tennis
it cards: Diners Club, Visa,
tercard
restaurant serves local
ine, using fresh pasta,
hrooms, truffles and game.

taurants

teca San Nicola ⸮⸮
trada dell'Ospedale,
0523932355
sed Monday and Tuesday
dit cards: American Express,
ers Club, Mastercard, Visa
omantic restaurant serving
ellent regional cuisine.
place and sitting room.

Ca' Longa ⸮⸮
Salvatore,
0523936948
sed Wednesday
dit cards: American Express,
ers Club, Mastercard, Visa
ional cuisine served in a
y setting with a brick floor,
ne walls and a fireplace.

iseums, Monuments
d Churches

seo dell'Abbazia
zza S. Fara,
0523936219
ening times: September-June:
urday and Sunday 11.00-
00, 15.00-17.00; July-August:
esday-Sunday 17.00-19.00.

OLOGNA

AT Bologna
Piazza Maggiore 6,
el. 051246541
www.comune.bologna.it/To
uringBologna

tels

Hotel Corona d'Oro 1890
** ★
a G. Oberdan 12,
0517457611
vw.bolognarthotels.it
rooms.
edit cards: American Express,
ners Club, Mastercard, Visa
cated in the old town, this
ilding has architecture from
rious periods: a small,
ernal courtyard with a 14th-
ntury portico, a welcoming
ll with an art nouveau
aircase, 19th-century rooms,
d meetings rooms with
ooden ceilings and open
eams.

Art Hotel Novecento **** ★
Piazza Galilei 4/3,
tel. 0517457311
www.bolognarthotels.it
25 rooms.
Credit cards: American Express,
Diners Club, Mastercard, Visa
Located in the heart of the city,
this Viennese succession-style
hotel has various rooms and
some suites (all different)
characterised by a calm feel and
attention to detail.

Best Western San Donato **** ★
Via Zamboni 16,
tel. 051235395
www.bestwestern.it/sandonato_bo
59 rooms.
Credit cards: American Express,
Diners Club, Mastercard, Visa
Located near the city towers,
this 16th-century building has
been carefully modernised and
now has numerous comforts.

Europa **** &
Via Boldrini 11, tel. 0514211348
www.zanhotel.it
101 rooms.
Credit cards: American Express,
Diners Club, Mastercard, Visa
Located in the old city in an
easy spot in reach. A cosy
setting and some rooms with
king-size beds.

Jolly Hotel de la Gare **** & ★
Piazza XX Settembre 2,
tel. 051281611
www.jollyhotels.com
156 rooms. Restaurant
Credit cards: American Express,
Mastercard, Visa
An elegant hotel with
comfortable rooms and suites
(on the 5th floor, all with scenic
balconies). The restaurant
serves regional and other
cuisine.

Jolly Hotel Villanova **** & ★
Villanova di Castenaso,
Via Villanova 29/8,
tel. 051604311
www.jollyhotels.com
209 rooms. Parking, pool,
restaurant
Credit cards: American Express,
Mastercard, Visa
Not far from the Bologna-San
Lazzaro di Savena highway exit,
this hotel is well located for
both the city and the Riviera.
Free shuttle bus (Monday to
Friday) to the city, station and
airport.

Novotel Bologna **** & ★
Villanova di Castenaso,
Via Villanova 31,

tel. 05160091
www.accorhotels.com/italia
206 rooms. Pool, tennis,
restaurant
Credit cards: American Express,
Diners Club, Mastercard, Visa
Located amid plenty of greenery,
it has a 'Sporting Club' in
summer. The restaurant is open
to midnight (homemade pasta
and desserts).

Savoia **** & ★
Via S. Donato 161,
tel. 0516332366
www.savoia.it
42 rooms. Sauna, restaurant
Credit cards: American Express,
Diners Club, Mastercard, Visa
Not far from the trade fair
district, a farm complex with a
shade-filled garden.

Sofitel Bologna **** & ★
Viale Pietramellara 59,
tel. 051248248
www.accorhotels.com/italia
244 rooms. Restaurant
Credit cards: American Express,
Diners Club, Mastercard, Visa
A comfortable hotel opposite
the train station. Breakfast can
be served in the rooms and
there is an agreement with a
fitness center. American bar
open to 2.00; garden and
Garden Side bar.

Starhotels Excelsior **** & ★
Viale Pietramellara 51,
tel. 051246178
www.starhotels.com
193 rooms. Parking, gym,
restaurant
Credit cards: American Express,
Diners Club, Mastercard, Visa
Opposite the central station,
this hotel offers the standards
you expect of this chain and has
a fitness center and high-speed
wireless internet. The restaurant
serves traditional local cuisine.

UNA Hotel Bologna **** & ★
Viale Pietramellara 41/43,
tel. 05160801
www.unahotels.it
99 rooms. Parking, restaurant
Credit cards: American Express,
Diners Club, Mastercard, Visa
Located near the old center, this
hotel has comfortable,
soundproofed rooms. The
restaurant serves regional
cuisine.

Art Hotel Orologio *** ★
Via IV Novembre 10,
tel. 0517457411
www.bolognarthotels.it
34 rooms. Parking
Credit cards: American Express,
Diners Club, Mastercard, Visa
Set in a completely refurbished
19th-century building, it is near
the old center. The rooms are
furnished with style and some
overlook Piazza Maggiore. The
good facilities meet most needs,
including an internet point and
bicycles.

Best Western Hotel Maggiore *** ⚒ ★
Via Emilia Ponente 62/3,
tel. 051381634
www.bestwestern.it/maggiore_bo
50 rooms. Parking
Credit cards: American Express,
Diners Club, Mastercard, Visa
A well-equipped meublé. Buffet
breakfast with sweet and savory
options. Bicycles available for
guests and an internet point.

Touring*** ⚒ ★
Via de' Mattuiani 1/2,
tel. 051584305
www.hoteltouring.it
36 rooms. Parking, pool
Credit cards: American Express,
Diners Club, Mastercard, Visa
A completely refurbished
meublé with a scenic terrace
overlooking the roofs of the old
city.

La Pioppa *** ⚒ ★
Via M. Emilio Lepido 217,
tel. 051400234
www.hotelpioppa.it
42 rooms.
Credit cards: American Express,
Diners Club, Mastercard, Visa
Not far from the Bologna-Borgo
Panigale highway exit and near
the airport.

Rural Lodgings

Cavaione ⚒ ★
Paderno, Via Cavaioni 4,
tel. 051589006
www.agriturismocavaione.it
Closed January-February
Only 6 km from the center but
in the hills surrounding the city,
it has a lovely view of the
environs. You can reach Bologna
by bus.

Restaurants

Battibecco ⅢⅢ
Via Battibecco 4, tel. 051223298
www.battibecco.com
*Closed Saturday midday and
Sunday*

Credit cards: American Express,
Diners Club, Mastercard, Visa
Regional cuisine in a warm and
welcoming restaurant decorated
with pastel colors, brickwork
and cane furniture.

Bitone ⅢⅢ
Via Emilia Levante 111,
tel. 051546110
www.ristorantebitone.it
Closed Monday and Tuesday
Credit cards: Diners Club,
Mastercard, Visa
A lovely, refined setting. The
menu specialises in Bologna
cuisine, making use of young
and tender fruit and vegetables.

Antica Osteria Romagnola ⅡⅡ
Via Rialto 13, tel. 051263699
*Closed Monday and Tuesday
midday*
Credit cards: American Express,
Diners Club, Mastercard, Visa
Situated in an 18th-century
building, some rooms have
brickwork floors and old prints.
Regional cuisine with both
seafood and meat specialities.

Rodrigo Ⅲ
Via della Zecca 2/H,
tel. 051235536
Closed Sunday
Credit cards: American Express,
Diners Club, Mastercard, Visa
Filled with atmosphere, it has
wooden walls and ceilings.
Bologna cuisine, using young,
tender fruit and vegetables in
season. Homemade pasta and
local desserts.

Da Sandro-al Navile ⅡⅡ
Via del Sostegno 15,
tel. 0516343100
Closed Sunday
Credit cards: American Express,
Diners Club, Mastercard, Visa
A restaurant filled with
atmosphere, serving traditional
regional cuisine. The lovely
terrace is used in summer.

Diana ⅡⅡ
Via dell'Indipendenza 24,
tel. 051231302
Closed Monday
Credit cards: American Express,
Diners Club, Mastercard, Visa
Central with a 1930s feel. In
summer, you can eat outside.
Traditional Bologna cuisine.

Drogheria della Rosa ⅡⅡ
Via Cartoleria 10,
tel. 051222529
www.drogheriadellerose.it
Closed Sunday
Cuisine: Emilia and creative
Credit cards: American Express,

Diners Club, Mastercard, Visa
In the old center, this pleasa
restaurant serves traditional
Emilia cuisine with numerous
creative touches using seaso
produce and products.

Grassilli ⅡⅡ
Via dal Luzzo 3, tel. 0512229
Closed Wednesday and Sund
Credit cards: American Expre
Diners Club, Visa
Traditional Bologna cuisine a
homemade pasta.

Rosteria Luciano ⅡⅡ
Via Sauro 19, tel. 051231249
*www.astratta.com/pointav/
rosterialuciano.htm*
*Closed Wednesday (Sunday i
summer)*
Credit cards: American Expres
Diners Club, Mastercard, Visa
A traditional Bologna restaura
that is refined and elegant. T
the homemade pasta.

Trattoria Leonida ⅡⅡ
Vicolo Alemagna 2,
tel. 051239742
*Closed Sunday (except during
trade fairs)*
Credit cards: American Expres
Diners Club, Mastercard, Visa
Set in a 15th-century building
this restaurant serves local
cuisine, including wonderful
fresh pasta. An outdoor sectic
is used in summer.

Trattoria Monte Donato ⅡⅡ
Via Siepelunga 118,
tel. 051472901
*Closed Monday (September-
June), Sunday (July-August)*
Cuisine: classic
Credit cards: American Expres
Visa
The view of the city is lovely
from the terrace of this rural
building on a hill outside
Bologna. This traditional
trattoria serves classic cuisine
focusing on dishes from the
mountains around Bologna.

Antica Trattoria del Pontelungo Ⅰ
Via Emilia Ponente 307,
tel. 051382996
Closed Saturday and Sunday
Cuisine: Bologna
Credit cards: American Express
Diners Club, Visa
An early 20th-century trattoria
neoclassical style with typical
local cuisine and homemade
desserts. A range of wines fror
Emilia.

Meloncello Ⅰ
Via Saragozza 240/A,

0516143947
ed Monday evening and
sday

it cards: Visa
old and typical local trattoria
flows out onto the portico-
d road leading to the
lica of S. Luca in Colle.
setting is pleasant,
a few tables on the covered
nda, and the rich menu
rs the classics of Bologna
ine.

ntegrappa-da Nello †
Montegrappa 2,
051236331
w.paginegialle.it
sed Monday
dit cards: American Express,
ers Club, Mastercard, Visa
erves the specialities of
gna cuisine, such as
ditional fresh pasta, cutlets
a bolognese' and local hams
d salamis.

night

vo Cafè
Mascarella 1,
051266112
elegant restaurant with a
o feel and live jazz music.

reria Meddix
Mascarella 26/c,
0515873830
s alehouse has live music,
aoke and a big-screen for
orts events.

blos
Marsala 17/19,
051226386
restaurant and pub with live
sic, including jazz.

ub '74
della Grada 10,
w.club-74.com
rious events are held here:
e music, dancing, cabaret,
ema and art exhibitions.

ostr...à
a E. Mattei 46/l,
. 051535905
ww.giostracafe.com
used in two old factory
ildings, it offers food, drink
d live music.

olem Caffè d'Arte
azza S. Martino 3/b,
. 051262620
ww.golemcafe.com
cated in the old Jewish
netto, this cafe offers, aside
om food and drink, art
hibitions and live music.

Rumba
a Nicolò dell'Arca 65/2,

tel. 051372104
www.larumba.it
This central American cafe has
appropriate music and frescoed
walls.

Never Comics Pub
Via Saragozza 67/b,
tel. 051331267
A modern pub where you can
dance and photographic
exhibitions are held.

Paladar Cafè
Via de' Griffoni 5/2,
tel. 051580894
A Latin American dance bar with
music and dance lessons.

The Cluricaune
Via Zamboni 18/b,
tel. 051263419
www.cluricaune.com
This pub, which uses the portico
section in summer, has food,
drink, pool and darts.

Museums, Monuments and Churches

Collezioni Comunali d'Arte ★
Piazza Maggiore 6,
tel. 051203526-051203629
www.comune.bologna.it/iperbole
/MuseiCivici
Tuesday-Saturday 9.00-18.30;
Sunday 10.00-18.30. Closed 1
January, 1 May, 25 December

Museo Civico Archeologico ★
Via dell'Archiginnasio 2,
tel. 0512757211
www.comune.bologna.it/museoa
rcheologico
Tuesday-Saturday 9.00-18.30;
Sundays and holidays 10.00-
18.30. Closed 1 January, 1 May,
25 December

Museo Civico Medievale ★
Via Manzoni 4,
tel. 051203930
www.comune.bologna.it/iperbole
/MuseiCivici
Tuesday-Saturday 9.00-18.30;
Sundays and holidays 10.00-
18.30. Closed 1 January, 1 May,
25 December

Museo dello Studio
Via Zamboni 33,
tel. 0512099020
Temporarily closed for
refurbishment

Museo di Palazzo Poggi ★
Via Zamboni 33,
tel. 0512099398-0512099360
museo.poggi@alma.unibo.it
www.unibo.it/musei/palazzopoggi
Monday-Sunday 10.00-17.00

Museo di San Domenico
Piazza S. Domenico 13,

tel. 0516400411
Weekdays: 9.30-12.30, 15.30-
18.30; Saturday only 15.30-
17.30. Sunday and holidays:
15.30-17.30

Museo di San Petronio
Piazza Maggiore,
tel. 051225442
Weekdays 9.30-12.30, 14.30-
17.30; Sunday and holidays
14.30-17.00

Museo di Santo Stefano
Via S. Stefano 24,
tel. 051223256
Monday-Sunday 9.00-12.00,
15.30-18.00

Museo Geologico "Giovanni Capellini"
Via Zamboni 63,
tel. 0512094555-0512094593
www.museocapellini.org
Monday-Friday 9.00-12.30.
Closed Sunday,
holidays and August.
First Saturday of the month:
15.30-19.00, with guided tours
and shows

Museo Morandi ★
Piazza Maggiore 6,
tel. 051203332-051203629
www.museomorandi.it
Tuesday-Sunday 10.00-18.00.
Closed 1 January, 1 May, 25
December

Museo Storico Didattico della Tappezzeria
Via Casaglia 3,
tel. 0516145512
www.comune.bologna.it/iperbole
/museotappezzeria
Tuesday-Sunday 9.00-13.00.
Closed on holidays during the
week

Pinacoteca Nazionale ★
Via delle Belle Arti 56,
tel. 0514209411
www.pinacotecabologna.it
Tuesday-Sunday, holidays 9.00-
19.00

Specola e Museo di Astronomia
Via Zamboni 33,
tel. 0512095701-
0512099360-0512099610
boas3.bo.astro.it/dip/Museum
Monday-Thursday 8.00-18.50;
Friday 8.00 and 14.30.
Closed Saturday and Sunday

Tesoro della Cattedrale
Via Indipendenza 9,
tel. 051222112
www.bologna.chiesacattolica.it/
cattedrale
Saturday and Sunday
16.00-17.30

BRISIGHELLA

IAT Brisighella
Piazzetta Porta Gabolo 5,
tel. 054681166

Hotels

La Meridiana *** ★
Viale delle Terme 19,
tel. 054681590
www.lameridianahotel.it
54 rooms. Restaurant
Credit cards: American Express,
Diners Club, Mastercard, Visa
A welcoming hotel with a
garden by the Lamone river.
Restaurant is only open from
June to August. An ideal starting
point for outings to Ravenna,
Bologna and Ferrara.

Rural lodgings

Corte dei Mori ★
San Cassiano, Via Valpiana 4,
tel. 054686489
www.cortedeimori.com
Closed mid January-February
Bicycle hire, restaurant
Credit cards: American Express,
Diners, Mastercard, Visa
An old country house nestled in
the greenery of the Apennines
with a panoramic view of the
Lamone valley.

Il Palazzo &
Via Baccagnano 11,
tel. 054680338
www.ilpalazzo.net
Open March-October
Located in the medieval part of
Brisighella, not far from the spa,
it has, aside from the restaurant,
three guest houses with rustic
furniture. Vegetarian menu,
bread and focaccia baked in the
wood oven and accompanied
with the house wine. Outings in
the Lamone valley and the Parco
della Vena del Gesso
dell'Appennino Romagnolo.

Relais Torre Pratesi &
Cavina, Via Cavina 11,
tel. 054684545
www.torrepratesi.it
Bicycle hire, pool, restaurant
Credit cards: American Express,
Diners, Mastercard, Visa
A stay with a 'castle flavor' in
the 16th-century tower and
neighboring farm. For leisure
time, it has various agreements
with nearby places.

Restaurants

Gigiolè ⫪⫪⫪
Piazza Carducci 5,
tel. 054681209

www.gigiole.it
Closed Sunday evening and
Monday
Credit cards: American Express,
Diners Club, Visa
Located within the old walls,
this restaurant strives for
traditional flavors from
Romagna.

Relais Torre Pratesi ⫪⫪⫪
Fognano,
Via Cavina 11,
tel. 054684545
www.torrepratesi.it
Credit cards: American Express,
Diners Club, Mastercard, Visa
Located in a tower, it serves
traditional dishes from
Romagna.

Museums, Monuments and Churches

Museo "La Signora del Tempo"
Via Torre dell'Orologio,
tel. 3474309838
www.comune.brisighella.ra.it

BUDRIO

Museums, Monuments and Churches

Museo Civico Archeologico e Paleoambientale
Via Mentana 32,
tel. 051803547-0516928322
www.comune.budrio.bo.it
Sunday 15.30-18.30;
first Sunday of the month also
10.00-12.30. Visits also by
arrangement

Pinacoteca Civica "Domenico Inzaghi"
Via Mentana 32,
tel. 051803547-0516928322
www.comune.budrio.bo.it
Sunday 15.30-18.30; first Sunday
of the month also 10.00-12.30.
October-June: visits by
arrangement

BUSSETO

IAT Busseto
Piazza Verdi 10,
tel. 052492487
www.bussetolive.com

Hotels

I Due Foscari ***
Piazza Rossi 15, tel. 0524930039
www.iduefoscari.it
20 rooms. Restaurant
Credit cards: American Express,
Diners Club, Mastercard, Visa
In an early 20th-century house,

it is full of atmosphere and h[...]
rooms with parquet floors an[...]
high ceilings.

Restaurants

Palazzo Calvi ⫪⫪⫪
Samboseto,
tel. 052490211
www.palazzo-calvi.it
Closed Monday and Tuesday
Credit cards: American Expres[...]
Diners Club, Mastercard, Visa
In a 17th-century noble
mansion, this restaurant also
has a few exclusive rooms.
Innovative Parma cuisine.

Sole ⫪⫪ ★
Piazza Matteotti 10,
tel. 0524930011
www.albergosole-busseto.it
Closed Friday evening
Credit cards: American Expres[...]
Diners Club, Mastercard, Visa
Part of a small hotel, it serves
traditional Parma food.

Museums, Monuments and Churches

Casa Barezzi
Via Roma 119, tel. 0524931117
www.amicidiverdi.it
Summer: 10.00-12.30, 15.00-
18.30. Winter: Tuesday-Sunday
10.00-12.30, 14.30-17.30

Museo Civico Pallavicino
Via Provesi 35, tel. 052492239
www.bussetolive.com

CAMPOTTO

Museums, Monuments and Churches

Museo della Bonifica ★
Strada Saiarino, tel. 053280805
www.comune.argenta.fe.it
Guided tours only. Tuesday-
Sunday 9.00-13.00, guided tou[...]
9.00 and 11.00. Afternoon: visi[...]
by prior arrangement for group[...]
of 5 or more. Closed for the
second and third weeks of
August, New Year's Eve and Da[...]

Museo delle Valli d'Argenta ★
Via Cardinala 1/c,
tel. 0532808058
www.atalntide.net/ecomuseodi[...]
genta
Tuesday-Sunday 9.30-13.00,
15.30-18.00

CANOSSA

IAT Canossa
Via Val d'Enza Nord 167,
tel. 0522872225

...staurants

...ranera † ★
...Vedriano 188,
...0522870155
...sed Monday evening and
...dnesday
...dit cards: American Express,
...ers Club, Mastercard, Visa
...ustic restaurant serving
...nemade local cuisine.

...seums, Monuments
...d Churches

...seo "Naborre Campanini"
...Castello 8, tel. 0522877104
...w.tuttocanossa.it/musei.htm
...mmer: Tuesday-Sunday 9.00-
...30, 15.00-19.00. Winter:
...esday-Sunday 9.00-16.30

...RPI

> **...AT Carpi**
> *...orso Berengario 2/4,*
> *...el. 059649213-4*
> *...www.carpidiem.it*

...staurants

...Bottiglieria † ★
...Cesare Battisti 14/16,
...059681333
...w.bottiglieria.mo.it
...ly open in the evening
...sed Sunday and Saturday
...dday
...dit cards: American Express,
...ers Club, Mastercard, Visa
...cated in the center, behind
...e Duomo, it has wooden
...ults and serves traditional
...isine.

...seums, Monuments
...d Churches

...seo Civico «Giulio Ferrari»
...azzale Re Astolfo 2,
...'. 059649968-059649111
...w.carpidiem.it/musei

...ASTELL'ARQUATO

> **IAT Castell'arquato**
> *Via Dante 27,*
> *tel. 0523803091*
> *www.castellarquato.net*

...staurants

...occa ‖
...azza del Municipio,
...l. 0523805154
...w.castellarquato.com/cucina/
...cca
...osed Wednesday
...dit cards: American Express,
...ners Club, Mastercard, Visa

Located in the old town, this
rustic restaurant in medieval
style has a scenic veranda and
serves Piacenza cuisine.

Museums, Monuments
and Churches

Museo della Collegiata
Piazza Don Cagnoni 3,
tel. 0523805151
Monday-Sunday 9.00-12.00,
15.00-18.30

Museo Geologico "G. Cortesi"
Via Sforza Caolzio 57
tel. 0523804266-05233803091
www.museogeologico.it
March-October: Tuesday-Sunday
10.00-12.00, 15.00-17.00;
November-February: holidays
10.00-12.00, 15.00-17.00. Visits
also by arrangement

CASTELVETRO
DI MODENA

> **IAT Castelvetro di Modena**
> *Piazza Roma 5,*
> *tel. 059758880*
> *www.comune.castelvetro-*
> *di-modena.mo.it*

Hotels

Zoello ★★★ ♿ ★
Settecani, Via Modena 181,
tel. 059702635
www.zoello.com
60 rooms. Restaurant
Credit cards: American Express,
Diners Club, Mastercard, Visa
Surrounded by nature, this
building has various rooms,
suites, apartments and an
annex. The restaurant serves
traditional cuisine from Emilia.

Rural Lodgings

Cavaliera
Solignano Vecchio, Via Cavaliera
1/B, tel. 059799835
www.cavaliera.it
Bicycle hire, restaurant
Credit cards: American Express,
Mastercard, Visa
In the hills amid the vineyards,
it has rooms with a rustic feel.

CASTROCARO
TERME

> **IAT Castrocaro Terme**
> *Viale Marconi 81,*
> *tel. 0543767162*

Hotels

Rosa del Deserto ★★★★ ♿
Via Giorgini 3, tel. 0543767232

---

www.hotelrosadeldeserto.it
48 rooms. Parking, restaurant
Credit cards: American Express,
Diners Club, Mastercard, Visa
Opposite the entrance to the
spa (health treatments at
reduced rates for guests), it has
a sun terrace and a restaurant
favoring local dishes.

Eden ★★★ ★
Via Samorì 11,
tel. 0543767600
www.hoteledenterme.it
40 rooms. Restaurant
Credit cards: American Express,
Diners Club, Mastercard, Visa
Located in a scenic and green
spot, the restaurant serves
regional cuisine.

Restaurants

La Frasca ‖‖‖‖
Via Matteotti 38,
tel. 0543767471
www.lafrasca.it
Closed Tuesday
Credit cards: American Express,
Diners Club, Mastercard, Visa
A true taste experience with
some age-old Romagna recipes.

La Cantinaza †
Via Garibaldi 45,
tel. 0543767130
Closed Wednesday
Credit cards: American Express,
Diners Club, Mastercard, Visa
Located in a refurbished late
15th-century building, it serves
traditional regional cuisine.

CATTOLICA

> **!AT Cattolica**
> *Via Matteotti 46,*
> *tel. 0541963341*
> *www.turismo.provincia.*
> *rimini.it*

Hotels

Gabbiano ★★★★ ♿
Viale Carducci 132,
tel. 0541954267
www.hotelgabbiano.com
58 rooms. Parking, sauna, pool,
tennis, restaurant
Credit cards: Mastercard, Visa
Central, 50 m from the sea, with
technologically innovative
services. Air conditioned, well-
equipped rooms, air conditioning (also shower or spa bath).

Kursaal ★★★★ ♿ ★
Piazzale I Maggio 2,
tel. 0541962305
www.kursaalhotel.it

60 rooms. Parking, pool, restaurant
Credit cards: American Express, Diners Club, Mastercard, Visa
On the main square, it has comfortable suites. Reserved access to the beach.

Regina * ★**
Viale Carducci 40, tel. 0541954167
www.hotelreginacattolica.it
62 rooms. Pool, restaurant
Credit cards: Mastercard, Visa
By the beach, it has a pool with hydro-massage, a sun area and air conditioned areas.

Restaurants

Lampara 🍴🍴🍴
Piazzale Galluzzi 3, tel. 0541963296
www.ristorantelampara.it
Closed Tuesday (except in summer)
Credit cards: American Express, Diners Club, Mastercard, Visa
A typical marina restaurant serving traditional cuisine favoring seafood. The terrace is used in summer.

Museums, Monuments and Churches

Museo della Regina
Via Pascoli 23, tel. 0541831464
www.cattolica.net
Summer: Tuesday 9.30-12.30; Wednesday-Sunday 16.00-19.00, 20.00-23.00. Winter: Tuesday-Thursday 9.30-12.30; Friday and Saturday 9.30-12.30, 16.00-19.00; Sunday 16.00-19.00

CENTO

IAT Cento
Via Guercino 41, tel. 0516843334
www.comune.cento.fe.it

Hotels

Al Castello ** ♿**
Via Giovannina 57, tel. 0516836066
www.halcastello.it
68 rooms. Parking, restaurant
Credit cards: American Express, Diners Club, Mastercard, Visa
A pleasant spot away from the centre. There is also an annex.

Grand Hotel Bologna e dei Congressi ** ♿**
Via Ponte Nuovo 42, tel. 0516861070
www.grandhotelbologna.com
142 rooms. Sauna, pool, restaurant
Credit cards: American Express, Diners Club, Visa
An elegant feel with hydro-massage in the suites. The restaurant serves traditional dishes from Emilia.

Restaurants

Osteria Vino e... 🍴🍴
Via Malagodi 8/A, tel. 051902663
Closed Tuesday
Credit cards: American Express, Diners Club, Mastercard, Visa
A former synagogue and now a frescoed restaurant, it serves dishes from Bologna and the Po valley.

Museums, Monuments and Churches

Galleria d'Arte Moderna "Aroldo Bonzagni"
Piazza Guercino 39, tel. 0516843390
Friday, Saturday and Sunday 9.30-12.30, 16.00-19.00. Visits also by arrangement

Pinacoteca Civica
Via Matteotti 16, tel. 0516843390
www.comune.cento.fe.it/pinacoteca
Friday, Saturday and Sunday 9.30-12.30, 16.00-19.00. Visits also by arrangement

CERVIA

IAT Cervia-Milano Marittima
Via Matteotti 39, tel. 0544993435

Hotels

Ascot * ★**
Viale Titano 14, tel. 054472318
www.hotelascot.it
30 rooms. Pool, restaurant
Ideal for families with children. Heated pool.

Cinzia * ♿**
Pinarella, Viale Italia 252, tel. 0544987241
www.severihotels.it
33 rooms. Sauna, pool, tennis, restaurant
Credit cards: Mastercard, Visa
Separated from the beach by a pine grove, it has a heated pool on the scenic terrace, hydro-massage, a sun area and a Turkish bath. The restaurant serves regional and Italian cuisine.

K2 Cervia * ♿**
Viale dei Mille 98, tel. 0544971025
www.hotelk2cervia.com
70 rooms. Restaurant
Credit cards: Diners Club, Mastercard, Visa
Close to the sea, port and old town, it has a garden with a gazebo. The restaurant serves regional cuisine.

Globus ** ♿**
Milano Marittima, Viale 2 Giugno 59, tel. 0544992115
www.hotelglobus.it
55 rooms. Parking, sauna, pool, tennis, gym, restaurant
Credit cards: American Express, Mastercard, Visa
Central and near the sea. Good amenities (from the sauna to the gym).

Le Palme ** ★**
Milano Marittima, VII Traversa 1, tel. 0544994661
www.premierhotels.it
102 rooms. Parking, sauna, pool, gym, restaurant
Credit cards: American Express, Diners Club, Mastercard, Visa
Right by the sea and surrounded by a garden, it has a pool with hydro-massage, a fitness center and a scenic sun terrace.

Miami ** ★**
Milano Marittima, III Traversa, tel. 0544998189
www.hotelmiamibeach.com
78 rooms. Pool, restaurant
Credit cards: American Express, Diners Club, Mastercard, Visa
Right on the beach, with the pine grove behind, the rooms have a terrace or balcony. Buffet restaurant on the beach.

Restaurants

Al Teatro 🍴🍴
Via Circonvallazione Socchetti 3, tel. 054471639
www.ristorantealteatro.com
Closed Monday
Credit cards: American Express, Diners Club, Mastercard, Visa
Regional cuisine, using only seafood, homemade bread and raw fish.

Tortuga 🍴🍴
Tagliata, Viale Sicilia 26, tel. 0544987193
Closed Wednesday
Credit cards: American Express, Diners Club, Visa
Good fish or a simple pizza. The kitchen is open after 22.00. Plenty of outdoor space for the summer.

Museums, Monuments and Churches

Museo del Sale - MUSA
Magazzini del Sale Torre,
Via Nazario Sauro,
tel. 0544977592
www.comunecervia.it/turismo
June-14 September: Monday-
Sunday 20.30-23.00. November-
March: Saturday, Sunday and
holidays 15.00-18.30. 23
December-6 January: Monday-
Sunday 15.00-18.30. April-May
and 15 September-30 October:
Saturday, Sunday and holidays
9.30-19.00. Visits also by
arrangement.

CESENA

IAT Cesena
Piazza del Popolo 11,
tel. 0547356327
www.comune.cesena.fc.it

Hotels

Alexander **** &. ★
Piazzale Karl Marx 10,
tel. 054727474
www.albergoalexander.it
4 rooms. Parking, sauna, gym,
restaurant
Credit cards: American Express,
Diners Club, Mastercard, Visa
A hotel complex with well
equipped rooms.

Casali **** ★
Via Croce 81, tel. 054722745
www.hotelcasalicesena.it
8 rooms. Parking, gym,
restaurant
Credit cards: American Express,
Diners Club, Mastercard, Visa
An old house with a picturesque
little dining area where
traditional dishes with modern
touches are served.

Meeting ****
Via Romea 545, tel. 0547333160
6 rooms.
Credit cards: American Express,
Diners Club, Mastercard, Visa
A pleasant two-storey meublé
with well equipped, comfortable
rooms.

Restaurants

Osteria Michiletta ¶¶
Via Fantaguzzi 26,
tel. 054724691
www.osteriamichiletta.it
Closed Sunday
Credit cards: American Express,
Diners Club, Mastercard, Visa
In the old center, this typical
tavern serves seasonal regional

cuisine. A lovely little courtyard
is used in summer.

Teatro Verdi ¶¶ ★
Via Sostegni 13,
tel. 0547613888
www.teatroverdi.it
Closed Monday
Credit cards: American Express,
Diners Club, Mastercard, Visa
An unusual setting: lunch in the
stalls and dinner on the stage or
in the boxes of this 19th-century
theatre. Music and variety
shows. Seasonal traditional
specialities.

Cerina ¶
San Vittore, Via San Vittore 936,
tel. 0547661115
Closed Monday evening and
Tuesday
Credit cards: American Express,
Diners Club, Visa
Some rustic rooms and a garden
for open-air meals where you
can enjoy the tastes and aromas
of Cesena and the Savio valley.

At night

Circolo Culturale Arci Intifada
Via Parini 12, tel. 0547611217
Live music.

Teatro Verdi Ristorante Varietà Discobar
Via Sostegni 13,
tel. 0547613888
Live music.

Museums, Monuments and Churches

Museo Archeologico ★
Via Montalti,
tel. 0547355727-0547356327
www.comune.cesena.fc.it
Tuesday-Saturday 9.00-12.00,
15.30-18.30; Sunday 10.00-
12.30. Visits at other times by
prior arrangement

Museo della Cattedrale
Corso Mazzino, c/o Duomo,
tel. 0547613304

Museo di Scienze Naturali ★
Piazza Zangheri 6 -
Loggetta veneziana,
tel. 0547356442-0547356443-
0547355727
www.comune.cesena.fc.it
June: Tuesday-Saturday 10.00-
13.00, 16.30-19.30; Sunday and
holidays 10.00-13.00, 15.30-
19.30. July-August: Tuesday-
Saturday 10.00-13.00, 17.00-
20.00, Sunday and holidays
10.00-13.00, 16.00-20.00

Museo di Storia dell'Agricoltura ★
Via Cia degli Ordelaffi 8,
tel. 054722409

www.comune.cesena.fc.it
June: Tuesday-Saturday 10.00-
13.00, 16.30-19.30; Sunday and
holidays 10.00-13.00, 15.30-
19.30. July-August: Tuesday-
Saturday 10.00-13.00, 17.00-
20.00, Sunday and holidays
10.00-13.00, 16.00-20.00

Pinacoteca Comunale ★
Via Aldini 26, tel. 0547355727
www.comune.cesena.fc.it
Tuesday-Saturday 9.00-12.00;
Sunday: 15 September to 31
March 15.00-18.00, 1 April to 14
September 16.00-19.00

CESENATICO

IAT Cesenatico
Viale Roma 112,
tel. 0547673287
www.cesenaticoturismo.com

Hotels

Executive Meeting Place Hotel **** &. ★
Viale Cesare Abba 90,
tel. 0547672670
www.executivemph.it
140 rooms. Sauna, pool, tennis,
gym, restaurant
Credit cards: American Express,
Diners Club, Visa
A hotel resort with an esthetic
center, a large garden with a
pool, and summer and piano
bars.

Valverde *** &. ★
Valverde,
Viale Carducci 278,
tel. 054786043
www.riccihotels.it
70 rooms. Parking, pool, tennis,
gym, restaurant
Credit cards: American Express,
Mastercard, Visa
On the beach, with sports
facilities, activities, bicycle
outings and hydro-massage.
Various different rooms and 30
apartments with sea views.

Rural Lodgings

Ai Tamerici &. ★
Via Mesolino 60,
tel. 0547672730
Pool, restaurant
Credit cards: American Express,
Diners, Mastercard, Visa
Only 2 km from the sea, but
immersed in greenery, it offers a
genuine stay in the countryside.

Restaurants

Magnolia ¶¶¶
Viale N. Bixio 3,
tel. 054781598

Only open in the evening
(Sunday midday from
October to May) Closed Monday
(Tuesday from October to May)
Credit cards: American Express,
Diners Club, Mastercard, Visa

A good place to go where
emphasis is placed on quality
cuisine. Regional cuisine with
traditional local flavors.

Buca ⁈
Corso Garibaldi 41,
tel. 054782474
www.labucaristorante.it
Closed Wednesday

Credit cards: American Express,
Diners Club, Mastercard, Visa

In summer, you can eat on the
old terrace overlooking the
canal harbor home made.
Innovative cuisine that respects
local traditions. The neighboring
Osteria del Gran Fritto focuses
on typical seafood dishes.

Titon 1954 ⁈
Via M. Moretti 10,
tel. 054780622
Closed Tuesday
(in summer also Sunday
evening)
Credit cards: American Express,
Diners Club, Mastercard, Visa

Set in an 18th-century building,
it serves genuine regional
cuisine using seafood and
homemade egg pasta.

Museums, Monuments and Churches

Antiquarium
Via Armellini 18,
tel. 054779264
www.cesenatico.it
Summer: Monday-Sunday 17.00-
23.00. Winter: Saturday, Sunday
and holidays 15.00-19.00

Museo della Marineria
Via Armellini 18,
tel. 054779264
www.cesenatico.it
Summer: Monday-Sunday 17.00-
23.00. Winter: Saturday, Sunday
and holidays 15.00-19.00

COMACCHIO

IAT Comacchio
Corso G. Mazzini 4,
tel. 0533314154
www.ferrarainfo.com

Restaurants

Antica Trattoria la Barcaccia ⁈
Piazza XX Settembre 41,
tel. 0533311081
www.comacchio.it

Closed Monday (except in Aug)
Credit cards: American Express,
Diners Club, Mastercard, Visa
Local seafood and lagoon
specialities, especially eel.
Homemade desserts.

Vasco e Giulia ⁑
Via Muratori 21,
tel. 053381252
Closed Monday

A typical trattoria in the old
town with a flame grill. Cuisine
based on fresh fish and
homemade desserts.

Museums, Monuments and Churches

**La Nave Romana
di Comacchio** ★
Via della Pescheria 2,
tel. 0533311316
www.comune.comacchio.fe.it/
sistemamuseale
June-August: Tuesday-Sunday
10.00-13.00, 15.00-19.00.
September-May: Tuesday-
Saturday 9.30-13.00, 15.00-
18.30; Sunday and holidays
10.00-13.00, 15.00-19.00

CORREGGIO

URP Correggio
Corso Mazzini 33,
tel. 800218441
www.comune.correggio.re.it

Hotels

**Best Western Hotel Dei
Medaglioni** ★★★★ ♿ ★
Corso Mazzini 8,
tel. 0522632233
www.bwhoteldeimedaglioni-re.it
35 rooms. Restaurant
Credit cards: American Express,
Diners Club, Mastercard, Visa

In an old building in the old
town, it has some suites
and a restaurant serving
traditional dishes from Emilia
and other excellent cuisine with
local flavors.

Museums, Monuments and Churches

Museo Civico ★
Corso Cavour 7,
tel. 0522693296-0522691806
www.museo.comune.
correggio.re.it
September-May: Saturday
15.30-18.30; Sunday 10.00-
12.30, 15.30-18.30.
Group visits by prior
arrangement. Closed August

FAENZA

IAT Faenza
Piazza del Popolo,
tel. 054625231

Hotels

Vittoria ★★★★ ★
Corso Garibaldi 23,
tel. 054621508
www.hotel-vittoria.com
49 rooms. Parking, restaurant
Credit cards: American Express
Diners Club, Mastercard, Visa

In a building in the old center,
it has frescoed ceilings and
early 20th-century furniture.
Italian and Emilia cuisine with
local specialities.

ClassHotel Faenza ★★★ ♿ ★
Via S. Silvestro 171,
tel. 054646662
www.classhotel.com
69 rooms. Restaurant
Credit cards: American Express
Diners Club, Mastercard, Visa

The annexed restaurant
overlooks the internal courtyard
Italian and Emilia cuisine with
traditional specialities.

Rural Lodgings

La Sabbiona ♿
Oriolo Fichi, Via Oriolo 10,
tel. 0546642142
www.lasabbiona.it
Closed Epiphany-mid February
Bicycle hire, pool, restaurant
Credit cards: Mastercard, Visa

Amid the hills in an old
farmhouse, it is rustically
furnished. Regional cuisine
with traditional local flavors.

Il Laghetto del Sole
Via Pittora 37,
tel. 0546642196
www.illaghettodelsole.it
Credit cards: American Express,
Diners, Mastercard, Visa

Set in the greenery of the
Faenza hills, this lovely farm
has a sizeable lake for fishing
and a range of interesting
activities and festivities.

Ca' de' Gatti
San Mamante, Via Roncona 1,
tel. 0546642202
www.cadegatti.it
Pool, restaurant
Credit cards: Mastercard, Visa

The building has about 1000
years of history (the medieval
floor is partly visible) and lies
amid woods, vines and olive
groves in the hills between
Faenza and Brisighella. The

⋆⋆⋆ ⋆⋆⋆ ⋆⋆⋆ ★★★ ★★ ★ Hotels ⁞⁞⁞⁞⁞ ⁞⁞⁞⁞ ⁞⁞⁞ ⁈ ⁑ Restaurants ♿ Disabled ★ Special TCI Rates

splendid surrounding area can be explored, on bike or by foot, along the various trails that explore the land, culture and past.

Trerè ★
Via Casale 19,
tel. 054647034
www.trere.com
Bicycle hire, pool, restaurant
Credit cards: American Express, Diners, Mastercard, Visa
In the hills, just 6 km from Faenza and 7 from Brisighella, this functioning farm grows grapes and makes wine.

Restaurants

Raita ⅂⅂
Via Naviglio 25/C,
tel. 054621584
Closed Sunday and Monday
Credit cards: American Express, Diners Club, Mastercard, Visa
Near the main square, this tavern offers traditional regional cuisine with traditional local flavors. Garden used in summer.

Enoteca Astorre ⅂ ★
Piazza della Libertà 16/A,
tel. 0546681407
www.enotecaastorre.it
Closed Sunday
Credit cards: American Express, Diners Club, Mastercard, Visa
Set in Palazzo Laderchi, near the Duomo, it serves traditional regional cuisine, a seafood menu, hams, salamis and local cheeses.

Museums, Monuments and Churches

Museo Internazionale delle Ceramiche MIC ★
Corso Baccarini 19,
tel. 0546697311
www.micfaenza.org
April-October: Tuesday-Saturday 9.00-19.00; Sunday and holidays 9.30-18.30.
November-March: Tuesday-Friday 9.00-13.30; Saturday, Sunday and holidays 9.30-17.30.
Closed 1 January, 1 May, 15 August and 25 December

Pinacoteca Comunale
Via S. Maria dell'Angelo 1,
tel. 0546660799
www.faenza.provincia.ra.it
Friday-Sunday 10.00-16.00.
Visits also by arrangement

FANANO

IAT Fanano
Piazza Marconi 1,
tel. 053668825
www.comune.fanano.mo.it

Rural Lodgings

Del Cimone la Palazza ♿
Canevare,
Via Calvanella 710,
tel. 053669311
www.agriturismodelcimone.it
Bicycle hire, restaurant
A stone building on a grassy hill. Horses and cattle are reared on the farm. The cuisine is typical of the mountains, using homemade products. Various excursions/walks and scenic viewpoints.

FERRARA

IAT Ferrara
Castello Estense,
tel. 0532209370-299303
www.comune.fe.it

Hotels

Annunziata **** ★
Piazza Repubblica 5,
tel. 0532201111
www.annunziata.it
24 rooms.
Credit cards: American Express, Diners Club, Mastercard, Visa
An elegant and calm hotel overlooking Castello Estense, within the 18th-century walls. Access to parking in a pedestrian area, free bicycle hire and two internet points. The rooms are well equipped. Relaxation area with open beams and a reading corner. Some accommodation in the Prisciani Art Suite annex. Parking available at an extra cost.

Best Western Astra **** ♿ ★
Viale Cavour 55,
tel. 0532206088
www.bestwestern.it/astra_fe
69 rooms. Parking, restaurant
Credit cards: American Express, Diners Club, Mastercard, Visa
In the old town, it has rooms and suites with computer connections. The restaurant serves local and vegetarian cuisine.

Ferrara **** ♿ ★
Largo Castello 36,
tel. 0532205048
www.hotelferrara.com
42 rooms. Restaurant
Credit cards: American Express,

Diners Club, Mastercard, Visa
Opposite Castello Estense, it has rooms and suites. The restaurant serves traditional cuisine with modern touches.

Il Duca d'Este **** ♿
Via Bologna 258,
tel. 0532977676
www.ilducadeste.it
73 rooms. Restaurant
Credit cards: American Express, Diners Club, Mastercard, Visa
A hotel with elegant and comfortable rooms. The restaurant serves local cuisine.

Principessa Leonora **** ♿
Via Mascheraio 39,
tel. 0532206020
www.principessaleonora.it
22 rooms. Parking, gym
Credit cards: American Express, Diners Club, Mastercard, Visa
Set in the heart of the city in a 16th-century mansion with brick floors, fireplaces and antiques. The rooms are romantic and there are also a suite and an internet point. Bicycles and even a carriage are available to tour the city.

Carlton *** ♿
Via Garibaldi 93,
tel. 0532211130
www.hotelcarlton.net
58 rooms. Parking
Credit cards: American Express, Diners Club, Mastercard, Visa
In the old center, this hotel is modern, comfortable and well furnished. Some accommodation also in the Carlton Residence and Casalbergo Carlton annexes.

Corte Estense *** ♿ ★
Via Correggiari 4/A,
tel. 0532242168
www.corteestense.it
20 rooms. Parking
Credit cards: American Express, Diners Club, Mastercard, Visa
In the old center, this hotel in a 17th-century noble mansion has a lovely internal courtyard, bicycles to hire and guided tours. Homemade bread and croissants for breakfast.

Europa *** ♿ ★
Corso Giovecca 49,
tel. 0532205456
www.hoteleuropaferrara.com
46 rooms. Parking
Credit cards: American Express, Diners Club, Mastercard, Visa
In the old center, this Renaissance building has frescoed areas and period furniture.

Rural Lodgings

Alla Cedrara
Porotto, Via Aranova 104,
tel. 0532593033
www.allacedrara.it
Bicycle hire
Credit cards: American Express,
Diners, Mastercard, Visa
In the countryside, you stay in
the old hayloft of a farmstead.
Rooms have wooden beams,
period furnishings and modern
features, such as a bar fridge
and air conditioning. In summer,
breakfast is served outside, and
in winter, in a room with a
fireplace. Not too far away are
Comacchio, the abbey of
Pomposa and the Parco
Regionale del Delta del Po.

Ca' Spinazzino &
Spinazzino, Via Taglione 5,
tel. 0532725035
Closed Epiphany-February and
for some of December
Pool
Amid poplars and fruit trees in
an early 20th-century
farmhouse. Camping possible.

Restaurants

Antico Giardino ⫴
Ravalle, Via C. Martelli 28,
tel. 0532412100
Closed Monday and Tuesday
midday
Credit cards: American Express,
Diners Club, Mastercard, Visa
An elegant restaurant with a
garden used in summer. Local
cuisine and homemade fresh
pasta.

Antica Trattoria Volano ⫴ ★
Viale Volano 20, tel. 053276142
Closed Friday
Credit cards: American Express,
Diners Club, Mastercard, Visa
Near the Po di Volano river, a
rustic restaurant serving local
cuisine.

Borgomatto ⫴
Via Concia 2, tel. 0532240554
www.borgomatto.it
Closed Monday and Saturday
midday
Credit cards: American Express,
Diners Club, Mastercard, Visa
A small restaurant in the center
that focuses on local flavors.
Homemade pasta.

Il Don Giovanni ⫴ ★
Corso Ercole I d'Este 1,
tel. 0532243363
www.ildongiovanni.com
Open in the evening from
Tuesday to Saturday (lunch by
prior arrangement), Sunday
midday
Closed Monday
Set in a charming 18th-century
building right in the old town,
this restaurant serves excellent
food.

Lanzagallo ⫴
Gaibana, Via Ravenna 1048,
tel. 0532718001
Closed Sunday and Monday
Credit cards: Mastercard, Visa
A simple trattoria where the
food is tied to the seasons.
Many of the vegetables are
grown in the garden behind the
restaurant.

Oca Giuliva ⫴
Via Boccacanale S. Stefano 38,
tel. 0532207628
Closed Monday and Tuesday
midday
Credit cards: American Express,
Diners Club, Mastercard, Visa
Traditional Ferrara cuisine in line
with the seasons. The porch is
used in summer.

Viaragnotrentuno ⫴
Via Ragno 31/A,
tel. 0532769070
Closed Tuesday
Credit cards: American Express,
Diners Club, Mastercard, Visa
Set in a building from the
Middle Ages, it serves local
cuisine with modern ideas.

I Tri Scalin ⫰
Via Darsena 50,
tel. 0532760331
Closed Monday and Sunday
evening
Credit cards: American Express,
Diners Club, Mastercard, Visa
A typical trattoria serving local
dishes.

Trattoria la Botte ⫰
Pontelagoscuro,
Via Padova 169,
tel. 0532462311
Closed Sunday (in summer also
Saturday midday)
Credit cards: Mastercard, Visa
A lovely trattoria near the Po. A
simple place filled with local
flavors.

At night

Bar Aldo's
Viale Po 7/7
Latin American and group
dancing.

La Fabbrica
Via delle Erbe 24
Board games, cards, table
football and darts.

Madame Butterfly
Via Bottego 5
Live music.

Matiz
Via Piccolomini 2
American bar and pub with live
music.

Pelledoca
Via Arianuova 93,
tel. 0532248952
Pub with live music.

Quo Vadis
Via Calamandrei 8,
tel. 0532253480
Ballroom dancing and theme
evenings, orchestral events.

Museums, Monuments and Churches

Casa dell'Ariosto
Via Ariosto 67, tel. 053244949
www.comune.fe.it/musei-
aa/schifanoia
Tuesday-Saturday 10.00-13.00,
15.00-18.00; Sunday 10.00-
13.00. Closed on holidays

Casa Romei
Via Savonarola 30,
tel. 0532240341
Tuesday-Sunday 8.30-19.30

Civico Museo di Schifanoia ★
Via Scandiana 23,
tel. 053264178-0532209988-
0532244949
www.comune.fe.it/musei-
aa/schifanoia/skifa.html
Tuesday-Sunday 9.00-18.00.
Closed 1 and 6 January, Easter,
November, 25 and 26 December

Il Castello Estense di Ferrara ★
Piazza Castello,
tel. 0532299233
www.castelloestense.it
Tuesday-Sunday 9.30-17.30.
March, April and May also open
Monday

Mostre di Palazzo dei Diamanti ★
Corso Ercole I d'Este 21,
tel. 0532244949-0532209988
www.comune.fe.it
Monday-Sunday 9.00-19.00;
Opening times may change
according to the current
exhibition

MusArc, Museo Nazionale dell'Architettura
Via XX Settembre 152,
tel. 0532742332
www.comune.fe.it/musarc
Open during exhibitions:
Tuesday-Sunday 10.00-13.00,
15.00-18.00

Museo Archeologico Nazionale
Via XX Settembre 124,

el. 053266299-0532244949
www.archeobo.arti.beniculturali.i
t/Ferrara/index.htm
Tuesday-Sunday 9.00-14.00

Museo della Cattedrale ★
Via S. Romano,
tel. 0532761299-0532209988-
0532244949
www.comune.fe.it/turismo/mcatt
ed.htm
Tuesday-Sunday 9.00-13.00,
15.00-18.00

Museo Lapidario Civico ★
Via Camposabbionario 1,
tel. 053264178-0532209988
www.comune.fe.it/musei-
na/schifanoia/lapi.html
Tuesday-Sunday 9.00-18.00

Pinacoteca Nazionale ★
Palazzo dei Diamanti,
Corso Ercole I d'Este 21,
tel. 0532205844
www.pinacotecaferrara.it
Tuesday-Saturday 9.00-14.00;
Thursday 9.00-19.00; Sunday
and holidays 9.00-13.00. Closed
1 January, 1 May, 25 December

FIDENZA

IAT Fidenza
Piazza Duomo 16,
tel. 052483377
www.comune.fidenza.pr.it

Rural Lodgings

Il Tondino
Tabiano Castello,
Via Tabiano 58,
tel. 052462106
www.agriturismoiltondino.it
Open mid March-mid December
and New Year's Day
Pool, restaurant
An old farming possession of
the Tabiano castle. An ideal
place if you want something
interesting to do every day: old
towns, castles, excursions and,
on the actual farm, fishing. For
sale: hams, salamis and lard.

Museums, Monuments and Churches

Museo del Risorgimento "Luigi Musini"
Via A. Costa 3,
tel. 0524526365
www.comune.fidenza.pr.it
Summer: Tuesday, Thursday
16.00-18.00; Wednesday, Friday
10.00-12.00; Saturday 10.00-
12.00. Winter: Tuesday-Saturday
10.00-12.00. Thursday by prior
arrangement. Closed Sunday
and Monday

Museo dei Fossili
Via Berenini 136, Via Costa 2,
tel. 0524576431
Open 1st and 3rd Friday of each
month from 21.00 to 22.30.

Museo Diocesano del Duomo
Via Don Minzoni 10/a,
tel. 0524514883
www.museoduomofidenza.it/ind
exf.htm
Tuesday-Saturday 10.00-12.30,
14.30-17.30

FIORENZUOLA D'ARTA

Restaurants

Trattoria Baracchino †
Baselicaduce, Via Baracchino
104, tel. 0523984374
Closed Tuesday and Thursday
evenings
A typical Piacenza trattoria.
Various hams and salamis as
well as local specialities, tortelli
pasta and wine from the area.

FIUMALBO

IAT Fiumalbo
Via Capitano Coppi 11,
tel. 053673909

Hotels

Val del Rio ★★★ &
Dogana Nuova, Via Giardini 221,
tel. 053673901
www.valdelrio.it
31 rooms. Parking, gym,
restaurant
Credit cards: American Express,
Diners Club, Mastercard, Visa
Simple yet refined hospitality.
Regional cuisine.

FONTANELLATO

IAT Fontanellato
c/o Rocca Sanvitale,
Piazza Matteotti 1,
tel. 0521823220
www.fontanellato.org

Restaurants

Europa † ★
Via Pozzi 12,
tel. 0521822256
Closed Sunday evening
Credit cards: Diners Club,
Mastercard, Visa
300 m from the Rocca del
Santuario di Fontanellato, it
serves Emilia cuisine.

FORLÌ

IAT Forlì
Corso della Repubblica 23,
tel. 0543712435
Piazza Morgagni 9,
tel. 0543714223-714339
www.delfo.forli-cesena.it
www.turismoforlivese.it

Hotels

**Best Western Premier Hotel
Globus City ★★★★** & ★
Via Traiano Imperatore 4,
tel. 0543722215
www.bestwestern.it/globus_fo
98 rooms. Parking, sauna, pool,
gym, restaurant
Credit cards: American Express,
Diners Club, Mastercard, Visa
Rooms and two suites with spa
baths, a fitness area with a
heated pool. Romagna cuisine.

Della Città et de la Ville ★★★★
Corner of Corso della Repubblica
and Via Fortis 8,
tel. 054328297
www.hoteldellacitta.it
57 rooms. Restaurant
Credit cards: American Express,
Diners Club, Mastercard, Visa
In the heart of a large park, this
modern and functional complex
is by Giò Ponti.

Masini ★★★★ &
Corso Garibaldi 28,
tel. 054328072
www.hotelmasini.com
51 rooms.
Credit cards: American Express,
Diners Club, Mastercard, Visa
In the old centre, with a largely,
scenic terrace. There are
agreements with the La Vecchia
Forlì and Osteria del Medio
restaurants, where you can enjoy
Romagna cuisine.

Ramada Encore Forlì ★★★★ &
Viale Vittorio Veneto 3/E,
tel. 054322038
www.ramadaencoreforli.com
84 rooms.
Near the center with good
facilities.

Rural Lodgings

La Sarzola
Magliano, Via Maglianella 9,
tel. 054389470
www.sarzola.it
Bicycle hire
Credit cards: American Express,
Diners, Mastercard, Visa
Located on the Fiordalisi golf
course and the Oasi Faunistica

di Magliano, it has rooms and apartments set in 18th-century rural buildings. The proximity of the Adriatic Riviera makes it possible to spend that day at the sea, or you can go for a boat trip and take a guided tour of the Po delta park.

Restaurants

Casa Rusticale dei Cavalieri Templari ⅋⅋
Viale Bologna 275,
tel. 0543701888
Closed Sunday and Monday
Credit cards: American Express, Diners Club, Mastercard, Visa
In the 14th-century the Templars stayed in this building, then it became a church. Now it is a restaurant with genuine furnishings and a pergola for the summer. The cuisine is based on the traditions of Emilia.

Don Abbondio ⅋
Piazza Guido da Montefeltro 16,
tel. 054325460
www.donabbondio.info
Closed Sunday
Credit cards: American Express, Diners Club, Mastercard, Visa
Opposite the convent of S. Domenico, this tavern and wine bar also has a range of salamis, hams, cheeses and, of course, wines. Local cuisine.

Gusto ⅋ ★
Via Zampeschi 7, tel. 0543720165
www.italiaabc.it/az/gusto
Closed Saturday
Credit cards: American Express, Diners Club, Mastercard, Visa
A restaurant with a lovely veranda. The kitchen, open to midnight, serves cuisine from Romagna.

La Cantina di Tulio ⅋
Via Torelli 3, tel. 054330411
Closed Thursday
Credit cards: American Express, Diners Club, Mastercard, Visa
Set in the cellars of a 16th-century building in the old town, it serves Romagna cuisine. Good selection of salamis, hams and local cheeses, served in hot, homemade piadinas.

At night

Caffè della Repubblica
Corso della Repubblica 105,
tel. 054332732
Alehouse, pub and small restaurant.

Diagonal loft Club
Viale Salinatore 101,
tel. 054321974

This pub, near Porta Schiavonia, has live music.

Moquette Bar & Shop &
Via dell'Aste 17,
tel. 054332751
An interesting place in the center where you can have a bite to eat and buy books or CDs.

Naima Club
Via Somalia 2, tel. 0543722728
www.naimaclub.it
Various events, especially jazz and blues concerts.

Oltremodo
Corso Garibaldi 56,
tel. 054332799
Pub serving snacks and other food, karaoke.

Pride Irish Pub
Viale Italia 12, tel. 0543370239
A pub with a lovely outdoor area and live music.

The Abbey
Piazzetta XC Pacifici 2,
tel. 0543370172
Right in the old center, this pub is on a small square not far from Piazza Saffi.

Wild Horse Irish Pub
Piazza Porta Ravaldino 5,
tel. 054333538
Pub serving food and snacks.

X-Ray
Via Forlanini 1,tel. 054325539
Pub serving light food and snacks.

Museums, Monuments and Churches

Museo del Risorgimento "Aurelio Saffi"
Palazzo Gaddi, Corso Garibaldi 96, tel. 054321109
www.comune.forli.fo.it/cultura/villasaffi.asp
Tuesday-Saturday 9.00-13.00; Sunday 9.00-12.30. Closed on holidays and 4 February

Museo del Teatro "Angelo Masini"
Palazzo Gaddi,
Corso Garibaldi 96,
tel. 054321109
www.comune.forli.fo.it/cultura/sdmuseo.asp
Tuesday-Saturday 9.00-13.00; Sunday 9.00-12.30. Closed on holidays and 4 February

Museo Etnografico Romagnolo "Benedetto Pergoli"
Palazzo del Merenda,
Corso della Repubblica 72,
tel. 0543712606
www.comune.forli.fo.it/cultura/sd

museo.asp
Wednesday, Friday, Saturday 9.00-13.30; Tuesday, Thursday 9.00-13.30, 15.00-17.30; Sunday 9.00-13.00. Closed on holidays and 4 February

FORLIMPOPOLI

IAT Forlimpopoli
c/o Rocca Albornoziana,
Piazza Pompillo,
tel. 054349250
www.comune.forlimpopoli.fc.it

Museums, Monuments and Churches

Museo Archeologico Civico "Tobia Aldini"
Piazza A. Fratti 4,
tel. 0543749234
www.comune.forlimpopoli.fc.it
Thursday 10.00-12.00; Sunday 10.00-12.00, 15.00-17.00. Visits also by arrangement

GALEATA

IAT Galeata
c/o Museo Civico "Mons. Domenico Mambrini",
tel. 0543975424

Hotels

Museo Civico "Mons. Domenico Mambrini" ★
Pianetto, Via Borgo Pianetto - Convento dei Padri Minori Conventuali, tel. 0543975424
www.museocivicomambrini.it
Thursday 9.00-13.00; Saturday and Sunday 9.30-12.30, 15.00-18.00. Visits also by arrangement

IMOLA

IAT Imola
Via Massini 14,
tel. 0542602207
www.comune.imola.bo.it

Hotels

G.H. Donatello ★★★★ &
Via Rossini 25, tel. 0542680800
www.imolahotel.it
140 rooms. Parking, pool, restaurant
Credit cards: American Express, Diners Club, Mastercard, Visa
A welcoming hotel with plenty of wood in the common areas. The Il Veliero restaurant, under separate management, serves

...egional and Mediterranean ...uisine.

Molino Rosso ** ♿ ★**
Via Statale Selice 49,
tel. 054263111
www.molinorosso.it
20 rooms. Parking, pool, tennis, gym, restaurant
Credit cards: American Express, Diners Club, Mastercard, Visa
Located in an old mill amid plenty of greenery, it has avante-garde rooms in terms of technology and comfort. The restaurant serves traditional cuisine.

Olimpia ** ♿**
Via Pisacane 69, tel. 054228460
www.bestwestern.it/olimpia_bo
35 rooms. Parking, restaurant
Credit cards: American Express, Diners Club, Mastercard, Visa
Large rooms and suites with modern furnishings. The L'Artusi restaurant serves Romagna cuisine and has a lovely fireplace.

Restaurants

Naldi ⅏ ★
Via Santerno 13, tel. 054229581
www.ristorantenaldi.com
Closed Sunday (except race days)
Credit cards: American Express, Diners Club, Mastercard, Visa
A refined restaurant serving excellent Emilia cuisine.

Osteria del Vicolo Nuovo ⅏ ★
Via Codronchi 6, tel. 054232552
www.vicolonuovo.it
Closed Sunday and Monday
Credit cards: American Express, Diners Club, Mastercard, Visa
Set in a 17th-century building, it has two levels: one with a fireplace, the other in the vaulted cellar. Traditional food using local raw materials and produce. Salamis, hams, local cheeses and homemade desserts.

E Parlaminté ⅃ ★
Via Mameli 33, tel. 054230144
www.eparlaminte.com
Closed Sunday evening (in summer, for the whole day) and Monday
Credit cards: American Express, Diners Club, Mastercard, Visa
A restaurant in the old town serving traditional dishes from Romagna.

Museums, Monuments and Churches

Museo Civico "Giuseppe Scarabelli" ★
Via Sacchi 4, tel. 0542602609

www.comune.imola.bo.it/musei comunali

Museo delle Armi e delle Maioliche della Rocca Sforzesca ★
Piazzale Giovanni dalle Bande Nere, tel. 054223472
www.comune.imola.bo.it/musei comunali
May-15 September: Saturday 9.00-12.00, 15.00-19.00; Sunday 15.00-19.00. 16 September-April: Saturday 9.00-12.00, 14.30-18.30; Sunday 14.30-18.30. Visits also by arrangement

Museo Diocesano d'Arte Sacra
Piazza Duomo 1,
tel. 054224362-054224156
Tuesday and Thursday 9.30-12.00, 14.00-17.00. Only by prior arrangement

Pinacoteca Comunale ★
Via Sacchi 4, tel. 0542602609
www.comune.imola.bo.it/musei comunali
Saturday and Sunday 16.00-19.00

Raccolta e Collezione d'Arte di Palazzo Tozzoni ★
Via Garibaldi 18, tel. 054235856
www.comune.imola.bo.it/musei comunali
May-15 September: Saturday 9.00-12.00, 15.15-19.15; Sunday 15.15-19.15. 16 September-April: Saturday 9.00-12.00, 14.45-18.45; Sunday 14.45-18.45. Visits also by arrangement

LONGIANO

IAT Longiano
Via Porta del Girone 2,
c/o locali ex peschiera,
tel. 0547665484

Museums, Monuments and Churches

Fondazione "Tito Balestra"
Piazza Malatestiana 1,
tel. 0547665850-0547665420
www.fondazionetitobalestra.org
Tuesday-Sunday 10.00-12.00, 15.00-19.00

Museo di Arte Sacra
Via Borgo Fausto,
tel. 0547666457
www.comune.longiano.fc.it
Saturday, Sunday and holidays 14.30-18.30. Visits also by arrangement

Museo Italiano della Ghisa
S. Maria delle Lacrime,
Via S. Maria,
tel. 0547652111-0547652172
www.museoitalianoghisa.org

Saturday, Sunday and holidays 14.30-18.30. Visits also by arrangement

LUGO

IAT Lugo
Piazza Trisi 31,
tel. 054522567

Hotels

Ala d'Oro ** ♿ ★**
Corso Matteotti 56,
tel. 054522388
www.aladoro.it
41 rooms. Restaurant
Credit cards: American Express, Diners Club, Mastercard, Visa
Set in a 18th-century noble residence, this hotel also has a restaurant serving regional cuisine (only by prior arrangement).

San Francisco ** ♿**
Via Amendola 14,
tel. 054522324
www.sanfranciscohotel.it
28 rooms.
Credit cards: American Express, Diners Club, Mastercard, Visa
A relaxing place with simple architectural lines, and interesting plays with light and shapes. Air conditioned rooms.

Restaurants

I Tre Fratelli ⅏
Via Di Giù 56,
tel. 054523328
www.paginegialle.it/trefratelli
Closed Monday
Credit cards: American Express, Diners Club, Mastercard, Visa
A refined restaurant serving local cuisine. Salamis, hams, fresh pasta and homemade desserts. An outdoor area is used in summer.

Antica Trattoria del Teatro ⅃
Vicolo del Teatro 6,
tel. 054535164
Closed Monday
Credit cards: American Express, Diners Club, Mastercard, Visa
Not far from Teatro Rossini, it specializes in local cuisine. The kitchen is open to midnight when there are shows at the theatre.

MODENA

IAT Modena
Piazza Grande 14,
tel. 0592032660
www.comune.modena.it

Hotels

Canalgrande ★★★★
Corso Canalgrande 6,
tel. 059217160
www.canalgrandehotel.it
68 rooms. Parking, restaurant
Credit cards: American Express,
Diners Club, Mastercard, Visa
This neoclassical building has
high standards of comfort.
Some areas have frescoed
ceilings and the dining area is
especially charming. Well
equipped rooms. Large garden
with age-old trees and a terrace.

Central Park Hotel ★★★★
Viale Vittorio Veneto 10,
tel. 059225858
www.centralparkmodena.com
48 rooms. Gym
Credit cards: American Express,
Diners Club, Mastercard, Visa
An elegant and well equipped
meublé near the center amid
tree-lined avenues. Internet
point.

Mercure Modena
Campogalliano ★★★★ ★
Campogalliano, Via del
Passatore 160, tel. 059851505
www.accor-hotels.com
97 rooms. Restaurant
Credit cards: American Express,
Diners Club, Mastercard, Visa
The hotel is surrounded by a
garden with a playground.
The restaurant serves Emilia and
Italian cuisine.

Mini Hotel Le Ville ★★★★ ★
Baggiovara, Via Giardini 1270,
tel. 059510051
www.minihotelleville.it
72 rooms. Sauna, pool, gym,
restaurant
Credit cards: American Express,
Diners Club, Mastercard, Visa
Set in an old farmhouse and
immersed in nature, it has a
pool, garden and gym.

Raffaello ★★★★ ★
Via per Cognento 5,
tel. 059357035
www.sogliahotels.com
127 rooms. Parking, restaurant
Credit cards: American Express,
Diners Club, Mastercard, Visa
A well-equipped hotel with
numerous suites.
The restaurant serves Italian
and traditional cuisine.

Real Fini ★★★★ &
Via Emilia Est 441,
tel. 0592051511
www.hotelrealfini.it
87 rooms. Parking, gym

Credit cards: American Express,
Diners Club, Mastercard, Visa
Various different, comfortable
rooms (some prestigious junior
suites).

Rechigi Park Hotel ★★★★
Fossalta, via Emilia Est 1581,
tel. 059283600
www.rechigiparkhotel.it
76 rooms. Sauna, gym,
restaurant
Credit cards: American Express,
Diners Club, Mastercard, Visa
A late 18th-century noble villa
decorated accordingly but
without giving up modern
comforts. Elegant and welcoming,
the rooms are well equipped and
the three suites have spa baths
and sizeable terraces.

Magnagallo ★★★ &
Campogalliano, Via Magnagallo
Est 7, tel. 059528751
www.magnagallo.it
30 rooms. Restaurant
Credit cards: American Express,
Diners Club, Mastercard, Visa
100 m from the Campogalliano
castle, this hotel has a lovely
restaurant set in an adjacent,
rustic building.

Restaurants

Fini ￥￥￥￥
Rua Frati Minori 54,
tel. 059223314
Closed Monday and Tuesday
Credit cards: American Express,
Diners Club, Mastercard, Visa
A true institution on the city, it
serves Modena cuisine in a
setting filled with atmosphere.

L'Erba del Re ￥￥￥
Via Castel Maraldo 45,
tel. 059218188
www.lerbadelre.it
Closed Sunday and Monday
midday
Credit cards: American Express,
Diners Club, Mastercard, Visa
In the most delightful and
authentic part of the old center,
this restaurant has a lovely view
over Piazzetta della Pomposa. It
also has works of modern and
contemporary art. The cuisine
focuses on variations of recipes
and local products, creating
traditional food with modern
touches.

Antica Moka ￥￥ ★
Fossalta, Via Emilia Est 1581,
tel. 059284008
www.anticamoka.it
Closed Saturday midday and
Sunday
Credit cards: American Express,

Diners Club, Mastercard, Visa
Set in a 20th-century villa, it
serves local cuisine specializing
in fish.

Laghi ￥￥ ★
Campogalliano, Via Albone 27,
tel. 059526988
Closed Wednesday
Located in the greenery along
the Secchia river, it has large
windows, a veranda and a
garden. The specialities are
dishes from Modena.

Quercia di Rosa ￥￥ ★
Fossalta, Via Scartazza 22,
tel. 059280730
Closed Tuesday and Sunday
evening
Credit cards: American Express,
Diners Club, Mastercard, Visa
A 19th-century villa with a large
garden and a little lake. Modern
cuisine.

At night

Bulldog's Club
Via Borelli 8,
tel. 059244913
Alehouse, restaurant and
pizzeria.

Caffè Concerto
Piazza Grande,
tel. 059222232
www.caffeconcertomodena.it
Restaurant, American bar,
literary café.

Central Club
Via Bolzano 41,
tel. 059440818
Music pub.

Cico's Cafè
Via Vaciglio 606,
tel. 059360306
Alehouse, sandwich bar, wine bar.

Clover Club
Via Scanaroli 22, tel. 059375003
www.cloverclub.it
Pub, alehouse, restaurant,
American bar.

Exalumeria
Via S. Agostino 9/a,
tel. 059221476
www.exalumeria.it
Café, pub.

Frozen
Via Argiolas, tel. 059460601
Dinner club, American bar.

Morsichino
Piazza Roma 5,
tel. 059243482
www.morsichino.it
Light food, snacks, wine bar.

Red Lion Pub
Via Rainusso 68/a,

l. 059331682
restaurant-pub, wine bar. Live
music.

ir Francis Drake Pub
ia Emilio Po 86
alehouse, sandwich bar.

Museums, Monuments
nd Churches

alleria Estense
iazza S. Agostino 337,
el. 0594395711
www.galleriaestense.it
uesday-Sunday 8.30-19.30

Musei del Duomo -
Museo Lapidario
ia Lanfranco 6,
el. 0594396969
www.duomodimodena.it
uesday-Sunday 9.30-12.30,
5.30-18.30. Also open for
roups on Monday by prior
rrangement

Mostra Permanente della
Biblioteca Estense Universitaria
argo di Porta S. Agostino 337,
el. 059222248-059222742
www.cedoc.mo.it/estense
Biblioteca: Monday-Thursday
8.30-19.15; Friday 8.30-15.45;
Saturday 8.30-13.45.
To examine the manuscripts,
ou need to submit your request
efore 13.00.
Sala Campori (Borso d'Este's
ible): Monday-Saturday
9.00-13.00. Closed Sunday

Museo Civico Archeologico
Etnologico ★
Viale Vittorio Veneto 5,
el. 0592033100-0592033101
www.comune.modena.it/museoa
cheologico
Tuesday-Saturday 9.00-12.00;
Tuesday and Saturday also
16.00-18.00; Sunday
and holidays 10.00-13.00,
15.00-19.00

Museo Civico d'Arte ★
Viale Vittorio Veneto 5,
tel. 0592033100-0592033101
www.comune.modena.it/
museoarte
Tuesday-Saturday 9.00-12.00;
Tuesday and Saturday also
15.00-18.00; Sunday
and holidays 10.00-13.00,
15.00-19.00

Orto Botanico Universitario
Viale Caduti in Guerra 127,
tel. 0592056011
www.ortobot.unimo.it
Open for schools in Modena and
the province by prior
arrangement

MODIGLIANA

Rural Lodgings
Malbrola
Via S. Martino in Monte 5,
tel. 0546941585
Open March-October and mid
December-mid January
Set amid olive trees and vines,
hills and streams, these rural
lodgings are divided between
two old farmhouses and
furnished with rustic period
furniture. The restaurant serve
regional cuisine. Sale and tasting
of the wine and extra-virgin olive
oil made on the farm.

Museums, Monuments
and Churches

Pinacoteca Comunale
"Silvestro Lega"
Palazzo Pretorio,
tel. 0546941019
www.comune.modigliana.fc.it
Sunday 15.00-18.00. Visits also
by arrangement

MONTEFIORE
CONCA

IAT Montefiore Conca
Via Roma c/o Rocca
Malatestiana,
tel. 0541980035

NONÀNTOLA

IAT Nonantola
Via Marconi 11,
tel. 059896555
www.comune.nonantola.
mo.it

Restaurants
Osteria di Rubbiara †
Rubbiara, Via Risaia 2,
tel. 059549019
www.acetaiapedroni.com
Closed Tuesday and in the
evening (except Friday and
Saturday)
Credit cards: American Express,
Mastercard, Visa
Local cuisine. The highlight is
the balsamic vinegar produced
by the family. Wine and spirits.

PARMA

IAT Parma
Via Melloni 1/b,
tel. 0521218889
www.turismo.comune.parma.
it/turismo

Hotels
Sofitel G.H. de
la Ville ***** ♿ ★
Largo Calamandrei 11,
tel. 05210304
www.grandhoteldelaville.it
110 rooms. Parking, sauna, gym,
restaurant
Credit cards: American Express,
Diners Club, Mastercard, Visa
Right next to a park, it has
soundproofed rooms and a
health area.

Starhotels du Parc **** ★
Viale Piacenza 12/C,
tel. 0521292929
www.starhotels.com
169 rooms. Parking, gym,
restaurant
Credit cards: American Express,
Diners Club, Mastercard, Visa
A 20th-century building with air
conditioned, comfortable rooms.
A small bridge links the hotel to
the Parco Ducale and makes it
possible to reach the center in a
few minutes.

Verdi **** ★
Via Pasini 18, tel. 0521293539
www.hotelverdi.it
20 rooms. Parking
Credit cards: American Express,
Diners Club, Mastercard, Visa
Opposite Parco Ducale, this villa
from the early 20th-century
has been refurbished and
elegantly furnished in art
nouveau style. Well equipped
rooms (and some suites) with
briar furniture, parquet floors and
marble coated bathrooms.
The common areas are furnished
with period furniture.

Villa Ducale **** ♿ ★
Via Moletolo 53/A,
tel. 0521272727
www.villaducalehotel.com
47 rooms. Gym, restaurant
Credit cards: American Express,
Diners Club, Mastercard, Visa
A villa and an old hayloft
surrounded by a park. The
restaurant serves regional
cuisine. Sports center nearby.

Best Western Farnese
International Hotel *** ★
Via Reggio 51/A,
tel. 0521994247
www.bestwestern.it/farnese_pr
76 rooms. Parking, gym,
restaurant
Credit cards: American Express,
Diners Club, Mastercard, Visa
Internet point, free bicycle hire
and a restaurant serving Parma
cuisine and local products.

Holiday Inn Express *** ♿ ★
Via Naviglio Alto 50,
tel. 0521270593
www.parma.hiexpress.it
70 rooms. Parking, restaurant
Credit cards: American Express,
Diners Club, Mastercard, Visa
Various different types of room
and an internet point. The
restaurant serves Parma cuisine.

Restaurants
Angiol d'Or ▥ ★
Vicolo Scutellari 1,
tel. 0521282632
www.angioldor.it
Closed Sunday evening and
Tuesday
Credit cards: American Express,
Diners Club, Mastercard, Visa
An elegant restaurant with a
garden used in summer
overlooking Piazza Duomo.
Local cuisine (also open after
theatre shows), cheeses
and local salamis.

Maxim's ▥ ★
Viale Mentana 140,
tel. 0521281032
www.palacemarialuigia.com
Closed Sunday
Credit cards: American Express,
Diners Club, Mastercard, Visa
One of the most famous
restaurants in the city, it serves
Parma cuisine, with both meat
and fresh fish specialities.

Parizzi ▥
Via Repubblica 71,
tel. 0521285952
Closed Monday
Credit cards: American Express,
Diners Club, Mastercard, Visa
A famous and elegant restaurant
in the old center. The cuisine
includes both traditional
specialities and creative modern
dishes.

Trattoria del Ducato ▥ ★
Via Paganini 5, tel. 0521486730
Closed Tuesday (Sunday from
June to August)
Credit cards: American Express,
Diners Club, Mastercard, Visa
The focus is on the local
specialities and the homemade
desserts.

Aldo ▯ ★
Piazzale Inzani 15,
tel. 0521206001
Closed Sunday evening and
Monday
Credit cards: American Express,
Diners Club, Mastercard, Visa
A rustic setting where you can
try some typical dishes from
Parma.

At night
Chelsea Pub ♿
Via Emilio Lepido 22,
tel. 0521481507
Sandwich bar and alehouse.

Discoteca Dadaumpa
Via Emilio Lepido 48,
tel. 0521483813
www.dadaumpa.com
In summer, this night club
extends outside to another
dancing area with two bars and
a pool. Also live Italian music
concerts.

Don Chisciotte
Strada delle Fonderie 15/a,
tel. 0521772730
www.luciferarts.it
Local cuisine and exhibitions.

Il Caffè del Prato ♿
Piazzale S. Francesco 1,
tel. 0521031118
In the heart of the old center,
near the Duomo, it hosts
various exhibitions.

Osteria Pub Ratafià Teatrobar
Via Oradour 14, tel. 0521243377
Set in an old stable, it is now
used for exhibitions and concerts.

Tapas ♿
Via D'Azeglio 67/b,
tel. 0521285688
Spanish cuisine with Catalan
furnishings help set the mood
for the Latin American evenings.

Tonic
Via N. Sauro 5, tel. 0521286066
Located in an old building in the
center, it hosts exhibitions and
jazz concerts.

Underground ♿
Via dei Farnese 2,
tel. 0521281587
A young and relaxed sandwich
bar.

Museums, Monuments
and Churches
Fondazione Museo Glauco
Lombardi ★
Via Garibaldi 15, tel. 0521233727
www.museolombardi.it
Tuesday-Saturday 9.30-15.30;
Sunday and holidays 9.00-18.30
(9.00-13.30 in July and August)

Galleria Nazionale di Parma e
Teatro Farnese
Piazza della Pilotta 5,
tel. 0521233309-0521233617
www.artipr.arti.beniculturali.it/ht
m/Musei.htm
Tuesday-Sunday 8.30-14.00.
Closed 1 January, 1 May, 25
December

Museo Archeologico Nazionale
Piazza della Pilotta 5,

tel. 0521233718
www.archeobo.arti.beniculturali
t/Parma/index.htm
Tuesday-Sunday 8.30-13.30

Museo Diocesano
Piazza Duomo, tel. 0521208699
www.fabbriceriacattedraleparma.i
Monday-Sunday 9.00-12.30,
15.00-18.30

PIACENZA

IAT Piacenza
Piazzetta Mercanti 7,
tel. 0523329324

Hotels
Best Western Premier Park
Hotel Piacenza **** ♿ ★
Strada Val Nure 7,
tel. 0523712600
www.bestwestern.it/park_pc
100 rooms. Parking, sauna, gym,
restaurant
Credit cards: American Express,
Diners Club, Mastercard, Visa
Not far from the center, it has
an internet point, some suites
and a restaurant serving local
specialities.

ClassHotel Piacenza
Fiera **** ♿ ★
Le Mose, tel. 0523606091
www.classhotel.com
80 rooms. Parking, gym,
restaurant
Credit cards: American Express,
Diners Club, Mastercard, Visa
Rooms with computer
connections; fitness area and a
restaurant serving cuisine from
Emilia.

G..A. Roma **** ♿
Via Cittadella 14, tel. 0523323201
www.grandealbergoroma.it
76 rooms. Parking, sauna, gym,
restaurant
Credit cards: American Express,
Diners Club, Mastercard, Visa
A seven-storey building that has
been completely refurbished.
Elegantly furnished. Some suites
with spa baths.

City *** ♿
Via Emilia Parmense 54,
tel. 0523579752
www.hotelcitypc.it
60 rooms. Parking
Credit cards: American Express,
Diners Club, Mastercard, Visa
Located in a quiet spot but not
far from the main city roads.

Holiday Inn *** ♿
Via Emilia Pavese 114/A,
tel. 0523493811
www.holiday-inn.com/piacenza

‡‡‡ ‡‡ ‡‡ *** ** * Hotels   ▥▥▥ ▥▥ ▥ ▥ ▯ Restaurants   ♿ Disabled   ★ Special TCI Rates

...o rooms. Parking, restaurant
redit cards: American Express,
)iners Club, Mastercard, Visa
.t the gates to the city, it is well
)cated for the highway. The
estaurant serves regional cuisine.

)vest * &**
/ia I Maggio 82, tel. 0523712222
www.hotelovest.com
9 rooms. Parking
Credit cards: American Express,
)iners Club, Mastercard, Visa
.ocated between the center and
he highway junction, it has well
.quipped rooms and junior
.suites.

Restaurants

Antica Osteria del Teatro 4
/ia Verdi 16, tel. 0523323777
www.anticaosteriadelteatro.it
Closed Monday and Sunday
Credit cards: Mastercard, Visa
n the city center, not far from
Teatro Municipale and Piazza
Cavalli, it is set in a noble
residence and has been around
for over 30 years. This truly lovely
place is a combination of Italian
tradition and modern trends.

Peppino ⅲ
/ia Roma 183, tel. 0523329279
Closed Monday
Credit cards: American Express,
)iners Club, Mastercard, Visa
A small restaurant in the old
center. The cuisine is based on
fish and homemade desserts.
Kitchen is open after 22.00.

Piccolo Roma ⅲ
Via Cittadella 14, tel. 0523323201
www.grandealbergoroma.it
Closed Saturday and Sunday
evening
Credit cards: American Express,
)iners Club, Mastercard, Visa
Period furniture and traditional
Emilia cuisine.

Vecchia Piacenza ⅲ
Via S. Bernardo 1,
tel. 0523305462
www.ristorantevecchiapiacenza.it
Closed Sunday
Credit cards: Diners Club,
Mastercard, Visa
Set in an 18th-century building,
with frescoed walls and ceilings,
it serves dishes prepared using
old Piacenza recipes. The cellar,
built in the 12th-century, can be
visited.

At night

Caprice &
Via Tortona 3,
tel. 0523482074
A night club. Also ballroom
dancing.

Disco Bar A21
Via I Maggio 65,
tel. 0523499082
Coffee house, snack bar and
pizzeria furnished in an original
way, using a highway theme.

Music Tavern Pub
Via Pietro Cella 68,
tel. 0523713121
An English-style pub serving
light food and a vast array of
drinks.

Taverna delle Fate
Via del Pontiere
On the river, it offers
entertainment and food from the
'food and wine kiosk'. Various
shows and live music.

Museums, Monuments and Churches

Musei Civici di Palazzo Farnese ★
Piazza Cittadella 29,
tel. 0523326981
www.musei.piacenza.it
July-15 September: Tuesday-
Thursday 9.00-13.00; Friday and
Saturday 9.00-13.00, 15.00-18.00;
Sunday 9.30-13.00, 15.00-18.00.
16 September-June: Tuesday-
Thursday 8.45-13.00; Friday and
Saturday 8.45-13.00, 15.00-18.00;
Sunday 9.30-13.00, 15.00-18.00

PREMILCUORE

IAT Galeata-Premilcuore
Via Nefetti 3,
tel. 0543971297

Rural Lodgings

Agroippoturistica Ridolla & ★
Via Valbura 2,
tel. 0543956829
www.ridolla.com
Bicycle hire, restaurant
Set in an old Apennine building,
it is the heart of a well known
center for horse tourism in the
lovely Rabbi valley on the edge
of the Parco Nazionale delle
Foreste Casentinesi.

RAVENNA

IAT Ravenna
Via Salara 8/12,
tel. 054435404
www.racine.ra.it

Hotels

Best Western Bisanzio ** ★**
Via Salara 30, tel. 0544217111
www.bisanziohotel.com
38 rooms.

Credit cards: American Express,
Diners Club, Mastercard, Visa
Set in an area restricted to traffic,
except to load and unload
luggage, it has a lovely garden.
An elegant setting with lovely use
of marble, chandeliers that frame
the columns and inviting
communal rooms. Internet point.

Jolly Hotel ** & ★**
Piazza Mameli 1, tel. 054435762
www.jollyhotels.it
84 rooms. Restaurant
Credit cards: American Express,
Diners Club, Mastercard, Visa
Close to the old center and the
major monuments, it has a
restaurant serving regional
culinary delights.

ClassHotel Ravenna * & ★**
Viale della Lirica 141,
tel. 0544270290
www.classhotel.com
69 rooms. Restaurant
Credit cards: American Express,
Diners Club, Mastercard, Visa
Not far from the highway,
it is set in a modern complex.
Sapori di Ravenna restaurant.

Diana * & ★**
Via Rossi 47, tel. 054439164
www.hoteldiana.ra.it
33 rooms.
Credit cards: American Express,
Diners Club, Mastercard, Visa
This meublé near the old center
is furnished in 19th-century style.

Italia * & ★**
Viale Pallavicini 4/6,
tel. 0544212363
www.hitalia.it
45 rooms. Restaurant
Credit cards: American Express,
Diners Club, Mastercard, Visa
Not far from the station and the
old center, it is set in a house
with a typical restaurant serving
regional cuisine.

Mosaico Hotel * & ★**
Via Darsena 9, tel. 0544456665
www.mosaicohotels.it
29 rooms.
Credit cards: American Express,
Diners Club, Mastercard, Visa
Behind the train station and
near the center. Bicycles
available for guests and a
reserved parking area.

Columbia * &**
Marina Romea, Viale Italia 70,
tel. 0544446038
www.columbiahotel.it
53 rooms. Sauna, pool,
restaurant
Credit cards: American Express,
Diners Club, Mastercard, Visa
Separated from the sea by a

pine grove, it has a restaurant serving local cuisine.

Rural Lodgings

L'Azdôra
Madonna dell'Albero, Via Vangaticcio 14, tel. 0544497669
Pool, restaurant
This rural lodging has three buildings, with two being for accommodation and one for the restaurant. Within easy reach, you can find splendid Romanesque monuments, Adriatic beaches and amusement parks.

Restaurants

Antica Trattoria al Gallo 1909 ⑪
Via Maggiore 87, tel. 0544213775
www.anticatrattoriadelgallo.191.it
Closed Sunday evening, Monday and Tuesday
Credit cards: American Express, Diners Club, Mastercard, Visa
Traditional Romagna cuisine, favoring vegetarian options. The first courses are the highlight.

Spasso Bistrot ⑪
Via Mura di S. Vitale 10, tel. 0544218100
Closed Monday
Credit cards: Diners Club, Mastercard, Visa
Near San Vitale, it serves traditional Romagna cuisine with innovative elements.

Taverna San Romualdo ⑪
San Romualdo, Via S. Alberto 364, tel. 0544483447
Closed Tuesday
Credit cards: American Express, Diners Club, Mastercard, Visa
A traditional restaurant on the northern edge of Ravenna. The cuisine combines local dishes with ethnic ones. Selection of cheeses and local salamis.

Flora ⑪ ★
Ragone, Via Ragone 104, tel. 0544534044
Closed Wednesday
Credit cards: American Express, Diners Club, Mastercard, Visa
A rustic setting in which regional cuisine is served (kitchen open also after 22.00). Homemade desserts.

Locanda del Melarancio ⑪
Via Mentana 33, tel. 0544215258
www.locandadelmelarancio.it
Closed Wednesday
Credit cards: American Express, Diners Club, Mastercard, Visa
Set in a 16th-century house (Casa Succi) in the old center, it is divided into a lovely tavern on the first floor and a refined

restaurant on the second one. There are also four rooms for accommodation. Regional cuisine with original touches.

Ustarì di Dù Canton ⑪ ★
Mezzano, Via Piangipane 6, tel. 0544523207
Closed Monday evening and Tuesday
Credit cards: American Express, Diners Club, Mastercard, Visa
A tavern as early as the mid-19th century, it still has a rustic and informal feel as well as a cool outdoor section. Regional cuisine, with the highlight being the filled pasta. There is also the famous 'fossa' cheese from Sogliano.

At night

Caffè Corte Cavour
Via Cavour 51, tel. 054430154
Open-air piano bar (summer only).

Lounge Bar Caffè Belli
Via A. Guerrini 9, tel. 0544217274
In the old centre of Ravenna, this café serves local cuisine and appetizers with a wonderful buffet. Music and appetizer specials on Friday and Saturday. Closed Sunday.

Silvano Art Cafè
Piazza Luigi Einaudi 7, tel. 0544212432
A small restaurant and coffee house with an open-air piano bar (summer only).

Museums, Monuments and Churches

Museo Arcivescovile ★
Piazza Arcivescovado 1, tel. 0544215201-0544541688
www.ravennamosaici.it
April-September: Monday-Sunday 9.00-19.00. October, March: Monday-Sunday 9.30-17.30. November-February: Monday-Sunday 10.00-17.00

Museo d'Arte della città di Ravenna – MAR ★
Via Roma 13, tel. 0544482356
www.museocitta.ra.it
Tuesday, Thursday, Friday 9.00-13.30, 15.00-18.00; Wednesday, Saturday 9.00-13.30; Sunday and holidays 15.00-18.00 (except during exhibitions)

Museo Nazionale
Via Fiandrini, tel. 054434424
www.comune.ra.it/citta/cultura_biblioteche/museonazionale.htm
Tuesday-Sunday 8.30-19.30

REGGIO EMILIA

IAT Reggio Emilia
Piazza Prampolini 5/c, tel. 0522451152
www.municipio.re.it/turismo

Hotels

Classic Hotel ★★★★ ⑆
San Maurizio, Via L. Pasteur 121 tel. 0522355411
www.classic-hotel.it
91 rooms. Parking, sauna, gym, restaurant
Credit cards: American Express, Diners Club, Visa
An elegant structure with a restaurant serving cuisine from Emilia, especially fish dishes.

Delle Notarie ★★★★ ⑆ ★
Via Palazzolo 5, tel. 0522453500
www.albergonotarie.it
51 rooms. Parking, restaurant
Credit cards: American Express, Diners Club, Mastercard, Visa
In the center, it has rooms with parquet and walnut root furniture. The common areas have coffered ceilings.

Mercure Astoria ★★★★ ⑆ ★
Viale Nobili 2, tel. 0522435245
www.accorhotels.com/italia
108 rooms. Parking, gym, restaurant
Credit cards: American Express, Diners Club, Mastercard, Visa
Near the public gardens, this comfortable hotel is right in the old center.

Posta ★★★★ ★
Piazza Del Monte 2, tel. 0522432944
www.hotelposta.re.it
39 rooms. Parking, gym
Credit cards: American Express, Diners Club, Mastercard, Visa
Set in the medieval Palazzo del Capitano del Popolo, this meublé is right in the old center and is well furnished with period furniture.

Airone ★★★ ⑆
Via Aeronautica 20, tel. 0522924111
www.aironehotel.it
56 rooms. Restaurant
Credit cards: American Express, Diners Club, Mastercard, Visa
Well located for both the trade fair and center, it is comfortable with sizeable, well equipped rooms. The restaurant serves regional cuisine.

Park Hotel ★★★ ⑆ ★
Via De Ruggero 1, tel. 0522292141
www.parkhotel.re.it
63 rooms. Pool, restaurant

⚲⚲⚲ ⚲⚲⚲ ⚲⚲⚲ ★★★ ★★ ★ Hotels ⑪⑪⑪⑪ ⑪⑪⑪ ⑪⑪ ⑪ ⑪ Restaurants ⑆ Disabled ★ Special TCI Rates

...edit cards: American Express, ...ners Club, Mastercard, Visa ...cated in a garden, it has ...oms with a balcony and an ...ternet point.

...estaurants

...elle Notarie ¶¶¶ ★
...a Aschieri 4, tel. 0522453700
...ww.albergonotarie.it
...osed Sunday
...edit cards: American Express,
...ners Club, Mastercard, Visa
...he cuisine remains faithfful to
...cal traditions without giving
...o innovative elements.

...noteca Morini ¶¶¶ ★
...ia Passo Buole 82,
...l. 0522323986
...ww.ristoranteenotecamorini.it
...osed Saturday midday and
...unday
...edit cards: American Express,
...ners Club, Mastercard, Visa
...refined restaurant serving
...uisine from Emilia.

...inque Pini-da Pelati ¶¶
...iale Martiri di Cervarolo 46,
...l. 0522553663
...ww.5pini.cjb.net
...osed Wednesday and Tuesday
...vening
...edit cards: American Express,
...iners Club, Mastercard, Visa
...his restaurant serves Emilia
...uisine with innovative,
...easonal elements.

...a Pozzo ¶¶
...iale Allegri 7, tel. 0522451300
...losed Sunday midday and
...onday
...edit cards: American Express,
...astercard, Visa
...he garden is used in the
...ummer. Emilia cuisine, with
...ocal cheeses and salamis.

...a Mangiare ¶
...iale Monte Grappa 3/A,
...el. 0522433600
...losed Sunday and Saturday
...idday (in summer)
...redit cards: American Express,
...iners Club, Mastercard, Visa
...n the old center, it is set in an
...rt nouveau building. A quiet
...lace where you can enjoy some
...onderful dishes from Emilia
...with some innovative touches.

...rattoria della Ghiara ¶
...icolo del Folletto 1/C,
...el. 0522435755
...losed Sunday
...uisine: Emilia
...redit cards: Mastercard, Visa
...A traditional trattoria in the old
...center, favoring regional recipes,
...ocal cheeses, hams and salamis.

At night

Brain and Soul Cafè
Via Monte S. Michele 4,
tel. 0522406287
Food, music and internet access.

Caffè Estate Amarcord
Via Martiri di Cervarolo 76,
tel. 0522332195
Restaurant and dance bar.

Discoteca Adrenaline
Corso Cairoli 25, tel. 0522433972
Trendy music.

La Rambla - Music Cafè
Via dell'Aeronautica 24,
tel. 0522512163
Live music.

Kanaka
Via del Quaresimo 2/g
Music and cabaret.

Transilvania
Via dei Gonzaga 41,
tel. 0522517406
Restaurant and night club with
live music.

Tutankhamon
Via P. Nobili 1, tel. 0522454155
Bar with live music.

Museums, Monuments and Churches

Civici Musei
Via Spallanzani 1,
tel. 0522456477
www.musei.comune.re.it
Summer: Monday 9.00-12.00;
Tuesday-Saturday 9.00-12.00,
21.00-24.00; Sunday 21.00-
24.00. Winter: Tuesday-Friday
9.00-12.00; Saturday 9.00-12.00,
15.00-19.00; Sunday 10.00-
13.00, 15.00-19.00

Galleria Civica "Anna e Luigi Parmeggiani"
Corso Cairoli 2, tel. 0522456477
www.musei.comune.re.it
Summer: Monday 9.00-12.00;
Tuesday-Saturday 9.00-12.00,
21.00-24.00. Winter: Tuesday-Friday
9.00-12.00; Saturday 9.00-12.00,
15.00-19.00; Sunday 10.00-
13.00, 15.00-19.00

Museo del Santuario della Madonna della Ghiara
Corso Garibaldi 44,
tel. 0522439707
www.municipio.re.it/IAT/iatre.nsf

RICCIONE

IAT Riccione
Piazzale Ceccarini 10,
tel. 0541693302
www.comune.riccione.rn.it

Hotels

G.H. Des Bains ★★★★★ ♿ ★
Viale Gramsci 56, tel. 0541601650
www.grandhoteldesbains.com
70 rooms. Parking, sauna, pool,
gym, restaurant
Credit cards: American Express,
Diners Club, Mastercard, Visa
A large villa luxuriously
furnished in Belle Époque style.
Two pools (one indoor) and a
beauty center.

Alexandra Plaza ★★★★ ★
Viale Torino 61, tel. 0541610344
www.alexandraplaza.it
60 rooms. Pool, restaurant
Credit cards: American Express,
Diners Club, Mastercard, Visa
Right on the beach, but
surrounded by a garden
(used for entertainment in
summer), it has rooms with
scenic balconies, an internet
point, activities for children
and bicycle use.

Atilius ★★★ ♿ ★
Via A. Boito 3, tel. 0541647624
www.atilius.com
51 rooms. Restaurant
Credit cards: American Express,
Diners Club, Mastercard, Visa
A central, elegant building
designed for easy access.
Lovely view from the terrace.

Novecento ★★★ ♿
Viale D'Annunzio 30,
tel. 0541644990
www.hotelnovecento.it
35 rooms. Parking, sauna, pool,
gym, restaurant
Credit cards: Diners Club,
Mastercard, Visa
Near the center and sea, it has a
large terrace, a gym with a sauna
and sunbathing area, hydro-
massage and a health area.

Restaurants

Azzurra ¶¶ ★
Piazzale Azzarita 2,
tel. 0541648604
www.ristoranteazzurra.com
Credit cards: Diners Club,
Mastercard, Visa
On the seafront, it has terrace
with a piano bar. Fish dominates
the menu. Booking
recommended.

Casale ¶¶ ★
Viale Abruzzi, tel. 0541604620
www.ilcasale.net
Closed Monday in winter
Credit cards: American Express,
Diners Club, Visa
It has a scenic terrace
overlooking the Riccione hills
and the sea. The menu is mainly
non-seafood with vegetarian
options. Local oils and cheeses.

Museums, Monuments and Churches

Museo del Territorio
Via Lazio 10, tel. 0541600113
www.comune.riccione.rn.it
21 June-August: Tuesday-Saturday 9.00-12.00; Tuesday, Wednesday, Friday also 21.00-23.00. September-20 June: Tuesday-Saturday 9.00-12.00; Tuesday, Wednesday, Friday also 15.00-18.00

RIMINI

IAT Rimini
Piazzale Federico Fellini 3, tel. 054156902
www.riminiturismo.it

Hotels

Grand Hotel ***** ★
Parco Federico Fellini 1, tel. 054156000
www.grandhotelrimini.com
168 rooms. Sauna, pool, tennis, gym, restaurant
Credit cards: American Express, Diners Club, Mastercard, Visa
Immersed in an age-old park, it offers a wide range of facilities. The halls have antique objects; refined suites; and the inevitable allure of the Fellini world.

Ambassador **** ♿
Viale Regina Elena 86, tel. 0541387207
www.ambassadorrimini.com
60 rooms. Pool, restaurant
Credit cards: Mastercard, Visa
Central, on the seafront, this welcoming hotel has a restaurant with large, glass walls.

Ariminum **** ♿ ★
Viale Regina Elena 159, tel. 0541380472
www.ariminumhotels.it
50 rooms. Sauna, restaurant
Credit cards: American Express, Diners Club, Mastercard, Visa
A comfortable hotel where the rooms are well equipped and decorated in art nouveau style.

Bellevue **** ★
Piazzale Kennedy 12, tel. 0541390490
65 rooms. Parking
Credit cards: American Express, Diners Club, Mastercard, Visa
By the sea in one of the most elegant parts of Rimini, Marina Centro, it has all the modern comforts.

Best Western Hotel Nettunia **** ★
Miramare, Viale Regina Margherita 203, tel. 0541372067
www.bestwestern.it/nettunia_rn
44 rooms. Sauna, gym, restaurant
Credit cards: American Express, Diners Club, Mastercard, Visa
By the sea, in the central Miramare area, this comfortable hotel is neoclassical. Elegant and spacious, it is also well equipped for physical treatments and relaxing, with a sunbathing area and a giant spa bath.

Le Méridien Rimini **** ♿
Lungomare Murri 13, tel. 0541396600
rimini.lemeridien.com
109 rooms. Parking, pool, restaurant
Credit cards: American Express, Diners Club, Mastercard, Visa
On the seafront, it is also a good spot for holidays. The restaurant serves regional cuisine with innovative elements.

Luxor **** ♿
Viale Tripoli 203, tel. 0541390990
www.riminiluxor.com
34 rooms. Restaurant
Credit cards: American Express, Diners Club, Mastercard, Visa
200 m from the sea, it has large glass windows. The rooms have balconies. The buffet breakfast consists of homemade products.

Parco dei Principi **** ♿ ★
viale Regina Elena 98, tel. 0541380055
www.parcodeiprincipi.net
39 rooms. Pool, restaurant
Credit cards: American Express, Diners Club, Mastercard, Visa
This Mediterranean-style hotel has rooms and suites with spa baths. The restaurant serves regional cuisine.

Rural Lodgings

Case Mori ★
San Martino Monte l'Abbate, Via Monte L'Abbate 9, tel. 0541731262
www.casemori.it
Closed for a period in October and November
Credit cards: Mastercard, Visa
The accommodation is in four farmhouses on a farm amid the first hills of inland Rimini where cereal crops, vines and olives are grown. The surrounding area has patches of natural vegetation, woods and cultivated fields. Behind lies the top of Mt Titano, while not far in front is the Rimini coast. Dinner is normally regional cuisine using produce from the garden.

Restaurants

Acero Rosso ¶¶¶
Viale Tiberio 11, tel. 054153577
www.acerorosso.it
Only open in the evening (Sunday and holidays also at midday). Closed Monday (also Sunday evening in winter)
Credit cards: American Express, Diners Club, Mastercard, Visa
A cool and inviting place near the Tiberio bridge. The excellent cuisine uses flavors, herbs and especially, fish. Good balance between tradition and innovation.

Il Melograno ¶¶¶
Viale Vespucci 16, tel. 054152255
www.hirimini.com
Only open in the evening; closed Sunday
Credit cards: American Express, Diners Club, Mastercard, Visa
A scenic restaurant serving regional cuisine with innovative elements.

Squero ¶¶
Lungomare Tintori 7, tel. 054127676
Closed Tuesday in winter
Credit cards: American Express, Diners Club, Mastercard, Visa
The food and the decoration is all about the sea, fitting its seafront location.

Vici e Ruscelli ¶¶
Torre Pedrera, Viale San Salvador 178, tel. 0541720500
Closed Monday and Tuesday midday
Cuisine: Emilia and creative
Credit cards: American Express, Diners Club, Mastercard, Visa
On the seafront, this simple restaurant has a small 'grotta' used as a cellar and a veranda used in summer. Regional cuisine with modern elements.

C'era una Volta ¶
Via Consolare 91, tel. 0541753268
Closed Tuesday
Credit cards: American Express, Diners Club, Mastercard, Visa
Set in an 18th-century country house, it serves regional cuisine. Meat and seafood dishes.

Grotta Rossa ¶ ★
Via Grotta Rossa 13, tel. 0541751707
Credit cards: American Express, Mastercard, Visa
A welcoming, rustic restaurant with a large, covered veranda where you can eat outdoors. Regional cuisine.

★★ṫ ★★ṫ ★★ṫ ★★★ ★★ ★ Hotels	¶¶¶¶¶ ¶¶¶¶ ¶¶¶ ¶¶ ¶ Restaurants	♿ Disabled	★ Special TCI Rates

night

lleria Giulio Cesare
azza Tre Martiri 16,
. 054151557
good alternative in the old
nter to the crowds of the
afront.

excal/Terrasamba
a Losanna 35,
. 0541373782
mix of ideas and sounds,
en with live concerts.

oe's
a Pomposa 55, tel. 0541776246
nadian cuisine and various
usic concerts.

ut Out
azzale Gondar 1
colorful spot where many
rties and concerts are held.

ock Island
olo di Levante, Piazzale
oscovich, tel. 054150178
ww.rockislandrimini.com
restaurant with concerts and
her events.

ondò del Tropico
ungomare Tintori 15,
l. 054123566
Vine bar with a gazebo in the
arden and live music.

ose & Crown
iale Regina Elena 2,
l. 0541391398
ww.roseandcrown.it
ritish pub with live music.

iki
ungomare Tintoti,
el. 054127058
ww.bagno26rimini.com
iadina house and restaurant
ooking essential) with various
orms of live music.

erbabuena
ia Cairoli 31, tel. 0541789095
ww.yerbabuena.it
n the old center, it has a good
election of rum and live music.

**Museums, Monuments
nd Churches**

Museo della Città ★
ia L. Tonini 1,
el. 054121482-054155414
ww.comune.rimini.it/cultura/mu
sei/musei_pagina.htm
6 September-15 June: Tuesday-
Saturday 8.30-12.30, 17.00-
9.00; Sunday and holidays
6.00-19.00. 16 June-15
September: Tuesday-Saturday
0.00-12.30, 16.30-19.30;
Sunday and holidays 16.30-
9.30; July and August, Tuesday
lso 21.00-23.00. Closed
Monday except when a holiday

SAN GIOVANNI IN PERSICETO

**URP San Giovanni
in Persiceto**
tel. 800069678

Hotels

La Posta ★★
Via IV Novembre 16,
tel. 051821235
22 rooms. Restaurant
Credit cards: American Express,
Diners Club, Mastercard, Visa
Classic furnishings and comfort.
The restaurant serves authentic
Bologna dishes.

Restaurants

Osteria del Mirasole �
Via Matteotti 17/A,
tel. 051821273
*Only open in the evening
(Sunday and holidays also at
midday)*
Closed Monday
Credit cards: American Express,
Diners Club, Mastercard, Visa
A small restaurant with a
fireplace serving Bologna
cuisine that makes good use of
products from the local markets.
Salamis, hams and homemade
desserts.

Sorsimorsi ⅰ
Via Poggio 2,
tel. 0516810768
www.sorsimorsi.com
*Closed Tuesday and Saturday
midday*
Credit cards: American Express,
Diners Club, Mastercard, Visa
Set in a rural homestead, it has
a garden used in summer.
Traditional Emilia cuisine where
fresh raw materials are crucial
and homemade products are
favored.

Museums, Monuments and Churches

Museo d'Arte Sacra
Piazza del Popolo 22,
tel. 051821254
*www.comunepersiceto.it/
Arte&Citta*
*Sunday 9.00-12.00; Saturday
open by prior arrangement*

SAN MARINO (REPUBBLICA DI)

Hotels

G.H. San Marino ★★★★ ★
Viale Onofri 31,
tel. 0549992400
www.grandhotel.sm

---

63 rooms. Parking, sauna, gym,
restaurant
Credit cards: American Express,
Diners Club, Mastercard, Visa
In a panoramic position with a
view of the hills. The restaurant
serves Romagna cuisine.
Annexed beauty centre.

Titano ★★★★ ♿ ★
Contrada del Collegio 31,
tel. 0549991006
www.hoteltitano.com
48 rooms. Parking, gym,
restaurant
Credit cards: American Express,
Diners Club, Mastercard, Visa
In the old center, this house
has a lovely panoramic terrace
(that can be enclosed with
mobile windows).

Quercia Antica ★★★ ★
Via Capannaccia 7,
tel. 0549991257
www.querciantica.com
26 rooms. Restaurant
Credit cards: American Express,
Diners Club, Mastercard, Visa
Near the old center, with
adjacent parking, it has a
restaurant and a fireplace for
winter evenings.

Restaurants

Righi-la Taverna ⅲ
Piazza della Libertà 10,
tel. 0549991196
Closed Sunday evening
Credit cards: American Express,
Diners Club, Mastercard, Visa
An old inn from the 19th-century
that serves Emilia and refined
cuisine in line with the seasons.

La Fratta ⅱ
Salita alla Rocca 14,
tel. 0549991594
www.omniway.sm/lafratta
*Closed Wednesday (except in
summer)*
Credit cards: American Express,
Diners Club, Mastercard, Visa
A welcoming restaurant with a
scenic terrace. The cuisine is
determined by local traditions.

Buca San Francesco ⅰ ★
Piazzetta Feretrano 3,
tel. 0549991462
Only open at midday
Closed Friday (in winter)
Credit cards: American Express,
Diners Club, Mastercard, Visa
This characteristic restaurant
favors Romagna cuisine.

Museums, Monuments and Churches

Museo di Stato ★
Piazzetta del Titano 1,
tel. 0549883835
www.museidistato.sm

2 January-19 March, 30 October-31 December: 9.00-17.00.
20 March-11 June, 18 September-29 October: Monday-Friday 9.00-17.15, Saturday-Sunday 9.00-18.15. Easter Monday 9.00-19.00. Closed 25 Dec, 1 Jan, 2 Nov (afternoon)

SANTARCANGELO DI ROMAGNA

> **IAT Santarcangelo di Romagna**
> Via C. Battisti 5,
> tel. 0541624270

Hotels

Della Porta ★★★★ ♿ ★
Via A. Costa 85, tel. 0541622152
www.hoteldellaporta.com
22 rooms. Sauna, gym
Credit cards: American Express, Diners Club, Mastercard, Visa
Overlooking a delightful courtyard, this equipped meublé has comfortable rooms.

Il Villino ★★★★ ♿
Via C. Ruggeri 48,
tel. 0541685959
www.hotelilvillino.it
12 rooms.
Credit cards: American Express, Diners Club, Mastercard, Visa
On the edge of the old center, this 17th-century villa is charming: brick and stone, barrel vaults, antique furniture.

Rural Lodgings

Locanda Antiche Macine
Via Provinciale Sogliano 1540, tel. 0541627161
www.antichemacine.it
Closed January
Bicycle hire, pool, restaurant
Credit cards: American Express, Diners, Mastercard, Visa
Not far from the Romagna Riviera, this rural lodging is an oasis for people desiring a comfortable stay in a tasteful place surrounded by nature. The sitting room has a fireplace.

Restaurants

Lazaroun ▦
Via del Platano 21,
tel. 0541624417 www.lazaroun.it
Closed Thursday
Credit cards: American Express, Diners Club, Mastercard, Visa
A delightful setting in an 18th-century structure made of stone with lovely floors and furnishings, matching the beautiful halls.

Osteria la Sangiovesa ▦
Piazza Simone Balacchi 14,
tel. 0541620710
www.sangiovesa.it

Only open in the evening
Credit cards: American Express, Diners Club, Mastercard, Visa
Set in the stables of a 17th. century noble residence, it has annexed volcanic grottos that date from the year 1000.

Museums, Monuments and Churches

Museo Storico Archeologico
Via della Costa 26
September-May: Closed Monday; Tuesday-Saturday 10.30-12.30; Tuesday, Thursday, Saturday and Sunday also 15.30-17.30. June-August: Closed Monday; Tuesday-Sunday 10.30-12.30 and 16.30-19.00.

SASSUOLO

> **IAT Sassuolo**
> Piazzale Avanzini Paggeria Nuova, tel. 0536807371

Museums, Monuments and Churches

Centro di Documentazione dell'Industria Italiana delle Piastrelle di Ceramica
Palazzina della Casiglia, Viale Monte Santo 40, tel. 0536818111
www.assopiastrelle.it
Visits by prior arrangement Monday-Friday

SCANDIANO

Restaurants

Bosco ▦ ★
Bosco, Via Bosco 133,
tel. 0522857242
www.ristorantebosco.it
Closed Monday and Tuesday
Credit cards: American Express, Diners Club, Mastercard, Visa
A classic restaurant with a fireplace in the main room.

Osteria in Scandiano ▯
Piazza M. Boiardo 9,
tel. 0522857079
www.osteriainscandiano.com
Closed Thursday
Credit cards: American Express, Mastercard
Set in a small 17th-century building in the old center.

SÈSTOLA

> **IAT Sestola**
> Corso Umberto I 3,
> tel. 053662324

Restaurants

San Rocco ▦
Corso Umberto I 39,
tel. 053662382

www.hotel-sanrocco.it
Closed Monday
Credit cards: American Express, Diners Club, Mastercard, Visa
A small and rustic restaurant in a gracious hotel. Emilia cuisine.

TERRA DEL SOLE

> **IAT Terra del Sole**
> Piazza d'Armi c/o Palazzo Pretorio, tel. 054366766

VERUCCHIO

> **IAT Verrucchio**
> Piazza Malatesta 21,
> tel. 0541670222

Rural Lodgings

Le Case Rosse ♿
Villa Verrucchio, Via Tenuta Amalia 141, tel. 0541678123
www.tenutaamalia.com
Closed mid January-February
Bicycle hire
Credit cards: Diners, Visa
In the Marecchia valley, it is set in a 19th-century country residence furnished with period furniture. Real country feel with comfortable rooms. The farm, with vineyards and orchards, has three restaurants specializing in meat, fish and fowl respectively.

Restaurants

Rocca ▯ ★
Via Rocca 34, tel. 0541679850
Closed Wednesday
Credit cards: American Express, Diners Club, Mastercard, Visa
Near the Rocca Malatestiana, this restaurant cut into the rock overlooks the Romagna Riviera.

Zanni ▯ ★
Villa Verrucchio, Via Casale 163, tel. 0541678449
www.casazanni.it
Closed Tuesday except in August
Credit cards: American Express, Diners Club, Visa
Ceiling with open beams; cellar that can be visited; courtyard with a well and a bonfire. Romagna cuisine and homemade ice-cream.

Museums, Monuments and Churches

Museo Civico Archeologico
Via S. Agostino 14,
tel. 0541670222
www.comunediverucchio.it
April-September: Monday-Sunday 9.30-12.30, 14.30-19.30. October-March: Saturday 14.30-18.30; Sunday and holidays 10.00-13.00, 14.30-18.00. Visits also by arrangement for groups.

METRIC CONVERSIONS

DISTANCE

Kilometres/Miles

km to mi	mi to km
1 = 0.62	1 = 1.6
2 = 1.2	2 = 3.2
3 = 1.9	3 = 4.8
4 = 2.5	4 = 6.4
5 = 3.1	5 = 8.1
6 = 3.7	6 = 9.7
7 = 4.3	7 = 11.3
8 = 5.0	8 = 12.9

Meters/Feet

m to ft	ft to m
1 = 3.3	1 = 0.30
2 = 6.6	2 = 0.61
3 = 9.8	3 = 0.91
4 = 13.1	4 = 1.2
5 = 16.4	5 = 1.5
6 = 19.7	6 = 1.8
7 = 23.0	7 = 2.1
8 = 26.2	8 = 2.4

WEIGHT

Kilograms/Pounds

kg to lb	lb to kg
1 = 2.2	1 = 0.45
2 = 4.4	2 = 0.91
3 = 6.6	3 = 1.4
4 = 8.8	4 = 1.8
5 = 11.0	5 = 2.3
6 = 13.2	6 = 2.7
7 = 15.4	7 = 3.2
8 = 17.6	8 = 3.6

Grams/Ounces

g to oz	oz to g
1 = 0.04	1 = 28
2 = 0.07	2 = 57
3 = 0.11	3 = 85
4 = 0.14	4 = 114
5 = 0.18	5 = 142
6 = 0.21	6 = 170
7 = 0.25	7 = 199
8 = 0.28	8 = 227

TEMPERATURE

Fahrenheit/Celsius

F	C
0	-17.8
5	-15.0
10	-12.2
15	-9.4
20	-6.7
25	-3.9
30	-1.1
32	0
35	1.7
40	4.4
45	7.2
50	10.0
55	12.8
60	15.5
65	18.3
70	21.1
75	23.9
80	26.7
85	29.4
90	32.2
95	35.0
100	37.8

LIQUID VOLUME

Liters/U.S. Gallons

L to gal	gal to L
1 = 0.26	1 = 3.8
2 = 0.53	2 = 7.6
3 = 0.79	3 = 11.4
4 = 1.1	4 = 15.1

Liters/U.S. Gallons

L to gal	gal to L
5 = 1.3	5 = 18.9
6 = 1.6	6 = 22.7
7 = 1.8	7 = 26.5
8 = 2.1	8 = 30.3

A

Agostino di Dùccio: Florentine Sculptor and Architect, c.1418-c.1481 - p. 105

Albani, Francesco: from Bologna, Painter, 1578-1660 - p. 23

Alberti, Leon Battista: from Genoa, Architect, 1406-1472 - pp. 35, 105

Alighieri, Dante: from Florence, Poet, 1265-1321 - pp. 21, 53, 115

Allegri, Antonio: see Correggio.

Ambrosini, Floriano: from Bologna, Architect, 1557-1621 - p. 22

Anselmo da Campione: from Campione d'Italia (Como), Architect and Sculptor, known from 1160-80 - pp. 54, 112

Antelami, Benedetto: Sculptor probably from Lombardy, known from 1178, died c.1230 - pp. 67, 68, 75

Antonio di Vincenzo: probably from Bologna, Architect, c.1350-1401/1402 - pp. 20, 21, 22, 23

Aretusi, Cesare: from Bologna, Painter, 1549-1612 - p. 70

Ariosto, Ludovico: from Reggio Emilia, Poet and Writer, 1474-1533 - pp. 36, 98

Aristophanes: from Athens (Greece), Playwright, BC c.444-385 - p. 87

Arnolfo di Cambio: from Colle di Val d'Elsa (Siena), Architect and Sculptor, c.1245-1302 - p. 23

Aspertini, Amico: from Bologna, Painter,

Illuminator and Sculptor, 1474-1552 - p. 20

B

Baglione or Baglioni, Cesare: Painter from Cremona, c.1525-1615 - p. 76

Bagnacavallo (byname of Bartolomeo Ramenghi): from Bagnacavallo (Ravenna), Painter, 1484-1542 - pp. 24, 87, 89

Balbi, Alessandro: from Ferrara, Architect, known from 1590, died 1617 - p. 98

Ballanti, Graziani: from Faenza, Sculptors and Modelers, G.B. 1762-1835 and Francesco ?-1847 - p. 91

Barbieri, Giovanni Francesco: see Guercino.

Barezzi, Antonio: from Busseto (Parma), Merchant and Verdi's Patron, 1787-1867 - p. 75

Barezzi, Margherita: from Busseto (Parma), Pianist and Verdi's first wife, 1814-1840 - p. 75

Baroncelli, Niccolò: known as Niccolò del Cavallo: from Florence, Sculptor, known from 1434, died 1453 - p. 35

Barozzi, Serafino: from Bologna, Painter, known from 1780, d. 1810 - p. 45

Bassani, Giorgio: from Bologna, Writer, 1916-2000 - p. 35

Bastianino (byname of Sebastiano Filippi): from Ferrara, Painter, 1532-1602 - pp. 35, 36

Bazzani, Cesare: from Rome, Architect and Engineer, 1873-1939 - p. 45

Beccadelli Antonio: from Bologna, Painter, 1718-1803 - p. 29

Benedetto da Maiano: Architect and Sculptor, 1442-97 - p. 90

Bernini Gian Lorenzo: from Naples, Sculptor, Architect and Painter, 1598-1680 - pp. 60, 63

Bertolani Gaetano: from Mantua, Painter, 1758-1856 - pp. 45, 47

Bibiena or Bibbiena, Antonio (byname of Galli Antonio): from Parma, Architect, Painter and Stage Designer, 1657-1743 - p. 94

Boiardo, Matteo Maria: from Scandiano (Reggio Emilia), Poet, 1441-1494 - p. 98

Bononi or Bonone, Carlo: from Ferrara, Painter, 1569-1632 - p. 37

Borghesi, Giovanni Battista: from Parma, Painter, 1790-1846 - p. 71

Borso d'Este: Lord of Ferrara 1413-1471 - p. 37

Bramante, Donato: from Fermignano (Urbino), Architect and Painter, 1444-1514 - p. 80

Bregno, Giovanni Battista: from Òsteno or Righeggia (Como), Sculptor and Architect, known from 1494, died before 1523 - p. 49

Byron, George Gordon: from London, Poet, 1788-1824 - p. 52

C

Cagnacci, Guido: from Sant'Arcangelo di Romagna (Forlì-Cesena), Painter 1601-1663 - p. 106

Callido, Gaetano Antonio: from Este (Padua), Organist, 1727-1813 - p. 89

Campi, Vincenzo: from Cremona, Painter, 1536-1591 - p. 75

Canova, Antonio: from Possagno (Treviso), Sculptor and Painter, 1757-1822 - p. 72

Cantarini, Simone: from Pesaro, Painter, 1612-1648 - p. 106

Carrà, Carlo: from Quargnento (Alessandria), Painter and Carver, 1881-1966 - p. 39

Carracci, Agostino: from Bologna, Painter, Carver and Sculptor, 1557-1602 - p. 26

Carracci, Annibale: from Bologna, Painter and Carver, 1560-1609 - pp. 26, 27

Carracci, Ludovico: from Bologna, Painter, 1555-1619 - pp. 22, 23, 26, 27, 40, 97

Carrari, Baldassarre the Younger: from Forlì, Painter, after 1460-1519 - p. 87

Cesi, Bartolomeo: from Bologna, Painter, 1556-1629 - pp. 23, 29

Chagall, Marc: from Vitebsk (Belorussia), Painter, 1887-1985 - p. 91

Charlemagne: Holy Roman Emperor, 742-814 - p. 63

Chierici, Alfonso: from Reggio Emilia, Painter, 1816-73 - p. 98

Cignani, Carlo: from Bologna, Painter, 1628-1719 - p. 46

…abue, Giovanni …name of Cenni di …o): from Florence, …nter, c.1240-1302 - p.

…reggio (byname of …onio Allegri): from …reggio (Reggio …lia), Painter, 1489-…4 - pp. 67, 70, 71, …73, 98, 102

…simo I de' Medici: …n Florence, Duke of …rence, 1519-74 - p. 53

…ssa, Francesco del: …m Ferrara, Painter …d Sculptor, c.1436-…/78 - p. 27

…sta, Lorenzo: from …rrara, Painter, 1460-…33 - pp. 20, 26

…espi, Giuseppe Maria …own as Lo Spagnolo: …m Bologna, Painter …d Carver, 1665-1747 -…. 24, 27

…eti, Donato: from …emona, Painter, 1671-…49 - p. 27

…e Chirico, Giorgio: …rn in Athens (Greece), …inter and Writer, 1891-…52 - p. 36

…e Sica, Vittòrio: from …ra (Frosinone), Actor …d Director, 1901- 1974 …pp. 35, 127

…etti, Cesare: Painter …d Collector, 1848-1919 …p. 98

…sraeli, Benjamin: from …ndon (England), …olitician and Writer, …804-1881 - p. 40

…onatello (byname of …onato di Niccolò Betto …ardi): from Florence, …culptor, 1382/83/86-…466 - p. 91

…cclesius: Bishop of …avenna from 521 to …34 - p. 83

…nzo (king): from …alermo, natural heir of

Federico II, 1225-72 - p. 16

Ercole I d'Este: from Ferrara, Duke of Ferrara and Modena, 1431-1505 - p. 35

Este Borso: Lord of Ferrara, 1413-71 - p. 37

Este, Francesco I: from Modena, Duke of Modena and Reggio, 1610-58 - p. 36

Este, Francesco III: from Modena, Duke of Modena and Reggio, 1698-1780 - p. 59

F

Facchetti, Giovanni Battista: from Brescia, Organ maker, 16th cent. - p. 80

Farnese, Alessandro: Duke of Parma and Piacenza, 1545-1592 - p. 78

Farnese, Ottavio: Duke of Parma and Piacenza, 16th cent. - pp. 73, 78

Farnese, Ranuccio I: from Parma, Duke of Parma and Piacenza, 1569-1627 - p. 78

Frederick I Barbarossa: Emperor, c.1123-90 - p. 63

Frederick II: from Jesi (Ancona), Emperor, 1194-1250 - p. 17

Fellini, Federico: Film director from Rimini, 1920- 1993 - pp. 107, 125, 128, 129

Fenzoni, Ferraù, known as Ferraù: from Faenza (Ravenna), Painter, 1562-1645 - pp. 29, 88, 91

Ferrari, Luca: from Reggio Emilia, Painter, 1605-54 - p. 97

Ferrucci, Francesco di Simone: from Fiesole (Florence), Sculptor and Engraver, 1437-93 - p. 23

Filippi, Camillo: from Ferrara, Painter, c.1500-1574 - pp. 36, 37

Filippi, Cesare: from Ferrara, Painter, 1536-c.1604 - p. 36

Filippi, Sebastiano: see Bastianino.

Fontana, Francesco: from Rome, Architect, 1668-1708 - p. 89

Fontana, Lavinia: from Bologna, Painter, 1552-1614 - p. 29

Fontana, Lucio: from Rosario (Argentina), Sculptor and Painter, 1899-1968 - pp. 39, 91

Fontanesi, Antonio: from Reggio Emilia, Painter and Carver, 1818-82 - p. 98

Francia (byname of Francesco Raibolini): from Bologna, Painter, Goldsmith and Medalist, c.1450-1517 - pp. 17, 26, 35

G

Galla Placidia: Roman empress, c.390-450 - p. 83

Gandolfi, Gaetano: from Décima di San Giovanni in Persiceto (Bologna), Painter and Carver, 1734-1802 - p. 27

Gandolfi, Mauro: from Bologna, Painter and Carver, 1764-1834 - p. 27

Gandolfi, Ubaldo: from Décima di San Giovanni in Persiceto (Bologna), Painter, Carver and Sculptor, 1728-81 - p. 27

Garelli, Tommaso: from Bologna, Painter, known from 1452-95 - p. 20

Garofalo (byname of Benvenuto Tisi): from Ferrara, Painter, 1476/81-1559 - p. 35

Geminianus (Saint): Bishop of Modena, 344-96 - p. 54

Giambologna (byname of Jean de Boulogne): from Douai (France), Sculptor and Architect, 1529-1608 - p. 16

Giani, Felice: from San Sebastiano Curone (Alessandria), Painter, 1758-1823 - pp. 45, 47, 91

Giannotti, Silvestro: from Lucca, Engraver, 1680-1750 - p. 24

Giotto or Giotto di Bondone: from Vespignano di Vicchio (Florence), Painter, Architect and Sculptor, probably 1267-1337 - pp. 27, 38, 106

Giovanni da Modena: Painter from Modena, known from 1398-1451 - p. 20

Girolamo da Carpi (byname of Girolamo Sellari): from Ferrara, Painter and Architect, c.1501-c.1556 - p. 35

Giunta Pisano (byname of Giunta di Capitini): from Pisa, Painter, known from 1229-54 - p. 23

Greco, El (byname of Domenico Theotokopulos): from Candia (Greece), Painter, c.1541-1614 - pp. 60, 98

Gregory VII (Hildebrand of Soana): Pope, 1020 c.-1085 - pp. 99, 112

Gregory XIII (Ugo Boncompagni): Bologna, Pope from 1572-85 - p. 22

Guarana, Jacopo: from Verona, Painter, 1720-1808 - p. 45

Guercino (byname of Giovanni Francesco Barbieri): from Cento (Ferrara), Painter and Carver, 1591-1666 - pp. 23, 30, 35, 39, 77, 106, 108

Guglielmo (Fra): from Pisa, Sculptor and Architect, c.1235-1310/11 - p. 23

Guttuso, Renato: from Bagheria (Palermo), Painter, 1912-1987 - p. 39

H

Henry IV: Emperor of Germany, 1050-1106 - pp. 99, 112

Holbein Hans the Younger: from Augsburg (Germany), Painter and Carver, 1497/98-1543 - p. 73

I

Innocenzo da Imola (byname of Innocenzo Francucci): from Imola (Bologna), Painter, c.1490- c.1545 - pp. 24, 26, 90

J

Jacopo della Quercia: from Siena, Sculptor, 1371/74-1438 - pp. 20, 26

Jacopo di Paolo: Painter from Bologna, known from 1378-1426 - p. 26

James of Ulm (Germany): Glass painter, 1407-1491 - p. 20

Justinian: Byzantine emperor, 482-565 - p. 83

L

Lamberti, Nicolò di Piero, known as Il Pela: from Florence, Sculptor and Architect, c.1370-1451 - p. 23

Lanfranco: Architect from Lombardy (Como?), known from 1099-1106 - pp. 55, 75, 112

Laureti, Tommaso: from Palermo, Painter and Architect, c.1530-1602 - pp. 16, 97

Lega, Silvestro: from Modigliana (Forlì and Cesena), Painter, 1826-95 - p. 52

Léger, Fernand: from Argentan (France), Painter, 1881-1955 - p. 91

Lelli, Ercole: from Bologna, Engraver, Painter, Carver and Medalist, 1702-1766 - p. 24

Leonardo da Vinci (Florence): Painter, Architect and Sculptor, 1452-1519 - pp. 73, 102, 103

Leonello d'Este: Lord of Ferrara, 1407-1450 - p. 36

Levanti, Antonio: from Bologna, Architect and Sculptor, known from 1611-64 - p. 24

Levi, Isacco Gioacchino: from Busseto (Parma), Painter, 1818-1909 - p. 75

Lippi, Filippino: from Prato, Painter, c.1457-1504 - p. 23

Lippo di Dalmasio: from Bologna, Painter, 1352-1410 - p. 24

Lombardi, Alfonso: from Ferrara, Sculptor, 1497-1537 - pp. 17, 21, 22

Lombardo, Pietro: from Carona (Canton Ticino), Sculptor and Architect, c.1435-1515 - p. 102

Lombardo, Tullio: from Carona (Switzerland), Architect and Sculptor, 1455-1532 - p. 87

Lorenzo di Bagno Marino or Lorenzo di Domenico: from Bologna, Architect, c.1341-c.1392 - p. 21

M

Master of St Geminianus: Sculptor, worked in the 12th cent. - p. 55

Magnani, Girolamo: from Fidenza (Parma), Painter and Stage Designer, 1815-1889 - pp. 71, 76

Malatesta, Galeotto: Lord of Cesena, 14th cent. - p. 49

Malatesta Novello (byname of Domenico Malatesta): Lord of Cesena, 1418-65 - p. 48

Mantegna, Andrea: from Isola di Carturo now Isola Mantegna (Padua), Painter and Carver, 1431-1506 - p. 30

Manuzio, Aldo: from Bassano (Vicenza), Humanist and Printer, 1450-1515 - p. 60

Manzù, Giacomo (G. Manzoni): from Bergamo, Sculptor and Painter, 1908-1991 - p. 39

Marfisa d'Este Cybo: daughter of Francesco, Protector of Tasso, second half of 16th cent. - p. 36

Marie Louise (of Austria): Duchess of Parma, Piacenza and Guastalla, 1791-1847 - p. 71

Masegne, Pier Paolo dalle: Venetian Sculptor and Architect, known from 1383-1404 - p. 23

Masini, Angelo: from Castrocaro Terme (Forlì-Cesena), Tenor, 1844-1926 - p. 47

Maximian: Archbishop of Ravenna from 546-556 - p. 94

Mastelletta (byname of Giovanni Andrea Donducci): from Bologna, Painter, 1575-1655 - p. 28

Matilda of Canossa: Lord of Canossa and Countess of Tuscany, 1046-1115 - pp. 55, 6 112, 113

Matisse, Henry: from Lecateau (France), Painter, 1869-1954 - p. 91

Mazzacurati, Marino: from Galliera (Bologn Sculptor, 1909-1969 - p. 71

Mazzola, Francesco: see Parmigianino.

Michelangelo Buonarroti: from Caprese (Arezzo), Painter, Sculptor and Architect, 1475-1564 - p. 102

Mona, Domenico: fro Ferrara, Painter, c.155 1602 - p. 37

Morandi, Antonio, known as Terribilia: Architect from Bologn known from 1535, d. 1568 - p. 21

Morandi, Giorgio: from Bologna, Painter and Carver, 1890-1964 - p. 17

Morelli, Enzo: from Bagnacavallo, Painter, 1896-1976 - p. 88

N

Niccolò dell'Arca (byname of Niccolò d'Antonio): from Bari? Sculptor, known from 1463, died 1494 - pp. 17, 21, 23

Nicola Pisano: Sculpto from Puglia or Tuscany c.1220-78/87 - p. 23

O

Onofri, Vincenzo: Sculptor who worked i Bologna, known from 1493-1524 - pp. 20, 24

Ordelaffi, Pino III: Lorc of Forlì, 1436-80 - p. 47

Orsi, Lelio: from Novellara (Reggio Emilia), Painter

, Architect, 1511-87 -
)8

avian Augustus:
nan Emperor, BC 63-
AD - p. 106

chioni, Francesco:
n Reggio Emilia,
ilptor, 1560-1631 -
)8

gno di Lapo: see
ctigiani Pagno.

lmezzano, Marco:
m Forlì, Painter,
455-1539 - pp. 46,
, 89

olo Veneziano: from
nice, Painter, known
m 1310-62 - pp. 26,

ris, Domenico di:
m Padua, Sculptor
d Smelter, known
m 1450-92 - p. 35

rmeggiani, Tancrédi:
m Feltre (Belluno),
inter, 1927-1964 -
98

rmigianino, Il
yname of Francesco
azzola): from Parma,
inter, 1503-1540 -
). 20, 27, 67, 73

assarotti or
asserotti, Bartolomeo:
om Bologna, Painter,
529-92 - p. 29

etitot, Ennemond-
lexandre: from Lyon
rance), Architect,
727-1801 - pp. 72, 73

etrocchi, Francesco:
om Torricella di
ugano (Switzerland),
rchitect, 1706-78 -
, 94

icasso, Pablo: from
Malaga (Spain), Painter,
881-1985 - p. 91

iero della Francesca:
om Borgo San
iepolcro, Painter,
.1420-1492 - pp. 105,
06

Pius VII (Luigi Barnaba Chiaramonti): from Cesena, Pope from 1800-23 - p. 49

Pistocchi, Giuseppe: from Faenza, Architect, 1744-1814 - p. 91

Portigiani, Pagno, known as Pagno di Lapo: from Fièsole (Florence), Sculptor and Architect, 1408-1470 - p. 23

Pseudo, Jacopino di Francesco: Painter, worked in Bologna in the first half of the 14th cent. - p. 27

R
Raphael (Sanzio or Santi): from Urbino, Painter and Architect, 1483-1520 - pp. 27, 80, 102

Raggi, Antonio: from Vico Morcote (Canton Ticino), Sculptor, 1624-86 - p. 63

Renée of France: from Blois (France), Duchess of Ferrara, wife of Ercole II d'Este, 1510-1576 - p.34

Reni, Guido: from Bologna, Painter, Carver and Sculptor, 1575-1642 - pp. 23, 27, 30, 40, 106

Romei, Giovanni: a well-known figure in the Este court, 15th cent., - p. 36

Rondinelli, Nicolò: from Lugo (Ravenna), Painter, c.1450- c.1510 - pp. 46, 87

Roseto, Jacopo: from Bologna, Goldsmith, known from 1380-83 - p. 23

Rossellino, Antonio (byname of Antonio di Matteo Gamberetti): from Settignano (Florence), Sculptor, 1427-79 - pp. 90, 91

Rossetti, Biagio: from Ferrara, Architect, 1445/47-1516 - pp. 37, 80

Rossi, Claudio: from Modena, Painter and Architect, 1814-63 - p. 62

S
St. Apollinaris: Bishop of Ravenna, 2nd cent. II - p. 94

Saffi, Aurelio: from Forlì, Patriot, 1819-90 - p. 45

Secchi, Riccardo: from Reggio Emilia, Sculptor, 1871-1938 - p. 98

Simone dei Crocifissi (byname of Simone di Filippo Benvenuti): from Bologna, Painter, c.1330-99 - pp. 25, 26

Sogari, Prospero: known as Il Clemente: from Reggio Emilia, Sculptor and Architect, 1516-84 - p. 95

Spani, Bartolomeo: from Reggio Emilia, Architect, Sculptor and Goldsmith, 1468-1539 - p. 95

Sperandio di Bartolomeo (Sperandio Savelli): from Mantua?, Sculptor and Medalist, c.1425-1504 - p. 23

T
Theodoric: King of the Ostrogoths, c.454-526 - p. 83

Theodore: Archbishop of Ravenna, 7th cent. - p. 86

Tiarini, Alessandro: from Bologna, Painter, 1577-1668 - p. 91

Tibaldi, Domenico: from Bologna, Architect, Painter and Carver, 1541-83 - pp. 22, 26

Tibaldi, Pellegrino, known as Il Pellegrini: from Puria di Valsolda (Como), Architect,

Painter and Sculptor, 1527-96 - pp. 22, 26

Tommaso da Modena (byname of Tomaso Barisini): from Modena, Painter, 1325/26-1379 - p. 59

Torreggiani, Alfonso: from Budrio (Bologna), Architect, 1682-1764 - pp. 20, 22

Trifogli, Domenico: from Torricella (Pavia), Architect, 1675-1759 - p. 29

Tura, Cosmè (byname of T. Cosimo): from Ferrara, Painter, before 1430-1495 - pp. 31, 35

V-W
Van Eyck, Jan: from Maaseik (Belgium), Painter, 1390-1441 - p. 98

Vela, Vincenzo: from Ligornetto (Canton Ticino), Sculptor, 1820-91 - p. 102

Verdi, Giuseppe: from Róncole di Busseto (Parma), Composer, 1813-1901 - pp. 67, 74, 125

Vignola (byname of Jacopo Barozzi): from Vignola (Modena), Architect, 1507-1573 - pp. 20, 73, 113

Vitale da Bologna (byname of Vitale degli Equi): from Bologna, Painter, known from 1309?-before 1361 - pp. 24, 27

Wiligelmo: Sculptor from Lombardy or Emilia, known from 1099-c.1110 - pp. 54, 63, 112

Z
Zaganelli, Francesco: from Cotignola (Ravenna), Painter, 1460/70-1532 - p. 87

Zucchi, Marcantonio: from Parma, Architect and Wood Carver, 1469-c.1531 - p. 70

GENERAL INDEX

A
Abbazia di Pomposa, 37, 210
Ancona di Bellocchio, 120
Argenta, 175

B
Bagno di Romagna, 50, 198, 210
Bagnacavallo, 88, 210
Bardi, 193
Bassona Beach, 121
Bellaria Igea Marina, 107, 210
Bertinoro, 51, 159, 210
Bobbio, 80, 149, 210
Bologna, 16, 124, 125, 130, 142, 147, 151, 176, 178, 182, 199, 208, 211
Bosco della Mésola, 39
Brescello, 135
Brisighella, 89, 143, 154, 159, 176, 199, 214
Budrio, 28, 214
Busseto, 73, 148, 193, 214

C
Campegine, 153
Campotto, 214
Canossa, 99, 153, 214
Caorso, 179
Carpaneto, 149
Carpi, 61, 215
Casola Valsenio, 153, 177
Castel Guelfo di Bologna, 178
Castel San Pietro Terme, 167, 199
Castell'Arquato, 81, 215
Castellarano, 99
Castelvetro di Modena, 62, 159, 215
Castrocaro Terme, 51, 191, 199, 215
Cattolica, 107, 118, 166, 195, 215
Cavriago, 167
Cento, 39, 152, 165, 191, 216
Cervarezza, 201
Cervia, 89, 143, 194, 201, 216

Cesena, 48, 147, 175, 176, 184, 217
Cesenatico, 51, 121, 166, 176, 184, 191, 217
Collecchio, 175
Comacchio, 40, 218
Coriano, 167
Correggio, 102, 149, 218

D
Delta del Po, 42, 127

E-F
Ex Colonia CRI Beach, 121
Ex Colonia Varese Beach, 121
Faenza, 90, 143, 160, 166, 167, 175, 177, 194, 218
Fanano, 62, 219
Ferrara, 31, 127, 132, 142, 147, 152, 165, 176, 183, 189, 208, 219
Fidenza, 75, 179, 221
Fiorenzuola d'Arda, 82, 143, 221
Fiumalbo, 62, 221
Fontanellato, 76, 148, 176, 221
Forlì, 45, 124, 133, 147, 159, 165, 175, 184, 208, 221
Forlimpòpoli, 51, 192, 222
Fornovo di Taro, 148
Fosso Ghiaia, 121
Fratta Terme, 202

G
Galeata, 52, 222
Gatteo, 179
Grazzano Visconti, 193
Grizzana Morandi, 167
Guastalla, 167

I
Imola, 28, 159, 222

L
Lido di Volano, 120
Longiano, 52, 223
Lugo, 91, 160, 166, 175, 188, 223

M
Maranello, 130

Marina di Ravenna, 121
Marina Romea, 120
Milano Marittima, 121
Modena, 54, 112, 142, 147, 152, 166, 176, 184, 192, 208, 223
Modigliana, 52, 159, 175, 225
Montecchio Emilia, 143
Montefiore Conca, 108, 225
Monteleone, 52
Montemaggiore, 134
Monteveglio, 134
Monticelli Terme, 202

N
Noceto, 175
Nonàntola, 62, 225
Novellara, 135

O
Oasi di Campotto, 41

P
Park "Ex Colonia Varese", 121
Parma, 67, 114, 125, 131, 143, 148, 152, 166, 186, 208, 225
Piacenza, 77, 149, 166, 187, 208, 226
Pieve di Cento, 165
Pinarella di Cervia, 121, 167
Pineta di S. Vitale, 94
Po Delta, 42, 127
Pontenure, 176
Porretta Terme, 183, 203
Portico di Romagna, 53
Porto Corsini, 121
Premilcuore, 53, 227
Punta Marina Terme, 203

R
Ravenna, 83, 166, 175, 187, 227
Reggio Emilia, 95, 114, 135, 143, 149, 153, 160, 166, 175, 188, 208, 228
Repubblica di San Marino, 108, 207, 231
Riccione, 109, 118,

119, 204, 229
Rimini, 103, 122, 12
143, 153, 166, 175, 177, 179, 188, 205, 208, 230
Riolo Terme, 205
Roccabianca, 175

S
S. Apollinare in Classe, 94
Salsomaggiore Term
153, 186, 206
Salvarola Terme, 20;
San Benedetto, 53
San Giovanni in Marignano, 179
San Giovanni in Persiceto, 29, 189, 231
San Lazzaro di Savena, 183
San Secondo Parmense, 149
Sant'Andrea Bagni, 207
Santarcangelo di Romagna, 109, 177, 232
Santuario della Madonna di S. Luca, 30
Sassuolo, 63, 179, 185, 232
Savignano sul Rubicone, 152, 159, 179
Savio, 119
Scandiano, 232
Sèstola, 66, 232
Sogliano al Rubicone
152, 167
Soragna, 149

T
Tabiano Bagni, 207
Terra del Sole, 53, 232
Torrechiara, 76

V
Verucchio, 109, 232
Vignola, 66, 175, 185
Vigoleno, 82
Viserba, 109

Z
Zibello, 149
Zola Predosa, 165

GLOSSARY

...roterion
...corative feature on a pediment

...bo
...aised pulpit in early churches
...m which the Gospels were
...d

...se
...emi-circular or polygonal
...ojection of a building, esp at
...st end of a church

...rium
...oby

...emin-de-ronde
...ternal raised pathway in
...edieval fortifications

...borium
...namental canopy over an altar

...ppus (cippi)
...one with inscription

...lipeus
...ield-like frame containing a
...lief or image

...dex (codices)
...rly, hand-written books

...osseret
...pplementary capital set above
...column capital to receive the
...rust of the arch

...mbrasure
...ith a splayed (angled) opening

...hibelline
...enoting support of the Holy
...oman Emperor

...uelph
...enoting support of the Pope

...oggia
...colonnaded or ardcaded space
...ithin the body of a building
...ut pen on one side

...unette
...n area in the plane of a wall
...amed by an arch or vault
...ontaining a painting or
...culpture

...ajolica
...type of early Italian
...arthenware covered with an
...paque tin glaze

Matroneum
overhead gallery in an early
church reserved for the worship
of women

Metope
decorative stone slabs with low
reliefs

Narthex
the portico before the nave of
an early Christian or Byzantine
church

Oculus (oculi)
circular opening especially at
the crown of a domenica

Paten
plate made usually of precious
metal used to carry the bread at
Communion

Parvis
the flat ground in front of a
church

Pentahedral
five-sided

Peribolos
ambulatory, walkway around the
edge of an apse

Piano nobile
upper floor occupied by the
nobility

Pilaster
shallow rectangular feature
protruding from a wall with a
capital and a base

Pluteus (plutei)
reading desk in an early library;
decorated square stone slabs in
Romanesque churches e.g. used
vertically as base for rood screen

Presbytery
the part of a church reserved for
the officiating clergy

Pronaos
a vestibule before the main part
of the church

Protesi and diaconicon
small altars at either side of an
apse

Rocaille
artificial rockwork made of

rough stones and cement, as for
gardens

Rood screen
stone or wooden balaustrade
separating the main part of the
church from the presbytery

Scriptorium
room set apart for scribes in a
medieval monastery

Stele
upright stone slab or pillar with
an inscription

Stoup
stone or marble container for
holy water

Tambour
the vertical part of a cupola

Telamon (telamones):
sculptured figure of a man used
as a column

Theophany
visible manifestation of God, or
a god

Tiburium
architectural structure enclosing
a dome, used in early and
Romanesque Lombard churches

Tondo
a round painting

Transept
the major transverse part of a
cruciform church

Triptych
a painting or panel with a main
central part and two lateral
parts

Tympanum
the space between an arch and
the horizontal head of the door
or window below

Westwork
the monumental western front
of a Romanesque church

PICTURE CREDITS

Notes

Notes

FUTURE
ON A HUMAN SCALE

LIA-ROMAGNA

www.regione.emilia-romagna.it

Regione Emilia-Romagna

A modern and elegant four-star hotel on Rimini sea front... 75 comfortable bedrooms each one with balcony and a pleasant sea view.
3 Km far from Miramare airport and Rimini railway station.
We offer a private wide car park, swimming pool, American bar, congress rooms and a special panoramic restaurant.
Here, at the Hotel Diplomat Palace every on of our guests is special and making them welcome is a pleasure as well as a tradition.
Be our guests and appreciate for yourselves the true meaning of hospitality!

Hotel Diplomat Palace**
Viale Regina Elena, 70
47900 Rimini - Italy
Tel. +39 541 380011
Fax +39 541 380414
www.diplomatpalace.it
diplomat@diplomatpalace.it

Situated in Rimini, in the marvellous Bay of Rivabella, in a quiet area right on the seaside, the Imperial Beach Hotel, stately and majestic, welcomes its guests with elegance, professionalism and kindness.
Brand new four-star hotel, it offers Panoramic restaurant overlooking the sea, American Bar, TV-room with maxi screen, Piano Bar, Meeting Room, Parking.
You can find us at 3 Km from Rimini railway station, 7 km from Miramare airport and just 1 km from the new fair district!

Hotel Imperial Beach**
Viale Toscanelli 19
47900 Rivabella di Rimini, Italy
Tel +38 541 26752
Fax +39 541 54403
www.imperialbeach.it
info@imperialbeach.it